A MODERN
SCRIPTURAL APPROACH TO
THE SPIRITUAL EXERCISES

DAVID M. STANLEY, s.j.

A MODERN SCRIPTURAL APPROACH TO THE SPIRITUAL EXERCISES

THE INSTITUTE OF JESUIT SOURCES

in cooperation with LOYOLA UNIVERSITY PRESS

Chicago, 1967

*Published through the aid of funds
donated by the late Mr. James L. Monaghan
of Milwaukee, Wisconsin,
1867-1963,
in memory of his brother,
Reverend Edward V. Monaghan, S.J.,
1879-1922.*

GEORGE E. GANSS, PH.D.

Director and General Editor
The Institute of Jesuit Sources
Chicago, 1967

THREE SERIES OF BOOKS are planned for publication by the Institute of Jesuit Sources: I, Jesuit Primary Sources, in English translations; II, Modern Scholarly Studies about the Jesuits, in English translations; III, Original Studies, composed in English.

The Institute is happy to offer, as the first book in Series III, the present study composed by Father David M. Stanley, S.J., professor of Sacred Scripture in the Jesuit theologate, Regis College, located at Willowdale, Ontario.

Under the stimuli which produced and followed Vatican Council II, Catholic piety is rapidly becoming more biblical and liturgical. Christian prayer is more clearly conceived as dialogue with God. God communicates himself to man through his words, especially those in the Bible, through his sacraments, made more fruitful by their accompanying ceremonial which is largely scriptural, and through the events of life. Man in turn responds to God, through dialogue and especially through the total commitment of himself to his Maker.

This growth in biblical stress is fortunate and promising. But it is also bringing problems of adaptation to many retreat masters and retreatants. Through experimentation and discussion, the wider modern knowledge must be put into the abiding forms of Christian piety or they may lose their attractiveness to present-day minds. For example, the knowledge, interpretation, and manner of using Sacred Scripture today differ considerably from those of the medieval era which were still common in St. Ignatius' day and even into the mid-twentieth century.

This problem is particularly grave for some retreat masters whose seminary training was completed ten or twenty years ago. Since then, they have been hard pressed by their daily duties in many fields. Meanwhile new approaches and more effective interpretations of Scripture, based largely on the study of literary forms recommended in the encyclical *Divino afflante Spiritu* (1943) and in the dogmatic constitution *Dei verbum* of Vatican Council II, have become prevalent among scholars and also among

vii

many retreatants. Hence these retreat masters have become aware of a danger of presenting obsolete interpretations of the Bible and of drawing so-called practical lessons from Scripture which say little or nothing to many in their audience. And yet, to assimilate the modern approach to Scripture and apply it fruitfully in giving the Spiritual Exercises are tasks difficult for one engaged in some field other than Scripture, no matter how zealous he is. The retreat master is puzzled about what he ought to do.

In this situation, the present book is timely for retreat masters and retreatants. Thoroughly familiar with modern scriptural studies, Father Stanley here offers a concrete example, coupled with some explanation of theory, of one way in which the modern scriptural approach can be employed in conducting the Spiritual Exercises of St. Ignatius of Loyola.

The substance of the book was first presented in an actual retreat which Father Stanley conducted in Holy Week of 1964 at St. Marys, Kansas, for a group of Jesuit theological students who were about to be ordained. He later revised the conferences in the form found here. Some readers may possibly feel that the structure of St. Ignatius' *Spiritual Exercises* does not stand out as prominently as it ought, or that there are not enough practical applications to daily life. However, emphasis upon that structure did not seem necessary, given the background of Father Stanley's auditors. According to St. Ignatius' own directives (*Spiritual Exercises* [18]), he felt obliged to adapt the Exercises to them. Each of these retreatants knew that structure well, having already made the Exercises some dozen times; and each had a copy of St. Ignatius' little book in his room. The practical applications were deliberately omitted because of St. Ignatius' directive (*Spiritual Exercises* [15]) that the director should allow God to deal directly with the exercitant, rather than run the risk of coming between the Creator and his creature. If such applications are to be effective, the exercitant himself must make them in response to the motions of the Holy Spirit.

The present writer had the good fortune to be present during the retreat itself. He gladly testifies that the young Jesuits to whom it was addressed had a profound and inspiring religious experience, one of true dialogue with God. They reacted to the retreat in a spirit of cooperation and enthusiasm. The book is published in the hope that it will help many others, whether directors or retreatants, to experience a similar reaction.

George E. Ganss, S.J.
February 2, 1967

DAVID M. STANLEY, S. J.

Regis College
Willowdale, Ontario

THE SUBSTANCE OF THIS BOOK was given originally as a retreat to the Jesuit scholastics of St. Mary's College, St. Marys, Kansas—the theologate of the Missouri, Wisconsin, and New Orleans Provinces of the Society of Jesus, among whose alumni I am privileged to be numbered. The retreat was specifically orientated towards the priesthood, since the theologians who followed the Spiritual Exercises in the Holy Week of 1964 were to be ordained priests the following June. While the conferences have been rewritten for publication, I did not think it necessary to edit out all the references to the liturgy which occurred during those days. The reader will also detect certain traces of the oral style, another reminiscence of the book's original *Sitz im Leben*.

It is to the suggestion of the Reverend George E. Ganss, S.J., professor of theology at St. Mary's College and director of the Institute of Jesuit Sources, that I owe the idea of publishing this retreat. Indeed, the notion that this eight-day version of the Spiritual Exercises of St. Ignatius should provide a concrete illustration of how the new approach to Sacred Scripture might be profitably employed in giving an Ignatian retreat was also his. Accordingly, I wish to acknowledge my deep indebtedness to Father Ganss for his initial inspiration, as well as for the persevering, generous, and painstaking labor which he expended as editor. Without his assistance this book would probably never have been published.

I also wish to thank the Reverend James Walsh, S.J., editor of *The Way*, for his kind permission to include the essay on "The Last Adam" which appeared in that periodical. I am grateful too to the Reverend Christopher Mooney, S.J., chairman of the Theology Department, Fordham University, for permitting me to use the material from a paper which I wrote for the American Institute of Spirituality, "Sacred Scripture as a Normative Guide to Religious Experience."

I also wish to acknowledge a debt to several distinguished contemporary Jesuit theologians whose friendship I value and whose thought in one way or another has influenced my own treatment of certain themes developed in one or other meditation or contemplation: Fathers Luis Alonso Schökel, Frederick E. Crowe, John Courtney Murray, and the late Pierre Charles.[1] Undoubtedly I am a debtor also to countless members of the Society of Jesus: to my master of novices, Joseph P. Monaghan, to my tertian instructor, Francis E. Keenan, and numerous other retreat masters. To all of these I express my sincere thanks for their instruction and inspiration. What is good in the following pages is simply part of our common heritage from the spirituality of St. Ignatius. What is imperfect or incomplete is the result of the limitations, spiritual and intellectual, of the author.

Finally, I should like to draw the reader's attention to two details. The translations of the biblical citations are my own work, as also the rendering of the ecclesiastical documents and the text of the *Spiritual Exercises*. Secondly, I have attempted, in Note A of the Reference Materials at the end of the volume, to provide a series of references to the text of the *Spiritual Exercises*, which hopefully will be of service to any retreatant who may wish to use this book and particularly to any retreat master who may ask how far I have followed the method and structures of the author of the "golden little book," St. Ignatius Loyola. May he, who was rightly acknowledged in his own age as a genius in adapting Christian spirituality to the men of his time, look with favor upon this attempt to utilize what is sound and useful in present day exegesis in the service of the Word.

NOTE: The numbers found in brackets [ ] throughout the book are references to the text of the *Spiritual Exercises*. They may be found most easily in the excellent English translation by Louis J. Puhl, S.J., *The Spiritual Exercises of St. Ignatius: a New Translation*, The Newman Press, Westminster, Maryland, 1965. This enumeration, already widespread since 1928, may become universally accepted when it is adopted in the revision of the critical edition, originally published under the direction of Frederick Cervós, S.J., in *Monumenta Historica Societatis Jesu* 19. *Monumenta Ignatiana autographis vel ex antiquioribus exemplis collecta* (*Series Secunda*): *Exercitia Spiritualia Sancti Ignatii de Loyola et eorum Directoria* (Madrid, 1919).

---

1 My deepest indebtedness is to my colleague, the Very Reverend R.A.F. MacKenzie, S.J., for innumerable insights into the text of the Bible; above all, for years of personal inspiration in the prosecution of our common task, the teaching of Scripture.

A MODERN
SCRIPTURAL APPROACH TO
THE SPIRITUAL EXERCISES

SCRIPTURE AS A NORMATIVE GUIDE
TO RELIGIOUS EXPERIENCE

THE PURPOSE OF THIS BOOK may appear to be a fairly grandiose one: to provide some exemplification of the way in which the twentieth century achievements of biblical scholarship may be pressed into service in giving the Spiritual Exercises of St. Ignatius to men of the present day. The work of the Form critics, the valid insights operative in Rudolf Bultmann's attempts at "demytholo-gizing" the Gospels, and the more theological preoccupations of the *Redaktionsgeschichtliche* school are all laid under contribution. Yet, this project has been undertaken not as any mere tour de force, but rather out of the conviction that, if the Spiritual Exercises are to fulfill the formative role in the spirituality of contemporary man which they certainly exercised upon countless Renaissance men, they should become instinct with that spirit of *aggiornamento* which Pope John has made the touchstone of modern Catholic orthodoxy.

Nature of this Book

The "scriptural revolution," which has affected modern Catholic theological thought so profoundly during the past two decades, is a phenomenon fairly familiar to all. It is beginning to have important repercussions also upon such more popular but crucially important areas as catechetics and homiletics. The Bible, it goes without saying, must be assimilated into the spirituality of each Christian in every age, for it has always been a tenet of the Church's faith that Sacred Scripture constitutes a normative guide for any valid Christian religious experience. Because this important truth needs, perhaps, to be restated in our day, it may not be unhelpful to discuss its significance here, by way of introduction to this attempt to show how modern biblical exegesis may be profitably employed in presenting the Spiritual Exercises to modern man.

Modern Scriptural Approach

Religious experience is defined as "the dialogue between God and man." That there is a clear and close connection between

Divine-Human Dialogue

1

religious experience and Holy Scripture may be easily appreciated by recalling that it has become the fashion nowadays to speak of the Bible as the record of the dialogue between God and man. In speaking of the structure of the Old Testament, R.A.F. Mac-Kenzie, S.J., finds this analogy of the dialogue particularly congenial. "An essential part of this structure, as it is traced through the Old Testament, is that it is an exchange. There is God's side of the work, and there is man's response. The salvation history is represented as a dialogue. God speaks to men, creatures with the gift of speech, and requires an answer from them. But speech on both sides is not mere utterance of words; it is as much deeds as words. God does things for these creatures, and expects a certain action from them in response."[1] Indeed, as Father MacKenzie points out in the same study (p. 161), the very arrangement of the Hebrew canon of the Old Testament would appear to indicate Israel's awareness that this dialogue quality was reflected in her sacred books. Holy Writ consisted of the law, the prophets, and the writings. "The concept apparently was that the Law and the Prophets were the word of God spoken to Israel, while the Writings contained Israel's response to that word, or reflections upon it."

Certainly one might present the New Testament in similar fashion, considering the Gospels (including Acts and the Apocalypse) as the Christian "word of this salvation" (Acts 13:26), while the letters of Paul and other apostolic writings might be viewed as the human response to "the message he [God] sent to the sons of Israel gospeling peace through Jesus Christ" (Acts 10:36).

In point of fact, however, the question is a more subtle one and ultimately requires a more complete answer. The Bible is truly the record of the dialogue between God and mankind; but it should be regarded as presenting *simultaneously* God's initiative in confronting man with the divine self-revelation *and* the human response of faith, which is man's contribution to this privileged conversation called sacred history. Salvation history is fundamentally God's autobiography; and God must in consequence be regarded as principal author of Sacred Scripture. But at the same time, the sacred books which contain the record of this divine condescension and initiative were written by human beings in human language, and hence are the concrete expression of these men's reply of loving obedience and faith to God's message. The Bible is at one and the same time God's self-revelation and that of the inspired writer. These two facets of Scripture are distinct or distinguishable, but

---

1 R. A. F. MacKenzie, S.J., "The Structure of the Old Testament," *The Basilian Teacher* (February, 1961), 157. See also Vatican Council II, *Dogmatic Constitution on Divine Revelation*, nn. 5, 21, 25.

they cannot be separated out in any material fashion. The entire biblical narrative is a divine-human Word, or, better perhaps, the Word of God incarnate in the human words of men.

This significant truth has not always been operative in the approach to the Bible as it is at the present day. Exaggerated insistence upon the *ipsissima verba Jesu*, characteristic of so many theology manuals, may serve to exemplify what I mean. It was made to appear as if the cited logia of Jesus were the divine element in our Gospels, while the remarks of the evangelists represented the human element. The fact is that these *ipsissima verba Jesu* do contain Christ's message; but they reproduce his teaching as already interpreted to a greater or lesser degree by the sacred writer, or the tradition which he records.

Since, as I believe, this question is germane to the discussion we have in hand, it may be well to remind ourselves at once that the sayings of Jesus in the Gospels, like the message of Yahweh expressed in the law or the prophetic writings, may be said to constitute a normative guide to our own religious experience precisely because they are not stenographic reports of the divine utterances, but the fruit of a specially privileged religious experience on the part of the inspired writers. Indeed, the intensely personal nature of these varying reactions to Jesus Christ, his message and his mission, make it possible to speak of the spirituality of John as distinct from that of Paul or Matthew. And therein lies the paramount value of their inspired writings for evoking and regulating our own approach to Christianity, our own spiritual experiences. Moreover, it is because we are confronted by these various spiritualities, in the Old as in the New Testament, that the Bible can be rightly considered normative for the Christian life.

This point of view is one of the many good things which the recent instruction of the Biblical Commission has provided for us in its discussion of the historical truth of the Gospels. "For, out of the material which they had received, the sacred authors selected especially those items which were adopted to the varied circumstances of the faithful as well as to the end which they themselves wished to attain; these they recounted in a manner consonant with those circumstances and with that end. And since the meaning of a statement depends, amongst other things, on the place which it has in a given sequence, the Evangelists, in handing on the words or the deeds of our Saviour, explained them for the advantage of their readers by respectively seeing them, one Evangelist in one context, another in another. For this reason the exegete must ask himself what the Evangelist intended by recounting a saying or a fact in a certain way, or by placing it in a certain context. For the truth of the narrative is not affected in the slightest by the fact that Evangelists report the sayings or the doings of our Lord in a different order, and that they use different words to express what He said, not keeping to the very letter, but nevertheless preserving the sense."[2]

The Bible, Creative of Religious Experience

I have stated that Holy Scripture is a normative guide to religious experience. This somewhat ambiguous assertion may be understood in two ways: the Bible is to be thought of as actually creative of a validly Christian religious experience; or, the Bible is to be considered as the proper yardstick for correctly measuring the validity of one's personal religious experience. I believe it is possible to understand the assertion correctly in both senses. Through its prayerful consideration, Scripture is a specially fruitful source of the Christian spiritual life. It is in this fashion that the Rule of St. Benedict makes Holy Writ the object of *lectio divina*. In chapter forty-eight the author speaks of this monastic exercise, together with manual labor, as the remedy for *otiositas*, thereby expressing the conviction that the reading of Holy Writ demands the monk's careful attention and activity. Indeed, the same chapter informs us that *lectio divina* is understood to be the meditative or reflective reading of the Bible (*meditare aut legere*).[3] In treating of the monastic observance of Lent in chapter forty-nine, the Rule associates this *lectio divina* with *compunctio cordis;* hence it is no mere intellectual exercise, but one which is aimed precisely at effecting religious experience.[4] In fact, it is considered to have the same effect as the kerygma: *metanoia,* or, as St. Ignatius would describe it for a later age, *reformatio vitae.*

In this connection it is instructive to recall that the Vulgate translates the phrase which describes the effects upon his Jewish audience of Peter's Pentecostal preaching (*katenugēsan tēn*

---

2 The text of the *Instructio de Historica Evangeliorum Veritate* is cited according to the official English translation, which may be found in *Catholic Biblical Quarterly,* XXVI (1964), 308-309.

3 "Idleness is the enemy of the soul. Therefore the brethren should be occupied at certain times in manual labor and at other fixed hours in sacred reading [*in lectione divina*] . . . But if anyone should be so negligent and slothful that he is unwilling or unable to meditate or read [*meditare aut legere*], let some work be imposed upon him to keep him from being idle." *The Holy Rule of St. Benedict,* ch. 48.

4 "Although the life of a monk ought at all times to have about it the aspect of Lenten observance, nevertheless, since few have the strength for this, we exhort all to preserve their lives in all purity and also during these sacred days to atone for the negligences of other times. This is done worthily if we refrain from all vices and devote ourselves to prayer with tears, reading, compunction of heart [*compunctioni cordis*], and abstinence." (*Ibid.,* ch. 49.)

kardian), as *compuncti sunt corde* (Acts 2:37). The *compunctus corde* of the Vulgate Psalm 108:16 is a representative of the Old Testament class, the 'anawīm. *Compungere* was originally a medical term signifying "to lance," which came to denote the interior spiritual experience or state resulting from man's confrontation with the divine message.

This is probably as good a place as any to recall that when we speak of Scripture as a "normative guide" we mean something more than a merely intellectual criterion, or even some external law of conduct. The appeal of the Bible is to the whole man, his emotions and imagination as well as his understanding. The solemn, official doctrinal declarations of the magisterium of the Church are addressed to our intelligence for an orthodox comprehension of the truths of the faith. They were never intended to be something the Christian might live on. The statutes and prescriptions of canon law are certainly normative for the Christian life; but they do not operate with the rich unction and supremely human attractiveness of Holy Writ. "Whatever was written of old was written for our *instruction*, that by patience and the *consolation* of the Scriptures we might have hope," Paul asserts in his letter to the Romans (Rom 15:4). Thus the reading of Scripture should be carried out in such a way as to involve the whole person, affectively no less than intellectually. This should be borne in mind particularly when we come, as we presently shall, to discuss the Bible as the norm against which to measure and assess our own religious experience.

For the moment, however, we may profitably explore further the way in which Sacred Scripture provides the means of creating a truly Christian religious experience. For the Jesuit the most familiar method of attaining this goal is through the techniques St. Ignatius has bequeathed us in the Spiritual Exercises. I have in mind primarily the *contemplatio* with its preludes, the *historia*, and the imaginative "seeing the place," where I am to make myself part of the mystery, the *compositio loci*. As you are well aware, the Ignatian contemplation concerns itself with the events of sacred history, where the Ignatian meditation is taken up with the consideration of truths of the faith. While the contemplation, within the framework of the Exercises, is devoted to the events of Jesus' earthly and risen life, it can serve equally well for a prayerful, experienced assimilation of the events in Old Testament salvation history. As a matter of fact, the gospel embraces—as Paul was well aware (Rom 1:2)—the sacred history of Israel.

The Ignatian contemplation aims at showing the exercitant how

Ignatian Contemplation

5

to integrate himself into the dialogue between God and man in his own era and culture. For this, the work of one's understanding or even of one's imagination is not sufficient: the whole person must be caught up, engaged, committed to assuming his rightful place in the ongoing sacred dialogue which is contemporary salvation history. It is this "putting oneself into the picture," so to say, which St. Ignatius wishes us to accomplish by the *contemplatio*. I must endeavour, with grace, to put myself into the religious attitude symbolically represented by listening, seeing. Through the contemplation of some scene from the biblical narrative of salvation I can "hear" what Jesus Christ says to me in my own existential situation; or I can "see" what he intends to accomplish through me in my world of the twentieth century. In short, I must somehow learn to behold Christ as he confronts me in my own particular and personal chapter of sacred history. Through this religious experience of the Ignatian contemplation I am fashioned into a witness for Christ.

Biblical Spiritualities

To help me achieve this difficult assignment I have the aid of the various "spiritualities" in both Old and New Testaments. These can serve me as a normative guide inasmuch as they are actually the recorded religious experience of certain specially privileged members of the People of God—both Christian and Israelite. These inspired authors have left me their reaction of faith to the revelation enshrined in their writings. By my own prayerful appropriation of these sacred texts I am touched through Christ's grace in the innermost part of my being. From the perusal of the hagiographers' successful participation in the dialogue with God, I am taught to make my own response in my time and with the means at my disposal—historical, cultural, and ascetical.

Here perhaps it might be well to recall that this response of mine, though intensely personal, is in no sense an act of rugged individualism: I make my response necessarily as a member of God's people, or better as a son in God's family. The celebrated Ignatian phrase, *familiaritas cum Deo in oratione*,[5] might be well translated as the prayerful acquisition of a "sense of family," God's family. To integrate myself into sacred history means inevitably to

---

5 "In regard to the qualities which are desirable in the superior general, the first is that he should be closely united with God our Lord and intimate with him in prayer and all his actions . . ." (*Constitutions of the Society of Jesus*, [723], P. 9, c. 2, n. 1.) "For the preservation and development . . . of the Society, . . . the means which unite the human instrument with God . . . are more effective than those which equip it in relation to men. Such are, for example, goodness, . . . and familiarity with God our Lord in spiritual exercises of devotion . . ." (*Ibid.*, [813], P. 10, n. 2.)

integrate myself into this supernatural family of the Father of all mankind.

Permit me at this point to illustrate this somewhat abstract discussion by a brief reference to a central theme in Pauline spirituality. The divine initiative in effecting the redemption of rebellious man belongs, on Paul's view, to God *as Father*: it proceeds from his fatherly love of sinful man. "God demonstrates his love for us by the fact that, whilst we were still sinners, Christ died on our behalf" (Rom 5:8). Yet, while the work of our redemption stems from the Father's love in Pauline theology (as indeed in all other New Testament writers), Paul also speaks of the "wisdom of God," —a conception which represents the Father in his relations with fallen man as "a realist." God deals with man in his actual human dilemma; that is, taking cognizance of the fact that man, through the sin of Adam and his own personal sins, is constituted in a state of rebelliousness. He is "under condemnation." Mankind might be said to owe "a debt" to the Father, provided we understand such a figure of speech to connote that one act of filial obediential love which the Father desired to receive from man, yet which man in his fallen state was totally incapable of making. The divine action through which the Father made it possible for disobedient man to perform this necessary filial gesture of loving obedience Paul calls the "wisdom of God." "Since, in the wisdom of God the world through its wisdom did not know God, it has been God's good pleasure through the foolishness of the kerygma to save those who have faith" (1 Cor 1:21; cf. Rom 11:33ff.).

Christ's part in the working out of the Father's plan of salvation was to accept with total filial obedience his own death (and resurrection), as determined by God *in all its concrete reality*, thereby enabling sinful man to posit *in Christ* one perfect act of filial love towards the Father. Christ did this *instead of* (the Greek term is *anti*) rebellious man, since man in his existential situation was incapable of making such an act of obedience to his heavenly Father on his own behalf. In this sense Christ's death was vicarious, "in our place." But Paul is also aware that Jesus Christ by dying and rising did not exclude or excuse man from dying and rising personally. He died principally "on our behalf" (*hyper* in Greek), creating the possibility of personal participation in a "new creation," Christian death. That is to say, Christ's death and resurrection, far from rendering it unnecessary or impossible for mankind to share this supremely redemptive experience, actually opened up the possibility of man's participation in this saving action. Through his death and resurrection Christ involved mankind in this very process of salvation: he died and rose as the last Man, the second

7

Adam (1 Cor 15:21-22,45; Rom 5:19). "One died for all: therefore all have died. And he died on behalf of all (*hyper pantōn*) in order that the living might no longer live for themselves, but for him who died and was raised for them" (2 Cor 5:14-15).

Paul thus makes it clear that my most important response in the dialogue between God and man is the moment of my own death, when by the grace of Christ I make as perfect as possible my filial act of trusting, loving acceptance of my final self-denudation, by which I cooperate in my own redemption. This is what Paul calls elsewhere, "falling asleep through Jesus." "For if we believe that Jesus died and rose, so too God will bring all those who have fallen asleep through Jesus together with him" (1 Th 4:14).

The Bible, Normative for Religious Experience

It is time however to consider the second sense of our original assertion: Scripture as the norm for assessing the validity of one's religious experience. We might begin by reminding ourselves of the full meaning of the article of faith that the Bible is the Word of God. The statement is something of a paradox; for the Scriptures were written in human language, by human beings. God does not "speak" English—or even Greek or Hebrew! Nor does God write books. When we assert our belief that the Bible is the Word of God we mean that the authors of these sacred books enjoyed a special privilege, were "inspired" in a sense far surpassing that "inspiration" commonly attributed to the world's great literary artists. The hagiographer is endowed with the ability of expressing through his own language God's self-revelation. Accordingly, God speaks to us through him in a more direct, personal, immediate way than he speaks to us through nature or through the ordinary events of human history.

We may remind ourselves at this point that language has actually a threefold function; it is not merely a vehicle for the transmission of ideas. This is too narrow a view of the significance of speech. When I address myself to another, I may indeed transmit to him certain information which I possess; and this is certainly one of the purposes of speech. Yet inevitably in addressing another person I also communicate to him something of myself: I reveal my personality through whatever it is I say to him. There is a third function of language: I speak to another person, and thereby I involve him in a new interpersonal relationship with myself. I do not only pass on information, nor do I only tell him something about myself. I also awaken some reaction in the one I address. He is not quite the same after being engaged by me in this intercourse which we call language.

The Bible as the Word of God certainly communicates divine

8

truth to men; but intellectual instruction about God's action in history is not its sole, or even its principal purpose. It is also intended, as Paul points out, for our "consolation." By the very fact that it is God's Word, it reveals God in a most intimate, personal way. And moreover it contains a message by which God seeks to involve me as a person, to speak to me as myself, and as a member of his People. Thus the Bible presents itself to me with a divinely imperious demand for my submission and acceptance. Indeed, it presents itself thus to the Church; and in this sense the Bible may be rightly said to confront the Church in her daily life and in her journey through history.

The Constitution of Vatican II on Divine Revelation, *Dei Verbum*, states, in speaking of the place of the Bible in Christian preaching: "*Omnis ergo praedicatio ecclesiastica sicut ipsa religio christiana Sacra Scriptura nutriatur et regatur oportet*" ("Thus all preaching in the Church must, *like the Christian religion itself*, be nourished *and regulated* by Sacred Scripture") (No. 21). In this sense the Scriptures constitute the normative guide par excellence against which I can evaluate my religious experience. *Constitution "Dei Verbum"*

This of course implies the possibility of a real confrontation with the message, the personal communication, and the divine imperative contained in the Scriptures. In this connection there are two movements of which we should be aware: the tendency to up-date past events which is characteristic of the Bible, and the necessary task of our "going back in spirit to those remote centuries of the East" of which Pius XII speaks in *Divino afflante Spiritu*.[6]

By the updating tendency of Scripture, I mean the characteristic effort of the sacred writers to remain relevant to contemporary man in any age.[7] It is this quality which has led the Church to enshrine the Eucharistic action of her public worship in the setting of the liturgy of the Word. One of the most frequent examples of this forward looking tendency in the Gospels is the repeated phrase which accompanies so many of Jesus' logia, "Amen, amen, I *say* to you. . ." There is an informative instance of this up-dating movement in the book of Deuteronomy. As you know, this last book of the Pentateuch probably reached its present form only in the seventh or sixth century. The exilic or post-exilic author-editor directs his message, not to the generation of Israel in the desert, but *Updating Tendency of the Bible*

6 ". . . omnino oportet mente quasi redeat interpres ad remota illa Orientis saecula . . ." *Acta Apostolicae Sedis*, XXXV (1943), 314-315.
7 Cf. D. M. Stanley, S.J., "The Fonts of Preaching," *Liturgy for the People: Essays in Honor of Gerald Ellard, S.J.* (Milwaukee, 1963), 21-28.

9

to his own contemporaries, when he makes Moses say: "Hear, O Israel, the statutes and ordinances which I am delivering in your hearing *today*. . . . The Lord our God made a covenant *with us* at Horeb. It was not with our forefathers that the Lord made this covenant, but *with ourselves, who are all here alive today*" (Dt 5:1-3).

This same sensitiveness to the perennial modernity of the Word of God is evinced particularly by the evangelist St. Matthew, which is undoubtedly one of the reasons why his Gospel has proven so effective for purposes of public worship. The author frequently employs the present tense ("he says") when introducing the sayings of Jesus. He seems intent upon indicating the contemporary relevance of Jesus' message for his Christian readers. Like other inspired writers Matthew is aware that while God has revealed himself through a series of past events, yet by his will to have the past committed to writing God continues to reveal himself (above all in Christ) to us in the present. This continuing youthfulness and novelty of the scriptural Word of God is, I believe, one of the chief qualities which make of it a most effective normative guide to the Christian's religious experience. When the twentieth century believer reads, for example, Jesus' fiery excoriation of the bankrupt religious spirit of many of his Jewish contemporaries (Mt 23:2-39), he must consider this message as directed to himself in his own times—for such is the clear intention of the sacred writer.

Putting Oneself in the Biblical Picture The second movement towards this effective confrontation with Holy Writ, also ultimately designed to produce a truly Christian religious experience, is the effort on the part of the reader to put himself into the social, cultural, political, historical situations of the past, in which the events of sacred history were played out. This is accomplished by modern scholarship through the "proper use of the aids afforded by history, archeology, ethnology, and other sciences, in order to discover what literary forms the writers of that early age intended to use, and did in fact employ."[8]

At first sight this scholarly procedure might appear to be quite irrelevant to, or indeed even a serious distraction from, that religious experience which is our present concern. Yet it would seem to be of supreme interest to the Christian, for a salutary comprehension of the significance of the new covenant under which he lives, to have a profound, personal grasp of the meaning of covenant (*berīth*) as a sociological institution in the ancient Near East. It is only thus that he can appreciate the fact that the cov-

8 *Divino afflante Spiritu*, in AAS, XXXV (1943), 315.

enant which Yahweh had struck with his people was in the eyes of Israel primarily a pattern for life. One of Israel's most important contributions to the history of religion was her deep-seated awareness of the necessity of uniting religion with morality —a feature of her cult of God which is unique in the ancient Near East.

It is likewise essential for a receptive attitude to the message of Israel's prophets to realize that their pronouncements were directed first and foremost to the men of their own age. The prophets addressed themselves to the social and moral abuses present in their own contemporaries; they were, in Bruce Vawter's happy phrase, most truly the "conscience of Israel." As a consequence the prophetic word retains its urgency and its contemporary character for the Christian people. This message, the fruit of an intense experience of the otherness of Yahweh as well as of his profoundly personal nature (in contrast with the nature gods of the pagans [*goïm*]), of his loving condescension and utter reliability (in contrast with the freakish, whimsical, irresponsible character of pagan gods), retains its validity and dynamism for recreating in the modern man of faith a true religious experience of our God, who through his Son has made an everlasting covenant with us Christians.

If I may close with a final reference to the New Testament as a norm for genuine religious experience, I should like to recall the Johannine doctrine, echoing that of Paul (Gal 5:14; Rom 13:8-10), that the whole business of Christian living comes down to one divine command of Jesus, "You must love one another, as I have loved you" (Jn 13:34). If Israel's law and Israel's prophets make us conscious of the necessity of uniting religion with morality, our Lord has recreated this theme by insisting that the only way we can effectively love God is by loving one another. This is the burden of the Matthean parable of the last judgment (Mt 25:31-46). The possibility of observing this totally "new commandment" of Jesus is given us with the great gift of God's love, "poured forth in our hearts by the Spirit" (Rom 5:5). It is indeed through this supreme "law of the Spirit of life in Christ Jesus" (Rom 8:2) that the Christian is freed from all law as an extrinsic norm of conduct, from that "letter which kills" (2 Cor 3:6). Yet such freedom of conscience presupposes the proper formation of the Christian conscience. Such formation comes indeed most truly from the Scriptures—the valid, normative guide to genuine religious experience.

Feast of St. Ignatius Loyola
July 31, 1966.

THE FIRST WEEK

THE AIM OF THE FIRST WEEK of the Spiritual Exercises is to put *The Aim* oneself unresistingly, trustfully, as totally as possible, with the grace of Christ, into the hands of God our Father, author of that ongoing process which is called salvation history.

As a prelude to his work, St. Ignatius has set down the *Principle and Foundation*, [23] which epitomizes the entire message of the *Spiritual Exercises*. The author composed this statement after most of his book was completed, in order that he might help the exercitant to make a complete commitment of himself to God who is his creator.

Man, the Bible teaches us, has as his most basic vocation to *Man's Vocation* vindicate that "image and likeness of God" in which he was created, by exercising his God-given "dominion over the fish of the sea, the birds of the sky . . . and all the living things that creep upon the earth" (Gn 1:28). St. Paul echoes this teaching by viewing man as mediator of the redemption of the material universe (Rom 8:18-22). This stewardship of man also reaches out in various interpersonal relationships with his fellow human beings, St. Ignatius implies. Man can be redeemed only by adopting an attitude of mind communicated to him by divine revelation: "indifference." This is to be acquired by the prayerful consideration of the biblical record of sacred history, and it is essential to man's total fulfillment as a person. For it comprehends the free choice or rejection of "the other things" (*reliqua*), that is, all created reality, including other persons, which are not part of a person's own innermost self. These myriad choices, which make man the person he is or is to be, must be guided throughout life by a single criterion, the will of God. If man were to judge what helps or hinders him in his goal by any other standard, he can never be beyond the danger of turning into the dross of Stoicism a golden principle of action basic to Christian faith: to choose "what is *more* conducive to the end for which we are created."

15

*Sin in
Sacred History*   The first week begins properly with the Ignatian exercise on
"the first, second, and third sin" (that of the angels, the first parents, a man lost through a single serious sin). The recommended
methodology is the *meditatio*, which is performed by "employing
the three powers of the soul" [45] (memory, understanding, will—
a favorite Augustinian trinitarian image).

Whether or not one presents this meditation as formulated by
St. Ignatius, it is of paramount importance to note that he seeks
here to induct the exercitant into a true, personal experience of
salvation history. He wishes to give him an existential appreciation
of what existence outside the gospel actually means. This truly
biblical viewpoint is intended to help the Christian grasp the sin-
filled historical context in which his own sins have occurred, by
presenting before his eyes in prayer the principal events of sacred
history that have, or can have, a constant, baleful influence upon
his own personal sinfulness and actual sins.

The sequel to this consideration is the meditation upon one's
own sins. Here the aim is to bring home to one a realistic picture
of himself as a personality deformed by his past. At best, he has
an almost overpowering inclination to ratify, by actual sin, the
original sin of Adam. A further consideration is concerned with
hell, the total absence of the God who is truth, justice, mercy, love.
It is the ultimate and logical conclusion of an existence deliberately
lived outside the gospel of Jesus Christ.

One most significant feature of St. Ignatius' technique in the
first week is to confront the exercitant with the crucified Christ, as
he does in the colloquy in the meditation on personal sins [45].
Thus he reminds the Christian of the fundamental truth that the
Cross is God's continuing judgment upon history. Not only does the
Cross save sinful man from despair, it provides a divinely given
criterion for interpreting the meaning of all that happens in this
world.

*Discernment
of Spirits*   One of St. Ignatius' most significant contributions to the science
of spirituality is his formulation of "rules for the discernment of
spirits." The first series [313-327] he considers more appropriate
for the first week. Since his purpose is not information, even about
Christian truth, but an experiential knowledge (the biblical
sense of "knowing") of salvation history in which the exercitant
is to seek to become personally involved, the author of the *Spiritual
Exercises* is intent upon bringing him to a reflexive, conscious
awareness of his own spiritual reactions. Because St. Ignatius is a
realist he presupposes little, if any, spiritual formation in the one
who undergoes the Exercises for the first time. Hence his rules

of discernment for the first week are orientated towards winning the victory over cowardice and sloth.

We might say that the purpose particularly envisaged in the first week is the same as that of the apostolic preaching: *metanoia*, the personal, religious involvement with Christ, which means a total reorientation of a man's religious attitudes. St. Ignatius says *"ut homo vincat seipsum"* [21]. And this can only be accomplished by the response of Christian faith to the good news.

ISRAEL'S VOCATION, EFFECT OF YAHWEH'S FREE CHOICE
Isaiah 43:1-7

And now, so says Yahweh,
Who created you, O Jacob, and formed you, O Israel,
"Fear not! I have redeemed you.
I have called you by your name—you are mine!

2 If you pass through the waters, I will be with you,
Through the rivers, they shall not engulf you.
If you walk through fire, you shall not be scorched,
Through the flame, it will not burn you;

3 For I am Yahweh, your God,
The holy one of Israel, your saviour.—
Egypt I have offered as your ransom,
Ethiopia and Sheba in exchange for you,

4 Because you are worth much in my eyes,
You are precious—I love you!—
Men have I given in exchange for you,
And peoples instead of you.

5 Fear not! I am with you.
From the Orient will I bring your children,
And from the west I will assemble you;

6 To the north I will say, 'Give them back!'
And to the south, 'Do not keep them!'
Make my sons return from afar,
And my daughters from the ends of the earth!

7 Each that is called by my name,
Whom I have created and formed
And made for my glory."

Chapter 1

DIMENSIONS OF ISRAEL'S ELECTION
BY YAHWEH

"AND NOW, SO SAYS YAHWEH, who created you, O Jacob, and formed you, O Israel, 'Fear not! I have redeemed you. I have called you by your name—you are mine!'"

Dear brothers in Christ, I suggest that for our prayer tomorrow we reflect upon some of the ideas expressed in the forty-third chapter of Isaiah (Is 43:1-7). God is revealed here as the creator of Israel, that is to say, of his people. Hence God appears as the great motive power for Israel's optimism, an optimism that is based upon faith in Yahweh "who made sky and earth." This passage also suggests Israel's humility, Israel's acceptance of the fact that she was not the most ancient, the most cultured, the most successful in foreign affairs among the other nations of the ancient world. Israel's writers bear testimony untiringly to the fact that Israel was a latecomer in the ancient Near East. These authors never neglected to express Israel's creaturely dependence upon him who had made her what she was: God's people. *Israel's Notion of God*

But this creator God had another name which is suggested here. Israel knew him best by another title, one not of power, but of mercy. "Fear not! I have redeemed you." God had created this people by bringing them out of the bondage of Egypt. Egypt, in the prophets, was to become a symbol for sin. The redemption was God's act of "purchase." He had acquired this people for himself.

"I have called you by your name—you are mine!" A mother calls her child by its name. Thus she begins the long education towards self-identity as a person, which is the painful human process of growing up. And the prophet Isaiah here suggests that Israel's basic vocation was to be human. This is our fundamental call also. Before we are Christians, before we are religious, before we arc priests, we have a call, a sacred call from God, to be human. "I have called you by your name." *Israel's Call to Be Human*

From the biblical view, nothing can exist without a name. Accordingly in the opening chapter of the book of Genesis, the sacred writer represents his God, the God of Israel, as naming the various elements in the universe that they might begin to exist. Later, God was to call Jacob "Israel," since he was destined to become the eponymic ancestor of God's people, giving his name to them. By this act of changing the name Jacob, which meant "cheat" (Jacob was a liar!), to Israel, God was simply summoning the patriarch—and through him, his people—to be human (Gn 35:10).

What does it mean to be a human being? It means, first of all, that I know and—still more important—that I accept myself; that I have a good relationship with myself. This is what the child learns by being called by its name by mother or father. To be human means to be happy—not necessarily smiling, not merely "nice," but possessing basically a healthy relationship with other human beings, accepting their humanity and their inhumanity, not feeling threatened by the excellence of others. To be human also means to be responsible, to accept responsibility in making decisions, to have enough courage to be right and wrong. For as Isaiah goes on to suggest, human life contains an ineluctable element of risk. "If you pass through the waters, I will be with you, through the rivers, they shall not engulf you. If you walk through fire, you shall not be scorched, through the flame, it will not burn you; for I am Yahweh, your God, the holy one of Israel, your saviour."

The Risk of Being God's People

Thus the prophet describes Israel's vocation as a vocation to be a people, like any other people, like any other society of human beings, as a call fundamentally to be human. At the same time it was a summons to be God's people, to be *the* people. And God, in giving Israel her vocation, did not for a moment suggest that he would protect her from the risks entailed in being human. The prophet represents these risks by employing two of the most powerfully suggestive symbols that we find throughout the Bible: water and fire. The very ambivalence, the undifferentiated character of the symbol suggests this element of risk. Water as symbol represents at one and the same time life and death. God did not remove the element of risk from Israel's life as a people in giving her a vocation. As a matter of fact, if we read the history of Israel with attention, we see that, from the very moment when God called his people out of Egypt to offer sacrifice to him in the desert, the divine call was an invitation to risk, to hazard. Israel's real greatness, her fidelity to that vocation, was demonstrated not by being sheltered, not in being secure, not in withdrawing from

20

difficulties and the hazards of life, but in accepting the risks with faith in God's promise: "I will be with you." Her God was from first to last in Israel's eyes "Emmanuel," ("with us is God"). This was Israel's most characteristic conception of Yahweh: the one who remained with her faithfully.

According to Isaiah, Yahweh promises it is through risk, in time of crisis—"if you pass through the waters, I will be with you." This startling insight remains true for me. God *is* the risk in my life. The element of hazard discloses the divine element in my vocation. My calling, most fundamentally, the prophet tells me, is to be human, to be fully a man. And when, through baptism, I am called also to be a Christian, the risk is not diminished, rather it is increased. When I am called to be a religious, as well as a Christian, this risk is heightened yet again. When, in addition I am called to the priesthood, it is surely not to take me out of the world—if that means the avoidance of risk. For it is only in risk, in crisis, that I can find God.

And God is "the holy one of Israel." Israel's notion of holiness, the holiness of God, is that of a being totally other than any man, than any creature. And yet, though wholly other, he is intimately related to Israel. "I am your saviour." We may recall that the divine title saviour has already been given a specific content in v. 1 by the prophet, where Yahweh is equivalently named Israel's "*gōʾēl*," "kinsman-avenger." The historical reference is probably to the exodus from Egypt. Through a pact or covenant, two men or two families, two clans, two tribes or even two peoples pledged mutual loyalty. The Israelites, at least in the early period of nationhood, being primitive and nomadic were perhaps more aware of the element of risk in human life than were those peoples who lived in "the sown," the men who lived in towns and cities. For these, as Mircea Eliade has observed,[1] dwelt in safety within that magic circle, the town hedge or wall, which originated, most probably, as a fetish in order to keep out the demons and all the other enemies of man. The Hebrews were originally nomads, and risk was a familiar factor in their lives. Consequently, the kind of pact they entered into with their God was not made to eliminate risk but to engage in it more adequately and successfully. The sacred writers of Israel present Yahweh's role as covenant God through the notion of *gōʾēl*, the kinsman who can be counted on to avenge wrongs and uphold the rights of his people against all oppressors.

God
the Holy One

1 Mircea Eliade, *Patterns in Comparative Religion* (New York, 1958), 374.

You will have noted that in the middle of the third verse of this passage we encounter a new idea. Thus far the prophet has spoken of Israel's calling to be God's people as a summons to be human. Now he advances to the conception of that vocation as an election, the result of God's free choice. This suggests that the divine call possesses a much more mysterious quality. For now it is seen as the effect of Yahweh's love of preference. "Egypt I have offered as your ransom, Ethiopia and Sheba in exchange for you, because you are worth much in my eyes, you are precious—I love you!—Men have I given in exchange for you, and peoples instead of you."

In the seventh chapter of the book of Deuteronomy God lays bare the secret of his free choice of Israel. He reveals his heart to his people (Dt 7:7-8). "It was not because you were the greatest of all peoples that Yahweh set his heart on you and chose you (for you are the smallest of all peoples), but it was because Yahweh loved you. . . ." What the sacred writer has set down in the book of Deuteronomy is here repeated by the prophet Isaiah. While it is true that God loves all the nations of the world, as Israel was very well aware, and that God loves every human being, yet the inspired literature of Israel witnesses to the truth that God loves some more than he loves others. These individuals we call saints, because God's work in them is much more striking, so far as we can judge, than in the majority of men. Israel was very conscious of being herself the object of Yahweh's election, that is, of God's free, untrammeled, loving choice. "Because you are worth much in my eyes, you are precious—I love you!" "Fear not," the prophet makes God say again, "fear not! I am with you. From the Orient will I bring your children, and from the west I will assemble you; to the north I will say, 'Give them back!' and to the south, 'Do not keep them!' Make my sons return from afar, and my daughters from the ends of the earth."

The phrase "Fear not" is worthy of our attention here. In certain contexts of the Bible, it announces God's intervention, some special divine revelation, a significant historical act of God. "*Ne timeas, Maria*" ("Do not fear, Mary" Lk 1:30). It frequently has this meaning in Old Testament prophecy, as here in our passage. Fear not, God says, for I am Emmanuel. Fear not, for I am with you. This is the revelation that God had made to Israel when he acquainted her with the incredible fact that she was the object of his special predilection.

God's proper work in sacred history, as we see from the fifth and sixth verses of our pericope, is the task of unification. He created the universe to form a unity as one good thing. He formed Israel into one people out of a mob of nomads and runaway slaves, of nomadic Hebrews belonging to various tribes with no manifest desire for self-unification. The fusion of these freedom-loving clans into one people, as is clear from the book of Exodus, was solely Yahweh's idea. God made them one people. You are well aware of how this divine role runs through the Old and into the New Testament. Jesus one day upon the mountain of Galilee would speak of the angels who at the last judgment would be sent forth to assemble God's people from the ends of the earth (Mt 13:39).

Just as Israel's formation into a nation implied the call of each individual Israelite to belong to God, so in the Christian dispensation the work of unification, God's special prerogative, reaches each person, affects you and me personally. The integration of my personality is ultimately God's work. Was it St. Irenaeus who defined the Christian as consisting of body, soul, and the Holy Spirit? St. Bernard, pursuing that hobby of the Middle Ages, imaginative etymology, points out in one of his sermons that the word *monachus* (monk) signifies a fully integrated person, deriving the word from *monos*, "the man who is wholly one." This is of course not good etymology, but it is healthy spirituality. Now Yahweh, Isaiah informs us, not only unified the Hebrews as his people, he also effected the integration of each Israelite as a person. For the prophet asserts that the realization of man's basic call to be human waits upon the grace of God. What then is a person? What is it to be a Christian? Isaiah gives us an important clue, I believe, in the seventh verse of this passage: "Each that is called by my name, whom I have created and formed and made for my glory." In the opening verse, Yahweh was represented as saying that he has called Israel, by its name as a people. "I have called you by your name." Here however there is an advance in the thought. We learn that each individual Israelite "is called by *my* name," bears the name of God!

When a man loves a woman, he gives her his own name. When God loves man, he bestows his name upon that person. How better could Isaiah express the personal interest that God feels in every individual human being? And this personal interest is displayed by the God who is totally love! God permits, indeed, commands me to revise that pessimistic view of myself which is the result of so many sins, so many failures, so many abortive attempts at self-reformation. God brings me indeed to confess my sins. Yet in the Bible such confession by man is a form of glorifying God—man's highest function in the hierarchical order of the universe. To confess my sins and to proclaim God's glory are one and the same thing. And the miracle of it is that when man confesses his sinfulness, God deigns to listen. Moreover God is willing to listen even to me as a person, not as a mere cipher, a faceless individual. He heeds me as myself. Thus before I can ever begin to accept myself —one of the most fundamental acts of being human—God has already accepted me as I am. God has deigned to speak even to me. God has—it seems incredible!—given me his name. And so I may be described or designated as the man who is called by God's name. After all I am a Christian. I bear the name of—Christ, God's Son.

Accordingly, this basic vocation to be human has in very truth a divine dimension. My humanity is incomplete unless somehow my natural tendency towards God, the effect of my being called by God's name, is actuated and realized. That this is so, I have God's word. To reassure me of this overpowering truth, I have his call. He has called me out of nothingness, and he has called me to be supremely and totally myself. And when I reach this state of being myself, I can say that I am called by God's name. Moreover, God has not only called me, he has freely chosen me. I am the object, personally and as a member of the Christian people, of his free, deliberate, loving choice, of his divine election. And so in me also this work of unification and integration is principally the work of God. He labors to integrate me socially in his people; and to perfect me personally by recreating me in the image of his own Son. It is to achieve this goal that my God has summoned me to an existence which entails risk. For that he has called me into an existence which is truly a gamble. He has never once promised to eliminate the hazard, to withdraw me from the risk. He has however promised me the one thing that really counts: "I will be with you!"

THE INVITATORY PSALM
Psalm 95 [94]

Come let us shout with joy for Yahweh:
Let us acclaim the rock of our salvation!

2 Let us come before his face with thanksgiving:
Let us acclaim him to the sound of music.

3 For Yahweh is a great God,
A great king above all the gods.

4 In his hands are the depths of the earth,
And the summits of the mountains belong to him.

5 His is the sea—he has made it—
And the earth—his hands have fashioned it.

6 Enter his court! let us bow down,
Let us prostrate ourselves before Yahweh who made us,

7 For it is he who is our God.
We are the people of his pasturing,
The sheep of his hands.

8 Today if only you would heed his voice!
. . .

INITIAL ATTITUDES TO PRAYER

OBVIOUSLY, IN ANY GROUP of retreatants such as this there will be those who feel the need of stressing certain truths rather than others. All that one who is suggesting thoughts for the Exercises can do is to follow a kind of mean. So we should be free to exercise our responsibility in this, free to follow the points or not. But if we are to make the truths of the faith real to ourselves, we should react, we should adapt or change the rhythm of our life. And so in a certain sense the first day of a retreat—even an eight-day retreat—is a kind of lost day. It is spent principally in getting tuned in, changing from my habitual way of acting or thinking, getting ready to listen. Accordingly, one of the principal preoccupations of the first day ought to be to rid myself of my fears —those nameless, formless feelings and apprehensions that are, perhaps, the greatest distraction from hearing God speak to us.

The Psalter, Israel's Prayerbook "Come let us shout with joy for Yahweh. Let us acclaim the rock of our salvation! Let us come before his face with thanksgiving! Let us acclaim him to the sound of music." This psalm, as you know, forms the invitatory to the divine office. It is Psalm ninety-five in the Hebrew Bible (Psalm ninety-four in the Vulgate).

There is one wonderful and striking quality which characterizes the prayer of Israel. It is so very uninhibited, so "free-wheeling." It is completely and utterly candid and sincere. We learn, really, more about Israel from the psalter than we do from the rest of the Bible. We learn more about her spiritual life, her religious attitudes. This fascinating book has been called the "prayerbook of the second temple." As a matter of fact, the psalter is in many respects more relevant, more contemporary, for us than much of the rest of the Old Testament. We find it more appealing and congenial than those credal formulae through which Israel expressed her faith, in part because the psalter is poetry, and poetry speaks a universal language. This universal appeal is created with particular effectiveness by the use of the symbolism we find in the psalms. Moreover, the psalter gives us a much more balanced view of Israel, of her hopes and aspirations, of her religious spirit, than do, for example, the fiery denunciations of the prophets. As Father Bruce Vawter points out in his discerning book, *The Conscience of Israel*,[1] while the prophets were always claiming that no one listened to them, it is clear that someone must have heeded their message or we should not possess the written record of their gospel.

And, of course, for us who are priests the psalter is the gift of the Church to us. Today many, if not most, priests recite the breviary in the vernacular. Yet we should be aware that an intelligible translation is not the whole answer to the problem of acquiring a loving, profound acquaintance with this collection of prayers—the only prayerbook that the Holy Spirit has seen fit to inspire. We have to study it if we are to appreciate it. A deep love of the psalter is specially important for us who belong to the Latin rite, inasmuch as it provides the needed balance to the sober, sedate, somewhat calculated attitude of the Roman Mass form. The Byzantine liturgy is much more effervescent, more human, because more emotional and affective than our own. It is the psalter that gives us Latin priests the opportunity of developing this phase of our prayer-life. Yet as I say we must study it; and this means in the first place getting to know the life-situation of these prayers of Israel. It even helps, although here our conclusions may remain open to question, to ascertain the date at which these various prayers were composed. It is of paramount importance to recognize the specific literary forms they can assume. Some are thanksgiving prayers; many of them are "laments," that is, petitions; and there are also hymns, both personal and national. Above all, we should take note of the psalms of confidence and trust, for these exhibit a prayer-form that was peculiar to Israel. In the Moabite psalms we have parallels to the thanksgiving psalms, to the laments, the hymns. But there is nothing quite like Israel's psalms of trust and confidence, because these stem from Israel's unique and divinely revealed idea of God.

And so here in Psalm 94, the life-situation, the event for which this prayer was composed, was undoubtedly the public cultus, the liturgy of the temple. Whether it comes from the late regnal period, or whether it is post-exilic after the restoration of the temple need not concern us here. Liturgical worship was the setting in which the psalter was born.

You may have noticed this morning how the Church in the

1 Bruce Vawter, C.M., *The Conscience of Israel: Pre-exilic Prophets and Prophecy* (New York, 1961), 16.

Collect for the first Saturday in Passiontide emphasizes the pedagogical significance of our Christian public worship. The people
of God are "educated by the sacred rites" (*sacris erudita ac-
tionibus*). And we shall see how Israel in this psalm educated
herself, formed herself after the pattern for life that almighty God
had given her in the covenant. But liturgical worship, if it is to
be effective, cannot be mere antiquarianism. Nor can it be merely
a formalized assembly, even for such lofty reasons as the worship and the praise of God. It must somehow, through its conventions and its rubrics, give expression, sincere expression, to a
genuine religious experience, a true religious feeling, or it is an
empty show.

*Deus Praesens
in the Cultus*

"Come let us shout with joy for Yahweh: Let us acclaim the
rock of our salvation!" God is often represented in the Old Testament, as Christ occasionally is in the New, by the symbolism of a
rock. A rock ensures stability. This symbol suggests that grace
which all of us, all human beings, need and pray for—security,
inner peace. You will recall moreover that the God of whom the
Bible speaks is not God "as he is in himself," but God as revealed,
God as he has spoken to Israel. The figure of the rock here reminds
us of the sign-value in ancient, primitive religions of a mountain,
which can symbolize man's approach to God, the avenue or axis
along which human beings may encounter deity.

"Let us come before his face with thanksgiving." Yahweh was for
Israel the *Deus praesens*. And we Christians, we Christian priests,
stand before the face of God present to us in a marvelously new
manner through the incarnation. It may help to remind ourselves
that the incarnation gives a new Christian dimension to the psalter.
Hence it is before the face of the Son become man that we now
recite the praises of his Father. And the most basic attitude suggested by the present psalm is gratitude—that "plenary indul-
gence" for all our faults and failures and sins. There is no
earthly or human obstacle to familiarity with God, no impediment
to intercourse with him, which cannot be obliterated or absorbed
in the strong solvent of our thanks. "Let us acclaim him to the
sound of music."

*Worshiped as
Creator and King*

The next verse, in a manner typical of the psalm form, provides
the motivation for gratitude. Why ought we to enter God's presence
and sing his praise? "For Yahweh is a great God, a great king above
all the gods." Here we find expressed the principal motif of the
Jerusalem liturgy which springs from Israel's faith in God's position as king. As the creator God, Yahweh is world Lord. You will

28

recall the brief episode in the book of Genesis in which Melchisedek is represented as blessing Abraham: "Blessed," he says, "be
Abraham by the God who made the sky and earth" (Gn 14:19).
Melchisedek's God is *'Elyōn*, "the most high." He is king over the
entire universe. Here our psalmist employs some very ancient
titles, borrowed perhaps from the Canaanite cult, to praise the
unique God of Israel. Because he is unique, he is simply "great."
The term "great" is applied in the Old Testament to almighty God
without qualification. St. Luke contrasts Jesus with John the Baptist in his Infancy narrative by describing Jesus as "great," while
John is "great before God." The God of Israel is frequently acclaimed in the psalter as a great king above all the other gods. The
theological conceptions of the sacred writers of Israel were not so
sophisticated, religiously speaking, as ours are. Thus monotheism,
the fully conscious, reflexive rejection of the existence of any god
except the one God, appears only with the Second Isaiah in the
middle of the sixth century B.C. Prior to this writer, the people of
Israel believed firmly in only one God, since he alone had acted
for them, spoken to them. In their simple, direct way they affirmed
this "monotheistic" faith by saying that God stood above all other
gods and that since he was the universal creator, he was indispu-
tably king even "above all the gods." "In his hands are the depths
of the earth, and the summits of the mountains belong to him. His
is the sea—he has made it—and the earth—his hands have fashioned it." "The depths of the earth," of course, is a reference to
Sheol, the dusty, dingy, unhappy abode of all who pass from this
world, from life. Yet even this region of death, we are informed,
belongs to the God of Israel. Until relatively late in the religious
history of Israel, around the middle of the first century B.C., God
did not choose to reveal to his chosen people any consoling ideas
about the after-life—a point to be remembered when attempting
to assess the Hebrews' religious spirit and religious achievements.
Everyone, good, bad, or indifferent went to Sheol, the place from
which God was absent—a region devoid of life and living men,
enveloped in darkness and unhappiness.

And "the summits of the mountains" belong to him—those "high
places" over which controversy raged repeatedly throughout
Israel's history, until, under King Josiah, Jerusalem was selected
as the one place where God might be worshiped publicly in an
authentic way. The hills and the high places, the psalmist says, belong to this God only, not to those other gods whom the Canaanites
and the apostate Israelites worship on the mountain. "His is the sea
—he has made it—and the earth—his hands have fashioned it."
Out of the waters of the primordial chaos God had brought forth

dry land. And he had set limits to the ocean, bounds which it might not pass.

"Enter his court! let us bow down, let us prostrate ourselves before Yahweh who made us." The prostrations performed in the public worship of Israel were much more expressive than our staid, somewhat inhibited acts of adoration. With verse six, the psalmist adverts to the assembly of the worshiping community. And the high point of this worship is this prostration before the divine presence. "Let us bow down, let us prostrate ourselves before Yahweh who made us, for it is he who is our God. We are the people of his pasturing, the sheep of his hands." He is our God by the grace of the covenant. Yahweh not only created the world; he had created Israel. Through the covenant with his people he became their shepherd: "we are the people of his pasturing."

This idea is echoed in the twenty-second psalm, "The Lord is my shepherd." We are the sheep that attend upon his care, that await the largesse of his hands. He is Israel's God. He has a special love of predilection for this people. Here lies the primary reason why Israel prostrates herself. It is not merely because Yahweh is the all-high king, the God above all the other gods; but also because he is interested personally in Israel as his own people.

Prophetic Admonition   In the second and final movement of the psalm (vv. 7b-11), we have what commentators call a prophetic admonition, or warning. "Today if only you would heed his voice!" You recall that the author of Hebrews (Heb 3:7-11) has a long and very moving exegesis of this line. The great patriarch of religious life in the west, whose feast we celebrate today, St. Benedict, defines a religious vocation in the preface to his rule in terms of this line of the psalm. "And with our eyes open," he says, "to the deifying light, with ears attuned, let us hear what that divine voice tells us; which daily calls out, 'Today, if only you would heed his voice. Do not harden your hearts.' " (*Sancti Benedicti Regula Monachorum: Prologus*). "Today!"—the term is instinct with urgency. "Today" expresses also the contemporary relevance of the admonition. "Today" expresses, in a certain sense, Israel's religious ideal. It was each day that Israel, at least in the person of her great religious figures, listened for the voice of Yahweh. Her life as God's people, was thought to consist only of a day-to-day participation in the dialogue between God and herself, which we know is sacred history. "Today, if only you would heed his voice. Do not harden your hearts." God acts with me in no other way than he acted with Israel.

30

Israel recognized that the covenant was not merely a law, the charter or the constitution of her national existence and aspirations. The covenant was first and foremost a way of life. This is strikingly evident in the most ancient form of Israelite law, the code of the covenant (Ex 20:1—23:33). If you read this collection of laws with attention, you will be struck by one peculiar quality it possesses. Although it is the expression of God's covenant with his people (and hence a religious document containing divine revelation), still the greater part of it does not appear to deal with religion, with man's duties to God, but with the obligations of social justice. Israel's covenant with Yahweh provided simply a pattern for her daily living. To the Israelite, religion was not something to be donned like a new cloak on the Sabbath, an esoteric rite carried out with a specially composed face. Religion was the heart of Israel's everyday life as a nation.

The code of the covenant thus contrasts sharply with the authoritative declarations of the magisterium of the church—those enunciations or statements that we call *de fide definita*. They are not intended to be something to live by. They are addressed not to the whole man, but merely to his intellect. But the Bible, like the covenant, presents a pattern for life. To listen to the Word of God is a vitally religious act, as we can see from the lives of the Old Testament prophets who are concerned, indeed obsessed by the Word of God (*dābār Yahweh*).

Now my Christian vocation, my vocation as a religious and as a priest, will be seen to consist, if examined carefully, of just such a daily existential response to God's Word. My vocation remains always a piece of unfinished business. Some years ago there was a great deal of discussion about the question of temporary vocations, which so far as I am aware reached no very satisfactory conclusions. But is it not of the very essence of a religious vocation to be "temporary"? As long as I live, I am simply an unfinished chapter in sacred history. I am, if I am anything, a continuing participant in that dialogue with God, which is sacred or salvation history.

And so it is today, every day, that I accept or reject that divine call which is my vocation as a Christian, and a priest. Is not my retreat principally a time for undistracted listening? Does it not derive its main significance for my life as a time when I heed more attentively the voice of God. "Today if only you would heed his voice"—not the retreat master's, nor even your own. And yet it is true that when our Lord speaks to me the voice he uses is my own. Consequently, I must learn that prudence which St.

Ignatius calls discernment or discretion. For I must learn to distinguish my voice from God's, or rather God's voice when he uses my own voice to speak to me. If the time of retreat is a time of listening, as, indeed, my whole life is, I can only listen in the silence of my heart. And by the term "heart," I mean that innermost part of myself, as the Bible uses the term; that part of me which is unique; that part of me which is most authentic. I must listen with my whole personality. I must worship, I must pray with everything that is most truly myself. Prayer, as you know, engages the material side of my personality no less than the spiritual part of my nature with its intelligence and will. Indeed all that is included under the term "my body" is to be redeemed together with my soul. Moreover, I should be specially concerned to bring this side of myself to God in prayer, since it embraces that field of being where I actually live the greater part of my life—imagination, emotions, passions.

And so I have to pray with these things. I must worship with my body. Israel appears to have been very conscious of the importance of bodily attitudes in prayer. That is why there is so much talk of prostrations, and bowing, or standing before the face of God. There is undoubtedly a real significance for my prayer in the disposition of my body. St. Ignatius seems to have attached much importance to these physical attitudes [76]. We are taught this also through liturgical worship, which is prayer on a social scale. The very act on the part of many human beings of coming together, forming a fellowship to praise God is meaningful in itself.

Today, if only I would heed his voice. I remind myself that it is not a strange voice. It is a very familiar voice. I am bid by the psalmist not to harden my heart, like the generation in the desert. For this state of being closed, this refusal to listen to the voice of God, is the one obstacle I can place in the way of the dialogue which is prayer. This is that discontent with God which the Israelites manifested at Massah in the desert. I believe that St. Francis de Sales once said that the man who dies perfectly happy with God goes straight to heaven. The generation of Hebrews that wandered in the Sinai desert refused to heed God's voice; and persisted instead in tempting or trying him. A similar spirit is manifest in those attitudes which St. Paul deprecated in writing to the Corinthians (1 Cor 1:22). He warned them that the demands made by the Jews and the Greeks constituted a serious obstacle to their reception of Christianity. The Jews sought signs or miracles. They had to have faith proven to them. God had to show them; Christ had to show them. The Greeks made the mistake of reducing religion to the level of a philosophy. But Christianity is not a

32

philosophy. It is something very much more human, more "total," more demanding. Religion is—listening! Religion is my attempt with grace to participate in the dialogue that is my vocation as a Christian, between God and myself. And so if ever before we die, there comes one day, at least, when we truly, fully heed his voice, this life of ours will have been a successful religious life. "Today if only you would heed his voice!"

OUR HELP IS FROM YAHWEH!
Psalm 121 [120]

"I lift my eyes to the mountains—
Whence comes my help?"

2 "*My* help is from Yahweh,
Who made sky and earth!

3 He will not permit your foot to slip—
Your guardian does not slumber!

4 No, he does not slumber or sleep,
The guardian of Israel!

5 Yahweh is *your* guardian, *your* shade.
Yahweh at *your* right hand!

6 The sun by day will not smite you,
Nor the moon by night.

7 Yahweh will guard you from all evil:
He guards your life!

8 He guards your comings and goings
Henceforth and forever!"

Chapter 3

THE PRAYER OF THE CREATURE

I SAID EARLIER that the psalms of confidence or trust are quite *Prayer of Trust*
unparalleled in the Near Eastern religious literature that we
possess. There are psalms of petition, psalms of thanksgiving
among the Moabite prayers. There is no psalm or prayer of trust.
This is the result of that unique idea of God that Israel had. I
might put it another way and say that it is the result of the unique,
because revealed, conception of herself, as a people, and her conception of the human person which Israel had. Her acceptance, in
other words, of what we could call her creaturely condition. As a
people, the Israelites were well aware that they were newcomers
in the culture and the history of the Near East.

One of the traditional themes of the Christian spirituality is the *Quest for God*
quest for God. That is really what all of us, as Christians, are engaged upon, and this has been a matter of concern to all the great
founders of religious life. In the fifty-eighth chapter of the Rule,
Saint Benedict insists that the candidate who seeks admission to
the monastery must be asked whether he is seriously intent upon
the search for God.[1] There are many ways of seeking and there
are many ways of finding God. One, I suggest, that is helpful perhaps for our reflection is the hundred and twenty-first psalm (Ps
120 in the Vulgate), "Our Help is From Yahweh,"—a psalm of
confidence.

The situation that this psalm envisages is that of a layman pil- *God Found*
grim who has been to offer public worship in the temple of Jeru- *in Risk*
salem. At the termination of the feast, with the conclusion of the
liturgy, he suddenly feels very much alone as he turns his face
toward his homeward journey. "I lift my eyes to the mountains
—whence comes my help?" He realizes that he faces danger. The

---

1 "And let this elder watch carefully to see whether the novice is truly
  seeking God, and is zealous for the Work of God, for obedience, and for
  humiliations." *The Holy Rule of St. Benedict*, ch. 58.

mountains, particularly those to the east of Jerusalem, were notorious for the bandits that they harbored. One has but to recall Luke's parable of the Good Samaritan (Lk 10:30-37) to realize how dangerous these mountains were even in Jesus' day. The remainder of the psalm (it is only eight verses altogether) very probably contains the priest's reply to this diffident and timorous pilgrim. "*My* help," he asserts, "is from Yahweh, who made sky and earth." The priest in the holy place in Jerusalem feels secure. He is protected by the sanctuary, but more especially by the presence of the God of Israel enshrined above the cherubim in the holy of holies. He derives his sense of security also from the presence of the gathered community which has assembled to celebrate the liturgy. Hence he hastens to reassure the doubtful pilgrim. "*My* help is from Yahweh, who made sky and earth. He will not permit your foot to slip—your guardian does not slumber!" This God, the God of Israel, deploys his creative power in saving, protecting, watching over the people he has made. We moderns tend to think of the account of the creation in the beginning of the Bible simply as a kind of revealed cosmogony. Such indeed it is. But we should not forget that these pages were written not merely to explain how the world came to be, but chiefly to remind Israel that the first and greatest of God's saving acts—his "judgments" as they are called, his acts of redemption—was the creation of the universe for his future people.

"Your guardian does not slumber! No, he does not slumber or sleep, the guardian of Israel!" The Hebrews first came to know their God as one who had formed them into a people. The most basic characteristics of God as he revealed himself in the Old Testament is his relationship with the Israelite collectivity. "Yahweh is *your* guardian, *your* shade." The watcher of Israel not only guards the people, he guards each individual. The consciousness of this interpersonal relationship between Yahweh and each individual Israelite may be seen in the very formulation of the decalogue. "*I* am the Lord thy God, *thou* shalt . . . or shalt not . . ." And so here the priest reminds the pilgrim that God will look after him personally, because the God of Israel, the God who made a covenant with his people, is interested in him as an individual. "Yahweh is *your* guardian, *your* shade." The power, the suggestiveness of this symbol of shade in a world like that of the Mediterranean is a very powerful one. "Yahweh at *your* right hand." God is so interested in the pilgrim that he will stand at that side on which he is most vulnerable. Yahweh protects the individual Israelite to the very least and the most important detail.

"The sun by day will not smite you, nor the moon by night."

In the second book of Kings (2 K 4:18-20), which records the cycle of legends concerning the prophet Elisha, there is a story about a woman of Shunem who lost her little son when the lad followed his father at the harvest-time and died of sunstroke. The Babylonian moon-god was thought to cause fever, delirium, and, of course, lunacy, insanity. This popular belief in the baleful influence of the moon is reflected in the Gospels. There is the boy with the evil or unclean spirit, whom Jesus met as he came down from the mountain of the transfiguration. He was, Matthew tells us, a "lunatic" (Mt 17:15).

"Yahweh will guard you from all evil: he guards your life! He guards your comings and goings henceforth and forever." Yahweh, the priest in the psalm reiterates, is personally concerned with the intimate details of my human existence, of my personal life. And this God is the living, acting God of Israel. It is significant that in this brief psalm the sacred name Yahweh occurs four times. It is his power and his goodness manifested by his interest in the individual that are the pledge of my security. For he is Yahweh: "he who causes to exist," "he who makes live." At least this is a probable interpretation of that mysterious name.

So we find God once again in risk, in the midst of danger and trial. God is present in all threats to my life. Thus if my spirituality is not to be artificial, if it is to be truly operative in my life, I have to make use of my situation, my surroundings, to find God. I have to be open to all life's possibilities and contingencies. I must realize that there are many facets of human experience, including myself and others, that I must accept. The fish lives its whole life in salt water, and yet—at least to the Catholic palate!—fish tastes very flat. And so the secret, it would appear, of living, the secret of being human—my most basic vocation—is to let the things, and the persons around me season my existence. I must endeavor to acquire a shrewd estimate of all life's possibilities. Perhaps Abraham might well be regarded as the patron saint of such supernatural ingenuity. You recall the account (Gn 18:20-33) of Abraham's haggling with God over the fate of Sodom and Gomorrah—how time after time, he beat God down.

On the other hand, I have to accept myself. I have to accept my past first of all, because there is nothing outside of God himself that presents itself to me with such a face of stern necessity as my own past conduct. I can go on forever wishing that it might have been different, that it might not have left its mark upon me. Yet for all my wishing, there it is. I can do nothing with my past but accept it.

37

I have to adjust myself also to the limitations of my existence, the limits set by myself, by others, and by many situations upon my self-expression, my freedom. There is my own temperament, something that is not of my own choosing, handed on to me by my parents or grandparents. There are my acquired habits for which I have a large share of responsibility—good habits and some, perhaps, not so good. All these habits, virtues or bad habits, restrict my freedom. And yet habits are an absolute necessity of human existence. They keep me from going mad. I could not bear the strain of having to deliberate and choose each time I tied my shoe, every time I took a mouthful of food.

Other persons, as persons, certainly set a limit to my own possibilities. Their self-determination collides—more or less successfully—with my own plans and hopes. Yet, as I am a social being, I have to live in my society. I have to accept the social aspects of life with its conventions and taboos. The restrictive character of social activity may be illustrated by liturgical worship, which sets a certain restraint upon the personal individual expression of my own religious feeling, of my own religious experience.

And so between these two—what I must or cannot do, and what I am able or am permitted to perform—there is always a tension. The part of wisdom is to accept what is necessary and to exploit the openings which offer themselves to my initiative. Jesus reminds us of this in the Sermon on the Mount. God knows before you ask him what you need, and yet his conclusion is not that we give up the prayer of petition. Go on asking, he says. Keep on knocking, even though the Father knows.

God, Creator

As I face my future, I find its dark, mysterious face enlightened by three hopeful, encouraging thoughts set down by the Psalmist. In the first place, there is the unshakeable belief that my God is creator of sky and earth; and this creative, limitless power of his is made to operate also in his saving activity.

Guardian of His People

In the second place, I am reminded that God is the "guardian over Israel." My God is the one who looks after his people, who is ceaseless in his provident attention to the collectivity of Israel. He never takes his eyes off them. You may recall an ancient tale about the prophet Elijah, (1 K 18:17-40), how upon Mt. Carmel, the prophet on a memorable occasion pitted himself against the priests of Baal. It was intended as a test to see whose God "worked." When the Baal of these pagan priests did not produce the fire for the sacrifice, the prophet suggested tauntingly: "Cry out with a loud voice, for he is a god. Either he is meditating, or he is gone

38

aside, or he is on a journey, or perhaps he is asleep. He needs to be awakened" (v.27). The psalmist assures us that the guardian of Israel neither slumbers nor sleeps. The gods of the Gentiles fell asleep annually, because they were nature-gods; and in the inevitably recurrent cycle of nature, through summer into winter, these nature-gods shut up shop, so to say, ceased operation. They fell asleep. But throughout the Old Testament we find this truth asserted continually and confidently: the God of Israel is no nature-god; he is not to be confused with those manifestations of the gods of the Gentiles, the rivers or the sun or the moon.

In the third place, the God of Israel is the protector, the interested protector of the individual believer. Our psalm provides us with a striking illustration of this ceaseless vigilance. For the pilgrim harried by the threat of danger, worried and concerned about imminent catastrophe, God's spokesman, the priest in the sanctuary of Jerusalem, provides the comfort of faith. He must remember to live under the blessed protection of the God of Israel with complete hope and confidence. Now, in my own life such confidence and trust reposes upon my awareness of my creaturely position. This consciousness springs from faith in God's power and trust in his personal concern for me. Following the example of Israel I must admit that I am helpless before I can trust God for help. The priest in the psalm assures me that God is always present, unslumberingly present, to the pilgrim wayfarer. And what is my life but a quest for him, a pilgrimage? It is, in fact, a journey home to the Father.

Protector of the Individual

So, the first and most basic prayer that I can learn is the prayer that Israel teaches me—even as a Christian: the prayer of the creature dependent upon a creator who is not only powerful but concerned for me. God is interested in me as a person, interested in my troubles, my problems. He is concerned enough, not only to listen, but interested and powerful enough to give me the help that I cannot find in myself, that I cannot find in any other human being. Observe that the priest in the sanctuary does not volunteer to accompany the pilgrim on his homeward journey. The priest, like the pilgrim, is only a human being. Yet the priest promises something infinitely better—the help of the God who had made a covenant with Israel. That pact was indeed made with Israel as a collectivity, but it was extended in love to comprehend each individual member of the confederacy which we call Israel. "I lift my eyes to the mountains—whence comes my help?" *Our* "help is from Yahweh, who made sky and earth! . . . He guards your comings and goings henceforth and forever!"

39

EXORCISM BY ISRAEL'S FAITH
Psalm 124 [123]

"Had not Yahweh been on our side,"
Let Israel say,

2 "Had not Yahweh been on our side,
When men rose up against us,

3 Then they would have swallowed us up alive,
When their anger blazed forth against us!

4 Then the water would have swept us away,
The torrent would have engulfed us;

5 Then it would have engulfed us
With its seething waters!"

6 "Blessed be Yahweh,
Who would not let us become a prey to their teeth!

7 Our life, like a bird, has escaped from the fowler's net;
Remember, the net was broken, and we escaped!

8 Our help is in the name of Yahweh,
Who has made sky and earth."

Chapter 4

FAITH FACES THE
HUMAN SITUATION

I HAVE CHOSEN two psalms for our consideration of man and his place in the divine scheme of things: Psalm 124 and Psalm 8. Each of these in its own way throws the light of Israelite faith upon the human situation and clarifies the statement, "Man is a creature."

H. Gunkel has suggested that Psalm 124 was a prayer composed during one of the pogroms against the Jews in the Persian period, a situation like that envisaged by the book of Esther. However the situation is probably less specific. It may simply be a general description applicable to any one of the many occasions when God's people Israel was rescued by the Lord from danger. To make it more general still, more applicable, we may assume that this psalm represents a human situation in which each of us at times finds himself. Consequently, it really enters into that series of considerations on the human situation in general that is evoked by St. Ignatius' *Principle and Foundation* in the *Spiritual Exercises* [23].

The Human Predicament Mythicized

Mircea Eliade, as has been remarked, pointed out a tendency among primitive, prehistoric men to mythologize, or demonize the forces that threaten them.[1] As a consequence of the age-old fight between the nomads of the desert and "the sown," or inhabited parts of the world, the wall around ancient towns originated as a magic, protective circle, to keep out the "evil spirits," all those hostile powers which primitive man pictured as possessing demonic dimensions. By the magic of this protective ring, such forces were prevented from interfering with the life and culture and security of those who dwelt in town or village.

At any rate, we can see traces, even today in certain attitudes of man, of this prehistoric or primitive viewpoint in our contemporary culture. I am thinking, for instance, of the tendency among the peoples of the West to mythologize Russian communism and

1 Mircea Eliade, *The Sacred and the Profane: the Nature of Religion* (New York, 1961), "Sacred Space and Making the World Sacred," 49 ff.

grant to it a kind of demonic power, forgetting that the Russians are, after all, men like ourselves. In our lives too, this inclination to make bogies out of certain forces or persons or situations which threaten us is an experience that can occasionally plague any one of us. That is why I think this little psalm, which is so brief, has a deep lesson for all of us.

Sheol "Had not Yahweh been on our side, let Israel say, had not Yahweh been on our side, when men rose up against us . . ." There follow three graphic pictures, each introduced by "then," which exemplify the age-old human tendency to mythologize a difficult situation. "Then they would have swallowed us up alive, when their anger blazed forth against us." The first image reminds the Israelite of Sheol, so often pictured in the Old Testament as some sort of prehistoric monster, ready to devour God's people in its voracious maw.

Plaything of The second vignette is probably drawn from the spring floods
Nature Gods of Palestine. What may have been a very sluggish stream or even a dry torrent-bed for most of the year can suddenly become a raging flood. "Then the water would have swept us away, the torrent would have engulfed us." It is a symbol of the capriciousness (and in this sense it is a mythological symbol) of the forces of nature, represented for Israel by the gods of the Gentiles. Those nature gods acted according to no plan, nor did they display that reasoned activity and providence which Israel's God displayed towards her. The gods of the pagans acknowledgedly acted according to mere whim.

Primeval Chaos The third image is that of the chaotic world-sea, the huge flood, graphically described at the beginning of Genesis as inundating the universe, before almighty God with his creative power divided the waters from the earth (Gn 1:1-2). "Then it would have engulfed us with its seething waters!"

Note that it is nothing less than the presence of God which exorcizes this demonic picture. God's presence at Israel's side "demythologizes" this desperate situation. "Had not Yahweh been on our side, when men rose up against us . . ." Israel's faith in God reveals to her that her enemies are not demonic prehistoric monsters. They are only '*ādām*, merely men! We may reflect that in our own lives it is the function of our faith in Christ, and our trust in God's providence to help us recall that those situations, which may at times seem to threaten us, are always subject to the direction and the control of God. Hence, for us also, it is only faith,

42

Christian faith, which can "demythologize" our own human situation.

The rest of this brief psalm is a thanksgiving. It is a prayer of thanks to Yahweh, very short, but very deeply felt. How profound the feeling of gratitude is can be recognized by the sense of horror conjured up by the imagery employed in the beginning by the psalmist. "Blessed be Yahweh!" To bless God in the Bible is to recognize his power and his infinite perfection. In this psalm particularly, the sacred writer aims to make his audience realize that God's creative power is displayed in saving mankind, just as he saved Israel from this desperate situation. "Blessed be Yahweh, who would not let us become a prey to their teeth!" This is the ancient Israelite testimony to the provident care of God. Note too how, in this brief thanksgiving, the writer insists upon the truth that God's rescue of Israel is granted as a grace. It is something she had no right to expect. Her situation was like that of a bird caught in a fowler's net. In many of the tombs and in other illustrations of Egyptian art, we find pictures of such nets, with the birds struggling with all their strength to escape. It is just such a picture which is drawn for us here. "Our life, like a bird, has escaped from the fowler's net; Remember, the net was broken, and we escaped!" The net, the psalmist knows, was broken by the providence of God. Whatever the actual historical situation, whatever trial, catastrophe, or crisis Israel faced on this concrete occasion, like the crises and personal tragedies in our own lives, it was the hand of God that reached down to break the fowler's net.

Israel's faith recognized this. "Our help is in the name of Yahweh who has made sky and earth." Thus in the last verse, this faith of Israel which has demythologized the seemingly demonic situation, these superhuman threats to the people's existence, this same faith now issues in full, total commitment to the cause of God. "Our help is in the name of Yahweh." The "name of Yahweh," of course, indicates God as revealed to Israel. We may remind ourselves that God was not revealed to Israel in any abstract philosophical way—the Bible contains no speculation about the nature of God. God had revealed himself to Israel by acting in her behalf, by being on her side. "Our help is in the name of Yahweh," because God, to reveal himself, simply acted in defense of Israel. Moreover, the God who did this is the creator God, the God "who has made sky and earth."

He is also the God worshiped through the cultus within the sacred enclosure of the temple in Jerusalem. You will have noticed the cultic signature that we have in the very first verse of this psalm: "Had not Yahweh been on our side, let Israel say. . . ." The term "Israel" denotes God's people gathered for public worship at the liturgy carried out in the temple of Jerusalem.

And so this final *confessio*, this concluding praise of God stresses the miracle, as well as the gracious quality of God's help and protection. Israel is surprised to escape, just as the bird was probably surprised to escape with its life from the net of the fowler. For this is what Israel remembers with love and gratitude: that the net was broken, and she escaped; that the God who made the sky and the earth is the same God who deployed his creative power to save his people.

Accordingly, it is before the name of Yahweh, before God revealed in his saving activity on behalf of Israel, that Israel's enemies are revealed in their true light. They are not gods, not demons, not some preternatural force against which man is impotent. They are only *'ādām*, flesh and blood! Israel's perilous plight is discovered to be merely some sort of human situation, contrived by mortal men who cannot circumvent God's saving will. For Israel believed it was God's design to give his people freedom and salvation.

In the history of the Church this psalm acquires an even deeper significance, because the Church witnesses to the gracious protection which God has displayed towards herself, the new Israel, amid the dangers of the world. Moreover, for each Christian, and for us who are religious, this psalm ought to evoke deep gratitude. It is my faith in God, in Christ, and in his saving activity on my behalf, that makes me see through the situations which harry me, which may seem at times to be more than I can cope with, something beyond the strength of any human being. Then I recognize with Christian faith that men are only *'ādām*, that my trials are only human situations contrived by mortal men. So I too like Israel may thank God for my commitment of faith to him in Jesus Christ, because salvation comes to me only in this way.

II.

CREATION AND MAN'S DESTINY
Psalm 8:2-10

2 Yahweh, our Lord,
How glorious is your name in all the earth!
You, whose praise is sung to the heavens,

3 Have, from the mouths of babes and infants,
Established strength because of your enemies—
To still the enemy and the revengeful.

4 When I see the heavens, the work of your fingers,
The moon and the stars which you have formed,

5 What is man that you should think of him,
　The son of man that you should care for him?

6 Yet you have made him but little lower than God;
　You have crowned him with glory and splendor!

7 You have made him ruler over the works of your hands;
　You have put all things beneath his feet:

8 All sheep and oxen,
　And also the beasts of the field;

9 The bird of the sky and the fish of the sea,
　That traverse the paths of the seas.

10 Yahweh, our Lord,
　How glorious is your name in all the earth!

Our consideration of Psalm 124 provided one view of man, both *Antiphonal* his natural impotence and his divinely given strength. In the *Hymn* eighth psalm we have a rather remarkable description of the dignity of the human person. Since it is presented in a manner which may seem strange to us, although quite characteristic of biblical thought, it will require some explanation.

This hymn was probably composed to be sung antiphonally. At any rate, the second verse and the tenth are obviously meant to be sung by a choir, while the middle section, which begins with verse four, appears to be for a single voice. It is difficult to determine whether this psalm was originally part of the temple liturgy. If it were, then it was chanted at some nighttime festival. It seems clear, from verse four and following, that the prayer or the contemplation of the psalmist took place during the night. He observes the stars and the moon.

Whether or not the psalm is pre-exilic, it is entitled "a psalm for David." This would not necessarily indicate its date as the time of that king, nor even in the regnal period. However, some scholars believe it is quite possible that the poem contains a pre-exilic statement of that creation tradition embodied, perhaps later, in the hymn which now forms the first chapter of Genesis. This view depends on whether one considers the psalm an earlier version of the liturgical recital in chapter one of Genesis. It may well be a hymn written at a later period, modeled upon that same chapter.

The psalmist begins with an address to God as "our Lord"— *Yahweh* 'Adōnāi, an honorific title used in Israelite court life for the king. *King of Israel* God was acknowledged to be the king of Israel, and hence in the Bible the titles of etiquette addressed in ancient oriental courts to royalty were applied to God. "Yahweh, our Lord, how glorious is

45

your name in all the earth." Since the "name of God" denotes God as he had revealed himself to Israel, we should recall that, while this psalm is in a certain sense a meditation upon nature, the biblical authors never contemplated nature for its own sake. Indeed, they did not construct what we call theodicy or natural theology, based solely on deductions from the created universe. It is for this reason that the psalmist mentions the name of God at the outset of his poem. Whatever he finds in nature to remind him of God has been suggested because of God's self-revelation to Israel.

"You, whose praise is sung to the heavens, have, from the mouths of babes and infants, established strength because of your enemies —to still the enemy and the revengeful."

You will recall that in Matthew's portrayal of Jesus' triumphal entry, with its sequel, the cleansing of the temple, our Lord himself cites this section of our psalm. It provides an answer to the criticism of the religious leaders who demand to know why he permitted the children to shout "Hosanna!" in the forecourts of the temple (Mt 21:16). Actually the verse is difficult and several explanations are given. Might it be that there was actually a boys' choir employed in the temple liturgy? While this is not impossible, the thought may be similar to that in Paul's first letter to the Corinthians (1 Cor 1:27ff.), where the apostle asserts that God uses the weak things of the world to confound the strength of his enemies. Yet it is rather strange, when you think of it, that whatever this praise of God from children means, the psalmist would think it an answer to God's enemies, who are also the enemies of Israel.

Yahweh Repairs Disharmony in History Whatever be the meaning of the verse, we should remind ourselves of two themes which run through the psalter. The first is the belief that the enemies of God have introduced a discord, a disharmony into God's creation. We see this frequently alluded to in the psalms. The second is the conviction that the final overthrow of God's enemies begins in a hidden manner, almost in private, so to say, by the divine saving manifestations of the deity to individual Israelites, who are Yahweh's petitioners. This idea is found very frequently in psalms of thanksgiving and in laments or psalms of petition. The devout Israelite believed firmly that on the "day of Yahweh," the day of the last judgment, the enemies of God would be finally confounded. But he also believed that this judgment had already begun through God's interventions on behalf of the individual Israelite.

With verse four, we hear the voice of the soloist. This is obviously a night hymn. "When I see the heavens, the work of your fingers, the moon and the stars which you have formed, what is man that you should think of him, the son of man that you should care for him?" We now begin to see the reason the psalmist had for introducing his poem by praising God in his creation. He wishes to contrast the might and majesty of the universe with man's apparently infinitesimal smallness. How can the God who created the sky, stars, and moon ever have thought of man? The word that is used for "man" in verse five is *'enōsh*, a term which implies all the weakness and inconsistency of human nature. The amazing thought to the mind of the psalmist is this: despite man's apparent insignificance, the Creator-God, who is Israel's saviour, is capable of thinking not only of his chosen people as a group, but even of the individual Israelite!

"Yet you have made him but little lower than God!" The writer has referred to man in the second part of verse six as "the son of man," rather than *'ādām*. *'Adām*, as we learn from the early chapters of Genesis, suggests man's origins from the *'adāmāh*, from the soil of the earth. Yet God has made this creature "little lower than *'elōhīm*." The word is sometimes translated "angels," because the Hebrew plural, *'elōhīm*, which usually means God, can also designate the angels. Whether there is question here of the angels or of God himself, what the psalmist wishes to point out is, that despite man's apparent insignificance, he is of inestimable value in God's eyes. "You have made him but a little lower than God; you have crowned him with glory and splendor!"

As we learn elsewhere in the psalms, the two attributes, glory and splendor, belong in a special manner to God himself. We are told that glory is the prerogative of Yahweh (Ps 29:1), while splendor or honor is another divine attribute (Ps 104:1ff.). These have been communicated, our psalmist says, by God to man; and thus they form the basis of the dignity which belongs to the human person. Now it is not by any analysis of human nature as such, or some kind of metaphysical definition of man, that the psalmist arrives at this concept of human dignity. This precious prerogative is considered rather as the result of a gracious act of God. He has freely conferred these divine prerogatives of glory and splendor upon man. "You have made him ruler over the works of your hands; you have put all things beneath his feet!"

This sums up all that the first chapter of Genesis has to say about God's creation of man in his own image and in his likeness. Here again we are not given a metaphysical view of the concepts of image and likeness. Man is, according to the writer, created in God's image simply because God has entrusted him with a share

47

in his own divine dominion over the material and animal creation. Now, for the composer of our psalm as also for the author of the first chapter of Genesis, the basis of human dignity lies in the fact that God has given man a share in exercising dominion. This for both of them constitutes the basis of man's dignity. This is the significance of that glory and honor which God has communicated to man himself. Accordingly, man's privilege, as well as his duty, is to rule, to have dominion, to exercise responsibility. Man must then live up to this image and likeness implanted in him by God at his creation if he is to answer the challenge which God offers him. And it is an awesome challenge. God challenged man at the beginning of the world to imitate himself, man's creator, by exercising dominion, by accepting human responsibility.

In verses eight and nine we have a gradual widening of man's influence, a broadening of the area of his dominion so as to include all living things: sheep and oxen, the beasts of the field, the birds in the sky, and the fish "that traverse the paths of the sea." Thus are included even those sea-monsters considered in ancient mythology to be invisible and beyond man's power to tame or conquer. Even these invincible creatures God has set beneath the rule of man.

This passage (vv. 6-9) presents a very remarkable description of the dignity of the human person. You will immediately notice that no mention is made of the fall of man, of his sin. Nothing here suggests the picture which is found in the third chapter of Genesis. Yet even in Genesis, with its account of the original sin, there is a valid affirmation concerning the human condition even in its fallen state. The one thing man did not lose by his rebellion was the responsibility which God had bestowed upon him at his creation, to rule. This is the very foundation of the dignity of the human person. You will recall that even after the account of the fall in Genesis Adam begets Seth in his image (Gn 5:3); and the image which Adam retains is, of course, the image of God in which he was created. Moreover, in the story of the covenant with Noah (Gn 9:6), murder is declared a crime because man, now fallen man, is made in the image of God. Hence the exercise of dominion or responsibility is an inalienable human right according to the Bible.

After these reflections on man's true greatness, despite his apparent insignificance in contrast with the mighty works of creation, the chorus takes up again the same praise of God with which it began. "Yahweh, our Lord, how glorious is your name in all the earth!" Notice that this time there is no reference to the heavens or the sky, for everything commemorated in the solo part of the hymn has reference to human history, that is, to man's part in the governing of this world.

You will doubtless remember that in Hebrews (Heb 2:5-9) the fifth through the seventh verses of this psalm are applied to Christ, to the risen Christ, and that the governance of the world, confided in our psalm to man, is there applied to the world to come. We are thus reminded that in the Christian revelation our psalm receives an eschatological dimension from the death and the resurrection of Christ. And we cannot afford to forget that even fallen man still retains this intrinsic human dignity, which in the risen Christ becomes transcendent, graced as it is with all the merciful work of the redemption. Thus ultimately man's true dignity appears only in the Christian revelation as the gracious act of Christ.

Ultimate Realized in Christ

FAITH IN DISILLUSIONMENT
Psalm 126 [125]

When Yahweh led the captives back to Sion,
We thought that we were dreaming!

2 Then our mouths were filled with laughter,
And our lips with psalms.
Then word went round, even amongst the pagan nations,
"What marvels Yahweh has wrought for them!"

3 Yahweh *had* wrought marvels for us,
And we *were* overjoyed!

4 "Restore our fortune, O Yahweh,
Like the brooks of the Negeb."

5 Those who sow in tears
Harvest with shouts of joy:

6 He who sows in sorrow and in tears
Shall come back bearing his sheaves with joy.

Chapter 5

LOVE WHAT YOU FIND

SOONER OR LATER every man or woman in this world faces a *The Human* crisis. There is one decision from which none of us is exempt: to *Dilemma* join the human race or resign from it. And the number of such resignations strikes one as astonishing. What is the secret of success? There is no automatic solution, no once-for-all formula; because the tension between my ideals and my daily living will go on, I suppose, as long as life is given to me. On the one hand, I cannot afford to relinquish what one might call the romantic view, "the vision splendid"; and yet, on the other, there are the hard, cold facts of life. I am always facing these tensions. It is my hope from the grace of ordination, which has been given to me or which soon will be mine, to serve God in Christ with fervor and indomitable perseverance; yet my priestly actuation of this grace that has been given to me will probably always fall short of the ideal before me.

To help us reflect upon this problem, this basic human problem, I suggest Psalm 126 (Ps 125, Vulg.)—"Those who sow in tears harvest with shouts of joy." The pattern that I find here in the history of Israel is significant, I believe, for the history of the Church; and it is relevant to my own personal history. Because I should not think that my difficulties in facing up to this problem arise out of a situation in which I find myself—I mean by that my religious situation, my priestly situation. In reality the problem is one from which no man is exempt. The man who is married, after a certain length of time, faces exactly the same problem in his existential situation as I must in mine. I can run away from the situation by relinquishing one vocation in the hope that in another I shall not have to find an answer to this problem. But the question remains to be answered; it will always require a solution, no matter what state of life I may pursue.

"When Yahweh led the captives back to Sion, we thought that *Israel's* we were dreaming! Then our mouths were filled with laughter, *Disenchantment*

and our lips with psalms. Then word went round, even amongst
the pagan nations, 'What marvels Yahweh has wrought for them!'
Yahweh *had* wrought marvels for us, and we *were* overjoyed!"
We should not miss the poignancy and nostalgia of those past
tenses in the last line. No mistake about it! No wish to deny it!
God had in history wrought miracles for this people. They had
reacted with faith; they had been overjoyed. But it is only too
evident now that in the situation described in this psalm joy has
vanished, those marvels have become only a mocking memory
from the past. It may well be, as some scholars point out, that the
reference here is to Israel's return from the Babylonian captivity
under Cyrus in the year 538. It is often difficult to be specific about
the historical situation of these psalms, for the very good reason
that through later editing they have been generalized to suit a
greater variety of situations. What is clear is that the psalmist
speaks of some poignant recollection of a great historical intervention by God, and asks himself: What did it all come to?

"When Yahweh led the captives back to Sion, we thought that
we were dreaming!" Israel's astonishment at this miracle is a
form of the praise of God. In the twelfth chapter of the Acts of
the Apostles, Peter is represented as experiencing a similar reaction upon his unexpected release from prison in Jerusalem. He
thought that it was a vision (Acts 12:9); he could not believe that
it was really happening to him. This sense of wonder at God's
efforts on her behalf is proof of Israel's faith. Throughout her
history Israel always reacted to God's works as his personal word
to her. On the occasion referred to by the psalmist, Israel was
astonished. Her mouth was full of laughter; her lips filled with
song. Even among the pagan nations, this striking event did not
pass unnoticed. Though lacking Israel's faith, the infidel had been
forced to admit that God had done great things for his people.
For it is characteristic of Yahweh, the God of history, to work in
history, through history, in order to reveal himself.

You will have noted the presupposition in the second part of
the psalm, where the psalmist voices his petition—God's works
continue unremittingly in history. It would be no compliment to
the power or the providence of almighty God if we imagined that,
to reveal himself to us, he had constantly to be correcting the historical process we call history. As if, in order to make himself
heard, the Lord had to shout above the noise of human commerce!
Nothing was farther from Israel's mind than the idea that these
divine interventions were a kind of interference with historical
events and human personalities. Israel's belief was that God
worked from within history to tell her of himself. That is what is

meant by saying that Israel's religion was an historical religion. Our Christian belief asserts this same truth; for it makes a similar claim to be historical. "The Word became flesh, and pitched his tent among us." He became a man like other men; he lived, in an utterly true sense, an ordinary human life. As Israel's faith made her see God's action in history, so Christian faith enables me to see in Jesus Christ the Son of God. Yet Jesus Christ was truly, fully a man, for all that.

After the psalmist's solemn commemoration of the great past event comes his petition to God to act again to help his people in their present distress. "Restore our fortune, O Yahweh, like the brooks of the Negeb." In common with many Mediterranean countries, Palestine has a number of brooks like Kidron, which in the spring of the year, as the snow melts, become fairly formidable torrents. As soon as the heat of summer strikes, however, they dry up completely. All that is left is a streak in the sand, or a scar on the rock, where water once flowed. Yet to the south in the Negeb, these winter torrents are longer lived because the brooks of the Negeb are fed by springs. Recent archeological explorations in the south of Israel by Nelson Glueck have proven that once there was a great irrigation system that sought to utilize these brooks, which lasted well into the summer heats.

"Restore our fortune, O Yahweh, like the brooks of the Negeb. Those who sow in tears harvest with shouts of joy." The torrent in the Bible is not infrequently a symbol of disillusionment—and well it might be, given the experience of the natives of Palestine. In the sixth chapter of Job, for instance, the protagonist is heard to declare, "My friends have been as disillusioning as a torrent, like the bed of dried up rivers" (Jb 6:15-17). In this season of drought, this time of disenchantment and frustration, our psalmist asks God to restore his people's fortunes. It may very well be that the historical incident envisaged here is the return of the Jews from Babylonian captivity. At least if it were, we can easily appreciate the disillusioning contrast between expectation and fulfillment. On the one hand, the Second Isaiah, in his prediction of this great event, compares it with the mightiest of the *magnalia Dei*, the most striking of God's miracles wrought in the past for his people. The return from Babylon is to be like a new crossing of the Red Sea. It will appear like a triumphant march back across the Fertile Crescent under the leadership of God, who like a shepherd will lead his people; thus it is to be greater than the exodus of old. The prophet also pictures the return of the exiles as a new deluge, another of the great salvation events of the Old Testament. Indeed, Isaiah even compares it to a totally new creation. But if we want to get

53

some idea of what we moderns are pleased to call "the historical reality," we have only to pick up a book like Nehemiah, or even to read a little farther in the book we call Isaiah in order to see how far from idyllic, how very frustrating the actual return from Babylon to their country was for the Jewish émigrés. They came back to a city in ruins; they came back to a sanctuary desecrated and destroyed. They had to reestablish the divine cultus which had been in abeyance over half a century. Economically the land was close to ruin. Politically there was no hope of restoring the monarchy: there were foreigners now in the land with whom they had to come to terms. Little wonder then that Israel, now become the Jewish people, turned in upon herself, surrounded herself with the hedge of the law behind which in isolation she might hold what little she had left.

Faith in Yahweh   Yet it was at this very period, when her fortunes were at their very lowest ebb, that Israel's sages and prophets gave the clearest and most striking expression to the people's eschatological hopes. The monarchy had disintegrated and fizzled out in the degradation of the Babylonian captivity—never to be restored. Still, it was at this moment in her history that Israel's hope in a future king, a David even greater than the historical David, took root and burgeoned. It was at this moment that Israel's hopes for the land, her ambitions for the people, became immeasurably more spiritual than ever they had been in the days of good fortune. Israel become the Jewish people caught sight of the ultimate direction of the divine plan; and she began at last to accept her basic vocation to be God's people, to be human. This *parousia* of Yahweh for which they yearn lies in the distant future. He will come—this they know. But when? "Restore our fortune, O Yahweh, like the brooks of the Negeb!"

There is one reality in the fifth and sixth verses that is very prominent: the certainty that future joy is going to spring from present sorrow. "Those who sow in tears harvest with shouts of joy." "He who sows in sorrow and in tears shall come back bearing his sheaves with joy." This is the central message of the psalm. For me, in my contemporary situation, this message of the psalmist is still relevant today. It could be expressed in many ways, but I wish to paraphrase it as follows. If truly I believe that future joy will surely spring from present trials, that my surmounting some present frustration or disillusionment is going to count as my contribution to the reign of God, then I cannot afford to wait for the elimination of these threats, of this risk, in order to make my commitment to God. It is perfectly true that aeroplane travel is dangerous. It is perfectly true—and Monday morning's paper witnesses to it—that travel on the highway is a risky business. Yet the man who is so obsessed by the possibility of such dangers as to remain at home is no man at all. There is no pat answer to the problem which the psalmist faces—which I too must face—because none of us knows for sure how long our own life will continue. None of us knows for sure what is to happen to us. None of us knows with any certainty what direction our own development, our own reaction to various experiences, is going to take.

What then is the solution? I believe the answer may be illustrated by a very common human experience. A young man falls in love with a woman, after a certain period of time spent in her company. He can accordingly make a prudential judgment that she is the person he ought to marry. And so they marry. But by the next month, or the next year, or twenty years later, he undoubtedly discovers that the reality of married life is very different from what he thought he was going to find. This is what I mean when I say that there is no simple or automatic solution for this problem of facing the concrete contingencies of life. The only practical answer that can be given is this: I must love whatever I find. For I can be fairly sure of this, that what I am going to find in my life as a priest, in my life as a religious, is going to be very different from what I now imagine it will be. All I have to do to prove this to myself is to look back over my past life, as the psalmist looks back in this psalm, and see how differently things have worked out from the way I conjectured. There is no one of us who has a periscope that can pierce the future. And even if we had, even if we knew precisely what was going to happen to us, how could we predict with certainty our own reactions to those events?

I can ask however for the grace to love whatever it is that I am going to find. I can ask for the grace, as the psalmist begs in this psalm, of supporting whatever experiences I may meet and must cope with. That this was the psalmist's petition, we can see by his clear affirmation of faith that future joy will spring from this present state of sorrow in which the chosen people found itself historically when this psalm was written.

Here it may help to recall the continual tension in the Bible between historical reality and its literary presentation by the sacred writers. It would be unwise to wish to dispense with such literary presentation, even though it frequently presents a difficulty to our modern mentality in grasping the writer's intention. For the manner in which Israel's writers presented certain events

55

in her history bears witness to Israel's faith, to Israel's sense of commitment to God. We might take the account in Exodus of the crossing of the Red Sea. We do not know for sure just what happened at the crossing of the Red Sea. We can be quite certain however that Mr. DeMille's presentation of it in the movie, "The Ten Commandments," has missed the main point, the religious message, of the biblical presentation. For Mr. DeMille attempted to depict a spiritual reality, an action of almighty God in history, from a materialistic point of view, with the ineffectual techniques which are all that materialism has to offer. The poetic and epic presentation found in the fourteenth and fifteenth chapters of the book of Exodus witnesses to Israel's unshakeable faith that in everything which happened to her—and this is the lesson that the Bible has to teach me in my life—God was present dynamically. This should come home to us when we read the biblical descriptions of those great national crises in the story of Israel, and we see the deep faith with which that people met calamity and national disaster. When "the Assyrian came down like a wolf on the fold," Israel's prophets, the men "who saw" and interpreted God's action in history declared, "God has visited his people." The misfortunes of their people were perceived to be a visitation of their God. The divine purpose was not merely to punish a people that even on its own admission was a sinful people, but to make them "turn," as the Hebrew idiom expresses it, to make them react, to convert them to God's will.

So also in my own personal history, I should endeavor to learn the precious lesson which Israel's sacred writers teach me: to love whatever I find. Actually, there is no other reaction to the happenings of my life that makes sense. Any other reaction will only rob me of the possibility of becoming truly human. It is this attitude of faith which alone can keep me truly a member of the human race. The secret is simply to love what I find. It is this open-hearted attitude towards all the eventualities of my earthly existence which alone can ultimately bring me true fulfillment. "He who sows in sorrow and in tears shall come back bearing his sheaves with joy."

THE STORY OF THE FALL
Genesis 3:1-19

The serpent was the shrewdest of all the wild animals that Yahweh God had made; and he said to the Woman, "So God has said that you may not eat of *any* of the trees in the garden?" 2The Woman answered the serpent, "We *may* eat the fruit from the trees in the garden! 3—It is only with regard to the fruit from the tree in the middle of the garden that God said, 'You shall not eat it; you shall not even touch it, under pain of death.'" 4"Not at all" the serpent rejoined, "You wouldn't die! 5God knows very well that the day you eat this fruit, your eyes will be opened, and you will be like God, knowing good from evil."

6The Woman saw that the tree was good to eat and tempting to the eye, and that it was desirable for [acquiring] understanding. She took the fruit, and she ate it. And she gave some to her husband, who was with her; and he ate.

7Then the eyes of both of them were opened; and they saw— that they were naked! So they sewed fig-leaves together and made themselves girdles.

8They heard the foot-steps of Yahweh God, as he took a stroll through the garden in the afternoon breeze; so the Man and the Woman hid themselves from Yahweh God among the trees of the garden. 9Yahweh God called the Man, "Where are you?" he said. 10"I heard your foot-steps in the garden," the Man replied; "and I was afraid since I am naked; and I hid myself." 11God rejoined, "Who told you that you were naked? Then you have eaten from the tree, which I forbade you to eat!"— 12"The Woman you gave me as companion—she gave me some fruit from the tree; and I ate it." 13Yahweh God said to the Woman, "What ever have you done?"; and the Woman replied, "The serpent deceived me—and I ate!"

14Then Yahweh God said to the serpent, "Since you have caused this, you shall be the most cursed of all animals and of all the wild animals. You shall crawl upon your belly, and you shall eat dust as long as you live! 15I will put enmity between you and the Woman, between your offspring and hers. He will crush your head, while you attack him in the heel."

16To the Woman, he said, "I shall increase your pain at childbirth...."

17To the Man, he said, "Because you heeded the suggestion of your wife and ate from the tree, which I forbade you to eat, the soil will be cursed on your account.... 19In the sweat of your brow you shall eat your bread, until you return to the soil, since you were taken from it. For dust you are, and to dust you shall return."

THE BIBLICAL VIEW
OF SIN

St. Thomas'
Notion of Sin

IN THE *Summa Contra Gentiles* (Book III, Chapter 122), St. Thomas gives a technical or theological definition of sin. He states that "God is not offended by us except insofar as we act against our own proper good." As theologians, this definition pleases us. We sometimes have difficulty with the ordinary description of sin as an offense against God, because it strikes us as perhaps somewhat ingenuous. For we know that God is infinitely happy and unchangeable. How can the eternal, undiminishing beatitude of the Blessed Trinity be affected by anything that I do, anything that I am? In the technical language of theology, we are told that it is only by extrinsic denomination that God can in any sense be truly said to be angry, grieved, or outraged with us for our sins. And yet there is a problem—one might even say a danger—in insisting upon such a clinical view, contenting ourselves with such a technical diagnosis of sin. If it be true—and we have it on the authority of St. Thomas that it is—that God is not offended by us except insofar as we act against our own proper good, do we not run up against a psychological difficulty? If sin properly speaking is to be regarded not so much as an offense against God, but simply an offense against myself, may not this very exact definition diminish the aversion and horror that I must feel in regard to sin? Is it not possible that I may cease to experience that sense of positive horror, which the old, untechnical view of sin most effectively instilled (and let us honestly admit it) in those persons who love God?

From this technical point of view, sin is a "surd." It has in itself no explanation; it is unintelligible, because it is not-being. It has no cause, in any proper sense. God's collaboration is necessary for every act of mine, even my sinful acts; and yet he does not collaborate in sin itself, as he does in helping me act. Perhaps the most terrifying truth about sin from this point of view is that in itself it is due entirely to my own perversity. God's collaboration may be necessary for me to produce a sinful act; but God does not cause sin as such, simply because sin is a lack of goodness, a not-something.

It is well at this point, I suggest, that we rethink the problem of anthropomorphism in the Bible. It is also important to recall that our theological, scholastic viewpoint is also a human manner of thinking about divine truth. I mean that since it is human it can only express certain aspects of the divinely revealed truth. Theological language, while exact, as scientific language ought to be, can give me but a tiny insight into the Christian mystery. We must also recall the fact that any kind of language, including theological language, comes to us with the mark of its own cultural and historical context indelibly stamped upon it by that civilization or human situation in which this expression of the truth emerged.

Now we all well know that God who is infinite goodness, complete and unlimited, has been so utterly good as to permit me to share in his goodness. "You are of infinite value," he says to me paradoxically, "because you are a creature. I have created you only that you may share in my goodness, in myself, in my happiness."

We know also that God's happiness and glory are infinitely complete without any creature at all. God would be just as great, just as glorious, just as much God, whether he chose to create the world—whether he chose to create me—or not. We know however that he willed to create me simply and solely because he loves his own supreme happiness, his own infinite, unchangeable goodness, to perfection. He loves himself so much (if I may put it this way), that he chose to share himself with me.

And yet it would seem, when we reflect upon it, that God does somehow obtain something from me. May we not say that God must in some sense receive glory from myself which he would not otherwise have received had he not created me, some honor he would not have had were I not to attain heaven? God is so good, so great, so powerful, and so infinitely perfect that he can make his purpose in creating myself coincide exactly with my own personal fulfillment, with my purpose in attaining him. He is so gloriously infinite a God that he can receive his glory from making me share in his goodness forever.

So we must, as I have said, rethink this problem of anthropomorphism, of our human way of expressing the other-worldly, the divine, those realities that are beyond us. It is necessary, in other words, to plumb the meaning of this mythicized vision—for that is what it actually is—of supernatural realities.

We are all well aware that when the sacred writers speak of

God's anger or God's good pleasure at man's response to his Word, we are dealing with an anthropomorphic expression. God has no "right arm." God is not a "rock," nor is he like "a warrior aroused from a drunken stupor" (Ps 78:65). In fact, we should realize that the statement, "God is spirit" (Jn 4:24), that is, "breath," "wind," is just as much a figure of speech as David's description of Yahweh in 2 Samuel 22:9: "smoke went up from his nostrils, and a devouring fire came out of his mouth." The Bible is in fact full of anthropomorphisms for the very good reason that there is no other way to speak about God in human language. Moreover, even the highly technical language of theology, less strange to us because it comes from a culture with which we are more familiar, is also human language, and hence also an anthropomorphic expression of divine truth.

There is another very important facet of this problem of biblical anthropomorphisms. It is very striking that they are employed most frequently by those authors who possessed without a doubt the loftiest, the most spiritual, the theologically most sophisticated conception of God. I refer, of course, to the classical prophets, the men whose writings present the idea of God in its purest form in the Old Testament. Thus, for example, the Second Isaiah, who in many respects represents the ultimate in Old Testament theology, can represent Yahweh as saying: "For a brief moment I abandoned you, but with great tenderness I shall take you back. In an outburst of wrath for a moment I hid my face from you, but with enduring love I take pity on you" (Is 54:7-8).

Now this use of anthropomorphic expressions by the prophets has a very essential purpose. They mean to emphasize God's personal character. They wish, so that there will be no confusion in the minds of the Israelites, to set their conception of Yahweh in contrast with those impersonal, frivolous, unpredictable, irrational, whimsical gods of the Gentiles, which are simply personifications of the blind forces of nature and nothing more.

Let us return to our problem concerning the definition of sin. When we say that my sins can really make no difference to God, but only to my own proper good, we are expressing a truth about God. We thereby declare him immutable, unchangeable, infinitely perfect. Yet there is another aspect of the relationship between God and myself which I cannot afford to neglect. The Bible insists over and over again, as we have seen the psalmist state, that God does care for me as an individual, that God loves me as a person, that God does desire that I attain my own proper good, which is to participate as fully as my creaturely capacity warrants in his own happiness and goodness.

60

I point this out to you because I have often felt that this problem is one which those who are trained theologically in a system
noted for its exactness and precision sometimes experience. Such
theologians have passed the stage where they can be content with
the ordinary, somewhat unsophisticated conceptions of sin. On the
other hand, we experience a difficulty also with such a carefully
formulated view of sin as that found in the *Summa Contra Gentiles:* it omits all that can touch us humanly. This is of course true
of any scientific language. To be scientific, ordinary human
speech must be emptied of all its emotional overtones; it must
be freed as far as possible from the thralldom of the imagination;
it must rise from the concrete, particular situation to include every
possible instance where this particular reality is found. The di-
agnoses of various diseases found in medical books can be read
by most men without so much as the shedding of one tear.

However, it so happens that when we meditate upon sin, it is
precisely this being moved emotionally and imaginatively as
human beings that we wish to achieve. I suggest, then, that we turn
again to the Bible, to the Old Testament, in order to find a more
existential description of sin, and hence a more vivid, concrete
realization of what sin means or ought to mean to me personally.
You are all familiar with the little story in the third chapter of
Genesis, in which the sacred writer uses a kind of parable or myth
—it is actually taken from the mythological collections of the
ancient Near East—in order to illustrate the tragedy which sin
had caused in the lives of men and women around him. Another
variant account of this same myth may be found in the twenty-
eighth chapter of Ezekiel, and I suggest that this passage may
serve as an introduction to our reflections upon sin, since it illustrates very graphically the aspect of sin of which St. Thomas
speaks so technically in the *Summa Contra Gentiles*—sin as an
evil for man himself.

Ezekiel's poem is employed as a satire against the king of Tyre,
who has been dethroned, but you will see in a moment that there
is question of the same myth as in Genesis. God is represented
here as addressing the fallen king.

"You were a model of perfection,
full of wisdom, admirable in beauty.
You lived in Eden, in the garden of God;
all kinds of precious stones formed your raiment . . . .
I placed you there with a cherub as your
guardian on the day of your creation:

you lived upon the holy mountain of God;
you walked in the midst of burning coals.
You were a model in your conduct from the day
of your creation,
until the day when evil was found in you.
By the machination of your conduct, you
filled yourself with violence and sin;
so I threw you down from the mountain of God,
and your guardian cherub caused you to perish
in the midst of the coals.
Your heart had been puffed up with pride
because of your beauty;
you corrupted your wisdom for the sake of
your splendor.
And I threw you down to the earth
and offered you as a spectacle to kings,
because of the number of your faults.
Because of the dishonesty of your conduct,
you have befouled your sanctuaries;
and I made fire come forth to devour you;
I reduced you to ashes upon the earth
in the eyes of all who looked upon you.
Among the peoples, any man who knew you
was struck with horror at your condition;
you are an object of terror—you are finished,
destroyed forever"   (Ez 28:12-19).

The Fall in Genesis

The story that we have in the second and third chapters of Genesis comes to us from a source we generally call the Yahwist, a man who in many respects takes a very human view of God. Yet, for all that, his notion of God is very lofty and pure. Perhaps the greatest quality of this writer is his deep insight into human psychology. He makes us aware in his own "folksy" way of the great privilege that was man's from the beginning. You will recall how he represents God as a potter, who scratches around in the earth, makes a little doll, blows in its nose—and the Man comes into existence. And having made man out of this clay, God takes him, puts him in a place where the Man has no right to be—the garden of Eden. God, in the homely view of this author, has a little country villa,—an oasis, the only proper place in the ancient Near East, for a pleasance, or country seat, admirably fitted up with every sort of water supply, the greatest luxury in a dry land! It is a place where almighty God, like the inhabitants of the Mediterranean world even today, takes a little walk towards four or five in the afternoon to enjoy the breeze that blows over the hot earth from the Mediterranean. This garden of God is a place of privilege, a place that belongs solely to God himself. And yet here, without any merit on his part, is where God places the Man he had made from the soil. And when God looks around his creation, among the creatures he has made, to seek a companion for the Man, he can find none. So he creates the Woman by making use of part of the Man's side. We call it a rib, but the term is not that specific in Hebrew. God might have been represented as repeating what he did the first time—taking a little clay and making another little doll, a female doll this time, and blowing in its nose. But our author does not put it that way, because he wants to show the equality and the close solidarity which exists between the Man and the Woman.

In the third chapter we reach the celebrated story of the fall of this privileged pair who, without any merit of theirs, were permitted to live in God's country seat. "The serpent was the shrewdest of all the wild animals that Yahweh God had made" (Gn 3:1). Did this author really think that serpents could talk, or did he realize that this malevolent beast was merely a symbol for Satan? We cannot be sure, but we do know that by the time the book of Wisdom was written, some fifty years before Jesus' birth, its author certainly realized that this serpent was identifiable with the devil (Wis 2:24).

The serpent approaches the Woman with considerable finesse. "So God has said that you may not eat of *any* of the trees in the garden?" This is obviously an unwarranted generalization. And the Woman corrects him at once: "We *may* eat the fruit from the trees in the garden!—It is only with regard to the fruit from the tree in the middle of the garden that God said, 'You shall not eat it; you shall not even touch it, under pain of death.'" Here we have an interesting detail. God had not said, "You shall not even touch it."—Did the Man tell the Woman this in order to keep her from coming too close to danger? The serpent seizes upon the Woman's weak point—curiosity: "Not at all. You wouldn't die! God knows very well that the day you eat this fruit, your eyes will be opened, and you will be like God, knowing good from evil." Observe how the Yahwist now exteriorizes the psychology of temptation by having the Woman look at the tree and realize how good to eat it appeared, how desirable to look at, how desirable too, for acquiring this special understanding. And, "She took the fruit, and she ate it. And she gave some to her husband, who was with her; and he ate." No argument! The male of the species does not display his customary domination: he is very easily led.

63

Now our author tells us the tragic sequel: "Then the eyes of both of them were opened" (just as the serpent had indeed promised!) "and they saw—that they were naked!" It is a highly dramatic presentation of the fall. What does this "knowledge of good and evil," of which the Yahwist speaks, mean? In order to understand it, we should recall that knowledge in the Bible is not simply intellectual as it is usually with us. Knowledge is not an ivory-tower occupation for the Semite. It is too closely related to reality, too much a part of life. For the biblical writers knowledge is nothing less than experience. When Adam "knew God," when Adam "knew his wife" (through sexual intercourse), each of these activities are capable of being included under knowledge. When Adam "knows God," he lives God's truth. As John will tell us later, the truth is something we must do, not merely think about (Jn 3:21). "To know God" is to honor, praise, worship him, as is his due. Knowledge is practical: it involves man's activity.

Sin, Denial of Man's Creatureliness — Now the knowledge of good and evil in our story is depicted as something which properly belongs to God alone. It is God's own proper preserve. This is why God placed the ban on the fruit of the tree of knowledge, so far as the Man and Woman were concerned. Knowledge, we have seen, is a taking possession of someone or something: it is an exercise of dominion. Thus, in the second chapter of Genesis, the Man is said to name all the animals, which means that he is exercising that dominion over the animal world which almighty God had commanded him to exercise. The Man is the king, in other words, of the animal creation.

But what does it mean to exercise dominion over good and evil? It means to create one's own categories of right and wrong. I decide what the norms of morality are—for me! This would seem to be the sense of the phrase in this passage, as St. Thomas Aquinas rightly perceived: "The first man sinned principally by desiring likeness to God with respect to the knowledge of good and evil, as the serpent had suggested to him, that is to say, that he might be able, through the power of his own nature, to determine for himself what was good to do and what was evil" (*Summa Theologica*, II-II, q.163, a.2).

The self-deception, I need not remind you, that is involved in such a fatuous course of action on the part of the first Man and the first Woman is dramatically presented in Genesis. "You will be like *'elōhīm* (you will be like God)," the serpent had said in his invitation to these creatures to become something more than creatures, to rise above the limitations of their very being—in other words to be what they were not. With deliberate and very

64

dramatic irony, the author tells what happened to them as a result of their sin. He repeats the first part of the serpent's promise —for it was true—that their eyes would be opened. It was unfortunately also very misleading. Their eyes were opened,— "and they saw that they were naked!" Thus the Yahwist expresses the inner change, the psychological crisis they underwent, by having them cover their nakedness.

In the sequel we are shown a very clear distinction between the effect of their action on themselves and the punishment which God inflicts upon that action. They had, in a certain sense, actually acquired the knowledge of good and evil. They foolishly thought that this would make them like God. But to be like God is not the same as to be God; and to act like the gods, while remaining human, must inevitably end in disaster. Here we see described, in a very human, homely way, St. Thomas' notion of sin as acting against our own proper good.

You will note that the only way out of the calamitous situation to which the Man and the Woman have brought themselves lies with God's initiative, indeed, with God's loving kindness for fallen man. Sin is something that man can "create," so to say. It is, at the same time, something from which man cannot liberate himself. In Genesis 3:15, we are told that the divine initiative actually entered the tragic picture. God's love and condescension came to remedy the evil, to bring grace—a divine favor totally unexpected. This is the surprise ending to this sad story. Thanks only to God's liberality and graciousness man is enabled to act for his own proper good once again.

It is not a very pleasant subject—sin. Perhaps it may not help me to find God in Christ as easily as contemplating, through the pages of the Gospel, the actions and the words of God's Son made man. But it is part of the human situation. It is a fact. It is an historical reality, and as such we cannot afford to neglect it.

THE DIVINE MERCY
Psalm 130 [129]

2 From the watery depths I cry to you, Yahweh!
  O Lord, hear my voice!
  Let your ear be attentive
  To the voice of my petition.

3 If you should record men's sins, Yahweh,
  O Lord, who could bear it?

4 But near you stands pardon—
  It is then we fear you.

5 I put my hope in Yahweh: my whole being waits hopefully;
  I count upon his Word.

6 My whole being puts its hope in the Lord
  More than the watchmen for the dawn.

7 More than the watchmen for the dawn
  Let Israel hope in the Lord!
  For gracious kindness stands near Yahweh!
  Near him stands bountiful redemption!

8 He it is who will redeem Israel
  From all her sins.

Chapter 7

DEEPER KNOWLEDGE OF GOD
THROUGH REPENTED SIN

IN PSALM 130 (129 in the Vulgate), the *De profundis*, we learn that repented sin brings me a new revelation of God. One purpose of meditating upon the fact of sin is to provide me with an experiential, personal knowledge of God, by bringing home to myself the truth that God really cares for me. In order to accomplish this, I am taught in this psalm that the essential attitude is, with God's grace, to throw myself upon the divine mercy, to await God's word of pardon.

Antisocial Character of Sin

The regulation of the Church known as the law of integral confession can create a serious difficulty for many people. The great danger is that the process of self-examination can turn into a system of self-justification. If only I can tell all my sins, according to species and number, so that I succeed in getting the whole story completely off my chest, then I am *ipso facto* justified! And this, of course, we know is not true.

"From the watery depths I cry to you, Yahweh: O Lord, hear my voice! Let your ear be attentive to the voice of my petition." This psalm is post-exilic, but no clues are given us concerning the concrete situation in which the psalmist finds himself. The prayer would appear to be that of an individual Israelite: it was not composed for the worshiping community. This prayer was made at night time (cf. verse six); and that is about all that can be said. It is clear from the first verse however that the petitioner feels himself cut off, isolated from God and from his fellow men, from all living beings. The symbol employed here, the waters of the primordial chaos, represent Sheol. The petitioner is so far sunk in the depths of the world sea, that God must bend his ear to catch his plaintive voice. Yet his prayer somehow gets through the watery depths of the abyss, and we note how deeply conscious he is that his relationship to God is that of slave to master, or lord. The suppliant addresses Yahweh in this case as *'Adōnāi*. "O Lord, hear my voice! Let your ear be attentive to the voice of my petition. If you should record men's sins, Yahweh, O Lord, who

67

could bear it?" The answer, of course, to this rhetorical question is: nobody!

One of the most striking features of this psalm is to be found in the fourth verse: "But near you stands pardon—it is then we fear you." In this beautiful line of the *De profundis,* we hear the petition for forgiveness expressed so hesitantly and delicately that it can easily be overlooked. The psalmist voices his plea in a very indirect manner. He seems to be almost shy in asking God for pardon. Thus he presents this divine forgiveness in his prayer as a personification, standing in the presence of God. He had already implied in the third verse that God will not record men's sins, because no man could successfully face such a record. What gives him hope is his confidence that pardon stands, like one of the angels, before the face of God; and this pardon moreover is a grace, a free gift that God is only too ready to bestow upon those who beg for it.

God's Creative Forgiveness

Even more interesting is the remark that follows: "Near you stands pardon—*it is then we fear you.*" Forgiveness of sin lies totally within God's creative and merciful power. Man must not presume that God is ready to accord this to him without some change on his own part. Yet, the psalmist tells us, when God does grant pardon—and the psalmist is confident he will grant it to him—there is a new grace given; and this he calls "fear." What is meant by this fear? Actually, it signifies a new revelation of God. When man experiences the forgiveness of God he comes to know God in a way in which he has not known him before. We find this illustrated very graphically in the book of Exodus. You recall that, in the thirty-second chapter of Exodus after Israel had made the covenant with Yahweh, while Moses is on the mountain to speak again with God, the people fell into sin by worshiping the golden calf. As Moses descended the mountain, he heard the jubilant shouts which this ritual had evoked, and in his anger he broke the tablets on which the decalogue was written. Almighty God is described as becoming very angry. Indeed he is said to repent of the pact that he made with this people, until, at Moses' intercession, God decides to give them one final chance. So Moses ascends the mountain once again in order to renew the covenant with God.

New Knowledge of God

It is at this point in the book that we see how, through her repented sin—and Israel has repented of her sin—the chosen people gains an entirely new knowledge of God. Israel perceives a new dimension in the covenant, of which certainly she was not aware before she sinned and repented. I am thinking of those verses (Ex 33:18ff.) where, after Moses had begged Yahweh to permit him to see his face, the Lord causes a vision of himself to pass before Moses. The words which accompany the vision are noteworthy: "Yahweh, a God of tenderness and pity, slow to anger, rich in grace and fidelity, who keeps his favor for thousands, who tolerates faults and transgressions and sins, yet he does not permit anything to go unpunished. . . ." Here is the new knowledge which the psalmist had called the fear of God. This term expresses the experiential knowledge of her God which Israel attained through repentance for her sin of idolatry. She came to know her God in his act of forgiving her, in a way she had not known him the first time she made the covenant (Ex 19:1ff.).

In the *De profundis* also the psalmist expresses this same idea. Pardon stands before the face of God, and when this is granted to man he receives, with the grace of divine pardon, an additional favor, the "fear of God"; that is, a more personal knowledge of the God with whom he deals.

"I put my hope in Yahweh: my whole being waits hopefully; I count upon his Word." Having made his petition so discreetly and indirectly, the psalmist now expresses his confident trust that he will be forgiven. He throws himself upon the mercy of God. And his whole being, his *nephesh* (his life), waits hopefully and counts upon God's Word, his *dābār*.

The Word of God is creative. On the very first page of the Bible, God is represented as creating everything through his Word. "And God said: 'Let there be light,' and light came into being" (Gn 1:3-4). Man, the psalmist knows very well, can create sin. But only God can remedy the tragic situation that man has brought about; only God can cure sin. So the psalmist waits upon the Word of God's creative forgiveness.

Actually this "Word" which the psalmist awaits so hopefully and confidently, is really only fully spoken through the coming of Jesus, the Word incarnate, in the New Testament. What the psalmist longs for is the saying reported in St. Matthew's Gospel, where Jesus turns to the paralytic and says: "Courage, my son, your sins are forgiven you!" (Mt 9:2). It is this Word that the author of the *De profundis* is hoping to hear.

"My whole being puts its hope in the Lord more than the watchman for the dawn." In the Bible night is a symbol of God's absence, of God's withdrawal, while the dawn, in many of the psalms especially, is thought of as the appropriate time for God's entry, or

God's return into the life of his suppliant. The symbol of the watchman occurs elsewhere in the Bible. The most famous passage is found in Isaiah: "Watchman, what of the dawn—watchman, what of the dawn?" (Is 21:11). In the picture sketched here by the prophet, the Edomites, allies of the Philistines in their fight against Sargon, call out to the seer: "How long is the time of our incarceration, our enslavement?" For they had lost, as you will remember, the war to Sargon II of Assyria. The prophet dramatically depicts them as men who call out to the watchman upon the ramparts of the city to ask the time. "How long until the dawn breaks?" And the watchman reassures them that they have not long to wait.

Similarly in our psalm we find that this hopeful longing for forgiveness, for the Lord's return into the life of the sinner, is expressed through this image of the watchman awaiting the dawn. "More than the watchmen for the dawn let Israel hope in the Lord! For gracious kindness stands near Yahweh! Near him stands bountiful redemption! He it is who will redeem Israel from all her sins."

Hope Based on the Covenant Israel's hope in Yahweh is based upon the covenant that he had made with her ancestors. Thus in this seventh verse mention is made of one of the great virtues of Israel's covenanted God—his *ḥesed*, his gracious, loving kindness. It is that virtue which the head of the clan, the patriarch, is expected to display towards the members of his family. The word may be paraphrased as merciful kindness, or loving condescension. It resembles the Latin word *pietas*, which denotes that quality governing the relations of the father towards the children in a family. Our psalm represents this gracious kindness as standing in the presence of God. This divine characteristic, Yahweh's covenanted *ḥesed*, gives confidence to the sinner. For he now realizes that that divine pardon, which also stands before the face of God, will be given him in virtue of his covenanted relationship with Yahweh. "Near him stands bountiful redemption." God is the redeemer. He is the *gōʾēl*, the kinsman-avenger. It is God "who will redeem Israel from all her sins."

Hope Fulfilled in Christ In the first chapter of St. Matthew's Gospel, the evangelist explains the meaning of the name Jesus. It is *Yēšuʿa*—Yahweh saves. Matthew asserts that the child was "named Jesus, because he is to save his people from their sins" (Mt 1:21). The incarnation gives a completely new dimension to the psalter; hence it acquires a new relevance for us who are Christians. This hope of the psalmist for forgiveness comes to us incarnate in Jesus Christ. He is the

70

dābār, he is the Word of God become man. He it is who "will redeem Israel from all her sins" (Ps 130:8), indeed, rescue all mankind from all sin. He, who as the Word of God stood in God's presence, who was the very embodiment of this gracious kindness, this covenanted quality of God, has, through the incarnation, brought forgiveness to us and pardon from the throne of God.

Through our experience of sin, or, rather, through our personal experience of sin repented, we advance by this new grace of Christ to a deeper knowledge of our Lord. It is for this reason that in the sacrament of penance we must throw ourselves upon the mercy of Christ. This should be the fruit of our reception of this sacrament. The sacrament of penance abolishes the anti-social consequences of sin; for the favor of God in Jesus Christ reunites me not only with God himself, but also with other men, from whom sin has cut me off.

That is why the Church in the rite of confession, which is a liturgical action, has always been conscious that I confess my sins not merely to the priest insofar as he represents Jesus Christ, but also to the priest as a man, to the priest, in other words, as he represents the other members of the Body of Christ from whom I have become estranged through sin. It is particularly necessary to remind ourselves of this facet of confession because, through the concern in the Latin rite to preserve the anonymity of the penitent—and the Church has good reason for this precaution—we are liable to forget that we are really performing an act of public worship when we go to confession. We might think of ourselves—quite wrongly—as telling our sins through this man to God; as obtaining, through the priest as a kind of supernatural transmitter, the forgiveness which Christ has promised in this sacrament. We are in danger of forgetting, in other words, that this man, the priest, offers us in the name of the Church, as well as of Christ, the means of returning to the fellowship of the people of God.

The psalmist is well aware, from the symbol he uses for Sheol in verse one, that he is cut off by sin, not only from God, but also from the cultic assembly of Israel. Sheol is a place where there are no living men. It is the kingdom of the dead, the abode of lifeless shades. My sin too cuts me off from the other members of the Church. In the sacrament of penance this social rupture, this separation from one's fellow Christians, must be repaired, no less than that from God and Jesus Christ.

This psalm serves to remind us that the pardon which God gives through the sacrament of penance is a grace, a free gift. The psalm can teach us also that it is through repented sin that I gain

71

a more profound knowledge of God, that I bring home to myself one aspect of God's character which I probably could not learn in any other way. As we see from his remark about fear, and as we see perhaps more clearly illustrated in the thirty-second to thirty-fourth chapters of Exodus, Israel came to learn about her divine covenant partner, Yahweh, in quite a new manner once she repented of the sin of idolatry and came humbly to ask again that the covenant with her God be renewed. She now knew him as the God who would graciously deploy his creative power to forgive, instead of destroying, the people of his acquisition.

St. Ignatius had a profound sense of the value of repentance as an aid to advancing in that "sense of family" towards God our Father (*familiaritas cum Deo in oratione*), which he considers in the Constitutions as the hallmark of the Jesuit. He was wont to recommend that prayer be short, and not protracted; but he assumed that the man of prayer should be mortified—dead to sin. His peculiar insistence—and in this Ignatius was unique among Christian mystics—upon the practice of the daily examination of conscience is proof that he shared our psalmist's conviction that through repented sin a man will advance in the knowledge and the love of God in Christ.

THE SECOND WEEK

THE PURPOSE OF THE SECOND WEEK in the context of the com- *Aim*
plete Spiritual Exercises, planned to last a month, is to bring the
exercitant to choose a state of life. This phase opens with a consideration of the *Kingdom of Christ* [91-98], which is calculated
to inaugurate the following of Christ by a general and very
generous self-oblation. Later, the retreatant is aided in his
consideration of the different states of life open to him by two
key meditations, that on *Two Standards* or Banners [136-148],
and that on *Three Classes of Men*. He is to reflect also upon *Three
Degrees of Humility* [165-168], and then further practical rules
are given for his "election" [169-188].

The most characteristic feature of the second week, however,
and one which should dominate even an abbreviated course of
the Exercises, is the continued contemplation of the earthly life
of Jesus from the incarnation to the final week of his public
ministry in Jerusalem. The Ignatian *contemplatio* is orientated to
the *imitatio Christi*, the following of Christ, in love and total self-
commitment. Since this imitation of Christ is so central to the
second week, and since it presents certain difficulties to the modern mind, we must endeavor to establish its true nature.

It is perhaps easier to say what the following of Christ is not. It *Imitatio Christi*
is not mere "monkey business," the slavish aping of the words
or gestures of Jesus. Neither does it consist simply in allowing
one's ethics to be influenced by Jesus' example. Certain moral
qualities, which may well be exemplified in our Lord's conduct,
have a value intrinsic to themselves, without being referred necessarily to him. For this reason "moralizing" on the mysteries of
Jesus' earthly life risks the danger of remaining superficial in one's
relationship with him.

In the language of modern psychology, the *imitatio Christi* involves the arduous process through which the contemporary
Christ operates with a man on a long term basis. The Spiritual

75

Exercises are a condensed plan for one's spiritual growth through an ordered, graduated series of religious experiences, which are to issue ultimately in an untrammeled freedom of relationship with the risen Lord. In the second week, I am to discover for myself the supreme attractiveness of Jesus simply because he operates well in any human situation.

Most fundamentally, however, it is our Christian faith in the reality of the incarnation and our appreciation of its far-reaching significance for our own existence that provides the final, and only thoroughly satisfactory, reason for *imitatio Christi*. The Word of God, his Son, the perfect self-expression of the Father, became man so completely that by contemplating the events of this utterly human life we can, we believe, discern the mysterious features of the invisible God. Indeed, once this present order of salvation was ordained by God, the incarnate Word, his human, no less than his divine life, becomes the determining factor in the lives of all men—whether or not they are aware of him. When theologians state that there is no grace except the *gratia Christi*, they understand that there can be no divine favor conferred upon any man that is independent of Jesus Christ. Grace is a participation in the human-divine life of our Lord. Now the explicit purpose of the New Testament revelation, above all in the four Gospels, is to acquaint us with the saving truth that our lives are orientated wholly towards our incorporation in Jesus Christ. The Christian, of course, is thus incorporated sacramentally in baptism; and the other sacraments aid and further this incorporation.

But it is also clear by the fact of the incarnation that God has willed that men know of his loving purpose in thus communicating himself in his Son become man to our history. It is a primary thesis in Johannine theology that the final significance of the mission of the Son is to reveal "the God no man has ever seen" (Jn 1:18). Here then is the ultimate reason for our contemplation of the earthly life of Jesus. As free beings, persons, we are intended by the Father to make our own "decision for Christ"; that is, to imitate or follow him by reproducing in our own inimitable fashion the "spirit of Jesus." We can only do this by developing consciously in our Christian living an intense awareness of our necessary, ontological relationship to the incarnate Word. This is the goal which St. Ignatius sets us in the second week.

We may obtain a more concrete insight into the meaning of the *imitatio Christi* by considering the letters of Paul, the only place in the New Testament where the terms "imitate," and "imitation" occur. One striking feature of Paul's teaching on this point is that he normally proposes, to the communities which he himself has

founded, the *imitation of himself* (2 Th 3:7; Phil 3:17; 1 Cor 4:16),
only occasionally and indirectly the imitation of Christ (1 Th 1:6;
1 Cor 11:1). The explanation for this strange injunction lies in
Paul's profound consciousness that the glorified Son of God is
mysteriously present within him—a truth he learned in the hour
of his own conversion (Gal 1:16). It is then by observing the concrete form of Christian existence in their apostle, exhibited
supremely in his universal service of all men (1 Cor 10:33), that
his converts are to imitate Christ. Paul means that while the specific style of the *imitatio Christi* must inevitably vary from age to
age, from culture to culture, indeed, from person to person, yet
Jesus has revealed himself and his Father through his earthly life:
he is the way to the Father, apart from which there is no other.
Paul was intensely aware of the *ecclesial* character of the following of Christ: there is no authentic *imitatio Christi* independent of
the Church. Thus it is to his own manner of Christian living that
he points, which he commands his Christians to "imitate," because
only in this way can they receive the genuine apostolic traditions
concerning Jesus Christ.

The Election, which makes its appearance in the text of the
Spiritual Exercises only in the middle of the second week, is in
reality a continuing process that began with the *Principle and
Foundation* and is operative through the *Contemplation for Obtaining Love.* It is of the utmost importance to grasp the fact
that for St. Ignatius "election" possesses a profoundly biblical
sense (cf. the election of Israel described in Isaiah 43:1-7). It is
only in virtue of the fact that God has "elected" me in Christ that
I am empowered to make the Ignatian "election" of God in Christ.
This election is not merely an ethical act of my free choice, nor
is it simply a question of effective psychology. "You have not
chosen me: I have chosen you," Jesus tells me. That St. Ignatius
was well aware of this primacy of God's free choice of man, which
creates the possibility of a supernatural "election," that is, of
openness to the divine initiative, may be seen from a favorite
formula which reappears constantly in his letters. "I beg God our
Lord that he may deign in his generosity and goodness to grant us
a superabundance of grace, in order that we may fully experience
his most holy will and carry it out entirely."

JESUS' MESSIANIC ENTRY INTO THE CITY AND TEMPLE
Matthew 21:1-17

And when they drew near Jerusalem and came to Bethphage on the mount of Olives, Jesus sent two disciples on ahead [2]with these instructions, "Enter the village straight ahead of you, and you will at once discover a she-ass and her colt tethered together. Untie them, and lead them back to me. [3]And if anyone says anything to you, just say, 'The Lord needs them, but he will return them shortly.' "

[4]This took place in order that the oracle contained in the words of the prophet might be realized, [5]"Tell the daughter of Sion, See, your king comes to you in all gentleness, astride a she-ass and a colt, the foal of a draft animal."

[6]So the disciples went off and did all that Jesus had bid them do: [7]they brought the she-ass and the colt, and laid their cloaks on them. Then he sat on top of them. [8]The huge crowd spread their cloaks on the road, while some of them began to cut branches from the trees and strew them on the road. [9]The section of the crowd preceding him, as also the part following kept shouting, "God save the Son of David! May he who comes be blessed by the Lord's name. Let the angels sing, 'God save him!' "

[10]Now as he entered Jerusalem, the whole city was stirred to its depths, demanding, "Who is this?" [11]But the crowd kept replying, "This is the prophet Jesus from Nazareth in Galilee."

[12]Now Jesus entered the temple area, and drove out all who were busy buying and selling in the sacred enclosure. He overthrew the tables of the money-changers and the dove sellers' stalls. . . .

[14]Now the blind and the lame approached him in the temple area, and he cured them. [15]But the chief priests and scribes became indignant as they observed the wonders he worked and the children shouting out in the sacred enclosure, "God save the Son of David!" [16]They said to him, "Do you hear what they are saying?" But Jesus replied, "Of course I do! —Did you never read that 'Upon the lips of infants and babies, you have created for yourself a hymn of praise?' "

[17]With that he left them abruptly, and went off outside the city to Bethany, and spent the night there.

Chapter 8

JESUS' MESSIANIC ENTRY
INTO JERUSALEM

IT IS A MOST HAPPY CIRCUMSTANCE that, as we begin the second week of the Exercises, the Church in her liturgy is preparing to enter the second Passion week by celebrating the procession with palms. We may then employ this procession as a liturgical composition of place, which will introduce us to the "principle and foundation" of the second week: the consideration on the *Kingdom of Christ.*

Procession with Palms

The purpose of this procession is to remind the faithful of their commitment to Christ as the king who has gained the initial victory over his enemies and those of mankind by his death and resurrection, and so has entered upon his reign. Yet, as Paul reminds the Corinthians, "he must reign until he puts all his enemies beneath his feet" (1 Cor 15:25). Like the Christ of the Ignatian consideration, he tells me that, if final victory is assured by his work of redemption, much remains yet to do; and for that he calls me to offer myself whole-heartedly to labor with him, to suffer with him, that I may join him in glory. The prayer for the blessing of the palms today is inspired with the same theme: ". . . grant that what your people express outwardly today, they may bring to perfect inward realization, by gaining the victory over the enemy and by loving that work of mercy, which is the redemption." My participation in today's procession is a symbol of my commitment to Christ, the offering which I must make with my whole being, my whole person. This following of Christ is the principal object of the Ignatian *contemplatio,* the characteristic exercise of the second week.

St. Ignatius tells us that I accomplish this work of *contemplatio* in the Spiritual Exercises successfully if I "derive some spiritual profit" [cf.106]. That expression is vague, and I believe it was left vague intentionally. St. Ignatius did not mean what are popularly called "practical conclusions," "practical applications." He meant much more than that. He intended that by this contemplation of the recorded events of Jesus' earthly life I should help myself to see where I can enter into the contemporary plan of salvation in my world today, in my world here and now.

To return to the liturgy of today—we should be conscious that this is precisely the aim of the liturgical procession of the palms. Note, in the first place, that the liturgy very appositely employs two psalms (Pss. 23 and 46 in the Vulgate enumeration) in connection with the blessing. These psalms ("To God belongs the earth in its fullness, the world and all its peoples," and "All you peoples clap your hands and acclaim God with joyous shouts, for Yahweh the most high is awesome, the great king of all the earth") were both composed for a processional liturgy, which, in the era before the Babylonian exile, was held in the temple to honor the kingship of Yahweh. There has been for some years now a very vigorous debate among scholars as to whether this liturgical procession was an annual enthronement ceremony of Yahweh modeled upon the New Year's festival in honor of Marduk held at Babylon. There are good reasons for asserting that the Jerusalem feast was of a very different character from that of Babylon, if indeed it existed at all. Marduk was a nature god who died annually, and this enthronement of Marduk was, of course, his resurrection, a new accession to royal and divine power, after death and resuscitation in the springtime. Yahweh was no nature god. It may well be, however, that such processional psalms as these formed a liturgy, even one celebrated annually, which commemorated the entry of God's throne, the ark, into the holy city in the days of King David. It may even be that, for some time at least, the ark was taken again from the holy of holies, out of the city gates, to be carried triumphantly in procession back to its resting place in the sanctuary. Actually, we do not know. The point is that Psalm 23 and Psalm 46 recall the truth that Yahweh, by choosing this people, became king of Israel and, through her, of all the earth.

Mystery of the Messianic Entry

What has all this to do with the narrative of Jesus' messianic entry into Jerusalem, the Gospel reading for today's liturgical celebration? What was Jesus trying to teach us by this living parable of a solemn entry into the holy city? We may recall, in the first place, that this event is unique in the public life of our Lord. It is the single occasion in his whole career when he acted contrary to his habitual practice of refusing to allow anyone to acclaim him as Messiah. We should not allow ourselves to overlook the very significant fact that on this occasion Jesus took the initiative in arranging this public acknowledgement of his messianic function by Jerusalem in the last week of his life.

80

Secondly, we may note the paramount importance of this event in the evangelical traditions. It is one of those relatively rare episodes which is repeated by all four evangelists. Each author, it is true, recounts it in his own way. In the basic outline of the apostolic kerygma, the official testimony of the early Church upon which our Christian faith reposes, we have a well-defined series of events in our Lord's earthly life. This has been described for us by Peter's statement in Acts (Acts 1:21-22). This apostolic testimony covered a movement which began with John the Baptist's ministry and terminated with Jesus' ascension. We shall return to this point again. For the moment, I should like to recall that in this particular sequence of events which provided the outline for the Synoptic Gospels, Jesus' public entry into Jerusalem marks the first time during his public life that he comes to Jerusalem and its sanctuary. The recognition of this enables us to understand what might otherwise seem a very abrupt termination of the Marcan narrative of this event (Mk 11:11). That evangelist concludes his story with the words: "Jesus entered Jerusalem and the temple area; and after he had looked around him at everything, since it was already late, he left to go to Bethany with the Twelve." The whole significance, for Mark, of the episode is that Jesus enters Jerusalem and comes into contact with its sanctuary. This is the principal meaning of this very dramatic happening.

Matthew has taken very much the same view. This author represents the whole city of Jerusalem as in turmoil, disturbed by the announcement that, "This is the prophet Jesus from Nazareth in Galilee" (Mt 21:11). In Matthew's version of the story, the episode ends, as I pointed out before, with Jesus' reference to the eighth Psalm: "By the mouths of children and babies you have procured praise." This psalm, as we saw, was applied by Hebrews 2:5-9 to Jesus' eschatological kingship, his domination of "the world to come."

Now at last, perhaps, we begin to understand the message of this parable-in-action which is Jesus' messianic entry into the temple. By that I mean that we begin to see it *as mystery* by turning once again to the author of Hebrews to see how he uses this event as the vehicle for presenting the whole pattern of Christ's redemptive activity. The pertinent passage is altogether too long to read (Heb 9:11—10:22), and I shall only cite selections from it. "But when Christ appeared as highpriest of the good things to come, he entered once for all through the greater and more perfect tent not made with hands, that is, not of this creation . . . into the sanctuary, by virtue of his own blood, having secured our eternal redemption. . . . How much more will the blood of Christ, who through the Holy Spirit offered himself unblemished unto God, cleanse our consciences from dead works to serve the living God? . . . For Christ has entered, not that sanctuary made by men's hands, a mere symbol of the real one, but heaven itself to appear now before the face of God on our behalf. Nor yet has he entered to offer himself over and over again (for in that event he would have had to suffer death over and over, ever since the beginning of the world.) But as it is, he has appeared once for all at the end of the ages, to put an end to sin by the sacrifice of himself. . . . Christ was offered in sacrifice once for all to take away the sins of many. The second time he will appear, with no relation to sin, to those who await him eagerly to bring them salvation. . . . Since, then, brothers, we are free to enter the sanctuary in virtue of the blood of Jesus, by that new and living way which he inaugurated for us through the veil, I mean his humanity, and since we have in him a highpriest set over the house of God, let us draw near to God with a sincere heart with perfect faith, having our hearts cleansed from an evil conscience by sprinkling and our body washed with pure water."

This whole conception has been inspired by the Old Testament liturgy of the day of Atonement. The sacred writer has also employed the theme of Jesus' messianic entry into the sanctuary of Jerusalem. For the author of Hebrews this event of Jesus' earthly life is significant for its symbolic value. It functions as a kind of parable exemplifying the pattern of Jesus' redemptive work. Through his death and resurrection and ascension Christ has entered *the* sanctuary, the heavenly tent of testimony, in order to intercede for us during the lifetime of the Church. One day he will reappear (as did the priest on the day of Atonement after sprinkling blood upon the propitiatory), returning to us, his people, in order to lead us processionally into the celestial holy of holies before the throne of God.

The author of Hebrews, like Paul himself, is very much aware that our Lord did not undergo death and rise to sit at the right hand of God in order to exclude our personal experience of this same redemptive process. Jesus truly suffered and died, and rose in our stead, because only he who is the Son of God incarnate could effectively achieve what the Father desired mankind to perform. But Christ did not act, so to speak, in a private capacity. The vicarious character of his death is but one aspect of his work of salvation. Jesus Christ also involved man in his own redemption. He made it possible for man to enter into a new solidarity with his saviour. Thus Hebrews represents Jesus as the great highpriest who leads his followers in procession into the heavenly sanctuary. By this is meant that the Christian people is caught up in the very movement of the redemption.

Here then we have an illustration, within the New Testament itself, of this method of prayer which is called "contemplation" in the *Spiritual Exercises*. One begins from some significant event in Jesus' earthly life, in order to become more aware of one's own involvement in the contemporary rhythms of salvation history. It will be recalled that St. Ignatius has arranged the book of the *Exercises* with very few meditations. Almost all the most basic Exercises are *contemplations*. For, Father Nadal tells us, St. Ignatius was a "contemplative in action." Now if I read Father Nadal's description of St. Ignatius' characteristic prayer correctly, he seems to be saying this. Prayer for the Jesuit is "practical," in the sense that it is always orientated to the Jesuit's collaboration in the divine plan of salvation here and now today. The aim of the Ignatian contemplation upon the mysteries of the life of Christ is to assist me to learn thereby Christ's will for me. It was Ignatius' conviction that, through the contemplation of the mysteries of Jesus' earthly life, I shall infallibly learn where I am to be inserted by Christ's grace into today's unfolding of God's plan for the redemption of the world. The liturgy in its own characteristic way through this procession of palms is attempting to teach us this same truth. Our participation in this procession is only a symbolic act, but there precisely lies its value. We should not forget, as the author of Hebrews points out in the passage cited above, that Jesus' passion and death—indeed his whole earthly life—was simply a series of symbolic acts, bodying forth that one efficacious act of will by which, on entering the world, the Son announced to the Father, "I have come to do your will, O God!" (Heb 10:7).

Now it is precisely this attitude of mind, which we find expressed here by the incarnate Word, that the Ignatian consideration on the *Reign of Christ* is calculated to arouse in the exercitant. Christ here calls each to the "more" of the *Foundation*—at least, each man who wishes to be *"insignis."* There is no question, as yet, of any specific resolution, of any call to a particular course of action or state of life. The response of the generous man is articulated by St. Ignatius in the prayer of self-oblation at the conclusion of this consideration.

"Eternal Lord of all things! I make my commitment with your favor and help, before your infinite goodness and in the sight of

Ignatian Contemplation

83

your glorious Mother, and of all the saints of the heavenly court. I bear witness that it is my earnest desire and deliberate resolve, provided only it be for your greater service and praise, to imitate you in bearing every injustice and affront, actual poverty as well as spiritual poverty, if your most holy Majesty has willed to choose and admit me to such a state of life."

Chapter 9

PREFACE TO THE CONTEMPLATIONS
OF THE SECOND WEEK

WE HAVE BECOME ACCUSTOMED to represent divine revelation as a conversation between persons (God and man), with all that that implies of interpersonal reaction. Indeed this same conception may be taken as a definition of the spiritual life. By means of what St. Benedict in the Rule has called *lectio divina*, or Ignatius in the *Exercises* calls *contemplation*, I attempt to live my "spiritual" life, that is, existence under the divine domination of the Holy Spirit, by integrating myself into this conversation or dialogue. My purpose is to become involved personally, with the grace of God, in this sacred history, because I believe that I have a part to play in this history. I must become caught up in, I must experience, principally by means of the liturgy and the Spiritual Exercises, this *divinum commercium*, for the very good reason that this is the only way I can be saved.

Revelation as Dialogue

This integration of myself into sacred history is not accomplished without a certain struggle because it involves an opposition between my past and my future participation in this saving dialogue. It is surely obvious to us all at this stage of our spiritual lives, that it will take us a lifetime to bring this experience to its full fruition, to its complete realization. As I said earlier, I am simply an unfinished chapter in this sacred history as long as I live.

Moreover, my responsiveness to the divine initiative, inviting me to participate in this conversation, is not an automatic process, because it involves me in the most personal area of my whole being, my own freedom. I have to acquire and—more difficult still—I have to maintain an ever deepening awareness of Christ's operation in my own life. I must contrive somehow to hold myself in readiness to live my life with him right now in this the twentieth century.

I suppose we might look upon a retreat as consisting of a particular series of actions by which, as a religious, I attempt to increase, or at any rate maintain, this responsiveness to Christ's dynamic activity in my life. This is the way I advance in the spiritual life.

But what is freedom?[1] In this context freedom, I should say, is my power to break with my past; my capacity to respond to the future, which is as yet only a possibility, so that I am able to collaborate with Christ, to work with him, who comes on his own terms, for the purpose of shaping my life in his image and likeness. Obviously, the decision to acquiesce in this plan introduces novelty into my life; and I must remember that the genuine character of any decision can only be perceived when it is embodied in action. It is a truism that no real choice exists except embodied in action. Otherwise, it is, as you know, a mere velleity.

However, before I can reach a real decision of this nature there is a battle to be won. There are always areas within myself which are not submissive to Christ. There remains a sector within me which is not engaged in this dialogue, unresponsive to our Lord. Whatever has caused that wrong orientation, that tuning-out to the voice of the Spirit, it has been embodied in my conduct in the past, as I know only too well. For it has produced habits which, if I am going to make a new decision for Christ, must be broken or changed. Otherwise my future is already determined by the past. Such is simply the function of any habit, bad or good. As a consequence of my bad habits I shall not be able to hear the voice of Christ, to hear the Gospel. I will be incapable of responding to his invitation to take my part in the dialogue which is contemporary salvation history.

Accordingly I must attempt somehow to interrupt the automatic process set in motion by my past habits. How can I accomplish this? I have to stop, to recollect myself, in the most literal sense of that word, because this is the time I have set aside to prepare for my future response, my future engagement with Christ. Now this "recollection," if I can call it that, moves in two directions: it has a twofold orientation. In the first place, I aim to break with my past, to see its absurdity, inanity, shamefulness. Put in other words, my goal, from this point of view, is the same as that designated by the New Testament as the purpose of the kerygma, or apostolic preaching: repentance, reform of life, *metanoia*. To achieve this aim is not enough, however. This is just the negative aspect of my intent which we have set in prominence thus far in our retreat. But to break with the past without looking hopefully to future positive action is to court disaster, as is

1 Frederick E. Crowe, S.J., "Complacency and Concern," *Cross and Crown* 11 (1959), 180-190.

illustrated by the parable in Matthew 12:43-45. It is a story about a foolish fellow who cleaned up the devil's apartment when he was gotten out, but left it vacant. So the devil came back and settled in again with a pack of cronies.

The element in my reform of life which is far more important (and this is my main reason for devoting most of our time to it) is to make present to myself, as well as I can, the new course of action because it still lies in the future, and, as future, still exists only as a possibility for me. I must try to represent it as concretely and attractively as I can. All I am saying is that I must try to make my future life, as yet placed merely in the realm of possibility, as real to myself as I can. The only way I am able to do this is, of course, by using my imagination, my feelings, my desires, and by some shrewd planning. It is essential that this be done, however, so that such positive preparation, though future, will counterbalance the pull of habits from the past. This recollection, by which the future is balanced off successfully against my past, is a condition of paramount importance for an authentic, efficacious decision.

This positive side of the radical change in Christian existence, directed to this future new life in Christ, my attempt to prepare for a real decision, demands the grace of Christ. I propose nothing less than to live with him and for him. By my contemplation of the earthly life of Jesus, I inaugurate this positive program for the future. The result of contemplating these scenes from the Gospels is my ability to put myself in the position of one listening, in an attitude of responsive attentiveness to the grace of Christ. We cannot afford to forget that St. Ignatius never intended that this effort by which the attention of the entire person is caught up in the earthly career of Jesus, the essence of contemplation in the Ignatian sense, should remain merely an intellectual exercise. That intellectual phase of Ignatian contemplation is called, in the *Spiritual Exercises* [2, 102, 111], *historia*—the statement of the theme, or the brief narration of a mystery in our Lord's life. The Ignatian concept of contemplation, however, demands that I put myself into the picture, seeing the Jesus of history in order that I may know more intimately, love more deeply, follow more effectively [104], the contemporary Christ, the exalted and glorified Lord of history. For my purpose is not a retrojection of myself into a series of events already played out some twenty centuries ago, but rather the insertion of myself in salvation history which is being enacted in my own day.

I must, of course, accomplish this task in a manner congenial to

Contemplation of Jesus' Earthly Career

my own twentieth century mentality. St. Ignatius illustrated his intent in terms which would appeal to a sixteenth century man, examples which may or may not appeal to me. To the highly imaginative medieval mind (and St. Ignatius was one of the last men of the Middle Ages highly endowed with imaginative powers), to "see the persons," "hear their words," "observe their actions," [cf. 106-108, etc.] was very natural and easy. You will remember the little maid-servant and the "little unworthy slave" in the contemplation on the Nativity [114] (Ignatius doubtless found her in Ludolph's *Life of Christ*). This example may not appeal to you: frankly, it strikes me as artificial, play-acting. Yet St. Ignatius did discover a sound pedagogical principle: he desired that I should learn to play my personal role in contemporary sacred history by inserting myself into the mysteries I contemplate.

Let us candidly admit that we face a serious problem here in trying to be faithful to St. Ignatius' goal in our contemplations of the second week. The difficulty is one of adjusting ourselves to the seemingly naive viewpoint so dear to medieval piety. The glorified Christ found little, if any, place in the devotion of the Middle Ages. For the Christian of that era was wholly engrossed in what he believed to be the "historical" details of Jesus' earthly career. His devotion was directed to the new-born infant in the crib (as by St. Francis of Assisi), to the gruesome character of Jesus' Passion (as in the writings of St. Gertrude), to the lonely "abandonment" of the Eucharistic Christ (as with St. Colette, and even as late as St. Margaret Mary in the seventeenth century). The general effect of such piety was the proliferation of imaginative and sentimental trivialities, created to fill out the often stark, schematized narratives of the Gospels. Alternatively, the vision of the Christian life was given a certain theological substance by employing concepts borrowed from scholastic theology (*gratia sanctificans, institutio, mactatio, character, satisfactio*). The Ignatian *Contemplation for Obtaining Love* [230-237] provides an instance of this.

Thanks to the modern theological renaissance, which was created and came to flower in the renewal connected with Vatican II, we are perhaps more than ever aware of how obsolete and unattractive such piety is to modern man. His is a mentality which feels itself more at home with Pauline Christology, where the accent is upon the death and resurrection as the unique Christ-event. He finds more congenial the fundamental theorem of Johannine spirituality, constructed upon the vision of the Jesus who was "dead, and is alive forevermore" (Ap 1:18): viz. that the exalted Christ is more dynamically present in our contemporary world as Lord of history, than ever he was when he walked the hills of Galilee during his mortal life.

As a consequence of these attitudes the present-day Christian is confronted with a real difficulty in making the Spiritual Exercises, particularly those of the second week. He demands to know why he should pray to any other than the glorified Christ, the *only* Christ who actually exists. He is, moreover, not much interested in a technique which seems to him an exercise in spiritual archeology. He is keenly aware also that the antiquated insistence upon the *ipsissima verba Jesu* springs from an ingenuous view of the Gospel record, and is, in any event, irrelevant so far as he is concerned. He finds much more meaningful the modern scriptural view that these words (and deeds) of Jesus come to us refracted through the lived experience of the apostolic Church.

We can only find satisfactory answers to this crucial problem by widening and deepening our appreciation of the nature of our written Gospels and by more attention to the attitude of the primitive Christian community towards the traditions regarding Jesus.

Since we shall have occasion later, in discussing the contemplations of the fourth week (pp. 285-286), to describe more fully the stance of the early Church vis-a-vis the living traditions regarding Jesus' life, we will for the moment content ourselves with pointing out its two most salient features, which explain the somewhat puzzling way in which the apostolic age handled the *dicta et facta Jesu* in a manner at once serious and mindful of their historical importance, and yet quite creative and uninhibited by the modern bogey of "historical accuracy." In the first place, the Gospels reveal that the apostolic Church evinced an essentially forward-looking orientation of mind. She was deeply concerned with the events of her own contemporary history and with the hope of the triumphant return, seemingly quite imminent, of the parousiac Christ. If the evangelists looked back to recall the words and deeds of the "Christ in the flesh" (2 Cor 5:16), as indeed they did in writing their Gospels, they did so simply to interpret them in the light of Easter, or to employ them to deepen their readers' faith in the paschal mystery. Consequently, what must be borne in mind in employing the Gospels as sources for our Ignatian contemplations is that they consist basically of a dialogue between the author and his Christian reader. It is their character as documents of Christian faith written by believers for believers that gives them their deepest significance for use in the Spiritual Exercises.

In the second place, we should not allow ourselves to forget

89

that the first inspired New Testament writings were not the Gospels, but the letters of Paul. This simple fact of history tells us a good deal about Paul's personal attitude towards the "history of Jesus,"—an attitude most probably representative of the Church of the apostolic age. Paul did not feel called upon to record the sayings and deeds of Jesus, that is, to write a Gospel. He wrote letters in his own name with the full awareness that his words carried an authority given them by the Holy Spirit (1 Cor 2:16; 7:40). Indeed, he ordered these letters read to the community assembled for public worship, as at Thessalonica (1 Th 5:27; cf. also Col 4:16),—and this, "in the Lord's name"! This apostolic self-assurance explains the conundrum of Paul's treatment of the sayings of Jesus (which he rarely cites), and the events of Jesus' life (to which he almost never refers).

It is only as the second generation of Christians begins to replace the first generation (towards the year 70 A.D. and thereafter) that our canonical Gospels come into existence. And when they do we find little evidence of concern on the part of their authors to provide word-for-word transcriptions of the *logia* of Jesus, or to avoid in their narratives of Jesus' life what not infrequently seem like contradictions to an age (like our own) plagued by scrupulosity over historical accuracy. Even the four inspired accounts of what Jesus said and did at the Last Supper, in the institution of the Eucharist, contain not a few variations.

This may be as good a place as any to remind ourselves of one most significant feature of the character of the authority with which the four Gospels present themselves to modern man. Grounded solidly as they undoubtedly are upon "eyewitness" testimony, the Gospels are not primarily authoritative for the Christian life because they repose upon the accuracy and fidelity of the human memories of "the original eyewitnesses" (Lk 1:2), but rather because the interpretation they present of the words and deeds of Jesus is "inspired," Spirit-filled.

Kerygmatic Character of the Second Week   We must, however, now attempt to give an answer to the modern man's problem: how is he to be helped to contemplate the scenes of Jesus' earthly life? I believe the answer lies in appreciating the *kerygmatic* nature of the Gospel record, and in making this kerygmatic quality operative in the presentation of the *historia* given to the exercitant by the director. The director must grasp the profound manner in which the paschal mystery itself, which is the heart of the Gospel, has influenced the interpretation and even the very narration of the events of our Lord's public ministry.

90

For the apostolic preaching was *kērygma,* that is, a message of hope, created under the direction of the Twelve, proclaimed to a despairing world as the "good news" that God had in Christ definitively "reconciled the world to himself" (2 Cor 5:19). This redeeming activity reached its climax in Jesus' death and resurrection. This twin event, then, was the quintessence of the gospel; so that, if—as appears to be the fact (Acts 2:21-22; 10:37-39)— the preaching also comprised references to Jesus' earlier life, these data were subordinated clearly to the principal message of salvation. Indeed, they merited to be included as "good news" only because of their relationship to the death and resurrection of Christ. The apostles were, first and foremost, "witnesses to his resurrection" (Acts 1:22). This gave the kerygma its primordial direction, made it "God's power unto salvation" (Rom 1:16), that is, imbued it with the dynamism to produce *metanoia,* the commitment to Christ, the response of Christian faith, in the hearts of its hearers.

It should be remembered moreover that this *testimonium apostolicum* was not only directed to outsiders: it was given continually within the Christian community itself (Acts 4:33), where its purpose was palpably different. Here, within the Church, it was an attestation "from faith to faith" (Rom 1:17), a message announced by believers to believers in order to deepen their comprehension of the Christian mystery. It is this living Christian tradition which we find written into our four Gospels.

These books then give us far more than the brute facts about Jesus' life. They are the Christian testimony, written down by four privileged members of the early Church, to Jesus' actions and teaching as selected, understood, interpreted for us, and— above all else—as lived by the Christians of the first and second generation. They do contain, beyond any doubt, the Christian revelation; but they preserve that revelation as incarnated in the Church's unerring response of faith. The *Sitz im Leben* or "life-situation" of the narratives about our Lord, as also of the record of his words, is not the historical context in which they originally occurred, but the daily life of the primitive Church. They tell us quite as much about the living faith with which the first Christians integrated themselves into the ongoing process of salvation history in their times as they do about the sacred history of Jesus of Nazareth.

It is then, I submit, the quality evinced by our Gospels as *veritas salutaris,* that "truth which God wanted to put into the sacred writings for the sake of our salvation" (Constitution *Dei Verbum,* No.

11), and not the mere "historical" truth they also possess which proves the value of contemplating the Gospel scenes for the twentieth-century Christian. Herein he learns how to incorporate himself in his own era into sacred history by observing the Master as he is depicted by the evangelists, and by obtaining an insight into the manner in which the early Church, through her contemplation of these same events, learned to insert herself into salvation history. Thus, what Vatican II has said about the role of the entire Bible in the Christian life applies *a fortiori* to the Gospels: "Therefore, like the Christian religion itself, all the preaching of the Church must be nourished *and ruled* by sacred Scripture" (No. 21).

Attention to the Contemporary Christ We might, by way of conclusion, reflect for a moment upon a cognate question which is often aired today because of our increased realization of the truth that it is the risen, exalted Christ who alone exists. To which Christ am I to pray? Can I pray to the baby Jesus, to the Jesus undergoing his Passion?

The Christian must learn to pray to the *contemporary* Christ, who continually confronts him in his own twentieth-century situation: the exalted Lord Jesus. Yet we cannot forget that this risen Christ is what he now is only in virtue of the past experiences of his earthly life, including his Passion. It is by contemplating the scenes in the Gospels that one learns in prayer to evaluate more deeply the significance for Christ himself of his various historical experiences.

Such a learning process is a very gradual one. Christian "wisdom," as Paul conceives it, is not acquired with baptism, but only after considerable maturation in Christ (cf. 1 Cor 3:1-2; 2:6ff.). In the various phases of his own personal spiritual growth towards Christian maturity, from spiritual childhood through spiritual adolescence to adulthood, the Christian can only pray to that Christ to whom, at these various stages, he is able to relate himself—to the "Christ in the flesh" (2 Cor 5:16), to Jesus in some phase of his mortal existence. St. Bernard told his Cistercians that a man must first acquire *amor carnalis Christi* (fall in love in a very human way with the Jesus of history) before he can advance to *amor spiritualis Christi*.[2] Until the Christian has attained his "religious majority," the maturity which enables him to relate to the risen Christ, he must undergo the developmental process in prayer, which is encompassed in its entirety by the Spiritual Exercises. For he must one day be able to confront Christ, become "life-giving Spirit" (1 Cor 15:45). He can indeed

2 Louis Bouyer, *The Cistercian Heritage* (Westminster, Md., 1958), 50.

catch sight of this development by observing the growth in the faith of the first disciples presented to him in the Gospels. The great value of the Spiritual Exercises is that they are precisely arranged as a graded series of experiences, in order to lead the Christian to that "mature manhood, measured by nothing less than the full stature of Christ" (Eph 4:13).

GOD'S WORD, THE SON, ENTERS HISTORY
John 1:1-18

In the beginning the Word already was;
The Word was at home with God;
Yet God he was, the Word!

2 He was in the beginning present with God.

3 All through him came into being:
Apart from him not one thing came to be.

4 What was made found life in him,
And this life was the light of men.

5 That light shines on in the darkness,
For the darkness has never put it out. . . .

9 He was the genuine light
That illumines every man.
He was making his appearance in the world.

10 He was present in the world—
The world was made by him:
Yet the world did not recognize him.

11 To his own land he came:
Still his own folk did not accept him.

12 But to those who did receive him—
To those who believe in his name,
He gave power to become God's children:

13 Those who were begotten,
Not by blood,
Nor by the desire of the flesh,
Nor by desire of any man,
But by God.

14 Thus the Word became flesh,
And pitched his tent among us.
And we have beheld his glory—
Glory from his Father as only Son,
Full of God's mercy and fidelity. . . .

16 Yes, of his fulness we have received our share,
Grace instead of grace!

17 The law was a gift through Moses:
This mercy, this fidelity came through Jesus Christ.

18 God no man has ever seen;
His only Son, who shares the secrets of his Father's heart,
Has personally acted as our interpreter.

Chapter 10

CONTEMPLATION ON
THE INCARNATION

THE FIRST CONTEMPLATION of the second week in the *Spiritual Exercises* is that on the Incarnation; and St. Ignatius has his own highly original way of presenting it [101-109]. Even a cursory reading of the *historia* which he outlines for the exercitant shows his concern to help him insert himself into salvation history. The exercitant is not only to imagine the confusion, injustice, sinfulness, despair of the world at the beginning of the Christian era; he should (indeed it is probably much easier for him to) confront himself with his own twentieth-century world, so badly in need of salvation.

St. John's Prologue

To present the contemplation on the incarnation today, I suggest that we consider the prologue to the fourth Gospel which is found printed on the opposite page. This inspired account has the advantage of presenting a *raccourci* of the entire biblical sacred history which reaches its culmination in the enfleshment of the Son of God. Moreover, it also reminds us of the necessary human response to the divine initiative of God the Father in thus directing the progress of this history, "for us and for our salvation." Thus our poem may be considered to fall into two distinct phases: the first, describing God's inauguration of the saving dialogue between himself and the human race (vv. 1-14); the second (vv. 14-18), depicting man's response and his return in the incarnate and glorified Son (who is "the way") to the Father. The announcement of the incarnation itself, accordingly, is placed so as to function as a hinge between the two main segments of the ode.

I.

The story begins in eternity, for the author's conception of sacred history is cyclic: from God, into history, and the return of history to the Godhead. The initiator of this cyclic movement is the Word, the perfect expression or image of "the God," as John here calls the Father.

Themes of Johannine Christology

"In the beginning the Word already was; the Word was at home with God; yet God he was, the Word!" This opening verse informs us that, while the Word is God, he is somehow distinct from "the God," since he is said to be "in the presence of," or "at home with" him.

Creation   The Word enters our world by means of three great events of sacred history. His first entry is through his act of creation and his abiding presence in the universe by which he preserves it in existence. John's thought is here inspired by the first page of Genesis, where the priestly editor employs a liturgical recital of the cosmogony, in which God is represented as summoning everything into being by his word, his creative command. "And God said, 'Let there be light!'—and light came into existence" (Gn 1:3-4).

"All through him came into being: apart from him not one thing came to be." Later on in this Gospel, in the allegory of the vine and the branches (Jn 15:1-5), Jesus will say, "Without me you can do nothing." That is how it has been, John informs us, from the creation of the world.

"What was made found life in him." The Word is the creative source of all life in our world; and that life which is found in its plenitude in the Word is called "the light of men." Here we meet, for the first time, those symbols which will characterize the fourth Gospel. The description of the Word as "light of man" suggests a theme which will play a preponderant role throughout this book: the Word of God comes to reveal the unseen Father to mankind and thereby to redeem man, to lead man back to God. In the fourth Gospel, Jesus' role as man's redeemer is subsumed under his primary function as revealer of the invisible Father.

Another theme characteristic of this Gospel is introduced by the words: "That light shines on in the darkness, for the darkness has never put it out." The author suggests, in his poetic manner, that there is a continuing struggle between the Word as light and the darkness—a symbol for all the anti-God forces in the universe. For the moment, John does not define these forces with precision, but contents himself with implying they include all that is "anti-Word," the creaturely refusal to respond with a reverent affirmative to the divine initiative in the dialogue.

The first coming of the Word, the evangelist ruefully concedes, was not an unqualified success, despite the fact that the Word was "the genuine light." In comparison with his function as revealer, as bearer of the divine self-communication to men, all created light, physical or intellectual, pales into insignificance.

They may, like the sun, serve as symbols of the Word; they may serve as types, like the illumination of the temple precincts on the feast of Booths (Jn 8:12), of which the Word is the perfect fulfill-ment. In every truth that men utter, as St. Thomas observes, we find the self-affirmation of the first truth, the Word of God. Yet the purpose of divine revelation in human language through the Scrip-tures cannot adequately be described as a mere communication of ideas. The modern student of semantics knows that in addition to this function language has two other essential functions: the self-revelation of the speaker, and the personal involvement of the one addressed. And here, as I have said, the author must admit failure. The Word, the genuine light, "was present in the world—the world was made by him—yet the world did not recog-nize him." The divine Word uttered at the creation of the universe, which continues to be spoken in the very preservation of all crea-tures, went unheeded.

And so the Word comes a second time, in more positive fashion. *The Tōrāh*
God attempts to reopen the dialogue with man in a more personal way. The Word renews his efforts to enter the human family by coming as the law of God, *tōrāh*. As you are aware, the term "law" is not an adequate translation for *tōrāh*, which means in-struction, teaching, revelation. It denotes God's speaking to man within a positive revelation. This new entry of the Word included the divine involvement with a particular people, to whom, through Abraham, God had promised a holy land—Palestine. The divine Word was spoken this time not to all creation, but to a people acquired by Yahweh for himself in their liberation from Egypt. Yet even this gracious gesture of God through his Word, the *tōrāh*, did not gain acceptance. "To his own land he came; still his own folk did not accept him." And now, without dwelling any further upon that second phase of the coming of God's Word, John imme-diately turns to the third and final entrance of God's Son as the incarnate Word.

To prepare his reader to appreciate the significance of this *Filii in Filio*
third coming of the Word, the evangelist details the benefits which the Son made man confers upon those who have received him— the Christian faithful. "But to those who did receive him—to those who believe in his name, he gave power to become God's chil-dren." It is significant that St. John confers the title, "Son of God," only upon Jesus Christ, Word of God incarnate. St. Paul will speak of all Christians as "sons of God." St. John (despite the Vulgate mistranslation—*filios Dei fieri*) speaks of us as "God's

97

children." The "power to become God's children" is conferred upon us by the Word in virtue of his unique divine sonship. We are children in the Son, that is, in virtue of that "power" which the glorified Christ communicates to us through his risen humanity. In reality, as the fourth Gospel will later state (Jn 7:39; 19:30), this "power" is none other than the Holy Spirit. Thus we are in very truth "begotten by God."

God's children are not begotten "by bloods" (it is to be noted that the term is plural in the Greek text), or as we might say "by ties of blood." We are indeed, as John is very conscious, begotten by blood—the blood of Jesus as he died upon the cross. The evangelist, however, wishes to insist that this divine power is not communicated by some kind of biological process. Nor is this power the result of some human urge, not even the innate desire of a man to father children in his own likeness. This begetting of "those who believe in his name" is the effect solely of the supreme event of salvation history: "the Word became flesh."

The Word of God became man: he "pitched his tent among us. And we have beheld his glory. . . ." For the first time in the fourth Gospel we hear the witness of the apostolic Church. It is the testimony of the first generation Christians. They are the "we," who were privileged to "behold his glory."

In the Old Testament the term "glory" had acquired a technical meaning. It signified the tangible, sensible manifestation of God's abiding presence—his protective presence—among his people. In the Bible "glory" means a theophany. The burning bush that Moses beheld in the desert of Sinai was an example of this "glory" (Ex 3:1ff.). The miracles which effected the Hebrews' deliverance from Egypt were instances, according to the psalmists, of this "glory." In the incarnate Word, however, who is the expression of God, we have the final form of divine revelation. We have the ultimate in theophanies, the last word in God's self-communication.

The Incarnation and Man's Salvation
    I wish to insert myself into this picture, into this history. I wish to rediscover this "glory" in my twentieth century situation. If I ask myself why the Word, the Son of God, became man, I begin to see that it was to save me, quite simply, from myself. For I am not, naturally speaking, because of egotism, concerned to save myself from myself. Jesus Christ entered human history to save me from the fate of being natural, of being helpless, of being useless even to myself. He came to give a supernatural "solution" (that is fundamentally what redemption or salvation means) to my own human life, to liberate me from myself.

And how does he effect this? He has found a way to become one with us more intimately than he had by functioning as the creator Word, or as the law Word. He has accomplished it for us by becoming "flesh," mortal man. And here I may remind myself that the Son of God did not become *"homo in genere."* The incarnation meant that he must limit himself. He had to belong to a particular race: he became a Jew, with all the rich advantages of temperament and talent, as well as the limitations which that race possessed. He chose, of necessity, to live at one particular period of human history. He could not live forever, if he were to be a genuine human being. He elected, in consequence, to live out his life in a specific geographical sector—rather small at that—of this globe of ours. He chose to become a man, not a woman; and thereby excluded himself from a whole special area of psychology and of experience.

Accordingly, it becomes evident that the incarnation meant a limiting of God's infinite Word in many, varying ways. Yet it is by these very limitations of himself that he saves me, provides a solution for my life. This great event has given me the means to see how I fit, in the twentieth century, into that rhythm of salvation which St. John described two thousand years ago. By the very fact that "the Word became a mortal man," that he became a Jew, that he entered a cultural milieu so very different from the one I belong to, our Lord disclosed his need of me. He chose to depend upon my collaboration in my era and my civilization. Accordingly, he saves me from frustration by the joyful news of the gospel that he has become man. In my world today the gospel must be preached. Men of my generation need to experience in their turn the salutary Christian witness to the truth of the gospel. To accomplish this, he must make use of *my* personality. He has real need of me. This is *my* vocation, revealed in the mystery of the incarnation. This is where I fit in. And this is the way in which the Word of God incarnate, who came to save me, has deigned to carry out his redemptive design: by integrating me into this segment of sacred history.

"The Word became flesh, and pitched his tent among us." He did not stay with us forever. He could not stay forever, if he were to be really human. And out of this divine necessity, this poverty flowing from his becoming mortal man, he created a doubly effective way of redemption for me and for the men of my century and my culture. Thus by the very event of the incarnation, the Word is already my redeemer. For this reason he is my saviour, because he saves me from being useless. He has made it possible for my life, my era, to become part of this history of salvation. He has provided me with the motives, through his incarnation, for my personal cooperation with his redemptive work; and, through the medium of his sacred humanity, he has made my life "graceful," as well as meaningful. This is the good news which he communicates to me through the message of the incarnation.

II.

Eucharistic Purpose of the Incarnation

The first half of the prologue to the fourth Gospel reached its climax in the announcement, "The Word became flesh, and pitched his tent among us." The second half of the poem provides us with an insight into the contemporary relevance, for the Christian, of the earthly life of Jesus. The author accomplishes this purpose by showing how this unique life of the Word of God actually means the divine establishment of the new covenant. The two most meaningful moments, as a reading of the fourth Gospel will reveal, are the incarnation and the "glorification" of Jesus— that is, his death on the cross.

The key to Johannine Christology lies in his assertion that, "the Word became flesh" (*sarx*). This Greek term in St. John does not have the pejorative sense which clings to it in the writings of St. Paul. *Sarx* for Paul is the theatre of sin, of temptation, of concupiscence. It is the symbol of the unredeemed part of man. In fact, even the Son of God himself, when he entered our world at his incarnation, came of necessity "in the likeness of sinful *sarx*" (Rom 8:3). In Pauline theology the work of man's redemption centers exclusively in Christ's death and resurrection. Paul has not, as John has, pushed back his soteriological synthesis to include the moment of the incarnation as a positive, saving act of God. The Son's becoming man, for Paul, is more in the nature of a preliminary presupposition for the redemptive work accomplished through his death and resurrection.

For St. John, on the contrary, *sarx* signifies what is human or creaturely, in contrast with the divine—without however connoting sinfulness. Hence John can employ the word in his statement of God's greatest gift to mankind: "the Word became *sarx*." It will be recalled, moreover, that this term is found also in the evangelist's very personal view of the purpose of Jesus' mission upon earth. In his discourse on the Bread of Life, John has managed to record Jesus' saying in instituting the Eucharist. He has done this however in characteristic fashion by employing his own inimitable terminology. While, as you are aware, the fourth Gospel does not contain an account of Jesus' institution of the Eucharist in the narrative of the Last Supper, still, for all that, the words of institution (a fact perhaps not so commonly appreciated) are not omitted.

"And this Bread which I shall give?—It is my flesh (*sarx*), [given] for the life of the world" (Jn 6:51b). Here we have the Johannine rendering of the logion reported by the Synoptics and by Paul. "This is my Body, which shall be handed over for you" (cf. Mk 14:22; Mt 26:26; Lk 22:19; 1 Cor 11:24). John probably employs the word *sarx*, "flesh," instead of *sōma*, "body," first of all, because it is closest to the word which Jesus undoubtedly used at the Last Supper. The Aramaic term, *bisri* ("my flesh"), was probably the only one available in that language, which like biblical Hebrew does not appear to have had (at least in Jesus' day) a proper word for body. St. John probably also chose *sarx* by preference, since it means living flesh, while the Greek word *sōma* is wide enough to include a cadaver. The Greeks indeed had a term meaning corpse also (*ptōma*); but the word *sarx* can only denote a living body.

Our reflection upon this usage of St. John enables us to understand how this evangelist envisaged the purpose of the incarnation. The Word became *sarx*, in order to give men his *sarx* as food, since it is only through this living flesh of the Word of God that life may come to mankind. For St. John, in short, the purpose of the incarnation is basically Eucharistic.

Now this relationship between the incarnation and the Eucharist is of paramount importance for discerning another dimension in the prologue. It is generally recognized that the Synoptic Gospels present the institution of the Blessed Eucharist, the Lord's supper, as Jesus' inauguration of the new covenant. St. John, on the other hand, at the outset of his Gospel, depicts the incarnation as the inauguration of the new covenant. It is this very enfleshment of the Word of God which constitutes the basis of God's definitive pact with the new Israel, the Christian people—with myself. And in the verses which follow John's announcement, "The Word became flesh" (Jn 1:14), this covenant theme dominates the movement of the poem.

We have already observed that John speaks of the incarnation as a pitching of "his tent among us," by the Word become man. And this, in turn, has provided the grounds for our contemplation of his "glory." There is little doubt, I believe, but that John is here thinking of the last chapter in the book of Exodus (cf. Ex 40:34-35) where we learn that after Moses built the tent of meeting, or reunion, where God came to meet Moses and, through him, his people, "the *glory* of Yahweh" came to take possession of this primitive sanctuary. Thus we may say that through the first covenant almighty God became a divine camper. Yahweh chose, as Israel's God, to live under canvas!

The technical term, "glory," as I said, in the Old Testament indicates a theophany, the manifestation of God's protective presence with his covenanted people. In the fourth Gospel the miracles of Jesus are termed a manifestation of his "glory," a first approach to his perfect revelation of God through his self-revelation (cf. Jn 2:11; 11:40; 12:41). This is why the author of the fourth Gospel prefers to call Jesus' miracles "signs," rather than "wonders." On his view, they function primarily as symbols of a deeper, hidden divine reality. And they are symbols, because they are Jesus' *doxa*, that is, an external sign—to the eyes of faith —of God's presence in Christ. But perhaps the most striking and certainly the most characteristic view of John is that the ultimate revelation, the final *doxa*, the definitive glorification of Jesus, begins, not with the resurrection, as with other New Testament authors, but with his Passion. The Passion inaugurates, in Johannine theology, Jesus' complete self-revelation. And so it signifies the initial phase of his glorification. It means also the first step in his exaltation. Jesus' Passion, for John, includes these two ideas: it is "glory," in the sense of revelation; it is also a "lifting up," because, as Jesus enters the Passion and mounts the cross, he begins, both for himself and for mankind, that last journey home to God through which man's salvation is once for all realized.

The "glory" that Jesus possesses is "the glory that belongs to the only begotten Son." In the fourth Gospel, John is very careful to reserve the title "Son of God" for Jesus only. The Son, the Word incarnate, comes to us, says John, "full of grace and truth." The Greek words that are used here are often found in the Septuagint as translations of the two great qualities or characteristics of Yahweh's activity as Israel's covenanted God. The terms which designate these qualities are very familiar to us all. We utter them each time we sing the psalm *Laudate Dominum*. They are contained in the motivation given in this psalm for glorifying God: *quoniam confirmata est* (the covenant) *super nos misericordia ejus et fidelitas Domini manet in aeternum*. The twin qualities, repeatedly mentioned in the Old Testament as characteristic of the saving actions of the God of the covenant, are *ḥesed*, translated by *misericordia* in the Latin psalter, and *'emeth*, rendered as *veritas*, or better, *fidelitas*.

The first term, *ḥesed*, denotes the loving condescension of God. It expresses Yahweh's personal interest in and loving relationship with his people. The other word, *'emeth*, evokes Yahweh's trustworthiness, his reliability. Israel can count on Yahweh! He is the covenanted partner of his elected people. No matter what happens, Yahweh will keep his part of the pact with Israel. The first word may be said to express the unilateral quality of this covenant. You will remember that the Alexandrian Jewish translators of the Hebrew Scriptures, rendered the term *berīth* (covenant) by a Greek word that does not normally mean covenant. The noun *diathēkē* signifies "testament," in the sense of a last will and testament. There is a word for pact or covenant in Greek —*synthēkē*: but this suggests an agreement between equals, a pact which is bilateral in its binding force upon both parties to a covenant. Hence, the Septuagintal translators employed the term *diathēkē* for the Hebrew word for Yahweh's covenant with Israel, since it was capable of expressing the essential grace-quality of this pact which God made. It does not suggest a bilateral pact. The covenant, in which Yahweh took the initiative, out of love for Israel (Dt 7:6-8), was really much more like a will, by which a man out of sheer goodness, benevolence, or condescension, binds himself to confer certain benefits upon his legatees in whose favor he makes his will.

The other word *'emeth*, or *fidelitas*, means that, despite this gratuitous character of the covenant which Yahweh made, he can be counted on to honor it. God has indeed bound himself freely by such a pact. It was a grace which Israel did not deserve; and Israel was ever conscious of this divine act of liberality towards her. Yet God would keep his part of the agreement.

St. John asserts that these two qualities, which in the Old Testament characterized the saving action throughout the centuries of Israel's covenant partner, are now incarnate in their fullest divine reality in the Word become flesh and blood. It is perhaps difficult for us to appreciate the significance of the biblical use of a sociological term like covenant to express the unique relationship with her God which Israel enjoyed. For we are not familiar with the ancient Near Eastern institution of the *berīth*. Being children of a totally different way of life, we do not have the same needs as the nomadic Hebrews. Our sense of security derives from different institutions. For the nomad clans wandering in the Sinai desert, liable to meet enemies, to be preyed upon, to encounter dangers of all sorts, the institution of the covenant was a matter of life or death. When two men bound themselves by covenant they became to all intents and purposes blood-brothers. Each covenant partner bound himself solemnly to protect the other, swore to take vengeance upon the other's enemies, to protect his partner's rights. And it was just such an agreement,

Israel believed, that God had graciously made with her—nothing more, nothing less.

When we reflect upon the significance of covenant making, we begin to see why the covenant was such a significant event in the history of the chosen people. It formed the very basis of her life as a people. It had, of necessity, to remain a living reality, a pattern of everyday life for Israel. Thus it comes as no surprise to learn that the covenant in Israel was concerned with social justice. If you take the trouble to read the code of the covenant in Exodus (Ex 20:1—23:33), you will be struck by several unique features of this set of laws. And here we may remind ourselves that in the code of the covenant we have the Mosaic law in its most primitive and ancient form. One quality which will surprise you, if you know anything about the law codes of the ancient Near East prior to or contemporary with the Israelite collection of laws, is the remarkable emphasis on the dignity of the human person. There is no offense for which a man must forfeit his life in the law code of Israel, except crimes like murder and kidnaping—both of them grave offenses against another person as a person. But for property damage, which was punishable by death in the code of Hammurabi, there was no death penalty in Israel. Hence persons are never considered of less value than things in the Mosaic law.

In the second place, you will remark the lofty conception of justice which Israel entertained. In her law there was but one set of laws that obligated everyone from the king down to the last peasant or slave. This was not true in other ancient Near Eastern law codes, where normally there was one law for the king or for the nobility, and another for the common people. You will recall the remark, in the book of Esther, of the king Ahasuerus (Xerxes), which is applied in the liturgy to our Lady: "This law was not made for you" (Est 15:13 Vulgate). Esther was queen; consequently, the law, which was meant for "the people," did not have any application to her. Such was Israel's idea of law and justice, however, that there was one law for all the members of the theocracy. King and peasant, slave and freeman, owed unconditional allegiance to the one God.

By employing this theme of the covenant in the second half of his prologue, the author of the fourth Gospel wishes to tell his readers that the Word of God become man has somehow assumed to himself all human institutions. He has given them all a part to play in the divine economy of salvation. In fact, John insists that the material components of the creation have, in consequence of the incarnation, been assigned a role in mediating God's definitive self-revelation. The incarnate Word comes to us as the very embodiment and recapitulation of all that was significant in the ancient covenant which Yahweh had made with Israel.

Of this "fullness," found already in the Word incarnate, "we have all of us received our share." It is specially characteristic of the Christology of the fourth Gospel to present the Word incarnate as at once our redeemer and the revealer of the invisible God. In fact, it is much more accurate to say that, in the eyes of St. John, Jesus Christ redeems us by revealing the Father to mankind. His very death and resurrection constitute simply the last word, or supreme "sign" of salvation. Perhaps we can appreciate this viewpoint better if we remember that for the sacred writers salvation or redemption must affect man in the totality of his person. Thus this revelation, which the Word become man is, cannot be thought of merely as the communication of ideas. It must be understood as a movement of the divine initiative which involves God's personal self-communication to us. This, John understands, was effected by the incarnation of the Word, whereby the Son, as a man amongst men, reoriented the whole of human existence to the Father quite as much through his earthly life and actions as by the words he uttered. Thus that very activity by which Jesus redeemed us may more properly be regarded as an "apocalypse," a revelation of his Father, and of that Father's love for man. We might restate this axiom of Johannine theology by saying that, since the divine work of redemption must touch man in the totality of his being, the revelatory words of the Word incarnate had to be supplemented by those deeds which effected man's redemption—Jesus' death and resurrection. This unique earthly life of the Word of God admirably exemplified those characteristic qualities of the activity of Israel's covenanted God: gracious condescension and fidelity. It is then in very truth the fullness of these covenant qualities which Christ has communicated to us.

In his narrative of the scene upon Calvary, St. John tells us that Jesus "handed over the Spirit" (*paredōken to pneuma:* Jn 19:30). Our evangelist has intentionally departed from the common expression signifying "to breathe one's last" found in the Synoptic tradition at this point (cf. Mk 15:37; Lk 23:46: *exepneusen;* Mt 27:50: *aphēken to pneuma*). On John's view, Jesus brings his mission to its final, successful conclusion by breathing forth the Holy Spirit upon our Lady and the beloved disciple, who represents all faithful Christians. In this last breath of the dying Christ, St. John has perceived a "sign." It is the communication of the new covenant of which Jeremiah had spoken (Jer 31:31), a covenant which consists essentially in the out-pouring of the Spirit of God.

105

The prophet had spoken of it as the substitution of a heart of flesh for the heart of stone that heretofore had characterized humanity. The moment of Jesus' death is the supreme "hour" of his exaltation, his glorification. Before this, St. John declared earlier in his Gospel, "the Spirit was not yet, since Jesus was not yet glorified" (Jn 7:39). Now, with the arrival of "the hour," the new covenant is struck with the new people of God. In the Synoptic tradition the new covenant is established at the Last Supper by Jesus' act of instituting the Eucharist. John, who omits this episode from his narrative of the meal at which Jesus took leave of his own, has chosen to identify it with the final, significant act of our Lord's mortal life.

It is not accidental that St. John has singled out the great redemptive act of Jesus Christ—his act of dying—as "the hour" of covenant-making. This interpretation is consistent with the characteristically Johannine view that Jesus is not only our redeemer, but, as the incarnate Word, he acts as the revealer of the unseen God. Throughout his earthly life the Jesus of the fourth Gospel constantly performs "signs": at Cana, in his act of mimed prophecy in cleansing the temple precincts, by curing the ruler's son, feeding the crowds in an out-of-the-way place, restoring a beggarman's sight, and by raising Lazarus from death. It is not the actual witnessing of these miracles which is the essential thing. It is much more the seeing the "sign" in the water made wine, in the bread, or in sight or even life restored where it was lacking. Jesus had come in order that men may see in him the Son of God, and thus find that life which is the purpose of the new covenant (Jn 20:31).

The new covenant, inaugurated in the hour of Jesus' leave-taking of this world, is maintained by the exalted Word incarnate in the glory of the Father. The risen Christ—and this is another theme of the fourth Gospel—continues to share with the new covenanted people that community of life, his "glory," through the sacraments of the Christian Church, notably baptism and the Eucharist. For St. John's thesis is simply this: the sacraments of the Christian Church are merely the prolongation of those gestures of mercy, and power, and loving condescension which characterized the earthly life of Jesus Christ. It is in the liturgical life of the Christian community that these healing, life-giving gestures are truly experienced by the faithful. The glorified Christ, who makes his presence felt in the sacramental life of the Christian, is the same Jesus of Nazareth whose miracles of healing and power were "signs" evoking the response of faith in his person and in his mission during his public ministry.

It is because he wishes to teach us this lesson that St. John in the fourth Gospel has imparted a sacramental dimension to his narratives of Jesus' "signs," or miracles. We can see this in the story of Cana, where at the request of his mother Jesus anticipates the miracles of his public life. The abundance of wine thus unexpectedly produced is a symbol of the heavenly messianic banquet, anticipated here below by the Church in her celebration of the sacraments of baptism and of the Eucharist. We see this same theme functioning in the Johannine narrative of the healing of the blind man, to whom Jesus gives the precious gift of faith in himself, symbolized by the restoration of his natural sight. Thus throughout St. John's presentation of the good news, Jesus stands revealed as the very incarnation of the new covenant communicating to men the divine qualities of mercy and fidelity. Now through the sacraments the glorified Christ continues to share his "abundance" of these covenant virtues, whereby he gives us "power to become God's children." They are the means of that grace which Christ bestows on us "instead of the grace" of the Old Testament.

"The law," the prologue continues, "was a gift through Moses." This statement indicates how sharply St. John's attitude to the Mosaic law contrasts with that of St. Paul. For the apostle of the Gentiles, the law of Moses was really a kind of detour interjected into sacred history. "Why then the law?" Paul asks the Galatians; and he answers his own question. "It was established for the sake of transgressions!" (Gal 3:19)—that scandalously candid remark, which centuries of copyists set themselves to alter, or erase from the record. For St. John, on the other hand, the law was a gracious act of divine generosity, to be recalled with gratitude. However, John must admit, it was given through Moses, a mere man. He was indeed empowered to communicate the *tōrah*, Yahweh's self-revelation, which provided Israel with a pattern for her religious and national life. But now in the Christian dispensation, through Jesus Christ, the incarnate Word of God, we receive an interior communication of the very covenant qualities of God himself. We receive the new covenant as "spirit and truth" within us.

John concludes his ode by carrying us back with the glorified Word incarnate "to the bosom of the Father." The prologue ends where it began, with the life of the Father and the Son for all eternity. Jesus Christ, the Word become man, is the way to the Father. And so the pattern of this poem traces out man's way to God through him. "God no man has ever seen." In the Old Testa-

*The Incarnate
Son as
Revealer*

ment, you will recall, tradition vacillated somewhat on this doctrine. While it was agreed that the majority of mankind might "not see God, and live" (Ex 19:12-13; 20:19), Moses was considered by some to be the exception. Did Moses behold the face of God, or did he not? In Exodus 33:11 we are told, "Yahweh conversed with Moses face to face as a man converses with a friend." Such was the view of the writer known as the Yahwist. Another ancient writer from the northern kingdom, the Elohist, a man somewhat more inhibited in his religious attitudes, much more reserved than the Yahwist so far as humanity's dealings with the deity are concerned, suggests that Moses did not see God. Hence we have the—to us—rather amazing confrontation of these divergent views in the Bible. Indeed, in the very same chapter in which we are told Moses actually saw Yahweh, we also read the remark of God to Moses: "You cannot see my face, for a man cannot see me and remain alive" (Ex 33:20).

All this is changed in the new covenant. There can no longer be any debate or any doubt as to whether men may see God. For the Word has become our "exegete"—the very word St. John employs. The Son of God incarnate has now become our interpreter of the Father, who does indeed remain unseen. Jesus, the only-begotten, who knows the secrets of his Father's heart, is thereby constituted man's guide to God. Such is the merciful condescension of the divine economy, moreover, that, when with Christian faith we perceive the Son in Jesus, we are enabled to behold the very face of God. "Philip, he who has seen me has seen the Father!" (Jn 14:9). This is the meaning of faith for St. John: that beholding God's Word in Jesus Christ we may contemplate deity itself. "We have beheld his glory!" That is to say, we have looked upon Jesus as the Son of God, the perfect image of the Father. Our hands have touched, our ears have heard, our eyes have seen this final manifestation of the eternal life of the Godhead (cf. 1 Jn 1:1), the Word incarnate.

This basic and crucial tenet of the Christian faith provides the fundamental validation of St. Ignatius' conception of the "contemplation" in the *Spiritual Exercises*. If during the earthly life of Jesus his disciples were led gradually to commit themselves and their lives to him as Master, and if with the coming of the pentecostal Spirit they saw in him the Son of God, I, too, by contemplating the scenes of the Gospel with the eyes of Christian faith, can learn to play my role as an apostle, a disciple of the glorified Lord. For the Bible assures me that God's action in history is ever consistent with itself. It was through the events of Jesus' earthly life and the sending of the Holy Spirit that the invisible

Father revealed himself and his divine will to Jesus' followers. Accordingly, in my own life, by contemplating Jesus in the episodes of his public life and death—listening for his words, observing his actions with faith—I shall assuredly dispose myself to assume my proper place in contemporary salvation history. It is this very contemplation of the doings and sayings of the incarnate Word which put me in contact with God, who is my Father.

"God no man has ever seen; his only Son, who shares the secrets of his Father's heart, has personally acted as our interpreter." The exalted Christ continues his work of interpretation for me through the activity of his Spirit. Thus at every instant of my reading of the Gospels, in my contemplation of Jesus' earthly activity, I am made aware that I behold the Father. This is guaranteed me by the new covenant, founded upon the incarnation, and completed by the moment of Jesus' death when he breathed forth, "handed over the Spirit," to me and all his covenanted people. There can no longer be any hesitation then for the Christian about man's ability to see the Father—thanks to the continuing reality of this new covenant, which centers in the greatest events of salvation history. For the Word, the perfect image of the invisible God, has become—and remains for all eternity—"flesh and blood."

Chapter 11

THE PROBLEM OF THE INFANCY
NARRATIVES

Literary Form SOMEHOW THE WORD has gotten round that biblical scholars, even Catholic biblical scholars, have been tampering with the Infancy stories. Consequently there is today, as you are well aware, no little uneasiness about the historical significance of these narratives. If I may be permitted to refer to my own experience, it seems that whenever I happen to give a lecture on the Gospels, we inevitably get round in the question period to "the case of the missing Magi!"

Accordingly, I thought that before we begin our contemplations of these beautiful episodes depicting the birth and childhood of Jesus we ought to talk quite frankly about this problem. We shall not discuss it in a highly technical way, which would certainly be out of place here. We wish simply to appreciate the decided advantage there is in an approach to these narratives which may still seem novel to some. When I speak of advantage here I mean the advantage for contemplating and praying about these narratives.

The professional student of Sacred Scripture has come to see— and I believe on solid grounds—that the kind of narrative which is found in the first two chapters of the Gospels of Matthew and Luke is of a quite different character from most of the episodes in these or other Gospels which deal with the subject of Jesus' public life.

Why do I say that there are solid grounds for such a viewpoint? The official apostolic testimony, which, in its oral form, constituted the Christian proclamation of salvation, the official witness of the Twelve to the resurrection of Jesus, included only the chronological sequence of events from the ministry of John the Baptist until the ascension of the risen Christ (Acts 1:21-22). This message of hope to a despairing world was, moreover, centered in the death and the resurrection of Jesus as the principal saving event. As a consequence, whatever episodes from the public life of Jesus were included in the apostolic preaching (or later, in the written Gospels) all were orientated towards this focal point in the gospel, Jesus' death and resurrection.

When we come to contemplate the Infancy narratives in our retreat, we should not ignore entirely the questions raised by modern Scripture studies regarding these stories, even though this is not the time for a critical and detailed dissection of them. You will note that I do not say we should try to defend them, because they need no defense. These narratives of Jesus' infancy in Matthew and in Luke are just as much the Word of God as the rest of the Scriptures.

I wish however to point out to you what I consider to be a decided advantage in this modern approach to these stories for the Ignatian exercise of contemplation. I believe we ought to capitalize on the very uneasiness we feel today concerning the historical character of certain details, or even entire episodes, in these narratives. And here I simply repeat a suggestion once made by my former colleague, now rector of the Pontifical Biblical Institute of Rome, R.A.F. MacKenzie, S.J. We should be on the alert to put the emphasis where Matthew and Luke, the inspired authors, put the emphasis; that is on the religious and doctrinal message of these narratives. We can rest assured that, in so treating them, we are employing them in our contemplation precisely as the Spirit of God desires, since it was for that very reason that he inspired the writing of them. *A Presentation of Christology*

I have said that these episodes fall outside the official apostolic proclamation of the gospel. The apostolic preaching, it will be remembered, possessed a twofold character. It was first of all based upon eyewitness experience, and it contained, in addition, the affirmation of Christian faith. This Christian belief of the apostolic preachers constituted in fact the hermeneutical principle by which they were empowered to interpret the meaning of the historical facts which, as eyewitnesses, the Twelve could attest.

Now, it is surely obvious that the Twelve had no personal experience of the events surrounding Jesus' birth and infancy. When consequently the evangelists Matthew and Luke wished to incorporate into their Gospels episodes relating to Jesus' first years, they could not rely upon the official witness of the Twelve. Where then did these sacred writers find the data for their Infancy narratives, and what method did they use in interpreting them?

At the heart of these stories there undoubtedly lie certain personal reminiscences, although the precise source of these memories, preserved within the family of Jesus, is now quite impossible to discover. It has been often suggested that the Infancy narratives in Matthew's Gospel, in which St. Joseph is cast in the principal role, came from his relatives; whereas the Lucan stories, which make our Lady the protagonist, come from her side of the family. This appears at first sight a quite satisfactory solution, until it be realized that Matthean and Lucan sequences have practically nothing in common with each other. Yet these narratives were written, not centuries after the events, but within a relatively few years.

It is thus very difficult to understand why, except for the virginal conception and birth of Jesus, these two accounts can present such a widely diverging, if not quite contradictory series of episodes. Indeed, it must be admitted that it is impossible to combine the elements in Matthew with those of Luke, so as to produce a consistent and harmonious sequence. Does one place the visit of the Magi (Mt 2:1-12) after the presentation of the child Jesus in the temple? Luke's assertion that immediately afterwards the Holy Family went back to Nazareth (Lk 2:39) makes this impossible, as the Magi found them in Bethlehem. Moreover, if Luke be right in stating that the presentation of the child Jesus in the temple occurred forty days after his birth, it is extremely difficult to insert the visit of the Magi and the flight into Egypt into so brief a span as six weeks.

Old Testament References

We should not, in the second place, overlook a salient feature of these narratives—the generous number of Old Testament citations and allusions scattered throughout them. The only other section of the written Gospels possessing a comparable number of references to the Old Testament are the Passion narratives. Throughout the fourfold account of Jesus' public life, citations from the Old Testament are surprisingly rare. This is particularly true of Luke's Gospel, where scarcely ever is a reference to "the Scriptures," to be found in the body of his book. Even in Mark, allusions to the Old Testament are not too frequent. Matthew, who interests himself in underscoring the relation of the Gospel to "the Scriptures," admittedly quotes them more in his story of Jesus' public ministry. But even so, there is no part of his Gospel, proportionately, that employs the Old Testament as consistently as his Infancy narratives.

The prominence of "the Scriptures" in these stories would seem to suggest that we are dealing with a kind of midrashic technique, found not infrequently in Old Testament literature. This literary genre was intended primarily for edification, with little concern for the historical as such. Thus, in the absence of any authoritative testimony by the Twelve regarding the facts of Jesus' infancy or

112

their authentic interpretation, these evangelists have gathered family reminiscences, vaguely enough remembered, and have filled out the sketchy data they obtained in this way by a rather generous introduction of Old Testament themes and quotations. Yet this very methodological treatment must be counted an advantage, because it underscores for us the religious message which Matthew and Luke mean their readers to grasp from these beautiful stories.

We ought also to bear in mind that these Infancy narratives are an integral part of the written Gospels, and are consequently (like the episodes recorded of Jesus' public ministry) also orientated to the center of the Gospel, the death and the resurrection of Jesus. St. Ignatius himself displays a certain awareness of this truth, by giving expression to the basic continuity between the Infancy accounts and the crowning events of our Lord's earthly career. You will doubtless recall the passage in the *Exercises* to which I refer. It constitutes the third point in the contemplation on the nativity. "The third point is to see and consider what they [our Lady and St. Joseph] are doing. That is to say, the journey and the labor that they undergo, in order that Our Lord may be born in extreme poverty and that, after such toils, after hunger, thirst, heat, cold, insults and affronts, he may die on the cross" [116]. St. Ignatius' awareness that the whole gospel is a continuum and that, consequently, to see the significance of its beginning we must bear in mind how it will end is something, I believe, which we are meant to keep in view throughout the Spiritual Exercises. All the episodes in the Gospel record, including the Infancy narratives, must somehow be made to throw light upon the heart of the Christian good news. For it is principally from the death and the resurrection of Christ that all these other episodes derive their salutary effect upon the exercitant.

Prologue to the Gospel

Finally, the Infancy narratives illustrate a pedagogical point which is important for the effective contemplation of Jesus' public life. They remind us, perhaps more strikingly than other Gospel narratives, that in reading and in contemplating the sacred text, we must attend principally to the dialogue between the author and his Christian reader. Matthew, Mark, Luke, or John did not propose to write books which might serve as the basis of Christian apologetics. Their Gospels were intended to be read with Christian faith. The evangelists did not indeed ignore or belittle the importance of basing their accounts, where possible, upon the personal, collective experience of the Twelve. They were con-

Dialogue Between Evangelist and Reader

cerned, however, to put first things first. Because they wrote as Christian authors for Christian readers, our evangelists, in addition to recording certain facts of Jesus' life, have attempted to provide us with insights of a Christological nature. Accordingly, the Gospel narratives must be seen to operate on two levels. They recount the traditional episodes of Jesus' earthly life, but they also provide us with an interpretation on a Christological level of the Christian mystery. We are thereby instructed in many essential truths of the Christian faith which the disciples learned only after Jesus' resurrection and the descent of the Holy Spirit.

Now, in evaluating the Infancy narratives, it is especially important to attend to this dialogue between the evangelist and the Christian reader. An example may make this clear. When Luke, recording the dialogue between the angel and our Lady at the annunciation, writes "The Holy Spirit will *overshadow* you . . . ," the Greek word he uses is a technical term in the Septuagint, signifying the presence of God in the holy of holies in the tent of testimony. The book of Exodus tells of how the glory of the Lord came to overshadow the ark of the covenant (Ex 40:34). St. Luke, by borrowing this consecrated terminology, is telling his reader that our Lady is the new ark of the covenant. She is, in other words, the mother of the Word incarnate.

I should like now to point out very briefly the thematic structure of St. Luke's Infancy Gospel and then that of St. Matthew. I take Luke first because he is a more accomplished writer, and hence his thematic structure is clearer than that of Matthew.

Luke's Infancy Narrative
Luke's first two chapters are inspired principally by two Old Testament passages. The first is found in Daniel (Dn 9:24ff.); the second occurs in Malachy (Mal 3:1-5). Each of these passages is very familiar to you, I know. The first is the famous prophecy *ex eventu* of seventy weeks, in which the angel announces the termination of Israel's guilt. We might state it more positively as the announcement of Israel's redemption at the close of seventy weeks. The angel also predicts that the sanctuary of Jerusalem will be reconsecrated at the end of that period.

Now, you will recall that one striking feature of these chapters is the refrain which recurs time and again, ". . . the time (or the days) was fulfilled." Luke does not think of these periods of time simply in terms of *chronos,* i.e. as they came round on the calendar: on his view, they are fulfilled. The *kairos,* or prophetic time, has become a reality. It should be noted how very carefully Luke points out the passage of time from the annunciation by the angel Gabriel to Zachary until the day when the child Jesus is presented in the temple. Elizabeth conceives; six months go by; and the annunciation is made to our Lady. Then nine months pass until she brings forth her firstborn son. Forty days later our Lady with the infant Jesus are presented in the temple. This whole time sequence, if one counts a month as thirty days, amounts to four hundred and ninety days, or seventy weeks.

This is undoubtedly one of the thematic devices which Luke uses to structure his version of our Lord's infancy. It has left its mark upon certain details of the Lukan narrative. For example, you will recall that the angel, who made the so-called prophecy of seventy weeks in the book of Daniel, was named Gabriel—hence the name of the celestial messenger in the Lucan annunciation scenes. The original prophecy, written in the apocalyptic genre, refers to the desecration of the temple under Antiochus Epiphanes IV and its reconsecration or rededication after the victory of Judas Maccabeus. St. Luke portrays the entrance of the child Jesus into the temple as its renovation, on which occasion salvation is proclaimed as an actual reality to the true Israelites like Simeon and Anna.

The other text which inspired Luke's literary creation is taken from the prophet Malachy (Mal 3:1-5). This text is prominent in the liturgy for the feast of the Purification. This mysterious prophecy was taken up in late Judaism time and again, meditated and commented upon. It speaks in obscure terms of an "angel," a messenger of the Lord, to be sent "before the face of God." Then suddenly "the Lord himself will come into his temple," for the eschatological consecration of the sanctuary at the end of time. Towards the close of the Old Testament period there was great speculation about the identity of this messenger. The Jewish scribes finally settled upon the notion that Elijah was to return to earth to prepare for the awesome appearance of Yahweh in the eschatological judgment. A later (inspired) editor of the prophecy of Malachy inserted this belief towards the end of the book, naming Elijah as this mysterious messenger (Mal 4:5-6). Ben-Sira, the author of Ecclesiasticus, in his "Praise of the Patriarchs," points out that Elijah is the one who is to come at the end of days, "to reconcile the hearts of the fathers to the children" (Sir 48:4-10). The New Testament itself bears witness to the vitality of this same tradition; and Jesus brings it to a final conclusion by pointing out that John the Baptist is Elijah (Mt 11:14). In the Lucan infancy the angel Gabriel announces that the child to be born to Zachary and his wife Elizabeth is to "go before God with the spirit and the power of Elijah" (Lk 1:17).

This whole prophecy of Malachy, as is clear, centers in the

temple. The temple and the holy city of Jerusalem in Luke's Infancy narrative also form the foci of interest. This is one way in which it is to be distinguished from the Matthean Infancy Gospel. The first scene opens in the temple at the hour of the evening sacrifice of incense. The series of episodes concludes formally with the presentation of the child Jesus in the temple. Luke appends a kind of postscript or epilogue, which narrates a pilgrimage made by the Holy Family to the temple when the child Jesus was twelve years old.

Some acquaintance with the literary structuring of these narratives can provide certain guide-lines for our contemplation. It reveals very clearly just what Luke is trying to tell us about the theological significance of these narratives. Thus the evangelist can show us what direction our contemplation of these mysteries ought to take.

Matthew's Infancy Narrative

When we turn to Matthew, although we may not find the same degree of literary artistry or even the depth of theological insight as in Luke's Infancy Gospel, we can observe a similar methodological approach. Matthew begins with the genealogy of Jesus because he wishes to demonstrate—Matthew is much more concerned with an apologetic interest than is Luke—that Jesus' roots are plunged deep in the past of his people. Accordingly, this evangelist constructs, quite artificially, a genealogy consisting of three series, each with fourteen links. The number fourteen, it would appear, is so important in Matthew's eyes that he has eliminated the names of three kings from his first series in order to arrive at that exact number. By this (to us) strange procedure, the evangelist shows that he wishes to prove that Jesus is the son of Abraham as well as the son of David—those two great Old Testament figures most intimately connected with the messianic hopes of Israel. God had promised Abraham that through him all the nations of the earth would invoke blessings upon one another (Gn 11:3). God communicated, through the prophet Nathan, to David the great promise that one day a son of his would sit upon his royal throne, of whose kingdom there would be no end (2 S 7:12-14).

In the second part of Matthew's first chapter the story of Jesus' miraculous conception and birth elucidates what in his genealogy appears as a mystery. Why was the name of Joseph introduced into the list of Jesus' ancestors, since it is clear that Joseph had nothing to do with Mary's conception of Jesus? The sequel explains this puzzling procedure. St. Joseph, as the angel's opening words to him make clear, is "son of David." It is then Joseph, who in the divine plan must act as father to this child, born of a virgin mother, by bestowing the name Jesus upon him, and thus hand on to him his Davidic lineage. When Joseph, awestruck at the great mystery of Jesus' miraculous conception, wishes to withdraw, fearing to intrude himself into this divine operation, he is reassured by the angel that he has his own special role to play in the economy of the redemption. Thus it is that Joseph accepts this mandate from God, with the happy consequence that Jesus is truly the son of David through Joseph, his foster father.

Matthew's second chapter provides a kind of preview of the main movement of the rest of the Gospel. The section of the Church to which this evangelist belonged, it would appear, was predominantly Gentile in membership. Matthew, like Paul, attempts to answer the agonizing question which obsessed the Jewish Christians of the first century: how has it happened that the very people with whom God had made his covenant have not obeyed the gospel and entered the Christian Church? The story of the Magi is used to illustrate how the pagans have answered the divine call to Christian faith more readily than the chosen people. By the use of mere natural science, under the guidance of divine providence (symbolized by a star), these oriental astrologers are led to faith in this child. In sharp contrast with the Magi, the religious leaders of Judaism with their half-pagan king Herod, although they possess the revealed word of God in "the Scriptures" (which plainly declare that this child is to be born in Bethlehem), do not believe. In the sequel, the episode of the attempted persecution of the child and his refuge in Egypt illustrates a theme that is very dear to Matthew. Almighty God's providential plan of salvation is being worked out, not merely despite but precisely because of human perversity exemplified here by the machinations of Herod. For it is because of such human perversity that Jesus Christ, the Son of God, will be handed over for execution. But this "handing over," (the word is to become a technical term in the Pauline vocabulary of the redemption) is, in the last analysis, not the work of the Jews; it is not the work of the Romans; nor is it the work of Judas or Caiphas or Pilate or Herod. It is the loving act of God the Father, who hands his beloved Son over for the rescue of all mankind (Rom 8:32; Jn 3:16).

We are accustomed to speak of "the flight into Egypt," but in point of fact it is a more accurate description of Matthew's point of view to call the episode "the return from Egypt into the land of Israel." It is important to advert to the fact that Matthew cites the prophet Jeremiah in connection with this event. The passage quoted is familiar to us all. The dead Rachel is pictured as weeping for "her children"—actually a group of captives from the northern kingdom herded together at Ramah, awaiting deportation at the hands of their Assyrian conquerors. According to the northern tradition, Rachel's tomb was not far from Ramah.

To understand Matthew's purpose in referring to this chapter of Jeremiah it is important to note how the mood of this poetic passage changes in the very next verse following that cited by Matthew. "Restrain your voice from weeping, and your eyes from tears! For your labour shall have its reward" (Jer 31:16), the prophet says. This serves to introduce the great promise, "See, days are coming," is the oracle of Yahweh, "when I will make a new covenant with the house of Israel and with the house of Judah, not like the covenant I made with their ancestors. . . . I will put my law within them, and will write it on their hearts. . . ." (Jer 31:31-34).

In Matthew's eyes the story of the flight to Egypt and the return of the child Jesus marks the beginning of the realization of this divine promise. This conception is underscored by a citation from the prophet Hosea, "out of Egypt have I called my son" (Hos 11:1). Thus the principal purpose for the flight into Egypt becomes clear. It has been arranged by God the Father that the infant Jesus might manifest his messianic vocation by being called out of Egypt. The Hebrews, according to the book of Exodus, had been formed into God's people, and so received their vocation as the *segullāh,* God's own acquisition, by being summoned out of Egypt (Ex 4:23). So too, by being called out of Egypt "into the land of Israel" (Mt 2:20), the "new covenant" foretold by Jeremiah moves close to realization.

Far from being impoverished by a frank recognition of the literary character of these Infancy narratives, our contemplations based upon these episodes are actually enriched by pursuing the advantages which modern scriptural scholarship provides. It has the great virtue of making us realize that, in the minds of these two evangelists, it is not the historical as such which is of primary importance in these episodes, but rather their religious message. It is this Christological teaching which Matthew and Luke are trying to convey to us through these beautiful stories. And it is for this value that the Christian Church has from the beginning held them dear to herself and used them in her liturgy, and in her prayer life, to introduce her children, throughout the centuries, to the gospel of Jesus Christ.

THE BIRTH OF JESUS IN BETHLEHEM
Luke 2:1-16

Now in those days an edict was promulgated by the Emperor Augustus ordering the census of the whole world. 2This census, the first of its kind, took place while Quirinius was governor of Syria. 3Every man went to be registered, each in his own hometown. 4Joseph also, leaving the town of Nazareth in Galilee, went up to Judaea to the city of David called Bethlehem, since he was of the house and lineage of David. 5He went to have himself registered with Mary, his betrothed, who was with child. 6While they were there, the time when she must give birth was fulfilled. 7She brought her firstborn son into the world, wrapped him in swaddling clothes and laid him in a manger since there was no room for them in the caravanserai.

8Now there were shepherds in the neighborhood, living out in the fields, who took turns at night guarding their flocks. 9When the angel of the Lord appeared to them, and the glory of the Lord bathed them with its splendor, they were overcome with a mighty fear. 10But the angel said to them: "Stop being afraid. Observe that I bring you word of a great joy, which belongs to all the people. 11Today, in the city of David a Saviour has been born for you, who is the Messiah, the Lord.

12And this will serve as a sign for you. You will find the infant wrapped in swaddling clothes and lying in a manger."

13Without warning a numerous troop of the heavenly host joined the angel and sang God's praises: 14"Glory to God in the heights of heaven and peace on earth to men of his good pleasure!"

15Now, after the angels had left them to return to heaven, the shepherds said to one another: "Let us go across to Bethlehem to see this event, which the Lord has made known to us." 16So they came with haste, and found Mary and Joseph, with the infant lying in the manger.

THE GOOD NEWS OF CHRISTMAS

Luke's Narrative

TO ST. LUKE REMAINS the undisputed honor of giving the Christian world the good news of Christmas. Without his narrative, the Christmas story would be immeasurably poorer. St. Matthew, it is true, promises to tell his readers "how the birth of Jesus Christ came about" (Mt 1:18); but he restricts himself to the message of the virginal conception and birth of our Lord, since he is chiefly concerned to explain how Joseph, though not the natural father of Jesus, was led by God's command to act *in a very real sense* as his father by giving the child his name, and so pass on to Mary's son his own Davidic lineage (Mt 1:18-25).

St. Luke's narrative illustrates his favorite technique of situating the event, as far as possible, in the context of contemporary history. More important still, the whole is presented as a gospel in miniature: "I bring you word of a great joy, which belongs to all the people," the angel announces, like an evangelist, to the shepherds. The chief Lucan theological themes are also to be found in the episode: his "social" interests, his love of actual poverty, his interest in women connected with Jesus, particularly his mother. Luke's awareness of the universalist nature of the Christian message may be seen from his formulation of the angelic kerygma, already alluded to. The Lucan picture of Jesus, dominated as it is throughout by insistence upon Christ's divinity, appears in the angelic proclamation of the birth of "a Saviour . . . who is the Messiah, the Lord." Luke, alone of the evangelists, gives this title, proper to the risen Jesus, to him during his earthly career. The note of joy which runs through this narrative is a hallmark of Lucan spirituality.

Bearing in mind the particular type of literature to which this story of Jesus' birth belongs, we shall do well to concentrate, in our prayerful contemplation of the Gospel text, upon its Christological orientation. St. Luke is mainly desirous of showing his reader that this event signifies the earthly manifestation of the incarnate Son, as Saviour and Messiah. As an epiphany narra-

120

tive, it may be compared with the story of the Magi in St. Matthew's Gospel. Yet where the first evangelist is primarily an apologete, intent upon proving that Jesus is Messiah, St. Luke is a theologian, who reflects upon the data of revelation, and exposes the Christology to be discerned therein. Thus he designates the infant Jesus as "Saviour,"—a title characteristic of his presentation of Christ.

What indications have we, from Luke's artistic arrangement of this narrative, that he intends it to serve as an epiphany of the Word become man? We may catch a hint of this purpose by taking cognizance of what seems a deliberately planned parallelism, a technique frequent in this Gospel, to provide a preview of future events, and so serve as a unifying principle. Here, the angel's joyous song will be echoed by the disciples' exuberant acclamation of Jesus at his messianic entry into Jerusalem (Lk 19:38). On that occasion, our Lord's followers chant, "Blessed is he who comes as king in the name of the Lord! Peace in heaven, and glory on high!" The angelic host sings, "Glory to God in the heights of heaven and peace on earth to men of his good pleasure!"

The last line of this translation, the much discussed "Peace on earth to men of good will" seems to have been cleared up for us by a passage in the Dead Sea scrolls found at Qumran, which suggests that it is probably God's good pleasure which is meant, not human good will.

Another indication that Luke intended to present this narrative as an epiphany is found in the phrase: "Stop being afraid!" (Lk 2:10). The force of this expression, in the Old as in the New Testament, is to serve as introduction to a new divine revelation (cf. Zeph 3:16; Jl 2:21; Lk 1:13; 1:30). There are additional details which point to the literary form employed throughout the Bible in descriptions of a theophany, or, as here, a "Christophany." There is, for example, the reference to "the angel of the Lord." This Old Testament expression does not signify one of these beings we call angels, but rather some tangible sign of God's providential care of his people. The book of Exodus depicts the burning bush as an appearance of "the angel of the Lord" (Ex 3:2). In Acts, the "angel of the Lord" who leads Peter out of prison conducts himself in a manner not usually associated with angelic behavior. Thus we may conclude that the phrase connotes simply some visible sign—whatever concrete form it took—of God's providential care over the primate of the Christian community (Acts 12:6-11). "The glory of the Lord," which bathes the shepherds in its awesome light, is another technical phrase, borrowed from the

Old Testament, to indicate a sensible manifestation of the divine presence. There is, in addition, the term "sign" (Lk 2:12), which points to some proof of the reality of a divine revelation. In the annunciation to Mary (Lk 1:36), the angel Gabriel had given our Lady a sign that the divine message regarding her own maternity of the Messiah was no delusion: her cousin Elizabeth would give birth to a son. We shall return to this "sign" given to the shepherds presently.

Pastoral Setting   The pastoral motif, which is particularly prominent in Luke's whole narrative, may well have been inspired by an Old Testament passage which Matthew made use of in his story of the Magi. I refer to the prophecy of Micah, particularly chapters four and five. You recall that St. Matthew cites the opening lines of chapter five: "But you, Bethlehem Ephrathah, tiny among the clans of Judah,—from you will come forth for me the one who will be ruler over Israel. . . ." The setting of Luke's nativity scene is reminiscent of an earlier passage in Micah where "the daughter of Sion" is about to give birth to a mysterious child, the eschatological king, mentioned in Isaiah's cantos concerning the Prince of Peace (Is 7:10—12:6). "And you tower of the flocks, Ophel of the daughter of Sion, to you will return the sovereignty of olden times, royalty upon the house of Israel. Why do you now utter cries? Is there not a king with you? Are your counselors lost, that travail has seized upon you like a woman in labor? Twist in travail and cry out, O daughter of Sion, like a woman in labor, for you are to go forth from the city and dwell in the open country. You will go even to Babylon. It is there you will be delivered. It is there that Yahweh will redeem you from the hands of your enemies" (Mi 4:8-10). A little farther on, the prophet continues: "But you, Bethlehem Ephrathah, tiny among the clans of Judah— from you will come forth for me the one who will be ruler over Israel. His origins go back to ancient times, to days of old. That is why Yahweh will abandon them, until the time when she who is to bear the child will have borne him" (Mi 5:2-3). This passage reflects the Isaian prediction of the great sign to King Achaz (Is 7:14). "And then the rest of his brothers will come, back to the children of Israel. He will shepherd his flock by the power of Yahweh, by the majesty of the name of his God. They will be established, for he will extend his power forever, even to the ends of the land. He himself will be peace" (Mi 5:3-4).

The suggestion that this pastorally orientated passage of Micah has had an influence upon the Lucan nativity scene is indeed an attractive one, which sheds light upon the intention of the evangelist. It may be helpful also to note Micah's reference to a "tower of the flocks." Mention is made in Genesis of a "tower of the flocks" in the vicinity of Bethlehem (Gn 35:21). In the Palestinian Targum, or commentary on this passage, it is asserted that this "tower of the flocks" is to be the scene of the revelation of the Messiah at "the end of days." Now, while the Palestinian Targum is more recent than this passage of St. Luke, it is rather interesting to observe in this document the presence of the same pastoral motif in a statement concerning the Messiah as we have in Luke. You notice too that the daughter of Sion, who is to give birth to a son, must leave the city and go into "the open country." St. Luke states that our Lady laid her newborn son in a "manger,"— an obscure Greek word, which could mean watering-trough located usually in the open fields.

We might remind ourselves in passing that there is no mention by Luke of a cave or of a stable, which we are accustomed to associate with the story of Jesus' birth. The stable theme, of which St. Francis of Assisi made such dramatic use, has been inspired by the remark found in Isaiah: "The ox recognizes its owner, and the ass its master's crib" (Is 1:3).

We might at this point organize our contemplation of this great mystery around the sign given to the shepherds as proof that a Saviour, the Messiah, has been born in the city of David. Luke, alone of the Synoptics, gives Jesus the title Saviour. This designation, not found in either Matthew or Mark, occurs but once in John (Jn 4:42). By contrast, the notion of salvation is a theme that runs through Luke. The Latin and the Greek words mean "health" as well as "salvation." There is a tradition, not entirely without foundation, which asserts that Luke was a physician. Indeed, he is probably the collaborator referred to by Paul in Colossians as "Luke, our dear physician" (Col 4:10). Moreover, there are indications in the writings of our evangelist that he was familiar with Greek medical terminology current in his day. His profession would explain why he presents Jesus to the Hellenistic world of his time, which was in search of salvation, as the divine answer to mankind's needs, both bodily and spiritual.

The angel's message to the shepherds was: "And this will serve as a sign to you. You will find the infant wrapped in swaddling clothes and lying in a manger." This Messiah is an infant—a word which comes from Latin, meaning one who cannot speak. By this sign, this infant, my place today in sacred history is indicated. If the Messiah cannot speak, his spirit dwelling in me enables me to be his voice. This Jesus, then, becomes my Saviour—he has come to save me, in a very fundamental sense, from the tragedy of a useless life. For I can supply him, my infant Christ, with a voice. Jesus is my Saviour, by the very fact that he cannot speak, and thus I am enabled to be his voice. You may recall how, at the foot of Mt. Sinai, Israel had cried out, "Do not let God speak to us, lest we die" (Ex 20:19). What a blessing then, that my God is an infant, and cannot speak! For were he to speak, the world of men must remain silent, since he, as the Word of God, upholds the mighty universe by the power of his word (Heb 1:3). He does not speak, however,—this infant Christ. Had not Isaiah written of him, "He will not protest or cry out, nor shall his voice be heard in the streets" (Is 42:2)? The priest may be aptly described as a man who is the voice of Christ—in the confessional, in the pulpit, most of all, at the solemn celebration of the Lord's Supper, the Eucharist, when, as he recites the historical narrative of the institution of this most blessed sacrament, the priest assumes the very accents of Jesus: "This is *my* Body." . . . "This is the cup of *my* Blood of the New Covenant." . . . "Do this as a memorial of *me.*"

He is moreover wrapped in swaddling clothes, this infant Saviour. He is a little bundle, incapable of moving either hand or foot. Consequently, I can be his gestures in my world, as well as his voice. Actions, after all, speak louder than words. Christ's voice was never heard, nor were his gestures ever seen, throughout the whole continent of the Americas. And yet his gestures of mercy, of compassion, of revelation, are seen everywhere in the gestures of his priests, in the gestures of his people: in the priest's hand upraised in absolution, in the Brother infirmarian's hands as he tends his sick, in those of the cook as he feeds the healthy. Above all we must not forget the most needed, because most meaningful, gesture which the world desires in our day—the gesture of my witness as a religious. My special religious gesture is my Jesuit gesture of obedience, my witness to Christ in the twentieth century.

And he is laid in a manger. He is a waif, this child: he is homeless. As a blessed consequence we may make a dwelling for our Saviour. He dwells in all the churches from St. Peter's in Rome to the last tin-roofed chapel in the Arctic. There are our own houses, our religious houses, that make a home for him. How fortunate for us! What a blessing that our Christ has no house, that he is laid in the manger of our tabernacles and of our hearts.

The Christmas   I suggest that we might complete this contemplation by recall-
Liturgy   ing the liturgical significance of the annual commemoration of

this nativity of our Lord. The epistle for the Mass of midnight provides an important clue to the meaning of Christmas. "God's gracious gift, the source of salvation of all men, has made his appearance in order to teach us how to live in this world waiting intently for the blessed object of our hope, the manifestation in glory of our great God and Saviour, Jesus Christ" (Ti 2:11-13). Each Christmas night we celebrate the birthday of God's Son. But this celebration possesses a unique character among birthday parties, and we should not miss its peculiar significance. Most birthday celebrations derive their meaning, and indeed their joy, from a look backwards over the years that have been lived thus far. I suppose there is no one in any family who thinks of a birthday as merely marking one year nearer the grave for the person who is thus feted. National birthdays which we observe, whether Washington's or the Queen's, are also characterized by this look backwards, because by them a people attempts to keep green the memory of distinguished men and women of the past. Similarly in the Church's calendar feastdays of the saints function as annual mementoes bidding us recall the lives of these heroic Christians.

Christ's birthday stands in contrast to all these commemorative occasions. Christmas, for us Christians, ought to remain in a class by itself. It appears unique among all other birthday celebrations simply because it is meant to be celebrated principally not by looking backwards, but by an anticipation of the future.

Each man makes but one entrance into this world, except the Son of God. Our Lord Jesus Christ is to make a second appearance. We are reminded at Christmas by the epistle of the Mass at midnight, that Jesus made his first appearance among us as the very incarnation of God's gracious kindness, that covenanted virtue of Israel's God, which is the source of salvation for all mankind. But this same reading also informs us that Christ is to come again for his manifestation in glory at the end of history. We should not forget that it is this second coming which has most absorbed the attention of the Church in the liturgical celebration of Christ's nativity. While it is true, of course, that we look backward at Christmas to Jesus' birth, yet if we are to grasp the main message of Christmas, we cannot afford to dwell solely upon this past event. We must look ahead with anticipation to "that blessed hope, the manifestation in glory of our great God and Saviour Jesus Christ."

Thus the lesson of Christmas is not primarily or principally a deeper love of poverty, an increased esteem for detachment. It does not consist even of the thrilling thought of God's approachableness, revealed in the baby of Bethlehem. The principal theme of Christmas is the message of hope—the unshakeable hope that Christ will come again in glory.

That the commemoration of Jesus' birth plays only a subordinate role in Christian faith and piety may be shown by several considerations. In the first place, the New Testament clearly indicates this. The Gospels do not enlighten us either as regards the day or even the year when this momentous birthday took place. What other birthday is celebrated amongst men whose very date is so shrouded in obscurity? All we can do is guess that Jesus was born somewhere between the years eight and six "before Christ." (This latter paradox can be explained by a mathematical error. When the first Pope John commissioned a Scythian monk named Denis to draw up a Christian calendar to replace the old pagan Roman method of dating time *ab Urbe condita*, Denis was some half dozen years off in his calculation.)

As for the day and the month on which Jesus was born, we can be sure only of one thing—it was not December twenty-fifth. What is important here is that we realize that it really does not matter. It obviously did not matter to God. It clearly does not matter to the Church, for she wishes us to celebrate this birthday principally by looking forward from Christ's first coming to his second advent. History provides evidence, I believe, that such was the very purpose for which the Church instituted the feast of Christmas. It was only in the fourth century, after she had been liberated by the conversion of Constantine, that the Church began to observe Christmas for the first time. Epiphany, the feast of the manifestation of the mystery of the incarnation, is more ancient. What was the purpose which the Church had in ordering her children to observe Christmas? The principal reason, it would appear, was the Church's concern that the Christian people might, through its new-found freedom, lose the intensity and eagerness of the hope in Christ's coming in glory. The situation in which the Church found herself under Constantine, though in many respects a great boon, also held a certain danger—the danger that Christians, by becoming too comfortable in this world once the world began to tolerate them, might forget what they had remembered vividly when they were outlawed and persecuted: that the Lord Jesus was to come again. Has not subsequent history shown how easy it can be for the Christian people to neglect this hope in Christ's return at the end of time?

The second indication that the celebration of Christmas consists essentially in looking to the future may be seen in the symbolism prominent in the Christmas liturgy. Why did the Church choose December twenty-fifth? It was because that date falls after the winter solstice. It occurs at that time of year when the days begin to lengthen once again, and men's minds and hearts turn towards the hope of springtime and the rebirth of nature, with the return of the sun's light into this world of ours. You will recall how the second Mass of Christmas is dominated by the theme of light, presenting Christ as Light of the world.

Perhaps the clearest indication that Christmas is intended to teach us to look forward to the future coming of Christ in glory is to be found in the futurist orientation of the entire liturgy from Advent to Epiphany. From the first Sunday of Advent the Church confronts us with one dominant theme for our prayer, "Stir up your power, O Lord, and come!" Since, as the new Constitution on the Liturgy asserts, the Church is most properly herself when she is assembled for public worship (Nos. 2, 7, 10), she always takes a very realistic attitude in the liturgy. She is well aware that the coming of Christ which she prays for at this season cannot be that birth which happened centuries ago. Nor can it be any kind of imaginary coming that she requests by this serious and oft repeated prayer. To be sure, Jesus' first coming as a little child, his life of poverty, his suffering, endeared him to the hearts of men. Yet this first coming of his, if we may say so, has simply whetted our appetite for his return, his second coming. It is for this reason that the Church celebrates each year the feast of Christ's nativity—to reawaken our longing for his return. For her fear is that this desire of ours, which belongs to the very essence of Christianity, may become jaded or disillusioned by so much waiting. This is the lesson which the liturgy, perhaps to our surprise, teaches us on Christmas Eve, in the Mass for the vigil of this great feast. We may be startled to find ourselves praying in the Collect, "O God, who causes us to rejoice each year at the prospect of our redemption, grant that we may without fear behold your only Son, Jesus Christ, whom we welcome with joy as our redeemer, *coming also as judge.*" The Christmas Preface bids us thank God for the mystery of the Word become man because through him whom we recognize as the God we can see, we are carried away towards the things we have still to see, the as yet invisible glory of the returning Christ. Thus it is principally the virtue of Christian hope which we must expect to nourish by our contemplation of the nativity.

The ancient Palestinian Eucharistic cultus of the first century contained a most moving acclamation—the only phrase which has survived from the Aramaic liturgy of the apostolic age, "Marana tha!—Come, our Lord!" In the closing lines of the Apocalypse the author presents the daily life of the Church as a continual liturgy of the *parousia*. "The Spirit and the bride say, 'Come!'" (Ap 22:17). And as the book ends we hear the voice of Christ, "the faithful Witness" (Ap 1:5), summing up his testimony to the Christian people: "He who gives this testimony says, 'Yes, I am coming soon!'" (Ap 22:20). And heartened by this promise, the Church cries out, "Amen! come Lord Jesus!" This prayer we must make our own through the contemplation of the nativity, "as we live in this world intently awaiting that blessed hope, the manifestation in glory of our great God and Saviour Jesus Christ."

JESUS IS BAPTIZED BY JOHN
Mark 1:4-11

John the baptizer appeared in the desert, proclaiming baptism with a view to repentance and the remission of sins. ⁵To him came the whole countryside of Judea, and all the inhabitants of Jerusalem; and they had themselves baptized by him in the Jordan river upon confessing their sins.

⁶John was dressed in camel's hair; his diet consisted of locusts and wild honey. ⁷In the course of his preaching he declared, "After me comes one mightier than I. I am not fit to stoop down and undo the thong of his sandals. ⁸As for myself, I have baptized you with water: he, however, will baptize you with a holy Spirit."

⁹At that time Jesus came from Nazareth in Galilee, and was baptized by John in the Jordan. ¹⁰Upon coming up out of the water, he saw the sky torn apart, and the Spirit like a dove descending upon him, ¹¹while from the sky came a voice, "You are my well-beloved Son, in whom I take delight!"

JESUS' BAPTISM: ESCHATOLOGICAL
DIMENSION OF HISTORY

Mark's Insight WE TURN NOW in our contemplations to that part of the gospel which is based upon the official, apostolic testimony to Jesus, his public ministry, his redemptive death and resurrection. I believe it is important to remind ourselves at the outset that the gospel constitutes a whole, and consequently we should, throughout our contemplations of Jesus' public ministry, constantly attempt to relate the various episodes to Jesus' death and resurrection. It is also necessary to bear in mind continually that, while the Gospel record is based upon the deposition of reliable eyewitnesses (hence its validity may not reasonably be dismissed out of hand), the Gospels are not mere "history." They are something much more significant for the Christian. The evangelists are well aware of the unique character of the events which they recount. The Gospel record is unique because it recounts the history of God's Son become man. There never was, nor ever will be, a history that can compare with this.

The Eschatological Dimension In order to impress ourselves again with this truth, so familiar to all of us, I suggest that we consider the eschatological dimension[1] in this history of Jesus as presented by St. Mark. If we were to do nothing else during our prayer than read in a leisurely, contemplative manner the entire Marcan account, concentrating our attention upon the various ways in which the evangelist insists upon this eschatological element, we should, I believe, have learned much about Christ, our redeemer.

I should like to suggest how, in the first thirteen verses of his book, which form a kind of prologue to his Gospel, Mark uses this eschatological viewpoint to show the unique character of Jesus' earthly career. He calls it "the beginning of the good news

---

1 I wish to acknowledge here my indebtedness in this chapter to a friend and colleague in New Testament studies, James M. Robinson, for the many insights he has provided in his brilliant book, *The Problem of History in Mark* (London, 1962).

of Jesus, the Messiah, the Son of God" (Mk 1:1). It is not easy to decide whether this title is to be applied to the whole of Mark's book, or simply to the ministry of John the Baptist as described in these verses. Let us assume here that Mark means to restrict it to the role of John in the Gospel. "In accordance with what has been written in Isaiah the prophet—'Remember, I am sending my messenger before you to ready your path,' 'a voice cries out in the desert: Ready the road of the Lord! Make his paths level!'— John the Baptizer appeared in the desert, proclaiming baptism with a view to repentance and the remission of sins."

According to Mark, the ministry of the Baptist is to be distinguished both from the economy of the Old Testament and particularly from the work of Jesus. Mark shows that he wishes to set John's function in contrast with the Old Testament dispensation by stating explicitly that John's role in sacred history fulfills the prophetic element in Israel's history. He attributes the prophetic texts, in a rather casual way, to the prophet Isaiah. Actually, though one verse from Isaiah is included, the first part of the citation comes from two other sources. There is a passage in Exodus (Ex 23:20) where, towards the end of the code of the covenant, almighty God promises his help in Israel's entry into the promised land: "Yahweh says: I am going to send an angel ahead of you to watch over you in the course of your journey and to bring you to the place I have determined." Reference is also made to Malachy (Mal 3:1), where God says, "Remember, I am going to send my messenger [or angel] to prepare the road ahead of me." The last part of this compound citation includes a verse of Isaiah (Is 40:3). John's work is described as the realization of this prophetic message from the Old Testament.

In what does John's ministry consist? John, says Mark, proclaimed a rite of baptism. Notice the kerygmatic quality of this symbolic rite. It is primarily a preparation for the coming of the Messiah. Thus, if it is plainly different from Christian baptism, it has little similarity to those lustral rites practiced in contemporary Judaism even though, as we see from the Qumran documents, they were intended only as an outward expression of that inner *metanoia*, or a change of mind. Johannine baptism was aimed at producing and expressing a deepened receptiveness of God's messianic designs; and it appears to have been received only once. Yet John's kerygmatic function is differentiated from that of Jesus. A little later in this first chapter of Mark, Jesus makes a proclamation also; but he proclaims the good news, the gospel (Mk 1:14-15). Jesus indeed also demands repentance, or reform

131

of life, but he does so because the kingdom of God has drawn near with his presence on earth.

John, then, is the hinge between "the Scriptures," by which term the New Testament writers designate the Old Testament, and the good news of salvation in Jesus Christ. In his function as the hinge, John has much in common with the spirit of Old Testament prophecy, even while his own ministry fulfills it. John is identified as Elijah by his costume. You recall that when King Ahaziah was seeking information about a mysterious character his messengers had met on the road, he asked for a description of the man. "He was a hairy man, with a leather belt around his loins," they said to him. And the King replied, "It was Elijah the Tishbite" (2 K 1:7-8).

St. Mark insists strongly upon the universal nature of Israel's response to John's message. "To him came the whole countryside of Judaea, and all the inhabitants of Jerusalem." It would be a mistake, however, to construe this mathematically. It must be understood theologically: John's message is meant for all Israel; hence Israel must respond as a collectivity. The Baptist speaks of a "mightier one," whom the reader of Mark will come to identify as Jesus of Nazareth. Why does the evangelist employ the term *ischyrōteros* (more powerful)? This term is a significant one in the vocabulary by which Mark will express the eschatological view of Jesus' history. You will recall the parable which Jesus uses so effectively in the debate with his adversaries, the religious leaders of Judaism who accuse him of connivance with Beelzebub. Our Lord replies: "No one can enter the house of a *strong man* (*ischyros*) and loot his property, unless first he tie up that *strong man*. Then he can loot his house" (Mk 3:27). Jesus is the mightier one who can accomplish this feat of binding Satan.

The Baptist remarks, when contrasting his function with that of Jesus: "I have baptized you with water; he will baptize you with a holy Spirit" (Mk 1:8). John's rite is merely symbolic. It is, in its turn, prophetic of a mysterious future baptism. Jesus, in Mark's story, is depicted from the moment of his own baptism by John as the bearer of the Spirit. For in the great eschatological combat, which Mark sees played out in the public ministry of Jesus, our Lord and the Spirit stand together as they fight against Satan, the adversary.

The Baptism of Jesus

Mark's summary account of the Baptist's function in sacred history comes to a climax with the account of Jesus' baptism. Here the Christian reader is faced with a difficult problem. Mark has already stated that this baptism, which John administered, entailed a public confession of sin on the part of the recipient. How then can the sinless One submit to this lustration, which in other men signifies an admission of sinfulness? What reason can the sinless Jesus have for undergoing such a baptism? When we read the ninth verse again, we realize that Mark has made a significant omission. Earlier the evangelist had said of the inhabitants of Judaea and Jerusalem: "They had themselves baptized by him in the Jordan River *upon confessing their sins*" (Mk 1:5). When however Jesus comes and is baptized by John in the Jordan, there is no confession of sin, because Jesus is without sin (Mk 1:9).

Yet why does Jesus subject himself to this humiliating rite? Mark tells us equivalently that it is because, as the Suffering Servant who is to redeem the rebellious descendants of the first Adam, Jesus wishes to associate himself as closely as possible with the sinful human family. Moreover, we see from the sequel to Jesus' baptism that his experience at the Jordan is unique. "Upon coming up out of the water, he saw the sky torn apart [Mark's violent expression is deliberately chosen], and the Spirit like a dove descending upon him, while from the sky came a voice, 'You are my well-beloved Son, in whom I take delight'" [a reference, surely, to the first of the Deutero-Isaian Servant songs, Is 42:1].

The most striking feature of this theophany is that the vision is enjoyed by Jesus alone. Mark does not say that there were any other witnesses of this manifestation of the Spirit and the Father. Accordingly, we must conclude that this theophany concerns Jesus personally, and has a bearing upon his mission in this world. You will remember that later Peter will refer to this episode as Jesus' messianic anointing with the Spirit (Acts 10:38). That is to say, it readies him in some way for his public ministry, the curing of men's ills and the waging of war against Satan. The Spirit descends upon Jesus like a dove. The image which Mark uses to symbolize the Holy Spirit, or rather, which Mark has received from the evangelical tradition, would appear to be taken from Genesis, where the Spirit of God is represented as brooding like a bird over the waters of the primordial chaos (Gn 1:2). Hence the appearance of the Spirit to Jesus is to be understood as the sign of the "new creation," in which he is to play the role of the new Adam. The divine voice from the sky declares that he is that "Servant of God" *('Ebed Yahweh)*, celebrated in the songs of the Deutero-Isaiah. Thus is Jesus informed (and through his experience, the apostolic Church) that it is his divinely conferred role, by his personal sufferings and his own glorification, to recapitulate the experiences of the people of Israel represented so poetically in "the Scriptures" by the Second Isaiah.

133

The Symbolism of the Desert   The Marcan sequel to Jesus' baptism and this theophany is briefly told. "Immediately afterwards, the Spirit drove him into the desert" (Mk 1:12). Again we note a certain violence in Mark's vocabulary. "And he remained forty days in the desert being tempted by Satan. He dwelt with wild beasts, while angels acted as his servants" (Mk 1:13). The immediate effect of Jesus' messianic anointing with the Spirit at his baptism is not, perhaps, what one might expect. The Holy Spirit does not lead him to engage in his public ministry of preaching and curing disease, but "drives him" into the desert where he will prepare for the inauguration of his mission, (which for Mark is basically a struggle against Satan) by hand-to-hand combat with the adversary. Mark does not tell us in so many words that Jesus is victorious in this struggle. He prefers to announce this inaugural victory symbolically by presenting him to his reader in this scene as the second Adam in the new Paradise. While at times in the Old Testament the desert appears as the abode of demons, the desert, particularly in the writings of the prophets, more frequently becomes a symbol of the presence of God. For in the minds of Israel's greatest prophets the period of the chosen people's march through the desert came to be regarded as the peak-point in the spiritual life of Israel. One need only recall how the great prophet of divine love, Hosea, thinks of his people's restoration as a new wandering in the wilderness, when Israel's jealous husband, Yahweh, after luring her into the desert, will, as in the days of her youth, make love to her once more (Hos 2:14-23). Jesus in the desert is like Adam in the first terrestrial paradise (Gen 2:19; Hos 2:18). He is the familiar of wild beasts, just as God had brought the beasts of the field to Adam to see what he would name them, thus signifying man's kingship over the animal creation. And just as Adam in that garden of God, Eden (the little pleasance that God had made for himself on earth), was privileged to enjoy a special and intimate companionship with God, so here Jesus as the new Adam is the familiar of angels who wait upon him. Thus there can be little doubt that, by such a description, Mark means to tell his reader that the victory belongs to Jesus from the very beginning.

With this introduction, Mark has sharpened our awareness that his story relates a combat of cosmic proportions, by means of the apocalyptic language he has employed in describing these unique experiences of Jesus at the Jordan and in the desert. This symbolic and figurative language, we begin to realize, is Mark's way of underscoring what he knows to be the fundamental thrust of Jesus' public life. It is, from first to last, a combat with Satan.

One other observation is pertinent here. We should not overlook the fact that the coming of the Spirit upon Jesus at his
baptism or the mysterious struggle with Satan in the desert—
events seemingly far removed from anything which we would
today call "history"—do not, as so frequently in ancient Near-
Eastern literature, cause the figure of Jesus to evanesce in some
kind of mythology. From this great spiritual experience and from
this combat, Jesus comes back to take his place in the world of
men, and carry out his mission of teaching and healing. Yet, all
the while he is thus engaged, Mark wishes us to realize Jesus in
a very real sense is fighting Satan. Mark has analyzed the activities
which engaged Jesus during his public life, and has placed them
in four main categories, each representing a facet of this
eschatological struggle with Satan. There are, in the first place,
the exorcisms; secondly, there are Jesus' miracles of healing;
thirdly, there are the debates or controversies with his adversaries;
and fourthly, there is Jesus' continual fight against ignorance,
tepidity, and obtuseness in his own disciples. These constitute for
Mark four areas of combat, so to say, in which the battle against
man's adversary, Satan, is waged by Jesus. While this view of our
Lord's public ministry is, to be sure, not absent from the writings
of the other evangelists, it is none the less stressed by Mark in a
special manner.

Accordingly, I suggest that we employ this Marcan theology
in our contemplation of Jesus' public ministry. We may, first of all,
contemplate Mark's presentation of Jesus' exorcisms. You will
recall that the first miracle recorded in Mark's Gospel is an exorcism (Mk 1:23-28). You will also remember that before Jesus
engages in this phase of the combat with Satan, he invites men,
Peter and Andrew, John and James, two pairs of brothers, to help
him in his ministry. It is significant, I believe, that Jesus solicits
and obtains the aid of mere human beings before doing battle
with Satan (Mk 1:16-20).

"It happened that there was a man in their synagogue possessed
by an unclean spirit, and he began to scream: 'What have you
to do with us, Jesus the Nazarene? Are you coming to destroy
us? I know who you are, the Holy One of God!' Jesus threatened
him: 'Keep your mouth shut! and get out of this man!'" It was
a violent scene, matched only by the crude language Mark uses
to describe it. The vulgar term employed here to render the word
which Jesus used in confronting the demon actually means "shut
your mouth!" Realist that he is, Mark has little in common with
that school of hagiography, which tended to sacrifice historical

truth in the interests of what was considered "edification."

Mark is well aware that this is a struggle to the death. The adversary, the demon, here attempts to gain the mastery over Jesus. You may recall, if you are acquainted with ancient works on magic, or with those manuals on exorcism from the Middle Ages, that there were lists of names for the devil. The medieval exorcist would read off these litanies of names in the hope that one of them might match the particular devil he was dealing with. Now, behind this practice lay the conviction, also shared by biblical authors, that, if you can learn the name of a person, you have him in your power. This view is probably the reason for the refusal, in late Judaism, to pronounce the sacred tetragram, Yahweh. Note how, in this Marcan narrative, the adversary attempts to get control of Jesus by naming him correctly. "I know who you are— the Holy One of God!" It is for this reason that Jesus silences him abruptly, almost impolitely, telling him to shut up. "And the unclean spirit, convulsing him violently, with a loud scream, left the man. Everyone was thoroughly frightened, and they asked one another as a result: What does this mean? Here is a new teaching [note the word], given with authority. He can command even the unclean spirits, and they obey him!" (Mk 1:27).

Thus, the exorcism for Mark is simply a form of Jesus' good news—his teaching. Yet it has a quality of complete novelty, this teaching, unlike that of the scribes, who taught solely by the authority of Rabbi So-and-so. By contrast, Jesus' teaching is dynamic: it produces results, like this exorcism.

The Healing Miracles   A second facet of this struggle with Satan appears in Jesus' miracles of healing. For Mark, as for his first commentators, Matthew and Luke, the miracles of Jesus' public life are a first assault on the kingdom of Satan established in this world. Jesus has entered history in order to inaugurate the reign, or kingdom of God; and the negative phase of that mission is to destroy the power of "the strong man," who is in possession of men—the devil. In Mark's account of Jesus' cleansing of the leper (Mk 1:41), there is a textual variant with every chance of being the original reading, which describes Jesus as "roused with anger" (instead of "stirred to compassion"). How explain this anger of Jesus at the request of a leper to be cleansed? The answer is to be sought in Mark's awareness that Jesus stands face to face with the adversary. This disease is the work of Satan; and consequently the anger Jesus here displays is a proof, no less than his subsequent healing of the sufferer, that he has taken the offensive against Satan.

136

In the second chapter of this Gospel, the first miracle recorded, that of the healing of a paralyzed man, makes the issue between Jesus and Satan very clear. Mark leaves his reader in no doubt about the real purpose of this cure. It is simply a symbol of a more profound, hidden reality—Jesus' fight against sin. Our Lord cures the man of his paralysis, "in order," as he says, "that you may know that the Son of Man has power *upon earth* to forgive sin" (Mk 2:10).

Closely associated with these exorcisms and miracles of healing, particularly in these opening chapters, is the third aspect of the eschatological struggle between Jesus and Satan—Jesus' debates with his adversaries, the religious leaders of Judaism. Mark gives his reader five examples of these controversies in the first three chapters of his Gospel. Throughout these narratives, but especially in the passage in the third chapter which I have already cited (Mk 3:22-27), it becomes increasingly clear that these debates are actually another facet of this perpetual combat with Satan. Jesus' adversaries are merely tools of Jesus' enemy, the devil.

Christ's Debates with His Adversaries

Finally, Jesus' struggle against ignorance, muddleheadedness, ambition, timidity, and jealousy in his own disciples, marks a fourth phase of his fight against Satan. It has become a commonplace to characterize the second evangelist as unsparing in his criticism of the poor disciples. Observe, for example, the severity of Jesus' reprimand in the fourth chapter, when the disciples seek an explanation of the parable of the Sower. It is to be remembered that this rebuff is found only in the Marcan account. "So you don't understand this parable? Then how will you ever understand all the parables?" (Mk 4:13). Jesus' impatience and criticism (Mark tells us equivalently) is due to his acute sensitivity to the fact that this ignorance, which he is fighting in his own followers, is the work of Satan. Perhaps the most dramatic example of this which Mark has recorded is the occasion when the disciples forgot to bring any bread with them on an excursion across the Lake of Galilee. Jesus warns them about the yeast of the Pharisees. In their deep embarrassment at being caught thus unprepared with provisions for this outing, "they began to argue among themselves and say: 'It is because we are without bread!' But Jesus, aware of this, said to them: 'Why do you think it is because you are without bread? Do you not yet perceive nor understand? Are you so completely muddleheaded? Though you have eyes, do you not see? Though you have ears, do you not hear? Don't you remember when I broke the five loaves among the five thousand?

The Disciples' Ignorance

—How many baskets of fragments did you retrieve?' They told him: 'Twelve.' 'When I broke the seven loaves among the four thousand, how many large baskets of fragments did you retrieve?' They said: 'Seven.' Then he said to them: 'How is it that you don't *yet* understand?' " (Mk 8:16-21).

This ignorance of the disciples is, for Mark, a sign of Satan's hold upon men—even those close to Jesus. The crisis is reached when, immediately after Peter's grand profession of loyalty (Mk 8:29), Jesus begins to reveal to his disciples the real nature of his messianic calling as the Suffering Servant (Mk 8:31). Peter is immediately horrified, and, in Mark's words, "began to scold him" (Mk 8:32). Matthew quotes Peter as saying "God forbid that this should happen to you, Master!" (Mt 16:22). Immediately Jesus wheels on Peter: "Get out of my way, you Satan! The view you take is not God's view, but a much too human one!" (Mk 8:33).

I suggest that in our contemplation we read through the entire Marcan account of the public ministry, observing how, throughout his narrative, the evangelist represents this series of episodes as a struggle between Jesus invested with the Spirit on the one hand, and that evil spirit opposed to God, who is Satan.

THE THREEFOLD TEMPTATION OF JESUS
Matthew 4:1-11

Then Jesus was led by the Spirit into the desert to be tempted by the devil. ²He fasted forty days and forty nights, and in the end he was hungry. ³Then the tempter approached with the suggestion, "If you are the Son of God, command these stones to become loaves of bread." ⁴But Jesus replied, "We read in Scripture, 'Man does not live on bread alone, but by every word that issues from the mouth of God.'"

⁵Next the devil took him to the Holy City, and set him upon the highest point in the temple precincts, with the remark, ⁶"If you are the Son of God, throw yourself down. We read in Scripture, 'He will issue orders to his angels for your sake, and they will support you with their hands, for fear you stumble over a stone.'" ⁷Jesus rejoined, "Scripture also says, 'You must not make trial of the Lord your God!'"

⁸Finally, the devil took him to a lofty mountain-peak, and disclosed to him all the kingdoms of the world with their brilliance, ⁹with the suggestion, "All that will I give you, if you will fall at my feet and adore me." ¹⁰Then Jesus said to him, "Off with you, Satan! We read in Scripture, 'The Lord your God you must adore: him alone must you worship.'"

¹¹At that the devil left him, and suddenly angels came and acted as his servants.

MATTHEW'S RECONSTRUCTION OF JESUS' TEMPTATIONS

Traditional Datum

THE EVANGELICAL TRADITION, as we have seen, guarded the memory of Jesus' testing by the devil. We realize upon reflection that, since there were no eyewitnesses to this struggle, the event must have been related to the disciples by Jesus himself. And it would appear probable, from the way Mark recounts the episode (Mk 1:13), that our Lord had only communicated to his followers the bare fact that at the beginning of his public life he underwent a particularly harrowing experience. This datum was considered of paramount importance by the apostolic Church as the authentic revelation of the true source of man's temptation. Just as Jesus brought the definitive revelation of God's plan of salvation for mankind, so also it is only in the Christian dispensation that the true nature of evil is discovered to us, and the real source of temptation is fully identified. This was the significance which the evangelical tradition perceived in Jesus' confrontation with Satan during forty days in the desert.

In the Old Testament, on the other hand, Israel had, during most of her history, attributed her temptations to God. The temptations of Jesus corrected that misapprehension by laying bare the real origin of such experiences.

Matthew's Amplification

St. Matthew, or perhaps some written source upon which he drew, has amplified the data received from the oral tradition concerning Jesus' temptation by Satan (Mt 4:1-11). I suggest that it can be most helpful in contemplating the event as presented in Matthew's Gospel to realize that the narrative is a construction, that is, an imaginative creation by the inspired writer, which seeks to explore the theological values present in the real event. What indication have we of the literary genre of this narrative? One sign, among several, that we are here dealing with a construction is the presence of Old Testament texts. Each time that Jesus rebuffs Satan, in Matthew's account, he cites a passage from Moses' second discourse to the people in Deuteronomy (Dt 8:3; 6:16;

140

6:13). It will be helpful to recall that although this book is classed as part of the Pentateuch, the books of the law, it is inspired rather by the prophetic than the legal spirit. Its true character may be judged from the fact that the apostolic Church saw in Deuteronomy the blueprint for the messianic community of the end of time. The first chapters of Acts contain frequent citations from, or allusions to, Deuteronomy. We shall have occasion to return to this feature of the book when we discuss this part of Matthew's presentation of Jesus' threefold temptation.

You will have noticed at the beginning of this narrative by Matthew a detail not mentioned by Mark, the fast of Jesus. The "forty days and forty nights" are actually a literary allusion to two famous episodes involving those two great figures of the Old Testament, Moses and Elijah. Of Moses we are told, in the narrative usually referred to as the renewal of the covenant after Israel's sin of idolatry (Ex 34:28), that he "remained with Yahweh forty days and forty nights without eating or drinking, and he wrote on the tablets the words of the covenant, the 'ten words.'" With regard to Elijah, it is narrated of him that, at the beginning of his prophetic career, an angel came to feed him, after which he fell asleep again. The angel came a second time, ordering him to get up and eat. "He arose and ate and drank, and in the strength of this food he walked forty days and forty nights to the mountain of God, Horeb" (1 K 19:8). Horeb is usually considered to be another name for Sinai; hence Elijah returned to the place where Moses had had his privileged experience of God. To Moses had been revealed God's special plan for Israel. Like Moses, Elijah in this same spot was vouchsafed the rare privilege of a theophany, which constituted the inaugural vision that opened his prophetic career (1 K 19:11-13).

You will recall that these two great representatives of the genuine spirit of Old Testament religion will reappear at Jesus' transfiguration. In addition, those two mysterious witnesses who appear in the Apocalypse (Ap 11:4-10) are described as the anti-types of Moses and Elijah. They have power to shut up the sky as Elijah once did (1 K 17:1-7). They have power also to turn water into blood and inflict other plagues like Moses (Ex 7:17-21). Thus Matthew employs this literary allusion, "forty days and forty nights" to depict Jesus' fasting as a recapitulation of the experience of the two greatest religious figures in Israelite history.

In any discussion of the literary development of the triple temptation of Jesus which Matthew has recorded in his Gospel, we cannot afford to forget the fact that Jesus was really tempted.

This fundamental datum of the tradition is unquestionably historical. It shows how truly human Jesus was; how completely he identified himself with the sons of men. Put yourself in his position. He is on the eve of the great mission which he has been sent to accomplish. He is about to embark upon his public life to carry out the mandate he had received from the Father. We all know well enough from our own experience that as we stand on the brink of some important decision and contemplate a project that simply must produce successful results we inevitably feel some hesitation, entertain some misgivings. Perhaps it is not beyond the bounds of possibility that we find ourselves wishing for some assistance far beyond the ordinary, to ensure the success of our venture.

Jesus Christ was human. Jesus was tempted. His temptations are represented in the Matthean narrative as colored by those travesties of the ancient messianic hope of Israel, which were current in the Palestine of Jesus' day. Legends concerning the Messiah appear to have assumed two principal directions. In the first place there was the conception of a prestidigitator Messiah. He was pictured as a kind of Blackstone or Houdini, possessing the occult art of turning stones into bread, or of flying through the air—as a publicity stunt. You may recall that towards the end of this Gospel, after Jesus' death, the religious leaders of Judaism, the "Establishment," tried to slander Jesus by calling him a "deceiver" —a conventional epithet for magicians in the Hellenism of the period (Mt 27:63-64).

The second caricature of his messianic vocation which Satan suggested to Jesus' mind and imagination is the figure of the warrior Messiah bent upon world-domination. That this was also part of the popular messianic mythology is clear from a remark in the fourth Gospel (Jn 6:15). That evangelist tells us that after Jesus had fed the crowd in a deserted spot they wanted to make him king. After all, would not the Messiah, so ran the popular legend, produce manna as Moses once did?

The second significant consequence of the fact that Jesus was really tempted and that he told his disciples about this experience is that he intended to encourage and console them. Indeed, the realization of this fact of Jesus' earthly existence ought to encourage me. Basically, Jesus underwent this experience simply because he was truly human. It would be natural or human enough to have thoughts like those pictured by Matthew flit across the consciousness of a man with a mission like Jesus. How well this mission of his might succeed with the preternatural assistance that Satan could offer! That our Lord repulsed such dangerous daydreaming goes without saying. Matthew shows this most effectively by the sequel to this episode in which we see Jesus call men to help him in his mission, rather than collaborate with the demonic powers.

I have already suggested that Matthew's narrative is a literary construction, inspired, in part at least, by three citations from the book of Deuteronomy. Thus the meagre data, preserved by the oral tradition, have been exploited or expanded following the classical scheme of the three major temptations which the Israelites underwent in the desert. For Matthew, Jesus' temptations are rightly regarded as a true messianic experience. That is to say, Jesus as the new Israel must submit himself to the same three trials once faced by the people of God. This messianic dimension appears to be suggested in the text by the form which two of the temptations take: *"If* you are the Son of God. . . ." (Mt 4:4-6). It had been by being summoned out of Egypt that the Hebrews, as God's people, became God's "first-born son" (Ex 4:22). This adoptive filiation of Israel is asserted by the prophet Hosea: "Out of Egypt have I called my son" (Hos 11:1). God made Israel his people, looked upon the Hebrews as his son, through the covenant struck with them at Sinai. Jesus stands before Satan in the temptation-scene as the representative of the messianic people.

In the desert Israel had been subjected to three great tests. The first is mentioned in the book of Numbers. After the Israelites had eaten the manna for some time, they lost their taste for this mysterious food, and demanded meat. God was angry, but eventually, though Israel had failed this first test, he gave them quail, meat in abundance (Nm 11:4-34).

There was a second occasion, "the day of temptation" at Massah (Ps 95:8—*Massāh* in Hebrew means temptation) when the Israelites demanded water; and they so provoked Moses that he struck the rock twice. As a punishment for this lack of trust in God, Moses was forbidden to enter the promised land (Nm 20:1-13). On this occasion Israel "tempted" God, by committing the sin of presumption.

The third failure of Israel when faced with temptation is the famous episode of the golden calf (Ex 32:1-8). Israel succumbed to a form of false worship, and experienced the divine wrath in consequence.

Matthew's narrative of the three temptations experienced by Jesus represents him as recapitulating the threefold experience of Israel in order to win the victory where Israel fell. Jesus triumphs over Satan, as I have said, by quoting from the very Old Testament book, Deuteronomy, which alludes to Israel's temptations. It is also the book which provided the blueprint for the messianic community, the new Israel—the Christian Church.

The Triple Challenge in Christian Life

There is another sense in which the temptation-scene in Matthew may be considered to follow a classical scheme—the threefold division of temptations found in 1 John 2:16. The author there speaks of "the concupiscence of the eyes, the concupiscence of the flesh, and the pride of life." Since we as religious counter this triple threat to the fulfillment of the will of God in our lives by pronouncing the three vows of poverty, chastity, and obedience, we might profitably consider briefly the risk or temptations which the religious state itself can occasion. No man can, even by taking vows, abdicate his basic responsibility of becoming and remaining a man. As we see from the priestly account of creation in Genesis, God challenged man to accept this responsibility to exercise dominion, to obtain the mastery of certain creatures (Gn 1:28). We might discuss this fundamental human problem under three main heads, suggested by the triple temptation of our Lord, as follows.

There is a threefold challenge which confronts me in fulfilling this vocation of mine to be a real human being: the challenge of earth, the challenge of woman, and the challenge of my own inmost self. It might be profitable to reflect, in this exercise, upon whether, by taking the three religious vows, we are not avoiding the challenge offered by these realities. The Bible appears to indicate that to face the challenge offered by the earth is one of man's ways to salvation. Did not Yahweh, after Adam's fall, command man to wrest his livelihood from the earth? "Because you followed your wife's suggestion and ate from the tree, of which I commanded you not to eat, cursed be the earth through you; in suffering shall you gain your living from it as long as you live. Thorns and thistles shall it produce for you, so that you shall have to eat wild plants. By the sweat of your brow shall you earn your livelihood. . . ." (Gn 3:17-19). It was a penal sentence, this divine decree. Yet in his goodness God also contrived to bring good to man from this very struggle with the earth. If even fallen man can find salvation by attempting to master the earth, as God challenged him to do when the world was young, then even religious men, supported and protected by the material security which a vow of poverty provides, cannot afford to avoid this struggle with the earth. Centuries ago St. Benedict displayed great sensitivity to this fundamental law of human psychology when he prescribed manual labor for all his religious in the Holy Rule (c.48): "because then they are truly monks, if they live by the toil of their hands, as did our fathers and the apostles."

The second challenge confronting every man is the challenge offered by woman. It is woman who provides man with the possibility of being the principle of another man, by begetting a son. Woman provides man with the means of satisfying a basic urge of his nature in a patterned manner. Thus woman helps man become a man by bringing his deepest instincts into subjection to reason, and by giving him a chance to rule. Here we may recall Yahweh's words to the woman in the third chapter of Genesis: "You shall be devoted to your husband, while he shall rule over you" (Gn 3:16). Man must be a principle of order to another. St. Paul, speaking out of his own era and cultural background, once remarked that "the man is the head of the woman" (1 Cor 11:3). Whatever is to be thought of such a statement in our age, it is surely true that, if I am to reach maturity as a man, my emotions, feelings, and imagination must be subject to my reason. Now one of the main contributions which a woman makes to man is to assist him in becoming fully a man, as source of law and order, not only for herself, but in his own life, and in that of their family. If, as a religious man, I decline the world of Eve by my vow of chastity, am I not incurring the risk of refusing the challenge of woman—and so becoming less a man?

The third challenge a man faces, if he is to become a real man is the mastery of his own soul. Any man worthy of the name must accept the responsibility of making decisions. He must choose a course of action and carry it out. A real man reflects upon the outcome of what he feels he ought to do, and he accepts the consequences. He is ready to pay the price. As a religious, who by vowing obedience has left the free disposition of himself to his superiors, I must ask myself whether I am not avoiding this third challenge, the free determination of my own life? Am I guilty of trying to slough off a responsibility which, like the corresponding right, is an inalienable duty to myself?

A real man makes his way purposefully through life. He is not swayed by every wind that blows. He does not blame his own mistakes or attribute his failures to someone else. Jesus Christ, we see from John, was just such a man. "I lay down my life," he says, "that I may take it up again. No man takes it from me: I lay it down of my own accord. I have the power to lay it down, and I have the power to take it up again. This commandment have I received from my Father" (Jn 10:17-18).

Perhaps we are now in a position to see that, in facing these

145

three temptations, Jesus was actually facing these basic human issues. Jesus successfully accepted this triple challenge to his manhood and achieved mastery, where Israel had failed. In imitation of this triumph of my Lord, I also, as a religious, must accept this threefold challenge successfully. I must face up to these same issues, if my life as a human being is to be a success. For my life as a religious cannot be a success unless I am successful as a human being. It is equally obvious, I think, that my life as a priest will not be successful unless, after the example of Jesus, I manage to cope with these problems successfully.

PAUL'S PRAYER FOR HIS PHILIPPIANS
  Philippians 1:9-11

And this is my prayer for you. May your love grow richer and richer yet, through fullness of knowledge and delicacy of apperceptiveness, [10]so that you may learn to prize the true values. May nothing cloud your conscience or hinder your progress until the Day of Christ. [11]May you reach, through Jesus Christ, the full fruit of holiness for the glory and praise of God.

"SIMUL IN ACTIONE CONTEMPLATIVUS"

ST. PAUL WAS VERY FOND of the Philippian community. In fact, the brief, informal note which he wrote to them would indicate that these converts at Philippi were the church of his predilection. The joyful note, struck already in the thanksgiving (Phil 1:3-8), is characteristic of the whole letter. Paul's great affection is revealed at the close of this first paragraph, when he tells them, "God is my witness, how I long for all of you in the heart of Christ Jesus" (v. 8).

His prayer for this struggling little community, which is printed on the preceding page, begs God that these Christians may increase in love and in that true knowledge, which may enable them, under the personal guidance of the Spirit, always to discern the better course of action, "to prize the true values" (v. 10). This prayer of Paul for his favorite church might well express the ambition which, we are told, St. Ignatius had for the Society. Indeed, there is a striking similarity between the spirituality of St. Ignatius and that of St. Paul, despite the fact that when St. Ignatius quotes Scripture (even Paul!), he often misinterprets it in some details. One thinks, for instance, of the popular but erroneous etymology by which he construes "Bethania" as "the house of obedience."

Yet it is perhaps no cause for astonishment that St. Ignatius had the mind and heart of Paul. Certainly Ignatius, like Paul, possessed the genuine Christian spirit, the "mind of Christ" (1 Cor 2:16). However, I believe that the affinity between these two minds was closer than that, and is not fully accounted for by saying that Ignatian spirituality is genuinely Catholic.

In this conference I should like to recall one striking point of resemblance between the mysticism of Ignatius and Pauline mysticism, because I think it reflects the quintessence of the spirit of the Society of Jesus. I mean the relation of mutual interdependence which exists, or ought to exist, between our prayer and our apostolic activity. We can sum it all up in that epithet, which Jerome Nadal used to describe the work and spirit of the Society as he found it embodied in Ignatius Loyola—*simul in actione contemplativus*.

We might begin by setting that famous expression in its context, Nadal's notes on the *Examen Generale,* in order to see just how Nadal understood the relationship which should exist between Jesuit prayer and Jesuit activity. In the second place, I should like to suggest to you the central position which this same conception occupies in the Pauline mystique of the apostolic life.

Here is the passage from Father Nadal: "Father Ignatius, we know, received from God the unique grace of great facility in the contemplation of the most Holy Trinity. This gift of contemplative prayer he received in a very singular manner towards the end of his years on earth, although he had enjoyed it frequently also at other times. At that period, however, he possessed it to such a degree that in all things, in every action or conversation, he was aware of God's presence and felt so great a taste for spiritual things as to be lost in their contemplation. In a word he was *simul in actione contemplativus*—contemplative even while engaged in action, a habit that he was accustomed to explain while remarking: 'God must be found in all things.'

Now we believe that this same privilege, which we are aware was bestowed on Father Ignatius, has been accorded to the whole Society. We feel certain that in the Society this grace of contemplative prayer awaits all of us. We declare it has been joined to [the grace of] our vocation."[1]

These remarks of Jerome Nadal raise two rather obvious questions. What did he mean precisely by describing Ignatius as a "contemplative, even while engaged in action?" Secondly, what grounds could he possibly have had for stating so confidently that the grace of prayer received by Ignatius has been given to each of us with our vocation to the Society?

Let us attempt to answer the second of these questions, which is the easier, first. It is clear to all of us, I am sure, that Nadal cannot mean that the great gift of mystical prayer, which Ignatius enjoyed during the years of his generalate, is going to be bestowed on each of us Jesuits. Nadal knew better than most men that infused contemplation is a completely free divine gift granted to those to whom God wills, when he wills, as he wills. On the other hand Jerome Nadal, as you are aware, was one of those who

1 *Monumenta Historica Societatis Jesu, Epistolae P. Hieronymi Nadal,* IV (Madrid, 1905), 651-652.

played a major role in the establishing of the Society. He was the man in whom Ignatius placed implicit trust because of his grasp of the *Spiritual Exercises* and his profound understanding of the spirit of the Society. For fifteen years, continuously under the first three Fathers General, Nadal toured Spain, Portugal, Germany, Austria, northern Italy, France, Belgium, and Bohemia as Visitor to promulgate the *Constitutions of the Society*. Accordingly, we can take it for granted that Nadal was well aware of that salient feature which, according to modern commentators on Ignatius' spiritual life, distinguishes him from all other mystics. I mean the perfect continuity, in structure or format, of his prayer from the very early period of his spiritual life at Manresa until, when as General, he reached the heights of mystical contemplation.

Father de Guibert, in his book on our spirituality, calls this "mysticism of service."[2] Note how the characteristic feature of this prayer can be discovered in the two famous exercises, that on *The Reign of Christ* [91—98] and that on *Two Standards* [136—147]. The first of these proposes the imitation of Christ as the Jesuit ideal. In it we learn that our apostolic activity is not a question of supererogation, but an essential part of our imitation of the incarnate Son, who, "for us and our salvation descended from heaven," who indeed marshaled every detail of his earthly life with divine singleheartedness, in view of his apostolic and redemptive mission. How then can we hope to be genuine companions of Jesus unless we walk in the steps of the Master and collaborate—to the extent his grace permits us—in this holy work of man's salvation? It is for this reason that in *The Reign of Christ*, Ignatius represents Jesus to us in the full course of his apostolic activity. He begins the series of contemplations on the earthly life of our Lord where the apostolic kerygma began: with Jesus' public ministry. Recall his "composition of place" for *The Reign of Christ*, by which Ignatius indicates that field of activity where, first in contemplation, then in action, I am to attempt to involve myself. "I am to see with the eyes of the imagination the synagogues, towns, and villages, through which Christ our Lord was wont to preach" [91].

Now, we are all quite well aware that those generous aspirations and that apostolic dynamism, which this contemplation aims at unleashing in us, is not meant necessarily to carry the exercitant off to the foreign mission fields. They are directed, rather surprisingly, against our disorderly affections, those basic obstacles to apostolic devotion found in all of us. For, to Ignatius' practical

2 Joseph de Guibert, S.J., *The Jesuits: Their Spiritual Doctrine and Practice* (Chicago, 1964), 50.

mind, this is where the reign of Christ must first be established—
agendo contra suam propriam sensualitatem et contra suum amorem carnalem et mundanum.

What is of paramount importance to appreciate here is the apostolic form of this *agere contra.* For Ignatius this is the characteristic pattern of my work as a Jesuit.

Two Standards, the typically Ignatian exercise, is orientated to an examination of the strategy of the adversary, as well as (and this is its principal aim) the redemptive plan proposed by "our sovereign and true leader, Christ our Lord." You will, upon reflection, realize that in this retreat we have already made the exercise called *Two Standards,* when we contemplated the Matthean account of the temptations of Jesus. You are aware, of course, that this meditation of two banners, or flags, two programs, is simply a concrete illustration of the rules for the discernment of spirits of the second week. It should be borne in mind that this characteristically Ignatian technique is also proposed under the form of service.

If at this point in our reflections we were to give a first approximation of the spirit of the Society, of the type of prayer which should distinguish its members, it is the contemplation of the contemporary plan of salvation in which I as a Jesuit must take my place in order to collaborate with my supreme Father General, Christ our Lord.

To specify this further, however, we must turn now to a consideration of that other question, the first proposed: what is the meaning of Nadal's celebrated phrase, *simul in actione contemplativus?* It is probably easier to say what it is not than what it is. It is certainly not necessarily a mystical grace, infused contemplation. Nor does it imply the subordination of my apostolic activity to the contemplative life, in the sense that I neglect the work assigned me by obedience—particularly that work which for most of us is carried out in the intellectual sphere. This is precisely the area where the problem of the relationship between our prayer and our work can become especially acute. Now, while Nadal explains the phrase by reference to St. Ignatius' aphorism "God must be found in all things," to find God in my work does not necessarily mean liking my work, attaining the goal of perfect self-fulfillment, successfully realizing all my own potentialities, becoming the perfectly balanced man. Nor does this "contemplation in the midst of action" demand some kind of attention to divine things that would distract from my work—even though St. Ignatius does at times appear to assume that the mature Jesuit

151

should entertain a kind of habitual, half-conscious attention to God. That he did not have this in mind is clear from the letter which he wrote regarding Father Oviedo, then rector of Gandia, who wished to lead an eremitical life. "What he [Oviedo] says of the supernatural manner of prayer, in which the presence of God is continual, seems fantastic and erroneous," Ignatius wrote. "Such a thing is not seen in the lives of even the greatest saints, although they have a recollection of God which is more frequent, a consideration of God more real than most men. Such continuity, however, is impossible in the ordinary course of things, even with the most spiritual and saintly man. Such a presence would demand a fixed, immobile attention of the mind which is repugnant to our state as *viatores.*"[3]

What then is the meaning of *in actione contemplativus?* To find the correct answer to this question, we have simply to recall two cardinal points of Ignatian spirituality: one involving the Ignatian concept of prayer; the other, Ignatius' notion of apostolic activity. The first of these concepts is defined by Jerome Nadal. "The prayer characteristic of the Society," he says, "favors execution." We should remind ourselves that when Nadal uses the word "contemplation," he is not speaking of any particular method of prayer, such as those found in the *Exercises.* It is clear from his conferences that he recommends all of them, without excluding even vocal prayer. On the other hand, he does not exclude infused contemplation. By the phrase, "the form of prayer peculiar to the Society," Nadal wishes to indicate the peculiar orientation of our prayer: to the greater glory of God. His remarks are strikingly reminiscent of the words of St. Paul. Nadal says, "the operative principle and the end of prayer is love. That is only to say that prayer tends to the greater glory of God by proceeding from the fullness of love, in such fashion that I should desire by my prayer what I ask and seek to obtain, in order to serve God more according to the vocation and Institute of the Society. Accordingly, *the prayer of the Society favors execution.*"[4]

Thus, for Father Nadal, the most basic and distinctive characteristic of the Jesuit's prayer is that it should immediately incite him to apostolic activity. In other words, our prayer normally should produce in us the conviction that the work we are about to engage upon, or are already engaged on, is good and desirable.

3 *MHSI, S. Ignatii . . . Epistolae et Instructiones,* XII (Madrid, 1911), 648-649.

4 M. Nicolau, *Jeronimo Nadal, Obras y Doctrinas Espirituales* (Madrid, 1949), 307, cited by Raymond Hostie, "Le cercle de l'action et de l'oraison," *Christus* N⁰. 6 (April, 1955) 204, as "le passage le plus décisif de Nadal sur ce point."

Ordinarily indeed, the effects of the divine grace given in answer to our prayer may be expected to furnish some attraction to that apostolic work we have in hand. Yet Nadal knows as well as any of us, that if such divinely conferred taste or relish for the apostolate is a great blessing to be received with gratitude, it is not a necessary consequence of our prayer. What is necessary if the Jesuit's prayer be genuine and not bogus? It should produce, I believe, the characteristically Ignatian virtue of *devotio,* that attitude of mind and heart which allows us to regard ourselves as expendable. It makes us determined to give ourselves promptly and magnanimously to Christ, to be disposed of according to his good pleasure. This awareness of our expendability, this state of readiness to serve, is a supernatural grace; one normally to be sought in our prayer. This *devotio* confers on our work its supernatural character and its meaning. The Jesuit's apostolic activity is born directly, by the special grace of his vocation, from his daily prayer.

This leads to the second Ignatian concept, that there is a necessary continuity between our prayer as Jesuits and our apostolic activity. It might be put more concretely and specifically as follows. There can be no dichotomy between our spiritual and our intellectual life. Nadal gives some illustrations from the life of St. Ignatius that may help us to understand this point. "I recall," he says, "that at the time of my first entry into the Society, Father Ignatius suggested that I devote myself to preaching and to the service of my neighbor. I begged to be excused because of my ineptitude, which was due to my sins and my spiritual poverty. The Father said to me, it is precisely in this way that you will make progress, if you concern yourself with the salvation of your neighbor."[5]

Elsewhere Nadal remarks, "This is what I would like to call the circle of occupations in the Society. If you are occupied with your neighbor and with the service of God in your ministry or in any office, God will help you afterwards more efficaciously in your prayer. And this more effective divine aid will in turn enable you to take care of your neighbor with more courage and spiritual profit."[6]

It seems that St. Ignatius was very sensitive to the fact that any activity, provided it be undertaken according to the divine will (concretely, this means by command of obedience), makes the Jesuit enter more effectively into the contemporary plan of sal-

5 *MHSI, Epistolae P. Hieronymi Nadal,* IV, 650.
6 Cf. Nicolau, *op. iam laudat.* 324-325, cited by Raymond Hostie, *art. cit.* 207 n. 2.

vation. The attitude that is to characterize the Jesuit in the eyes of St. Ignatius is the virtue of *devotio*—commitment—commitment of the whole person. Hence the practical necessity of carrying out in action what as a grace we have received in prayer. Thus, the spirituality of the Society may be represented as a kind of cyclic or circular motion: contemplation which results in action; action which in its turn leads us back with renewed ardor to contemplation. In this house, most of us are engaged in study; and so normally study ought to be the subject of my prayer. In prayer I attempt to gain some insight into the significance of these studies as my present apostolic activity. I should endeavor, with the help of grace, to convince myself that the purpose of my study is connected intimately with the contemporary twentieth century plan of salvation. This is true, not only because it is useful (not certainly because it is painful!), but primarily because, by learning whatever it is I am set to learn, I am cooperating with Christ's design in my world for its salvation.

And Father Nadal stands there assuring me that this prayer, given me with my Jesuit vocation, will be efficacious. I shall certainly receive this grace of *devotio*. I shall be more receptive of the attractiveness of that apostolic activity to which God calls me at the moment.

When we are actually engaged in study it is obvious that there can be no question of trying to recall the divine presence or of turning our thoughts to God. The intellectual life is too demanding, too jealous in itself. If we are going to acquire that academic competence which obedience requires, if we are going to acquire that solid learning, which St. Francis de Sales called an eighth sacrament in a priest, we must give ourselves wholly to this task. The Ignatian virtue of devotion can be practiced very effectively in my studies. Such apostolic activity, my study, is a supernatural operation because undertaken as part of the contemporary plan of the redemption. It is moreover assumed under obedience; and it is accomplished with the assistance of those many actual graces granted in prayer for this specific purpose. St. Ignatius promises us in addition that when we return to contemplation, we do so with renewed effectiveness because of a deepened attraction to prayer. This renewed effectiveness of our prayer will in turn win new graces enabling us to collaborate with Christ more devotedly for the advancement of his reign in our own times.

Paul As the Suffering Servant of God — As I suggested above, it is possible to see in this Ignatian method of contemplation an apostolic point of view which is similar to principles which are characteristic of Pauline spirituality. One of the very striking features of St. Paul's theology of the apostolic life is the original manner in which he makes use of the theme of the suffering and glorified Servant of God, found in the Second Isaiah. We are all familiar with the fourth Servant song (Is 52:13— 53:12), which the liturgy frequently employs during Passiontide. The primitive Christian community of Jerusalem saw in the conception of the Servant of God a prophetic description of Jesus' sufferings, death, and exaltation at God's right hand. The finest expression of this Christological development is found in the second chapter of Philippians, where Paul quotes what was probably a hymn from the Eucharistic liturgy familiar to his Philippians (Phil 2:6-11). This citation is proof that Paul was very much aware of this early Jewish Christian belief that Jesus had fulfilled the role of the *'Ebed Yahweh*. Thus it is all the more astonishing to find that in his letters he constantly applies these Deutero-Isaian texts concerning the Servant to himself. The reason of course for such a daring transposition is Paul's conviction that, in his own apostolic life, the work of salvation inaugurated by Jesus is being carried on. "We are the collaborators of God," he writes to the Corinthians (1 Cor 3:9). "We come as ambassadors on behalf of Christ, so that God exhorts you through us" (2 Cor 5:20). In this passage, Paul describes his apostolic work at Corinth by citing a verse from the second Servant song (Is 49:8): "Since we are Christ's collaborators, we also exhort you not to receive the grace of God in vain, for he says: 'At a providential moment I have heard thee: on the day of salvation I have called thee.' Note," Paul continues, *"now* is the providential moment, *now* is the day of salvation" (2 Cor 6:1-2). In thus considering his own apostolic career as a continuation of Christ's redemptive work as the Servant of God, Paul shows that he is fully conscious of cooperating with the divine plan for the salvation of men in his own day. This lofty view taken by Paul of his apostolic activity, so fundamental to his whole spirituality, is mirrored by the Ignatian concept of the Jesuit vocation as a *servitium sanctissimae Trinitatis*.

One question remains to be answered here. How can I discover the role I am to play in the contemporary plan of salvation? What guarantee have I that in my concrete activities I am in fact a "collaborator with God," "a steward of the mysteries of Christ"? So far as St. Ignatius is concerned, the answer is to be found by the use of the Rules of Discernment of Spirits for the second week [328—336]. Those rules are directed towards keeping generous, zealous souls on the right path. Their aim is to guard those advancing in perfection against delusion. The Rules of Discernment for the first week [313—327] are simply intended to get a person moving, to overcome timidity or sloth. The conception of Christian discernment is central in Pauline moral theology. It is, for him as for St. Ignatius, the principle which he urges his Christians to employ in order to integrate their lives into the contemporary plan of salvation. He writes to the Thessalonian community, "Do not stifle the Spirit: do not contemn the gifts of prophecy, but *scrutinize* them all. Guard what is good: reject every species of evil" (1 Th 5:19-22).

The word, which I have translated as "scrutinize," provides what Dr. Oscar Cullman once called "the key to New Testament morality."[7] We might well call it the key to Pauline spirituality. This act of discernment for Paul comes from the supernatural principle residing within each Christian, which in Romans he calls "the law of the spirit" (Rom 8:1ff.). This discernment, which is to be made by the Christian in every concrete situation of his existence, is carried out effectively with the help of the indwelling Spirit of God, whose dynamic presence provides the certainty that a correct moral judgment has been made. Thus in every individual action which he performs, the Christian must decide the issue for himself, and assume responsibility for it. The Christian must consider all his activity as his personal cooperation with the divine plan of salvation, under the dynamic control and direction of the Holy Spirit. It is upon this principle that Paul relies when, in his letters, he urges his Christians to their duty.

It is noteworthy that Paul does not restrict himself merely to repeating sayings of Jesus. Indeed, he only rarely quotes the Lord. As a matter of fact, Paul has been accused (unjustly) of neglecting Jesus' earthly life and his teaching. Yet it is a striking fact that he does not hesitate to add his own instructions, his own counsels, and even his own commands, to the precepts of Christ. What is more significant here, perhaps, is that the advice he gives in the so-called "moral" sections of his letters is only intended to illustrate or exemplify how the Christian ought to act in a given situation. For Paul is always conscious that the individual must make each decision afresh. It is for this reason he insists, in the text we cited in the beginning of this consideration, upon the need of prayer which proceeds from love and from which our action in turn proceeds. Thus Paul stresses that necessary correlation between contemplation and action, which for Nadal constitutes the specifically Jesuit form of prayer.

This key word in Pauline spirituality, "to scrutinize," I should

---

7 Oscar Cullmann, *Christ et le Temps* (Neuchâtel-Paris, 1947), 164.

like to point out by way of conclusion, also appears in an interesting passage in the letter to the Romans (Rom 12:1-2). It is of special significance for our present discussion, since it shows how well aware Paul is that the source of this Christian discernment is to be found in the Eucharistic sacrifice. Thus we discover another point of contact between St. Ignatius' teaching and Pauline spirituality. According to Father Joseph de Guibert,[8] another main characteristic of Ignatian mysticism, second only to its Trinitarian orientation, is its Eucharistic orientation. St. Paul writes to the Romans: "I exhort you, my brothers, by the mercy of God to offer your whole person as a sacrifice, a living oblation holy and pleasing to God—I mean the spiritual cult you have to offer. Do not fall in with the manners of this world. Let the Christian novelty of your spirit transform you and render you *capable of discerning the will of God*—what is good, what pleases him, what is perfect."

The famous phrase of Jerome Nadal, *simul in actione contemplativus,* expresses the Jesuit ideal incarnate in St. Ignatius. More than that, it defines the peculiar grace of prayer conferred by Christ on each Jesuit with his vocation to the Society. Far from degrading the notion of contemplation by orientating it thus to apostolic activity, it makes us, the members of the Society, conscious of the divine character of our work, because this action is a collaboration in our world today with Christ's plan for men's salvation.

8 De Guibert, *The Jesuits: Their Spiritual Doctrine and Practice,* 53.

SAYINGS FROM THE SERMON ON THE MOUNT
Matthew 5—7

5 [3]Happy, the poor in spirit: theirs is the Kingdom of heaven. [4] Happy, the meek; they will possess the land. [5] Happy, those who sorrow: they will be consoled. [6]Happy, those who hunger and thirst for holiness: they will be satisfied. [7] Happy, the merciful: they will experience mercy. [8]Happy, the single-hearted: they will see God. [9]Happy, the peacemakers: they will be called God's children. [10]Happy, those who suffer persecution for religion: theirs is the Kingdom of heaven. . . .

[48]Be perfect as your heavenly Father is perfect! . . .

6 [15]And whenever you are praying, do not carry on like hypocrites, who love to stand and pray in synagogues or on street corners, for people to see. . . . [7]While you pray, never prattle away like pagans. They think they will win a hearing by sheer force of words. [8]Do not imitate them. God your Father realizes what you need before you ask him. . . .

7 [7]Continue asking, and your petition will be granted to you. Go on seeking, and you will find. Keep on knocking, and the door will be opened for you. [8]Everyone who keeps asking receives. The man who keeps seeking finds. To him who continues knocking, the door will be opened. [9]Would one of you ever hand his son a stone, when he asks for a loaf of bread? [10]Or hand him a viper, when he asks for fish? [11]Now if you, with all your failings, know how to give your children what is good for them, how much more surely will your heavenly Father give what is good to those who keep asking him?

Chapter 16

SERMON ON THE MOUNT: PRAYER
OF PETITION

IN THE FOURTH of the notes for the exercitant during the second week [130] of the *Exercises,* St. Ignatius suggests that we bring to memory frequently the life and mysteries of Christ our Lord commencing with his incarnation down to the place or mystery which I am engaged in contemplating. This attention to the continuity which exists between the various episodes of the Gospel indicates that during the time when we are meditating on the public life of Jesus, the best reading we can take up is the fourfold account of the good news according to Matthew, Mark, Luke, and John. This is an excellent way of helping ourselves assimilate ever more deeply the primary sources of all genuine Christian spirituality.

Continuity in the Gospel Story

In the primitive Jewish Christian community of Jerusalem the Twelve, now become the college of the apostles, exercised a twofold role in their leadership of the Church. They preached the good news to outsiders, their former Jewish correligionists, in order to win them to Christian belief in Jesus Christ. In addition they also gave witness to the Lord within the community. Indeed, it is the written record of this apostolic testimony before the community of the faithful which primarily constitutes the four canonical Gospels. Written by believers for believers, these books are the official source of a deeper knowledge of Christ and Christianity. Accordingly, to return continually to a study of the Gospel text is, I believe, never wasted effort. It invariably produces some new insight, some fresh understanding of the gospel message.

St. Ignatius, being a Renaissance man, wisely arranged his version of the gospel in a manner calculated to catch the attention of his contemporaries. He chose to distribute the evangelical data over what he called four "weeks" in the *Spiritual Exercises.* This ordering of the materials should never cause us to forget that the purpose of the Ignatian Exercises is simply the assimilation of the Christian gospel. In the first week we are expected to grasp, in fact, to experience as far as possible, what life outside the gospel is like, what existence without Christ means. St. Paul has presented a dramatic description of man at enmity with God in the first three chapters of Romans, which has the same purpose as the Ignatian first week. In the contemplations of the second and succeeding weeks of the Exercises, we are guided through an ordered method of assimilating the gospel itself, in order to deepen our awareness of the various phases of the Christian mystery.

Matthew's Sermon on the Mount   I should like to suggest now that we make a contemplation on one of the great events in Jesus' public ministry, the Sermon on the Mount, as St. Matthew has presented it in his Gospel. Our particular purpose in making this exercise will be to impress ourselves with the great importance which Jesus seems to have attached to the prayer of petition. Occasionally, when reading modern writers on prayer and spirituality, one receives the distinct impression that the prayer of petition is low man on the totem pole of prayer. From the New Testament, particularly from the words of Jesus himself, one discerns a quite different scale of values.

The discourse which we call the Sermon on the Mount, like the other great sermons in Matthew's Gospel, is a creation of the evangelist. It has been put together from sayings of Jesus which this author gathered with loving care from many sources. The teaching is the teaching of our Lord: the arrangement, and probably also the presentation of the doctrine, comes from Matthew. What we have before us then is St. Matthew's view of Jesus' basic program for the Christian life. He here presents Christian existence as the perfect flowering of the Old Testament religious spirit. For Matthew, the newness of Christianity springs from one basic insight which Jesus revealed to his disciples: the truth that we are all sons of the heavenly Father. An important corollary flows from this fundamental fact: all men are brothers. I suggest that each of us reread the Sermon on the Mount in order to note how throughout Jesus invariably refers to God as Father: my Father, your Father, our Father, the Father in heaven. Practically no mention of God is made in this discourse which is not accompanied by the loving epithet, Father.

The Beatitudes   The introduction to the discourse consists of eight, or possibly seven Beatitudes. These present concrete examples, illustrated by two classes of saintly Israelites, of the attitudes towards God and our fellowmen, which the practice of the Christian religion demands. The first four Beatitudes are concerned with the poor (*'anawīm*). This Old Testament concept was not restricted merely to a social class. Rather, it denoted those Israelites, who through experience of suffering and continual threat to their very existence, came to acquire a profound sense of their complete need of God. The last four Beatitudes describe the prophet-protectors of the poor, those Old Testament champions of social justice, who in their day preached to their contemporaries the message of the brotherhood of man.

"Happy, the poor in spirit!" Matthew represents Jesus as declaring. By this he would seem to indicate the man who is conscious of his need of God—an attitude as basic to Christianity as it is difficult to learn. When we are young and robust we tend to rely upon our youthful zest and strength. Yet when we become old and wise we do not lean on God, but upon that wisdom which comes with experience and advancing years.

"Happy, the meek!" It is very difficult, if not impossible, adequately to translate the Greek term used in this Beatitude. "Meek" suggests an attitude that is much too negative. The 'anawīm in the Old Testament accepted suffering with courageous patience. This active embracing of misery is connoted by this word. To such men is promised the land, the holy land of Palestine, which in the thought of the prophets becomes a symbol of all the blessings of the messianic age.

"Happy, those who sorrow. . . ." This Beatitude canonizes the attitude of Israel during the Babylonian exile. It was then that she learned the great lesson that the covenant was not merely a privilege, but that it also entailed a grave responsibility. "Happy, those who hunger and thirst for holiness. . . ." Finally, the poor of the Old Testament are praised for their deep-seated longing for "holiness," for the accomplishment of the will of God. This desire is described by the most basic human appetites, hunger and thirst.

The prophets in a second series of Beatitudes are described first of all as "the merciful." The term that Matthew uses here does not mean mere compassion, a feeling of sympathy, but an active remedying of the distressful conditions under which others are forced to live. The "pure of heart," of course, are not those who remain sexually pure, but "the single-hearted," the men of single purpose: "Happy, those who have but one master!"

The prophets were peace-makers *par excellence*. Peace (*shālōm*) in the Old Testament is a symbol for the sum of all the messianic blessings. Peace in the New Testament is characteristically the work of Jesus Christ (Lk 2:14; Col 1:20; Eph 2:14). In the letters of Paul peace is a constant greeting and wish. The peacemakers —the prophets as well as the Christians—are rewarded with the right to be called God's children. If the Son of God has won the honor through his work of redemption to be called "our Peace," the Christian peacemakers actually share in this mission of Jesus Christ, and hence share in his sonship. The prophets suffered persecution for the sake of religion—Elijah, Elisha, Jeremiah, Isaiah. To such as they our Lord promises that, like the poor in spirit, they will obtain the kingdom of heaven.

Jesus' Renewal of Religion   Our Lord's renovation of the ancient religion of Israel, according to the Sermon on the Mount, is orientated towards man's increased awareness of his filial relationship to God as his Father—an awareness which necessarily involves a more profound consciousness of his ties of brotherhood with the rest of mankind. This is hinted at in the Beatitudes. It is seen also to be the main theme which inspires the six antitheses which follow the Beatitudes (Mt 5:21-48): "It was said to them of old . . . but I say to you. . . ." This whole development is summed up and explained by the concluding verse, "Be perfect as your heavenly Father is perfect." Not an easy verse, this, to understand; nor an easy counsel to put into practice. "Perfect"—the word in Greek means "mature." Paul uses the same term (*teleios*) to characterize the Christian who has attained his majority in the faith, and so possesses what Paul calls Christian "wisdom" (1 Cor 2:6). How can we be "mature," as our heavenly Father is "perfect" or "mature"? Clearly, of course, this perfection that is demanded of the Christian is not an attempt to rival God's infinite perfection.

It will help us understand Jesus' meaning here if we recall that the Bible does not speak of God as he is in himself. The Bible is the written revelation of God as he relates to man; hence it recounts God's activities as they affect the human race. Accordingly, to be "perfect as your heavenly Father is perfect" means, I think, that our human lives are to be patterned, as far as is possible for creatures, on the example that God gives us in his relation to us as our Father. We are to become "mature," by growing up into this ideal that we are children of the heavenly Father. God reveals his perfection supremely to us by acting towards us as a Father. We, on our part, will realize the Christian ideal in our lives by acting towards God as his children, and, consequently, towards one another as brothers.

This accent on the filial character of our relationship to God recurs in a later passage where Jesus describes the duties of the Christian people in terms of the three principal religious observances of Judaism: almsgiving, prayer, and fasting (Mt 6:1-24). Again it is the filial attitude of the Christian towards the heavenly Father which is to give these good works their particular character or stamp.

162

However, what concerns us particularly here is what Matthew says about the prayer of the Christian. He understands Jesus to have taught that the prayer characteristic of the Christian inculcates an attitude of preoccupation with God as our Father. Accordingly, at the beginning of chapter six exhibitionism is ruled out, because this kind of prayer demands our simple, single-hearted, filial piety, and that singleness of purpose and detachment from self which is an imitation of God's attitude towards us as displayed consistently throughout salvation history (Mt 6:5-6). Moreover, that mechanical, meaningless repetition, which springs from a superstitious belief that God can be manipulated by human insistence, is excluded. Yet, it is to be noted, perseverance in making our petitions is by no means forbidden (as the sequel will show). "Never prattle away like pagans," Jesus says. God is not deaf, nor is he insensitive to our needs. The ideal form of Christian prayer is exemplified by the Lord's Prayer (Mt 6:9-13).

Since, however, we wish to reserve our reflections on this prayer for a little later in the retreat, we shall review what Matthew adds by way of corollary to the *Pater Noster* (Mt 6:14-34). This filial attitude characteristic of Christian prayer has as its most basic presupposition the forgiveness of our fellowmen, because this is a prerequisite for the right relationship to God as our Father. Above all, whether we be rich or poor, whether we be secure or insecure, our Christian prayer-attitude must include trust in the Father's providential care of us. Perhaps nothing ruins prayer so quickly, or dries up our spirit so completely, as a lack of confidence in God as the Father. This is the burden of those verses (Mt 6:25-34) which state that, in our fight for the mastery of the earth, our dominion over all the threatening forces hostile to our survival, an uncontrolled desire for material security is not Christian. It can indeed afflict the rich, who are referred to first of all (Mt 6:25-30); but it can also afflict the poor (Mt 6:31-32). To those blessed with an abundance of this world's goods, Jesus suggests contemplation of the birds in the sky, the lilies of the field (those floral extravagances which the good God has permitted himself, to beautify the material creation). Your heavenly Father, Jesus says, feeds the birds in the sky, despite the fact that they do not bother to heap up material security. God lavishly provides grass for the countryside and beautifies it with those spring flowers, "the lilies of the field," although he knows full well that tomorrow they will all be cast into the fire and burned. The poor, on the other hand, are reminded by our Lord that their heavenly Father is fully aware how much they need the bare necessities of life, food and clothing.

163

And so upon all, whether secure or insecure, rich or poor, Jesus urges a basic commitment to the establishing of God's dominion in this world and the carrying out of his will. "Seek first the reign of God and his will; and all these other things will be given you" —as a bonus, as a free gift. Note that in urging this commitment Jesus makes mankind a promise which only the Son of God can make with assurance. "*All* these things *will* be given you!" He ought to know. He is God's Son in the fullest, most profound sense of that word.

St. Matthew ends this passage by reminding us that those elements in our human existential situation which are beyond our control remain safe in the hands of our heavenly Father. Our task is simply to cope with those problems in daily living that we can do something about, with which we can effectively deal. The rest is the concern of the Father in heaven.

Such a profound realization of his status as a son of the Father, which Jesus here urges upon the Christian, must ultimately issue in genuine fraternal love for all men. This consciousness of the brotherhood of man is of the very essence of Christianity. Thus, it is at this point in the Sermon on the Mount, at the beginning of chapter seven, that Jesus, who has already recommended the prayer of petition, returns anew to this subject, evidently so dear to his heart. By way of introduction, (Mt 7:1-6), our Lord is at pains to remove one of the greatest obstacles to fraternal love, judgment of our fellowmen. He presents three arguments against this vice, each more perfect, more Christian than the last, until the ideal is reached. Firstly, we shall be judged by our own criteria of judgment—usually rather exacting, when we are dealing with someone other than ourselves. In the second place, we should not judge other men, because we are quite incapable, in our imperfection, of passing any objective, supernatural judgment upon them. Finally, he reveals the best motive: all men are our brothers.

Perseverance in Asking

In the development which follows (Mt 7:7-11), Jesus returns to the theme he has already dwelt upon: the prayer of petition. Now however he insists on perseverance in asking. He urges this because, he assures us, it is always infallibly answered. "Continue asking, and your petition will be granted to you. Go on seeking, and you will find. Keep on knocking, and the door will be opened for you. Everyone who keeps asking receives. The man who keeps seeking finds. To him who continues knocking, the door will be opened." I believe that as we attempt to understand how our petitions are always answered it is essential to recall that the prayer of petition is recommended by Jesus because such asking is for our benefit, not the heavenly Father's. Our Lord has already implied as much when, in addressing the poor, he remarked, "The heavenly Father knows what you need before you ask him" (Mt 6:8). Obviously then the purpose of our requests cannot be to acquaint God with something of which he is unaware. Jesus recommends the prayer of petition to us, in the first place, because its main purpose is always achieved. What is this purpose? To make us conscious of our total dependence as sons upon the heavenly Father. This is that childlike attitude which our Lord will recommend later in this Gospel, by the "parable" of the little child whom he draws into the midst of the disciples (Mt 18:2-4).

In the second place, Jesus insists upon our perseverance in petitioning the Father, because our Father in heaven, who is infinitely more wise, infinitely more provident than any earthly father in acceding to his son's request, will give us what we really need, what we are most truly asking for. And among those "good things" which we shall unquestionably receive is a deeply increased sensitivity regarding our filial relationship to the Father, as also of our relation to all men, who are in fact our brothers. For it is persevering petition to God our Father which most effectively makes us conscious that we are all "in the same boat." By the prayer of petition we are thrown together, made newly aware of our brotherhood, since we are forced to admit that we all share the same existential situation. We are brothers—brothers in need of the help of our common Father. Awareness of our condition ought to help us to treat one another as brothers, as the law of Christ demands. Jesus is very well aware of how difficult it is for any one of us to experience, in a profound and personal way, this sense of family towards other men.

Accordingly, he insists upon perseverance in asking God for what we want. It is not that mechanical repetition (he has already ruled this out) is going to make the heavenly Father hear what he did not hear before! No! the need of repeating our requests lies in ourselves. It is for us, for our benefit. Only gradually, by the experience of humbly and repeatedly presenting our requests with filial piety to the one Father in heaven, do we come to see that we are just like the rest of men. The lesson which we are to learn is the lesson which the Pharisee in Luke's parable found impossible to learn (Lk 18:9-14). For that reason the Pharisee left God's presence unjustified, while the publican, throwing himself completely upon God's mercy and begging for forgiveness, came to realize that he was just like the rest of men; "and he went away justified."

JESUS CONSTITUTES THE TWELVE
Matthew 10:1-20

Jesus summoned his twelve disciples, and gave them authority to expel unclean spirits, and to cure every disease and all sickness. . . .

⁵These twelve Jesus sent on a mission, after giving them the following instructions. "Do not visit pagan territory, and do not enter any Samaritan town. ⁶Go instead after the sheep belonging to the house of Israel, that have been lost. ⁷As you travel, make the proclamation, 'The kingdom of heaven is at hand!' ⁸Cure the sick, raise the dead to life, cleanse lepers, expel demons. You have received a free gift: distribute it freely.

⁹Do not provide yourselves with gold, silver, or copper in your belts; ¹⁰ nor a traveling bag, nor a second tunic, nor a staff. The workman deserves his keep.

¹¹Whatever town or village you visit, make friends with some honest citizen, and stay with him until you leave. ¹²As you enter his house, bless it. ¹³If the house is a deserving one, your blessing will descend upon it. If it is not, your blessing will return to you. ¹⁴If any man refuses to receive you or will not listen to what you say, leave that house or town, and once outside, shake its dust from your feet. ¹⁵I assure you, it will go easier for the district of Sodom and Gomorrah on the day of judgment, than for that town.

¹⁶Remember, I am sending you out like sheep surrounded by wolves. So be shrewd as serpents, but innocent as doves. ¹⁷Be constantly guarded in your dealings with people. They will bring you into court; they will have you flogged in their synagogues. ¹⁸You will be brought to trial before governors and kings on account of me, to testify to your faith before them and the pagans.

¹⁹Now when they hand you over, don't worry about what you ought to say, or how to say it. In that hour, you will be inspired as to what to say. ²⁰It will not be you speaking, but your Father's Spirit speaking in you."

Chapter 17

THE TWELVE: INSTITUTION
AND MISSION

I SHOULD LIKE TO PROPOSE for our contemplation the event *The* recounted in the tenth chapter of St. Matthew's Gospel: the insti- *Life-Situation* tution and mission of the Twelve. One of the contributions made by Form Criticism to our understanding of the Gospels, which can be most useful in giving the Spiritual Exercises, has been to direct attention to the "life-situation" (*Sitz im Leben*). By "life-situation" is meant that historical context in the life of the primitive Church in which the narratives recorded in the Gospels attained their present formulation. It is important to recall that by "life-situa-tion" is not meant the original setting of the event or saying in Jesus' public ministry (when the full import of saying or happening was not comprehended). For their inclusion in the good news, the understanding of their significance brought by the presence of the Holy Spirit in the Church was necessary. Thus Form Criticism forces us to look into the very nature of the Church for the reason a particular episode or saying was preserved in tradition when, as St. John remarks, so very many episodes did not survive, and were not written down (Jn 20:30).

An example may illustrate this very significant point which I am attempting to make here. You recall that very early in Mark's Gospel (Mk 1:16-20; cf. also Mt 4:18-22 and Lk 5:1-11), there is a story concerning the call of two pairs of brothers by Jesus. Moreover, soon after this episode, in the Synoptic framework, there is the narrative of the vocation of Levi or Matthew (Mk 2:14; Mt 9:9; Lk 5:27-28). You may remember that in the *Vita Christi*, we used to read in the noviceship, these episodes were named— and I believe misnamed—the "first call" of these disciples. The impression was thus given that the men, who later became apostles were granted a kind of furlough, after which Jesus came along and called them definitively. Then they really got down to the business of being apostles!

Form Criticism however enables us to see the real reason why, in addition to the account of Jesus' call of the Twelve, these

167

stories of individual vocations should also be narrated in our Gospels. These stories are vocation stories, and they were preserved in the primitive Church to exemplify the ideal response to the call of Christ. If you examine any one of them with some care (the simplest and most skeletal is found in Mark 1:16-20), you will quickly realize that the whole episode comes simply to this. Jesus said, "Come;" and they came. We are not told anything about the disciples' psychological reactions to Jesus' personality. We are not told how these men went about winding up their affairs, how they took leave of those at home before they went. In fact, you receive the distinct impression that they merely walked off, and left their father to pick up the fishnets. Now, we have all had the experience of following a vocation, and I dare say that it was not at all like these stories in the Gospel. Why should we imagine that the first disciples acted in any very different manner from ourselves? The fact is, of course, that the story has been pared down to its bare essentials, because it was preserved only to illustrate the best response to the Christian vocation. This is the point; and anything else would be superfluous.

Jesus Creates the Twelve

Let us turn now to the other story which we wish to contemplate in our prayer: the institution and the mission of the Twelve by Jesus. Why was it recorded in addition to the previous episodes? The Form critic would reply that it corresponds to a different "life-situation" in the early Church. If we reflect a moment and seek to situate this episode in the context of the life of the apostolic Church, we will soon realize that this narrative, which at first might seem to indicate that certain disciples were called twice by our Lord, was actually meant to preserve the memory of an act on the part of Jesus, which the Church of the apostolic age considered to be essential to her own constitution and existence. Thus we come to see that the Church, from her earliest days, obviously believed that Jesus gave clear indications, during his public life, of his intention to found a Church —even though that Church came into being only after her Master's departure from this world; that is after his ascension and his sending the Holy Spirit.

St. Matthew's account of Jesus' institution of the Twelve is a very appropriate subject for contemplation during this ordination retreat. First of all, it is our vocation to be men of the Church. Consequently, we ought to attempt to know this Church very intimately, since we have chosen to live out the rest of our lives by making a very special commitment to the Church by a sacerdotal as well as a religious vocation. The fact that the early

Church carefully preserved this story should interest us, because it informs us that by assembling the Twelve as a collegial body, as the Christians of the apostolic age clearly saw, Jesus revealed his will to preserve unity amongst all Christians by means of this special group of disciples, who later became the apostolic college. True, they were twelve in number. Yet they did not found twelve churches. Rather, in accord with Jesus' intention, they formed one closely knit body whose function was to symbolize effectively that unity which Christ willed for his Church. This fellowship of the Twelve—the word "fellowship" is Paul's favorite word for unity—was to serve as the pattern, the exemplar, (one might almost say, the "efficient cause") of the unity of the entire Church. That the collegial character of the Twelve, that is their role as symbol of unity and catholicity, was recognized already in the apostolic age is indicated by the variations in the lists of the Twelve found in the New Testament. There are four lists of those who made up "the Twelve," you will remember: in the Gospels of Matthew, Mark, Luke, and in Acts—and the names vary perceptibly (Mt 10:2-4; Mk 3:16-19; Lk 6:14-16; Acts 1:13). Such disagreement should not be ignored, or glossed over. Nor should an attempt to harmonize them make us forget the significant fact that what the evangelical tradition considered of paramount interest was Jesus' constitution of the Twelve as a body, not the details of their personal identity. What the Church remembered and recorded in the Gospels was the all-important fact of "the Twelve": she was not concerned to recall them as twelve distinct personalities.

A second reason why this call of the Twelve deserves the attention of those of us who are priests or future priests, is the position of special privilege accorded to Peter in each of these four lists. Peter's primacy is commemorated by his being named invariably at the head of each of these lists. In fact, Matthew implies that Jesus called Peter "the first," not chronologically, but as leader. We ought to reflect upon this significant fact that the primacy of Peter is demonstrated by the forms which these lists had already assumed in the oral tradition. For it means that even within the Twelve, whose function was the preservation of unity, or fellowship, throughout the whole body of Christ, Peter stands as the unique symbol of the oneness of this special fellowship. In his own person (cf. Lk 22:31-32), Peter as head of the Twelve was intended by our Lord to body forth that unity which Christ willed to see amongst his followers, which he bequeathed as a precious heritage to the Church (Jn 17:22-23).

There is a third reason for contemplating this episode, one perhaps particularly significant for us who are not only priests but first and foremost religious—Jesuits. This is the fact that St. Matthew combines with his narrative of the institution of the Twelve, Jesus' instructions regarding their evangelical mission. This shows how conscious the apostolic age was of the essentially missionary character of the Twelve, and through them, of the Church. The Twelve as a group are given the task of spreading and preserving the Christian faith throughout the entire world. It is moreover very necessary for us, who share in it to some degree by our special devotion to the Holy See, that the apostolic office exists fundamentally as a form of service to all men. We learn indeed from this discourse that such service is to be freely rendered to all. Jesus declares, "Gratis have you received, gratis must you give." And Peter's horror, at a later date, over Simon Magus' appeal to his presumed venality—he tried to buy the gift of imparting the Spirit—shows how well the Prince of the Apostles learned that his primacy was principally a primacy of free service.

The final reason for taking this chapter of St. Matthew's Gospel for our contemplation is a very practical one for us who wish to live the Ignatian ideal by becoming "contemplatives in the midst of activity." For the technique, so characteristic of St. Matthew, of disclosing to his reader through the history of Jesus' public ministry the shape and character of the future Christian Church is well exemplified here, as I shall presently show. In consequence, this evangelist teaches me how, by involving myself through prayer in the scenes of the Gospel, I acquire the ability to transfer what I learn there to my own time, my own world, my own religious and priestly vocation in the twentieth century. I venture to suggest that this Matthean discourse provides a striking example of the manner in which the apostolic Church applied the teaching of Jesus to the contemporary situation in which, some twenty or thirty years after her master's death and resurrection, she found herself. I believe that this dynamic adaptation of our Lord's words, this living tradition, can be correctly said to be similar to the technique which St. Ignatius calls the "composition of place." By means of its devoted and profound contemplation of the significance of Jesus' action in instituting the Twelve, the apostolic Church learned, as Matthew here testifies, to solve what was perhaps the greatest problem in the first half-century of her Christian life.

Before discussing the nature and the solution of that problem, however, I must justify my statement that this discourse of Matthew illustrates the vital and dynamic way in which the early Church was accustomed to transfer Jesus' teaching, adapting it to her own "life-situation" (to borrow a term from Form Criticism). Matthew's discourse, as you are undoubtedly aware, consists of two quite distinct sections, each referring to two different historical situations. Verses five to fifteen clearly deal with the immediate task of the Twelve—a quite unpretentious catechetical tour of the hamlets of Galilee. With verse sixteen, however, the whole perspective suddenly changes, and we find ourselves contemplating certain experiences of the Church in the apostolic age. In the first part of the instruction Jesus tells the Twelve that they are not to go near any pagan town nor have anything to do with the Samaritans. Yet in the second section, the Twelve are discovered giving testimony before the pagans and their kings (Mt 10:18). We are thus given a graphic description, in verses sixteen to twenty-five, of the missionary activity of the apostolic college. Matthew's record is invaluable to us who desire to become adept in the Ignatian art of prayer since it reveals how the primitive Church learned to solve her problems and to take her place in the continuing salvation history of the second half of the first century A. D.

What was the problem which I asserted to have been the greatest question which the apostolic Church had to solve? It was, I believe, that of the significance, in Christian salvation history, of the era which lies between the first and second comings of Jesus. The problem may well strike the modern believer as a relatively simple one. Yet all the evidence of the New Testament clearly shows that this was a problem with which the great writers and theologians who created our sacred literature—Matthew, Paul, John, the authors of Acts and Hebrews—were preoccupied. The correct solution, which these men of the apostolic Church discovered by their contemplation of events like Jesus' choice of the Twelve, was this: the period between the first and the second comings of the Lord is significant as "the time of the Church," that period of history when Christian missionaries were given the mandate to bring to all men (and not only their former Jewish coreligionists) the good news designed by the Holy Spirit as a divine message of hope for a world in despair of its salvation. In other words, the theologians who wrote the New Testament learned that this "time between" was not intended by Christ to be spent, as the primitive Church appears at first to have thought, waiting for a proximate, indeed imminent *parousia* of their exalted Lord.

A thoughtful rereading of the first five chapters of Acts will reveal how far from understanding its mission in the world was

Significance of Christian History

the primitive Jewish-Christian community of Jerusalem in the first years after Jesus' departure from this earth. These Christians are depicted as waiting on the holy mountain of Sion for the return of Jesus on the clouds, promised by the two young men in white on the day of his ascension (Acts 1:11). The Christian realization of a truly universalist outlook, with the consequent centrifugal movement, which we recognize as the missionary spirit so characteristic of the Church, was almost entirely missing in these early days. Indeed, it does not seem to have developed to any notable extent until some years after the founding of the church of Antioch (Acts 11:19ff.). It was there during the Eucharistic liturgy that the Holy Spirit opened the age of the missions: "Set Barnabas and Saul apart for me, for the work I have in mind for them" (Acts 13:1-3).

Such then was the fruit of the Church's contemplation of the earthly actions and words of Jesus Christ. It should not be forgotten that our Lord did not tell the Twelve everything during his time with them on earth. Indeed, some of what he had taught them may well have been forgotten. At any rate, from what the Gospels tell us of his teaching concerning the salvation of the pagans, Jesus does not seem, during his earthly life, to have advanced beyond the Old Testament prophets. He announces but once or twice—not too clearly or specifically at that—that the Gentiles are to be called into the Kingdom (Mt 8:11). How or when the mission to the pagans would be inaugurated, Jesus does not appear to have disclosed to the disciples. One has only to read Acts' account of the conversion of Cornelius and his household to realize the trouble in which Peter became embroiled, although he was the acknowledged leader of the Jerusalem community, when he took the unprecedented step of admitting some Italians into the Jewish Christian Church (Acts 10:1—11:18). In its social aspect, of course, the problem was a problem of integration; and we all know very well that such problems are not solved quickly or easily. The question for the Jewish-Christian community was whether pagans might licitly be permitted to become Christians without first becoming Jews. The complexity of the whole issue may be gauged by the fact that evidently several extraordinary signs on the part of the Holy Spirit were necessary before anything effective was actually done. Such an unusual episode, however, serves only to remind us that, for the most part, the apostolic Church learned to live her life in faithful compliance with the will of Jesus by means of the contemplation of those episodes which had taken place during the time he spent on earth.

These the Church preserved in her living memory for some thirty or forty years before they were written down.

I should like to take cognizance here of an important principle of faith upon which the validity of such transfers as we have been speaking about reposes: the peculiar quality of the divine *commercium*. God's manner of bringing men to the knowledge of salvation is always consistent with itself in every age, in any culture, in either the old or the new dispensation. Paul's theology shows how deeply penetrated he was with this conviction. Stephen's *apologia pro vita sua* as we have it preserved for us in Acts, reposes upon this same belief (Acts 7:2-53). Accordingly, we are justified in concluding that by involving myself, through the Ignatian *contemplatio*, with the events and teaching of Jesus' earthly life, I may learn inevitably, by the operation of the same Spirit who informed the Twelve and guided them in their direction of the young Christian Church, how to insert myself into the contemporary plan of Christ for my own era, my own culture, my own country.

Permit me one brief illustration in evidence of my statement that Paul in his theology employs as an operative principle the conviction that God, in his relations with mankind, is always consistent with himself. In Romans 1:16-17, Paul states: "I am not ashamed [he actually means: I am proudly confident] of the gospel: it is God's dynamic power unto salvation for every believer, first the Jew, then the Greek. For through it God's justice is revealed from faith to faith. As Scripture has it: 'My just man shall live by faith.'" The "Scripture" which Paul cites here is the prophet Habakkuk (Hb 2:4). By "the justice of God" which the gospel reveals is meant that divine saving action of God, proclaimed by the Deutero-Isaiah (cf. Is 45:21; 46:13; 51:5; 56:1). This for Paul has been definitively revealed by the Father's action in the death and resurrection of Jesus Christ, which is the heart of the gospel (Rom 3:21-26; 4:25; 8:3-4).

What is the meaning of this citation from Habakkuk? At the time of the Chaldaean invasion, the prophet declared that the man who put his trust in Yahweh, instead of in power politics or military force, would save his life. He would live through this national crisis and come out unscathed. Paul sees a deeper meaning in this promise, which transcends the historical circumstances of the Chaldaean attack on Palestine. It is no longer a mere question of saving one's skin. He sees the Christian significance of this action of God in history, functioning through the gospel. Hence, from this specific historical instance referred to by

Habakkuk, he develops the following general theological principle: the man justified by faith in Christ will attain Christian salvation through God's dynamic action. But since it is by the hearing of the gospel that men come to believe (Rom 10:14), this "obedience of faith" (Rom 1:5), the hearkening to the good news, is the work of divine grace leading to salvation. For the gospel, in Paul's eyes, does not consist merely of the human words through which it is articulated. Nor does "gospel" mean a series of sound waves which a preacher may transmit on the ether. It signifies primarily that divine dynamism, or interior grace, which effects this salvation within man's innermost being. This activity of the Holy Spirit sent by the risen Christ into the hearts of the Christian faithful is the prophetic fulfillment, as Paul sees so clearly, of that power of Yahweh in the Old Testament which saved the trusting Israelite from the threatening might of the Chaldaean. For Paul, God's action whether in the Old or in the New Testament is consistent with itself. It is this theological principle, I believe, which justifies the Pauline technique of applying this text from Habakkuk to what appears to be a totally different context, and a completely different situation. For Paul has clearly transposed the prophet's meaning. He has, if you will, discovered the "fuller sense" of this Old Testament citation. The validity of Paul's interpretation is guaranteed by the truth that God deals with man in basically the same way throughout the course of sacred history.

Living Character of Tradition Our purpose in contemplating Jesus' actions and words in the episode of his sending the Twelve on an evangelical tour of the Galilean villages has been to observe Matthew's technique of employing a double perspective in his account of this important event (Mt 10:5-15; 16-25). To this evangelist, Jesus' mission of the Twelve is a symbolic act, which foretells the missionary work of the apostles in the first years of the Church. Thus Matthew testifies to an important characteristic of the living tradition: its continual adaptation by the apostolic Church to the concrete situations, the ever-changing experiences and new problems which she confronted. Our evangelist shows us how the leaders of the Church discovered answers to these contemporary questions through the contemplation of Jesus' earthly career. They did not hesitate to transfer his teaching to their own Christian lives and to the circumstances in which their missionary zeal involved them. They molded the living doctrine of the Master, in faithful conformity with his mind, to the current needs of the Christian people; and so they developed its potentialities through vital

174

contact with the historical process which is the life of the Church.

I suggest that we might profitably employ this striking example of the assimilation and evolution of Jesus' teaching, in order to appreciate how I may apply it to my own situation at the present day. Through my contemplation of this Matthean narrative, I may hope, with grace, to become personally involved in this scene from the Gospel, in order to learn better what position I ought to take in the continuing history of salvation in which I now, as once the members of the apostolic Church, am to become engaged.

THE MULTIPLICATION OF THE LOAVES
John 6:1-15

After that, Jesus went off to the other side of the lake of Galilee or Tiberias; 2but a large crowd followed him, because they had seen the signs that he was working upon the sick. 3Jesus went up the mountain, and sat down there with his disciples. 4Now it was near Passover, the feast of the Jews. 5As Jesus raised his eyes and saw that the crowd coming to him was large, he said to Philip, "Where can we buy bread enough for these people to eat?" 6This he said to test him, since he himself knew what he would undoubtedly do. 7Philip answered him, "All the bread you could buy with two hundred days' pay would not be enough to give each man a bite!"

8Andrew, one of his disciples (Simon Peter's brother), said to Jesus, 9"There's a lad here with five barley loaves and two fish. But what use is that among such a crowd?" 10Jesus replied, "Make the people sit down." Now there was plenty of green grass at that spot. So the people sat down, to the number of about five thousand.

11Then Jesus took the loaves, gave thanks, and distributed it to the reclining crowd. He did the same with the fish; and they had all they wanted. 12Now when they had eaten to satiety, Jesus said to his disciples, "Pick up the left over scraps, so that nothing be lost." 13So they picked them up, and filled twelve baskets with what had been left over from the five barley loaves by those who had eaten.

14At the sight of this sign which Jesus had just worked, the people said, "He is for sure the Prophet who is to come into the world!" 15Jesus however was well aware that they would come to take him by force and make him king; and so he fled again into the mountain—this time by himself.

Chapter 18

JESUS FEEDS THE MULTITUDE

I SUGGEST THAT WE TAKE for our contemplation an episode *Creative* which the apostolic Church regarded as a most significant event *Character of the* in Jesus' Galilean ministry: the feeding of the crowds in the wilder- *Gospel Record* ness. I propose that we contemplate this important happening as the author of the fourth Gospel represented it to himself (Jn 6:1-15). The story, as you know, is told by all four evangelists, each portraying it in the manner which appealed most to himself. Accordingly, if one of the other Gospel accounts is more helpful to anyone, he should feel free to use it as the *historia* for his prayer. The incident is found in Luke 9:10-17. Matthew has two accounts, which, I believe, are doublets, that is, two versions of a single happening (Mt 14:13-21; 15:29-39). Mark likewise has recorded two accounts, which probably came to him from two different traditions (Mk 6:30-44; 8:1-10).

It will appear, even on a casual reading of these various narratives, that they do not agree in a good many details. Rather than regard this as a disadvantage or a cause for concern, however, we ought to look upon this feature of these accounts as an advantage, because each account reflects the personal approach of its author to this mystery. It represents some facet of his Christian religious experience, of his spirituality. Moreover, each of these diverging accounts forms part of the word of Christ in the New Testament Scriptures. Accordingly, to follow the common tendency to choose but one inspired version of a given episode, while ignoring the others, is really to deprive ourselves of some of the treasure which Christ through the evangelists has left us to live upon.

It may not be out of place here to remind ourselves that the Gospels come to us incarnated, so to speak, in each sacred writer's response of faith to the mystery of Jesus Christ. This holds good not only for the Gospel accounts of Jesus' actions, but also for the record of his words. We can never afford to forget that all the words in Matthew's Gospel are, in a very real sense, Matthew's words—even those which Jesus is represented as uttering. I might emphasize this by reminding you that it is the words of the evangelists, not the words of Jesus, which are inspired. The words of Jesus were the very words of the Word incarnate; they had no need of any such aid as inspiration. Besides, Jesus did not write his words down: it was the evangelists who wrote them down. Now while our own devotion to our Lord—and perhaps also the demands of a certain nineteenth century Apologetic—might make us wish to recover the very words of the Master (*ipsissima verba Jesu*), we should not fail to see that no such concern is evinced by the evangelists or by St. Paul. This is only too obvious from the liberties which all these inspired writers habitually take in recording the sayings of Jesus. They do not hesitate to reformulate them, or, indeed, even to place them in a quite different context from that in which these logia were set in the oral tradition—a procedure which frequently gives them an almost totally new meaning. The real concern of the apostolic Church and of the sacred writers was to safeguard the true meaning of the Master's teaching with utter loyalty. To this orthodox interpretation the early Church clung with all the veneration and tenacity of her Christian faith. However once she had grasped the sense of Jesus' doctrine, she did not hesitate to apply his words to her own existential situation in her on-going history of the first Christian century. There are many examples of this in the Gospels. One striking instance is found in the Matthean explanations of the Sower (Mt 13:18-23), and of the Cockle (Mt 13:36-43). It appears probable that some of the applications derive from the experiences of the early Church, rather than from our Lord's ministry in Galilee. There is question, for instance, of organized persecution (Mt 13:21), of "the deception of riches" (Mt 13:22). Now in the agrarian, peasant culture of Galilee in Jesus' day it is very difficult to see what such phrases could have meant. When however we turn to the Acts of the Apostles, the story of Ananias and Sapphira illustrates how, even in the early Church, there were those who might fall away through "the deception of riches" (Acts 5:1-11).

In the explanation of the Cockle we are told that "the field" symbolizes the universe, the cosmos. This was assigned as field of activity to the apostolic preachers. Jesus, on the other hand, insists during his own lifetime that their efforts like his own are to be restricted to "the sheep that are lost of the house of Israel" (Mt 10:6; 15:24). Here again we seem to have an application to her situation in the early years by the apostolic Church of Jesus' words, rather than a literal recording of what he actually said.

178

To return to the subject of this contemplation, I said earlier that Matthew and Mark present two accounts of what was actually a single event: the feeding of the five thousand (Mt 14:13-21; Mk 6:30-44), and the feeding of the four thousand (Mt 15:29-39; Mk 8:1-10). The fact that both evangelists—the only two who give us two accounts of the incident—in an editorial passage present the reader with a reference by Jesus to these two accounts as separate happenings (Mk 8:18-21; Mt 16:9-10) is not necessarily any proof that there were two episodes. It is far more likely that they simply recorded two varying accounts of the same miracle.

Such a procedure as this should not surprise us. Our evangelists had a good precedent for it in the Old Testament. There is, for example, the famous story of Abraham and Sara and the ruse they pull on the pharaoh of Egypt (Gn 12:10-20). In a later chapter, they are represented as working the same trick successfully on poor Abimelech in Gerar (Gn 20:1-18). Now, one might feel that since Abraham had such success with this strategy in Egypt, he would naturally think it worth another try. However when, in a still later section of Genesis, we find Isaac and Rebecca in Gerar successfully employing the same technique on the same Abimelech (Gn 26:6-11), even the most credulous minds begin to wonder whether, as all modern Old Testament commentators assert, this is not simply the same story told over three times.

This of course puzzles us, makes us, perhaps, a bit uneasy. We would not write a story in this way. We might indeed fear lest such a procedure provide a handle for those who wish to attack the historical character of all biblical narratives. We should learn to "go back in spirit to the ancient Near East," as Pius XII has directed,[1] and attempt to appreciate the vast difference in methodology between Israel and that of the modern historiographer. The ancients did not have the sharply honed critical sense which characterizes present day historians. They simply accepted the sagas, legends, stories about the great men of the past without attempting to sift the evidence and recover the past "wie es eigentlich gewesen war." But Israel's writers possessed one incontrovertible advantage: they held in great respect the varying traditions, oral or written, which contained precious memories of their distant past; and they wrote them all down faithfully. This painstaking care to preserve all the memories concerning the patriarchs by the authors of the Pentateuch has been well known ever since the days of Julius Wellhausen. Modern scholarship recognizes at least four primary sources which stand behind

1 "omnino oportet mente quasi redeat interpres ad remota illa Orientis saecula. . . .", *Acta Apostolicae Sedis*, XXXV (1943), 314-315.

the composition of these books. Indeed, it is of paramount importance to appreciate the consummate art with which the writers combine these divergent traditions represented by these different sources. In the minds of the inspired writers, each of these traditions was sacred, and hence well worth preserving. Thus, in the account of the animals entering the ark, we are left wondering whether there were only pairs of all living creatures (Gn 7:14), or whether seven pairs of clean animals were admitted and a single pair from the unclean (Gn 7:2).

This solicitude on the part of the sacred writers to preserve the various modalities of the traditions handed on to them explains why Matthew and Mark have recorded a second version of Jesus' feeding of the crowds by multiplying the loaves and fish. The only notable differences in the two narratives are numerical—the number of persons fed—five thousand in the first instance, four thousand in the second—, the number of loaves and fish, and—perhaps most significant of all—the number of baskets of scraps collected at the end. Luke and John relate but one account of the incident (Lk 9:10-17; Jn 6:1-13). We may note the prominent part played by the Twelve in the Matthean and Marcan accounts of the first multiplication of loaves. Even though none of the evangelists expressly mentions the phrase, "the Twelve" in the beginning of his narrative, still, when each comes to the gathering up of the scraps of food, he points out that there were twelve basketfuls (Mk 6:43; Mt 14:20; Lk 9:17; Jn 6:13). In addition, Lk 9:12 explicitly refers to "the Twelve."

By contrast, the second account in both Matthew and Mark features the number seven. There are seven loaves (Mk 8:5; Mt 15:36). The number of fish is not mentioned; and "the disciples" (there is nowhere any reference to "the Twelve") gather seven baskets of scraps (Mk 8:8; Mt 15:37).

Now, while the traditions preserved in the early Church regarded the Twelve as an institution going back to Jesus, which ultimately evolved into the apostolic college, there was another body of specially selected men, not created by Jesus, but by the Twelve, who were called "the Seven" (Acts 6:1-6). They are popularly referred to as the first deacons. This group were appointed to assist the Twelve in the temporal administration of the primitive community (the phrase, *diakonein trapezais*, means either "to serve tables," or "to keep accounts"). They also preached the gospel and conferred baptism. These zealous men, you will remember, were Hellenists. The list of their names (Acts 6:6) would appear to indicate that their language was Greek, not Aramaic. Accordingly, it is not implausible that this second version of the feeding of the crowds comes down from traditions preserved by the Hellenistic branch of the Church, a sign of its veneration for the Seven who were Hellenists. On the other hand, the first account enshrines the Aramaic-speaking Christian tradition, deriving from some source in which the Twelve enjoy prominence. Whether or not such an explanation be correct, it has the merit of reminding us of the respect we should display towards all the traditions which the evangelists evidently regarded as sacred. There should be no question of having to sacrifice one, or attempting to select one which is considered to be more accurate. Since each account is equally inspired, each holds a message for us, each is the legitimate object of our loving contemplation.

We may now ask why this episode was considered so very important in the Gospel tradition? The answer to this question is not hard to find: this event was regarded as a parable-in-act, or a kind of mimed prophecy of the Eucharist. Among the many foci of interest, which the Form Critics enumerate as influences governing the selection and preservation of the episodes connected with our Lord's public ministry, the Church's liturgical interest figures prominently. Thus certain sayings and actions of Jesus were handed down in a liturgical formulation. Others, like the episode we are contemplating were meant to explain the principal act of the Church's public worship, the celebration of the Lord's supper, the Mass. Indeed, there are several narratives in the New Testament which display this same Eucharistic dimension. I am thinking, for instance, of the story of the two pilgrims returning to Emmaus, met by Jesus after his resurrection, who finally recognize him in "the breaking of bread" (Lk 24:13-35). There has been much discussion as to whether our Lord actually celebrated the Eucharist with these disciples. That Jesus did so is highly improbable. However, I do think that the story was told in such a way as to suggest the practice of the Eucharist, because in the apostolic age this incident was considered useful for the instruction of the faithful in the theology of the Blessed Sacrament. This was probably because it stresses the fact of the presence of the risen Jesus, even though that presence went unrecognized at first by his table companions.

There is another interesting illustration of stress on the Eucharistic motif in the famous narrative of the shipwreck on Paul's journey to Rome (Acts 27:33-36). You may recall that on that occasion Paul makes a speech in which he says, "Fourteen days now you have stood watch, without eating anything. I beg of you to take some food; it is necessary for your health. Not a hair of your heads will suffer harm!" The Greek word for health (*sōtēria*), as I have already pointed out, also means salvation, that "life" which the Eucharist nourishes (Jn 6:51). Now while it is quite inconceivable that Paul would actually have consecrated the bread in the circumstances, or distributed the Blessed Sacrament to the pagan Roman soldiery, yet the incident is narrated in such a way as to suggest to a Christian reader certain facets of the doctrine of the Eucharist.

With respect to the episode of the multiplication of the bread, the liturgical interest which inspired its preservation has also affected the manner in which the story is told. The Eucharistic significance of this event is implied in the Mass formula in our liturgy of the Roman rite. The recital of Jesus' institution of the Eucharist in the Latin Mass, which begins: "Qui pridie quam pateretur . . .," contains one little phrase found in no New Testament account of the Last Supper, "et elevatis oculis in coelum." The words are found, however, in all three Synoptic accounts of the feeding of the five thousand (Mk 6:41; Mt 14:19; Lk 9:16). This obviously important detail has been taken by the Church out of the Gospel accounts of this episode, and inserted into her liturgical recital of the Last Supper. The didactic purpose of such a procedure is clear: the Church wishes to underscore the Eucharistic relevance of this miracle.

Incidentally, our advertence to this technique on the part of the author of the canon of the Roman Mass provides us with a new insight into, and a deeper appreciation of certain techniques employed by the evangelists in the creation of the Gospels. They, like the sacred writers of Israel, are certainly concerned with the historical. Occasionally however this concern may be subordinated to some other higher purpose, viz. doctrinal instruction. The Church undoubtedly considers that in this part of the Mass she is dealing with an historical happening: Jesus' institution of the Eucharist at the Last Supper. Yet this narrative is intended to be principally a liturgical recital. Such a liturgical recital is surely based upon real events, still its purpose is broader than that of a merely factual account of what occurred on that solemn occasion. It has also a didactic and theological purpose. As a consequence, the Church introduced a detail into her account of the Last Supper, "raising his eyes to heaven," which she was perfectly well aware belonged in another historical context in the Gospels, because she wished to draw our attention to the relationship between these two episodes.

The Eucharistic motif is clearly operative in all six accounts of the feeding of the crowd (Mt 14:13-21; 15:29-39; Mk 6:30-44;

8:1-10; Lk 9:10-17; Jn 6:1-15). Throughout these narratives there is consistent effort to indicate the significant actions of Jesus by using the very terms employed in the description of what he did at the Last Supper. "Taking (*labōn*) bread ("the five loaves and two fish," or "he took the seven loaves and the fish") . . . he blessed (*eulogēsen*) it (or, "giving thanks: *eucharistēsas*"), and he broke (*eklasen*) the bread . . . and he gave (*edidou, edōken, diedōken*). . . ."

The variation on the second term, *eulogēsen*, which appears in Luke's single account and in the first of the two narratives in Mark and Matthew, is informative. The verb *eucharistein*, "to give thanks," became in the apostolic age a technical term for the celebration of the Eucharist. It replaces *eulogēsen* in both Mark's and Matthew's story of the feeding of the four thousand, as well as in the Lucan and Pauline versions of the Last Supper.

Another point to be noted is that in all these accounts the bread is considered much more important than the fish. This is especially noticeable in the second accounts of both Matthew and Mark, and in the single narratives of Luke and John. An example of this tendency to ignore the fish (which have no Eucharistic significance) may be seen in the form of Jesus' question (in three of the narratives by Mark and Matthew), "How many loaves of bread have you?" (Mk 6:38; 8:5; Mt 15:34). In fact, in the second Marcan episode, the fish are not mentioned in the disciples' response to Jesus: they are introduced merely as a kind of *hors d'oeuvre*, in passing (Mk 8:7); and at the end of the repast it is only the scraps of bread which are collected, according to John 6:13 at least, because it is the bread which is really significant in the purpose of this miracle.

The Johannine account is the version which I should like to suggest for our contemplation. "After that, Jesus went off to the other side of the lake of Galilee or Tiberias; but a large crowd followed him because they had seen the signs that he was working upon the sick" (Jn 6:1-2). These Galileans had witnessed Jesus' "signs" (John's favorite word for miracle); yet, as we learn later from Jesus' own words (Jn 6:26), they had not perceived the symbolic nature of this wonderfully compassionate action of his. A sign, after all, is meant to convey some meaning. The Eucharistic significance of this miracle went unheeded. "Believe me when I tell you this: you are looking for me because you ate your fill of the bread, *not* because you saw *signs!*"

"Jesus went up the mountain and sat down there with his disciples. Now it was near Passover, the feast of the Jews" (Jn 6:3-4).

Johannine Version

The Passover, of course, held a special Eucharistic significance for the early Church, because Jesus had instituted the Eucharist during a Passover meal celebrated with his disciples before he suffered. John alone mentions the proximity of this great Israelite feast.

"As Jesus raised his eyes and saw that the crowd coming to him was large, he said to Philip, 'Where can we buy bread enough for these people to eat?' " (Jn 6:5). In Matthew and Mark we are given the impression that the crowd came to Jesus to be taught (Mk 6: 34), or to have their sick cured (Mt 14:14). John however implies that they came simply to be fed: on catching sight of the crowd, the first question Jesus asks shows his concern about feeding them. Note that it is Philip—according to John—to whom our Lord puts this question. Philip is one in whom the author of the fourth Gospel has a special interest. In John's account of the Last Supper, it is Philip who says to Jesus: "Show us the Father, and we will be content" (Jn 14:8).

Of course, forty or fifty dollars worth of bread would not have been enough to feed this huge crowd of people, as Philip observes (Jn 6:7). "Andrew, one of his disciples (Simon Peter's brother) said to Jesus, 'There's a lad here with five barley loaves and two fish. But what use is that among such a crowd?' Jesus said: 'Make the people sit down.' Now there was plenty of green grass at that spot. So the people sat down, to the number of about five thousand. Then Jesus took the loaves, gave thanks, and distributed it to the reclining crowd. He did the same with the fish; and they had all they wanted" (Jn 6:8-11).

One typically Johannine feature of this narrative should not be overlooked: Jesus is here represented as handing out the food personally to the crowd. In the other Gospels it is explicitly stated that Jesus gave it to the disciples who in turn gave it to the crowd. St. John omits this detail deliberately: he wants to remind his reader that it is Jesus, the Messiah, who feeds his people in the wilderness, as popular tradition expected. More important—he wishes to point out and stress the important truth that, in the Blessed Eucharist, Jesus himself gives us his own body and blood as our food.

"Now when they had eaten to satiety, Jesus said to his disciples, 'Pick up the left over scraps, so that nothing be lost' " (Jn 6:12). This, once again, reveals the strongly Eucharistic orientation of the Johannine narrative. It commemorates the great care which the Church has always displayed towards the Blessed Sacrament. "So they picked them up, and filled twelve baskets with what had been left over from the five barley loaves by those who had eaten" (Jn 6:13). Observe that there is no mention of the fish at all, as John concludes his story.

"At the sight of this sign which Jesus had just worked, the people said, 'He is for sure the Prophet who is to come into the world!' Jesus however was well aware that they would come to take him by force and make him king; and so he fled again into the mountain—this time by himself" (Jn 6:14-15). The episode, John remarks, did not produce in the crowd even an elementary understanding of Jesus' mission. In fact, it seems to have distracted them from any proper insight into Jesus' vocation. These people come to the conclusion that he is the answer to Jewish popular messianic expectations, and so they want to honor him in their own way, by making him king. Jesus however has come into the world, has become flesh and blood (Jn 1:14), in order to give his flesh for the life of the world (Jn 6:51). He was indeed born to be king; but only to "give testimony to the truth" of the divine revelation he brings (Jn 18:37).

While this "sign" does not have its desired effect upon the Galilean crowd, it does constitute a fitting introduction, for John's Christian reader, to the discourse on the Bread of Life, which presents the evangelist's doctrine regarding the Eucharist.

It is perhaps significant that the episode of the multiplication of loaves is related by all the evangelists before they recount the event which forms the highpoint of our Lord's public life—Peter's profession of loyalty. It is narrated also before the account of Jesus' transfiguration, which forms the sequel to the Petrine confession of faith in the Master's messiahship. The facets of the mystery surrounding Jesus which these narratives reveal are essential for a fruitful understanding of the Eucharistic teaching which Jesus willed to suggest by his action on this occasion. He acts out through this miracle—as by parable—the significant elements of a central article of Christian faith which the early Church, in the light of the Holy Spirit, will expound to the faithful. This doctrine has received its classic New Testament expression in the Johannine discourse on the Bread of Life (Jn 6:26-65).

Chapter 19

OUR LADY IN THE LIFE OF THE APOSTOLIC CHURCH

The Mother
of Jesus

IN THE CONSTITUTION ON THE LITURGY, promulgated by the Second Vatican Council, the Church declares that she has always venerated the Mother of God in a special way, because in her she beholds the perfect image of what she herself is, and what she hopes to become.[1] I suggest that we consider here the place which our Lady held in the faith and the devotion of the apostolic Church from the evidence provided by the New Testament.

Mary's basic role, most frequently alluded to by the inspired writers of the apostolic age, is expressed by the title, "the mother of Jesus." In St. Mark's account of our Lord's visit to Nazareth, Jesus is described as "the son of Mary" (Mk 6:3). While this reading is not unanimously attested in the manuscript tradition, it is accepted as genuine by the better modern editors. Moreover, further evidence that this was the primary reason for the early Church's veneration of Mary is provided by Acts 1:14. After giving his list of the apostolic college, St. Luke depicts the disciples as united in prayer with "Mary, the mother of Jesus."

The third Gospel records the very beautiful testimonial tendered Jesus by an unknown woman (Lk 11:27-28). It was a custom of that age to laud a man by praising his mother. This woman calls Jesus' mother, our Lady, "happy," because she has given birth to such a son. "Happy, she who bore you and nursed you!" The Son of God in his reply concurs entirely with this evaluation of his own mother; indeed, he uses the occasion to point out her true greatness: her total, persevering commitment to God's will. "Indeed; happy, they who hear the word of God and keep it!"

In the fourth Gospel our Lady is twice referred to by the title,

---

1 "In celebrating this annual cycle of Christ's mysteries, holy Church honors with special love the Blessed Mary, Mother of God, who is joined by an inseparable bond to the saving work of her son. In her the Church holds up and admires the most excellent fruit of the redemption, and joyfully contemplates as in a faultless model, that which she herself wholly desires and hopes to be." (Constitution on the Sacred Liturgy, no. 103)

"the mother of Jesus": at Cana (Jn 2:1), and on Calvary (Jn 19:25). In the Apocalypse, the only prophetic book of the New Testament, we have that grand tableau in a series of symbolic images, where the mother of the Messiah appears as "a woman clothed with the sun, and the moon beneath her feet, and upon her head a crown of twelve stars" (Ap 12:1). These scriptural passages demonstrate clearly that the divine motherhood of our Lady was from the very earliest days of the church the principal reason and source of that great veneration in which she was held by the Christian faithful.

Nowhere perhaps is this devotion attested so strikingly as in Luke's account of our Lady's visit to her cousin Elizabeth in the Judean hill country. Elizabeth is represented by the evangelist as declaring, "Who am I, that 'the mother of my lord' should come to me?'" (Lk 1:43). There are two significant features of this verse which reveal the Mariological interest of the apostolic age. The first detail is Luke's application to Mary of the title "the mother of my lord." According to ancient Near Eastern court protocol this honorific title was conferred upon the queen-mother, who after the king was the most influential personage in the kingdom. In a society in which polygamy was practiced, no one of the royal wives, since the ruler had a plurality of them, could enjoy the security of a privileged position, until she had succeeded (as did Bathsheba, for instance, the mother of Solomon) in placing her son upon the royal throne. This is why in such a culture it was the queen-mother, rather than any of the king's wives, who ranked next to the sovereign.

We are shown the influence actually wielded by such a personage in the book of Daniel. You will recall the dramatic scene at Belshazzar's feast, when a mysterious hand wrote upon the wall of the royal banquet hall (Dn 5:1ff.). The king summoned his astrologers and soothsayers, but as they were completely at a loss in interpreting the sinister phenomenon, the king with the nobles was very much disturbed. Summoned by their cries of consternation, "the mother of my lord" enters and takes command of the whole desperate situation (Dn 5:10-12).

There is a scene in the first book of Kings (1 K 2:19-21), which illustrates graphically the power enjoyed by the queen-mother in the days of the monarchy in Israel. It is the occasion upon which, with Solomon established on the throne, Bathsheba, as "the mother of my lord," requests a favor from her royal son. The queen-mother enters the royal presence; "and the king arose to meet her and did obeisance to her, and sat down upon his throne. A seat was placed for the mother of the king; and she sat at his right hand." It is only then, when she was enthroned beside Solomon, that Bathsheba broached the subject which she had come to discuss with her son. " 'A small request I am about to make of you: do not refuse me.' 'Ask, my mother,' the king said to her, 'for I will not refuse you.' "

These illustrations from ancient Near Eastern court life of the powerful position of "the mother of my lord," help us to appreciate the significance of the application by Luke of this royal title to our Lady as the mother of Jesus. The evangelist testifies to the existence, before 80 A.D., of the Church's devotion to Mary, recognized even at this early period, and honored as the one person most closely associated with Christ in his work of redemption; and therefore the one after Christ himself, most powerful in interceding with God for the Christian people. We are also made aware of the close relationship which the apostolic Church perceived between our Lady's divine maternity and her queenship.

Ark of
the Covenant   We might also observe one other feature of the verse in Luke 1:43, "Who am I that 'the mother of my lord' should come to me?" A literary echo, which appears also to be intentional on Luke's part, suggests that our Lady is presented here as the new ark of the covenant. You will recall a passage in the second book of Samuel, which depicts King David as planning to bring the ark of the covenant, which had been recovered from the Philistines, up to his royal city, "the city of David"—Jerusalem. At the moment of the entry of the ark into the city, David is overcome with fear and awe, and he cries out, "Who am I that the ark of Yahweh should come to me?" (2 S 6:9).

There can be little doubt that St. Luke, in attempting to portray the scene between our Lady and her cousin, had that passage in mind when he composed this dialogue. This is confirmed also by the Lucan narrative of the annunciation to our Lady. Mary is there informed that the conception of her child will be effected by the operation of the Spirit of God. Luke verbalizes the divine communication in these words. "The power of the Most High will overshadow you" (Lk 1:35). The term *episkiazein* used here is that employed in the Greek version of the Old Testament to denote the coming of God's presence to "the tent of meeting," the sacred shrine where Yahweh was to dwell with his covenanted people. "Then the cloud overshadowed the tent of meeting, and the glory of Yahweh filled the dwelling. And Moses was unable to enter the tent of meeting, for the cloud overshadowed it, and the glory of Yahweh filled the tent" (Ex 40:34ff.). The divine presence manifested to Israel, "the glory of Yahweh," was enthroned upon the ark of the covenant. Luke's literary allusion to this passage leaves little room for doubt that his intention is to purposely point out to his reader that our Lady, who now carries within her womb the incarnate Son is the new ark of the covenant.

That Luke intends to present to the Christian reader the theological consequences of our Lady's maternity receives additional confirmation when we examine the form and structure of this annunciation scene (Lk 1:26-38). If one takes the trouble to compare it with similar events from Israel's sacred history, one realizes that our evangelist has modeled it upon the accounts of certain divine communications recorded in the Old Testament (cf. Gn 16:11-12; Jg 13:3-5; Is 7:14-15; Jg 6:12-16). In particular, there are three Old Testament scenes that seem to have had a special influence upon the composition of Luke's narrative of the annunciation to Mary. One is found in the prophet Zephaniah 3:14-17; another, in Zechariah 9:9-10; the third occurs in Joel 2:21-27. In all these passages the people of Israel is personified as "the daughter of Sion." Moreover, each contains a reference to some mysterious future king, an eschatological Messiah, to whom the daughter of Sion is to give birth. It seems altogether likely that Luke has patterned his account upon these Old Testament narratives, and consequently intends his reader to understand that our Lady is the real daughter of Sion. In her, this beautiful personification created by Israel's prophets has found its definitive fulfillment.

We might mention one other little passage in the New Testament which, in the opinion of some commentators, contains a reference to the divine maternity of our Lady. The text is to be found in 1 Timothy 2:12-15. Here the author is rather hard on women: he points out that they should have no right to teach in the Church because it was Eve, not Adam, who was deceived and fell into sin in her delusion. Yet, he adds optimistically, "she will be saved through childbearing, provided they persevere in faith and love and holiness." This puzzling change from singular to plural ("she," "they") and the presence of the Greek definite article before "childbearing," led the sub-apostolic fathers (Ignatius, Justin, Irenaeus) to see here a reference to *the* childbearing of our Lady, which led to the redemption of the world. As a consequence, womankind in its totality (the topic which concerns the inspired writer in this passage) may hope to be redeemed through the maternity of the one most illustrious representative of that sex, our Lady.

Mary's Virginal   Our Lady's virginity, that is to say, Mary's virginal conception
Motherhood   and birth of Jesus, are clearly attested both by Matthew and by
Luke. Matthew's presentation of Jesus' genealogy ends very
mysteriously (Mt 1:16). Though the evangelist has traced Jesus'
lineage through Joseph, he concludes by stating, "Jacob became
the father of Joseph, the husband of Mary. It was of her that
Jesus, who is called the Messiah, was born." He explains this mystery, in the second part of chapter one, by insisting that the
virginal conception and birth of Jesus were not only real facts, but
they were actually the realization of that prophecy made by
Isaiah 7:14, which Matthew quotes from the Septuagint translation of the Old Testament. "All this happened, in order that the
word spoken by the Lord through the prophet might be fulfilled,
'Behold, the virgin shall conceive and bear a son. . . .' " (Mt 1:22-
23). The Hebrew text was not quite so explicit on the virginal
character of this mysterious woman. The word *'almāh* in Hebrew
denotes simply a young girl of marriageable age, a maiden. The
quality of virginity is implied, but it is not explicitly connoted.
On the other hand, the Greek term *parthenos* expresses the idea
of virginity. It is certainly intriguing to conjecture why the Alexandrian Jews of the third or second century before Christ, who
translated Isaiah into Greek, should have chosen *parthenos* to
render *'almāh* in this passage. There can be no doubt, however,
that Matthew applied it in this sense to our Lady, thus attesting
the faith of the apostolic Church in the virginity of Mary.

    The same may be said of Luke, particularly in the passage I
have already referred to, which asserts that "the power of the
Most High" will "overshadow" her. The apostolic testimony of
faith to Mary's virginity in her conception and bringing forth of
Jesus is unquestionably asserted in both Infancy narratives. There
is no positive assertion anywhere in the New Testament, it must be
conceded, of the perpetual virginity of our Lady. This truth we
receive from the faith of the Church; hence this doctrine cannot
rightly be called in question, for nothing in the sacred books can
be said to contradict this Catholic belief. The numerous references
to "the brothers and sisters" of Jesus are an inevitable result of the
limitations of Semitic language, when it comes to expressing in a
nuanced manner certain relationships within the clan, or the
family. They have a word for mother, for father, for son, daughter,
mother-in-law and father-in-law, etc. They do not however possess
a word for cousin. In the book of Tobit there is the story of the
young man dispatched by his father to a distant clansman to ask
for his daughter's hand in marriage. This distant cousin, Raguel,
refers to "Tobit, our brother," (Tb 7:2) and young Tobit calls

his wife "my sister" (Tb 8:7). This is the effect of poverty of the language, or perhaps, better, of the deep awareness amongst the Semitic peoples of the significance of all family ties. Accordingly, the New Testament allusions to Jesus' "brothers and sisters" are not necessarily to be understood literally, and need not be interpreted as contradicting the teaching of the Church regarding the perpetual virginity of our Lady.

The most striking testimonial of the early Church's faith in our Lady's role in salvation history is provided us by the twelfth chapter of the Apocalypse. As a prelude to our consideration of that passage, we might remind ourselves briefly of the Church's Marian faith as recorded in the fourth Gospel. I have already referred to her title as "the mother of Jesus." Another theologically significant fact is that both at Cana and on Calvary Jesus addresses her as "Woman." Clearly there can be no question of any coldness or disrespect in Jesus' use of this term. Yet, since the Aramaic language has a word for "mother," which a son would normally use in such circumstances, we may rightly ask why these two passages represent Jesus as calling his own mother, "Woman"? It would seem probable that the evangelist wishes to establish some connection between these scenes of the Gospel and the text in Genesis 3:15. This text, which speaks about the enmity to be placed between the serpent and woman, is a vague one, because the word "woman" there means all womankind. But here in these two passages in John we have an explanation of the apostolic age at least that points to our Lady as the woman who, together with her son, is to fight the battle against Satan. She is, in other words, the new Eve.

This insight may well have inspired the panorama portrayed in the twelfth chapter of the Apocalypse. "A mighty sign appeared in the sky. A woman clothed with the sun. . . ." The author intends to describe the signs of the Christian zodiac; and the first and greatest of these symbols is this image of a woman, clothed with the sun, the moon beneath her feet, and twelve stars as a crown about her head. She is about to bear a child; and the child to whom she gives birth is the Messiah. Yet this is not an historical account of these happenings, but a symbolic picture. Immediately after the birth of the Messiah, though the dragon is there to devour him, the child is "taken up to God," a symbolic presentation of our Lord's death and resurrection. The woman is a symbol certainly of the Church. At the same time, I believe, she is a symbol of our Lady.

Accordingly the passage to which I referred in the Constitution on the Liturgy, promulgated by Vatican II, voices a very ancient tradition when it speaks of the close association of our Lady and the Church. For this figure in the twelfth chapter of the Apocalypse, though symbolic, does represent a profound reality. It is clear from the reference to her "other children" (Ap 12:17), whom the dragon attacks, that this woman is a symbol of the Church. Still it would appear also that, as the mother of the Messiah, the woman is a symbol of our Lady. This mysterious figure is given very special divine protection. She is carried away on "the wings of a great eagle," as God had promised to carry his people in the Old Testament. She is borne off to the desert— a symbol, in the Bible, of the protective presence of God. The woman's life is sheltered there, safe from the attack of the dragon, for all the rest of the Church's life. This practice of ranging back and forth from the individual to the collectivity our western mentality finds very disconcerting. But for the Semite it was a familiar procedure. It is to be found frequently in the Old Testament where, for instance, if the king sins, the people sin; and hence the people may justly be punished. It would seem probable that the woman in the Apocalypse represents not only the Church but also our Lady as the mother of the Messiah. This dramatic description thus constitutes the crowning expression of the faith of the apostolic Church in the efficacy of Mary's divine motherhood, since her maternity is so closely associated with her Son's triumph over evil.

In John's scene on Calvary, our Lord is represented as bequeathing our Lady to the beloved disciple (Jn 19:25-27). He asks his mother to accept the beloved disciple as her son in place of himself. The beloved disciple, in the eyes of the evangelist, represents the Christian people. This supreme test of our Lady's faith, this final demand of her divine Son that she exchange him for the people of God is an indication of our Lady's part in the redemption. Mary, by this heroic act of faith by which she accepts the divine plan of salvation in the death of her Son, has become more closely associated with him in his victory over "the ancient serpent," Satan, than any other human being. It is this victory of her faith which presages the victory of the Church's faith. And so our Lady is chosen to be the representative, the image, as the Constitution on the Liturgy says, of the Church herself.

At Cana, our Lady is given two brief lines to speak—the only words that she utters in the fourth Gospel. She turns to our Lord, when the wine fails, and says, "They have no more wine left" (Jn 2:3). And then, without expressing her request in so many words, she addresses the waiters with those words of the pharaoh of Egypt to his people concerning the patriarch Joseph: "Do whatever he commands you" (Jn 2:5; cf. Gn 41:55). These two very brief speeches illustrate our Lady's function in salvation history. She turns to her Son to present the poverty of humanity, and to intercede for his assistance, in that discreet, diplomatic, but efficacious way, which only a mother can effectively employ: "They have no wine left." Our Lady also turns to mankind, "the rest of her children," to impart that supreme lesson, of which her whole life was an exemplification: "Do whatever he asks." "Happy is she," Jesus had declared in effect, "because she heard the word of God and kept it." This is the chief glory of the Mother of God; and it was for this principally, her obedience and her faith, that the apostolic Church paid her homage from the earliest days, associating her in the cenacle, even before Pentecost, with the apostles. She was revered as "the mother of Jesus"; she was revered for her queenship; but most of all, she was dear to the apostolic Church as the unblemished image of the Church herself.

PETER VOICES THE FAITH OF THE TWELVE
Matthew 16:13-20

When Jesus came into the neighborhood of Caesarea Philippi, he asked his disciples, "Who do people say the Son of Man is?" 14They replied, "Some, John the Baptist; others, Elijah; still others, Jeremiah, or one of the prophets." 15"And you," Jesus asked them, "Who do you say I am?" 16Simon Peter answered, "You are the Messiah, the Son of the living God!"

17Jesus said to him, "Happy are you, Simon son of John! No mere man has disclosed this to you, but only my heavenly Father. 18Now I, for my part, say to you: you are Peter, and on this rock I will build my Church; and the power of the realm of Death shall not hold out against it. 19I will entrust to you the keys of the kingdom of heaven: whatever you shall declare unlawful upon earth shall be held unlawful in heaven; whatever you shall declare lawful upon earth shall be held lawful in heaven."

20Then he ordered his disciples not to tell anyone that he was the Messiah.

THE TRANSFIGURATION OF JESUS
Luke 9:28-36

Now it was about eight days after these words; and taking with him Peter, John, and James, Jesus ascended the mountain to pray. 29As he prayed, the aspect of his countenance became different, and his clothes changed to a brilliant white. 30Suddenly two men were conversing with him, Moses and Elijah, 31who, appearing there in glory, spoke with him about the *exodos* that he was destined to accomplish in Jerusalem.

32Meanwhile, Peter and his companions were overcome with sleep. However, they managed to wake up, and they saw his glory and the two men standing beside him. 33Just as Moses and Elijah were on the point of taking their leave of him, Peter said to Jesus, "Master, it is fortunate that we are here. Let us then erect three bowers, one for you, one for Moses, and one for Elijah."

34However, while he was yet talking, a cloud came and overshadowed them. They were seized with fear as they entered the cloud. 35From the cloud there came a voice, which declared, "This is my well-beloved Son, my chosen One. Listen to him!"

36As the voice died away, Jesus stood there alone. And the disciples kept silence, telling nothing at that time of what they had seen to anyone.

Chapter 20

JESUS "THE WAY" TO THE FATHER

WE CANNOT CONCLUDE our meditations on the public life of *Eschaton* Jesus without some attention to the two great events which form *in History* the climax and, in a sense, the conclusion of Jesus' public ministry: Peter's profession of loyalty to Jesus, made in the name of the Twelve; and the extraordinary experience granted to three specially chosen disciples, Jesus' transfiguration on the mountain.

The message of the gospel, the good news of Christianity, is that the *eschaton* has entered human history; the divinely transcendent has become a matter of common experience; the triune God has become personally involved with man's existential situation. To say this is to say a great deal in a short compass. It has always been the unshakeable Judaeo-Christian conviction that, through a specific series of events and by means of certain historical personalities, almighty God has revealed his will to men. The Judaeo-Christian conception of sacred history maintains that this privileged sequence began with Abraham, the first historical personage in the Bible, and continued on down the centuries to the close of the apostolic age.

The two events we wish to contemplate at the moment have a common distinctive characteristic. Of the various episodes in the Synoptic tradition, they are the only two which have been given an explicit chronological connection. This fact has so impressed students of the New Testament that the complex of events and sayings which cluster around these episodes are thought to have existed in written form anterior to the composition of our Gospels. For, as you know, it is characteristic of the Synoptic Gospels that while they display some kind of perceptible order, that order is almost never a chronological arrangement.

This exceptional character of the present phenomenon merits *Presented by* our attention here. It would appear to indicate that from earliest *the Evangelists* apostolic times, before the Gospels were composed, a clear connection was seen between these two events. We might say they form a kind of diptych, presenting two facets of Christian faith: man's act of total self-commitment and loyalty to Jesus Christ, and the naked reality of the mystery, which constitutes the object of that self-dedication. The first episode depicts the full-hearted and impulsive, if ill informed protestation of loving confidence by Peter, who, without knowing fully what he was reaching out for, could at least grasp, through grace and personal experience, enough of the mystery surrounding Jesus to make his act of self-commitment a responsible, humanly understandable leap in the dark. The experience of Jesus' transfiguration, on the other hand, reveals the ineffable, divine dimension of the person of Jesus Christ, as yet totally unsuspected by Peter and the Twelve.

A little reflection will disclose the profound truth that almost any truly human action is a symbol of some deeper, mysterious reality. The two short words "I do" in the marriage service, for example, represent a commitment comprising many years of self-sacrifice, and loyalty, and love. A handshake expresses a depth of sympathy that most men probably could not otherwise adequately express. The historian is dedicated to the task of dispelling the ambiguity which surrounds the happenings and personalities of real life. We may take the wounding of St. Ignatius at Pamplona as an illustration. In reality, this military action was certainly not of any major consequence. It was simply a little foray in a series of border raids on the confines of France and Spain which had been going on for centuries. Indeed, there probably were men killed in this particular engagement; there were others undoubtedly much more gravely wounded than Ignatius Loyola. Hence, considered in itself, this experience was quite insignificant. Yet the historian of the Counter-Reformation will see a meaning in this episode of Ignatius' life which extends far beyond the mere brute fact, because of the consequences for the Church stemming from the event. This trifling incident set in motion a whole chain of events leading to the founding of the Society of Jesus as a sequel to Ignatius' conversion.

The technique of historiography attempts to discern a patterned concatenation in what otherwise appears as an infinity of ambiguous, discontinuous facts. Such is the character of the phenomenon we know as war. In itself it comprises an uncountable catalogue of varying human experiences. The historian, who writes the history of the American Civil War or of World War II, writes it in much the same way as a playwright should, according to Aristotle, compose a good play. His war narrative consists of a beginning, a middle, and an end. Otherwise, it is unintelligible: it is simply not history. By creatively expressing the pattern which he has perceived, the historiographer is able to dispel the essential ambiguity surrounding such a series of facts, and communicate his precious insight into the significance of what otherwise appear as mere happenings to his reader. In so doing, he makes an intelligible picture out of what remains, to the uninitiated eye, an ambiguous progression in time, colored by a multitude of disconnected human experiences.

In the Gospels the authors, historians in their own right, wrestle with an obviously deeper, more difficult problem: the final breakthrough or irruption of the divine into man's world. In consequence, while the apostolic testimony reposes foursquare upon the personal and collective experiences of the Twelve (and hence it cannot, from this point of view, be reasonably called in question), still the element of supreme importance in creating the intelligibility of this unique history remains the testimony of Christian faith, the apostolic witness to Jesus' saving death and resurrection, which gives its ultimate meaning to the gospel. It was in the light of the paschal faith that these two scenes, Peter's confession of faith and Jesus' transfiguration were seen as complementary to each other. Whoever it was who wrote the little pre-evangelical essay and saw this relationship, did so as a Christian historian.

Peter's profession of loyalty to Jesus as the Messiah constitutes, in the Synoptic tradition, the highpoint—the "water-shed," as Vincent Taylor puts it—of the Galilean ministry. It is narrated by each of the first three evangelists; and moreover it is one of the rare episodes also recorded in the fourth Gospel (Jn 6:67-69). In Mark, it forms the conclusion of the first movement of the whole story (Mk 8:27-30). By the title of his work, inscribed in the very first verse, the author announced "the beginning of the good news of Jesus, the Messiah, the Son of God." The first of this twofold theme reaches its climax with Peter's recognition of Jesus' messiahship at Caesarea Philippi. Mark's Gospel will continue with an account of the ever deepening revelation by our Lord of the mystery surrounding himself, until finally his divine Sonship is proclaimed through the words of the centurion standing beneath the cross at Jesus' death: "Truly this man was Son of God" (Mk 15:39). The whole movement of Mark's narrative seems to be orientated towards these two significant professions of faith.

At Caesarea Philippi, according to Mark, Peter spoke in the name of the Twelve, and he expressed their conviction that Jesus was the God-given answer to the messianic hopes of Israel. In the sequel Jesus is represented as warning the disciples "severely" (Mk 8:30) not to reveal his identity. This profession of personal

Peter's Self-commitment in Mark

attachment and loyalty to himself moves Jesus to begin his instructions on the specific character of his messianic function: he is to be a suffering Messiah (Mk 8:31). The disclosure of such an unexpected vocation horrifies Peter, who has just voiced the disciples' confidence and faith in the Master; and he has to be harshly rebuked by Jesus: "Get out of my way, you Satan! You do not take God's view, but an all too human viewpoint" (Mk 8:33).

Now it is a strong temptation, in the light of this reaction of Peter, to conclude that he did not know what he was talking about when he declared, "You are the Messiah." One might be inclined to regard this profession of faith in Jesus as empty and worthless. Peter's notion of Jesus' mission as Messiah is a mere caricature of the reality signified by his words. We should not allow ourselves to forget, however, that Mark's literary arrangement indicates beyond any doubt that Peter's confession of faith is the high point in the disciples' collective experience of the public ministry of Jesus.

Actually, we here face a problem pertaining to common Christian experience, the growing pains felt by our faith in Jesus Christ. One can readily become disillusioned, and say: "I don't actually believe at all," or "I am practically without any real faith in Christ, when I reflect upon the myriad betrayals of this belief, which reveal the disconcerting inconsistency between my conduct and what I profess publicly." Accordingly, this experience of Peter can lead me to reconsider, and re-evaluate the painful limitations of my own profession of Christian loyalty. Peter's acknowledgement of the messianic mission of Jesus, while it was obviously lacking in depth of comprehension, was, nevertheless, as an act of devoted loyalty, a very significant act in the eyes of all the evangelists. It was of paramount importance already in the oral traditions which preceded the Gospels. Why? Because, though Peter did not yet grasp the full import of what he was saying, still with his heart, with the truest part of himself, he went out of himself, and made a total act of self-surrender to Jesus. Peter did not yet know the mystery of Jesus: the secret of his divinity. Peter's pledge of loyalty was to a person he did not know, for the person was the Son of God. Yet Peter's avowal was far from valueless. It was not, for all its limitations, an insincere commitment of himself and the Twelve to the Master—as later history will demonstrate.

Peter's Self-commitment in Luke and John   Luke's account follows that of Mark with two important variations. He presents Peter's profession by the words, "You are God's Anointed" (Lk 9:20). Jesus is acknowledged as the royal Messiah promised by God through Nathan the prophet (2 S 7:12-14). Moreover, Luke makes no reference to Peter's ignorance of the true meaning of Jesus' Messiahship, or to Jesus' rebuke.

We have already observed that the fourth Gospel records, in its own characteristic fashion, this profession of loyalty by Peter. Here it is associated with the later Christian belief in the Eucharist (Jn 6:67-69). After many of Jesus' disciples became disillusioned in him and went away, Jesus addressed the Twelve, "Do you wish also to go away?" It was then that Peter replied in the name of them all, "Lord, to whom shall we go? You possess the words of eternal life. We have come to believe, indeed we know that you are the holy One of God."

Matthew's version of the episode stands in marked contrast with all the other narratives of it; and possesses a quite distinctive character of its own (Mt 16:13-20). In the first place, when Jesus asks who, in men's opinion, he appears to be, Matthew states the question in a very significant fashion: "Who do men say that the Son of Man is?" The question does not have this form in Mark or in Luke, where it reads simply, "Who do men say that I am?" Moreover, the Matthean formulation of Peter's response is much more solemn than in any other account: "You are the Messiah, the Son of the living God."

In view of these considerations, it is clear that Matthew means to represent Peter's confession as a profession of Christian faith in the divinity of Christ. Such a procedure on the part of Matthew creates a problem, because, in the first place, the other evangelists leave little room for doubt about the nature of Peter's declaration in its historical reality and in its pre-resurrection context. It was meant to be a profession of faith in Jesus' messianic vocation. In the second place, as all the evangelists unmistakably testify, the disciples came to a supernatural awareness of Christ's divinity only after his glorification and his sending the Holy Spirit. Yet Matthew's interpretation of the tenor of Peter's statement appears clearly to anticipate this later Christian and paschal faith in Christ as the Son of God.

The first hint we receive that Matthew means to interpret this Petrine profession of loyalty in function of what it ultimately became is to be seen in his unique formulation of Jesus' question: "Who do men say that the Son of Man is?" In the Synoptic Gospels especially, this title, borrowed from Daniel 7:13 (where it designates a mysterious figure symbolizing redeemed Israel; cf. v.18), and imposed upon himself by Jesus, is a more apt expression for the divinity of Christ than even the title "Son of God." The explanation for such a paradox lies, in the first place, in the fact that "Son of God" was applied in the Old Testament to Israel, or to her kings or judges. The phrase thus acquired an ambiguity which it often retains even in the New Testament. The second relevant factor is the super-human character of the symbol in Daniel: this "Man" comes "upon the clouds of heaven," i.e. he comes from heaven to earth—thereby indicating that he is something more than human. Jesus' assumption of this title was due probably in part to its essential obscurity, and in part also to its openness to the possibility of connoting more than mere "man," as it actually suggested in Semitic idiom.

Matthew's purpose in thus construing Peter's profession as one of faith in Jesus' divinity is to remind his reader that the disciples' experience of Jesus during his earthly life resulted in a continuous growth in their devotion to him and in their consciousness of the import of his mission. They were attracted, at the beginning, like Andrew and the other disciple near the banks of the Jordan, by a mysterious quality in this man which drew them irresistibly to him. "Where do you live, rabbi?" they had timidly asked, and Jesus said, "Come; and you will see" (Jn 1:38-39). After some months in Jesus' company, the Twelve are selected for the special privilege of "being with him," as Mark puts it (Mk 3:14). As time went by, they learned to regard him as more than a rabbi—a prophet; and not merely "a prophet like one of the ancient prophets" (Lk 9:8), but as the Prophet or divine messenger enigmatically alluded to in the Old Testament (Mal 3:1ff.). The profession of loyalty at Caesarea Philippi formed the climax of the whole movement as long as "Jesus was not yet glorified," since as the fourth Gospel reminds us "the Spirit was not yet" given (Jn 7:39). Consequently, there can be no question of Peter making an act of faith in Jesus' divinity until after our Lord's resurrection; for such an act of faith is Christian faith which must await the presence of the Holy Spirit within the apostolic group.

Yet this enthusiastic loyalty, this persistent, if somewhat too human devotion, which grew in the hearts of the Twelve who saw in Jesus first an extraordinarily winning rabbi, then a prophet, and finally God's answer to Israel's messianic hopes, was to be transformed after his death and resurrection into faith in him as the Son of God incarnate. The organic character of this whole movement of the apostles' faith, the fairest fruit of their continued experience of the Son become man, is what Matthew has perceived and endeavored to express for his reader in his narrative of the scene at Caesarea Philippi. He has actually exercised his prerogative as an historian, who is also a theologian (or perhaps a mystic), to exploit the hidden dimension in Peter's pledge of loyalty in the light of what it subsequently became. Actually, a little reflection upon Matthew's technique here reveals it to be analogous at least to the methodology employed, for example, by the historian of the Counter-Reformation to whom we referred earlier. Indeed, the same procedure will be found operative in the Roman historian's attempt to answer the question: Why did Julius Caesar cross the Rubicon? One answer to the question, of course, might be given: to get to the other side. In the light of the subsequent destruction of republican Rome however, Caesar crossed the Rubicon to become the monarch of Rome, to overthrow the ancient *Res publica* and lay the foundations of the Empire. Similarly, Matthew sees in Peter's profession the basis or foreshadowing of that Christian faith which, under the action of the Holy Spirit, would eventually become the paschal faith of the Christian Church. Peter was unaware of all this at Caesarea Philippi. Peter did not even know, when he affirmed his conviction that Jesus was the Messiah, what being Messiah actually involved. He assuredly had no inkling about the deeper mystery enshrouding the person of Jesus. Yet to say all this is not to invalidate Matthew's point of view, or his interpretation of this significant episode.

The other side of the diptych, Jesus' transfiguration, is narrated by Matthew, Mark, and Luke. I suggest that we contemplate this awe-inspiring scene as St. Luke represented it to the reader of his Gospel (Lk 9:28-36). We might recall, however, that this mystery is also mentioned by Second Peter, where the author speaks of the apostolic testimony (2 Pt 1:12-18). He says in effect that through the kerygma the apostles testify to their belief that what was once a matter of personal human experience has been revealed as the Word of Life. Thus, for instance, the experience of Peter, John, and James upon the mountain of the transfiguration, mysterious as it appears to have been, was of a piece with their experience of Jesus during the ordinary (if indeed one may call it ordinary) life which they lived with him in Galilee. St. John states this same truth in his own inimitable manner. "What was from the beginning, what we heard and saw with our own eyes, contemplated, touched with our own hands of the Word of Life (for Life has manifested itself), we saw it, we testified to it, and we announced it to you, this eternal Word" (1 Jn 1:1-3). This is the heart of the Christian message, the presence in history of a divine reality that transcends all human experience.

Because it is transcendent, any human formulation of this

reality, as in the account of Jesus' transfiguration, tends to rely chiefly upon the symbol as the most effective means for suggesting this truly ineffable reality. Thus we shall discover that the sacred writers attempt to convey something of this tremendous mystery of Jesus' transfiguration by employing symbols related to the ritual of the Feast of Booths or Tabernacles.

Of the three great feasts in the life of Israel, the Feast of Booths was in many respects the greatest. The other two, mentioned together with it in the Mosaic Law, Passover and Pentecost, were of first-rate significance. But the Feast of Booths eclipsed them by the splendor and variety of its liturgy, as well as by the joy it evoked in the hearts of the participants. A thanksgiving festival at harvest time, its ritual involved processions in which Jewish men, clad in white garments, carried pomegranates and palms, while chanting Psalm 118 (117 in the Vulgate): Hosanna (O Lord deliver!). Tradition also prescribed the living in little booths, made of the branches of trees, during the octave of festivities. These details deserve mention because, as we shall see, they are reflected in the Gospel account of the transfiguration.

The fundamental orientation of this feast, as we find it explained in the Old Testament and in the writings of the rabbis, was eschatological: it announced the future realization of God's eschatological reign in the world and in history.

"Now, it was about eight days after these words," says Luke (about a week, in other words, after Peter's profession of loyalty), "and taking with him Peter, John and James, Jesus ascended the mountain to pray. As he prayed, the aspect of his countenance became different, and his clothes changed to a brilliant white. Suddenly two men were conversing with him, Moses and Elijah, who, appearing there in glory, spoke with him about the *exodos* that he was destined to accomplish in Jerusalem" (Lk 9:28-31).

Here we have the two greatest paragons of Israelite faith—the two, as we mentioned before, who, tradition claimed, were privileged to experience God intimately, face to face: Moses and Elijah. Moses, one might say, represents Israel's legalism. Yet such a characterization leaves much to be desired. Moses was the man who was privileged to mediate the covenant between God and Israel. Moses was the go-between at the very commencement of Israel's life as God's people. Elijah, in his turn, was the first, and in certain respects the greatest, of God's spokesmen, the prophets.

Luke represents them as conversing with Jesus (this detail is peculiar to Luke) about his *exodos*—that is the Greek term—which he was to carry out in Jerusalem. The word is often trans-

202

lated as his "death," but this highly charged expression obviously means a great deal more than that. The exodus out of Egypt was an event, which not only delivered the Hebrews from that land of sin and ignorance of the true God, but caused them to enter a new life of union with God through their tremendous experience at Sinai, where God made them his covenanted people. The term *exodos,* then, as Luke applies it to Jesus' work of redemption, comprehends not only his death, but also his resurrection and his glorification. Thus the evangelist depicts these two chief protagonists of the Old Testament religious spirit as speaking about the whole work of Christian redemption with Jesus, because it was to this event that the life of Israel, patterned upon the covenant and reanimated by the prophetic spirit, had been orientated through the centuries of her historical existence.

"Meanwhile, Peter and his companions," says Luke, "were overcome with sleep. However, they managed to wake up, and they saw his glory and the two men standing beside him. Just as they [Moses and Elijah] were on the point of taking their leave of him, Peter said to Jesus, 'Master, it is fortunate that we are here. Let us then erect three bowers, one for you, one for Moses, and one for Elijah.'" (Lk 9:32-33). The motif of this description as I said, comes from the Feast of Booths: the white garments, the bowers, or booths mentioned by Peter. Jean Daniélou, S.J.[1] has suggested that this privileged experience probably took place in the autumn, when the Feast of Booths was celebrated.

We may see in Peter's offer to build little bowers of leaves to house Jesus, Moses, and Elijah (although Mark states that Peter did not know what he was saying—9:6) an attempt to prolong this delightful revelation of the *eschaton,* so intimately bound up with the mystery of Jesus. "However, while he was yet talking, a cloud came and overshadowed them. They were seized with fear as they entered the cloud" (Lk 9:34). The disciples were overcome with awe, since they realized that they had entered the presence of God; for the cloud was a sign of the divine presence. "From the cloud there came a voice, which declared, 'This is my well-beloved Son, my chosen One. Listen to him'" (Lk 9:35). The same words which had been addressed to Jesus himself at his baptism in the Jordan are now directed to these three favored disciples. As the voice died away, Jesus stood there alone. "And the disciples kept silence, telling nothing at that time of what they had seen to anyone" (Lk 9:36).

The evangelists manage to convey the impression that, despite

---

1 Jean Daniélou, "Les Quatre-Temps de Septembre et la Fête des Tabernacles," *La Maison-Dieu,* N°. 46 (1956), 114-136.

this marvelous experience, which in itself expressed the mystery of Jesus' divine Sonship, the bewildered disciples could not yet understand its significance. Indeed, even when through the enlightenment of the Holy Spirit they did grasp its import with Christian faith, they found it next to impossible to express this apocalyptic event in human words. That is why the evangelists fall back upon the symbolism connected with the Feast of Booths in depicting the scene. This same set of symbols is employed habitually in the New Testament for the most striking representations of heaven. In the Apocalypse the hundred and forty-four thousand who follow the Lamb are pictured wearing white robes and holding palm branches in their hands. They sing the Hosanna —they are celebrating the Feast of Booths in heaven (Ap 7:9). It may well be, as Jean Daniélou has also suggested[2] that the description of Jesus' messianic entry into Jerusalem in the Gospels has been colored by the symbolism of this same feast—which would explain the presence of palm branches and the Hosanna with which the crowd greeted him.

Here "upon this holy mountain," as 2 Peter calls it, the disciples witnessed the ineffable, incommunicable mystery of Jesus. We see the same inadequacy of human words in the language which the mystics employ. St. Ignatius, for example, when attempting to communicate something of his tremendous vision at the River Cardoner, which he always regarded as the greatest mystical experience of his life, says that this revelation of the Holy Trinity was like three notes on an organ. Such a description does not really enlighten us very much. We are not even told whether it was a major or a minor chord! What we do learn from such an unsatisfactory description is that this is all human language can do.

The Mystery of Jesus   This mystery which confronts us here towards the termination of Jesus' public life at his transfiguration is the same mystery that confronts us throughout our own lives. The many-sided paradox of Christianity derives ultimately from the mysterious event of the incarnation. It is inextricably involved in the truth that the transcendent Son of God has somehow enclosed himself personally within the limitations of a set of human experiences. The reactions of this supreme event upon the creation, upon history, upon human experience we are taught through the pages of the New Testament. You will recall that in presenting Jesus' critique of Jewish observances and ritualism, based upon the distinction between the clean and the unclean, Mark says that by his remarks Jesus declared all food clean (Mk 7:19). This is part of the

2 *Ibid.*

meaning of the incarnation: that the old distinction between clean and unclean has been abolished forever. Peter would later learn this lesson fully through the vision granted to him at Jaffa (Acts 10:10-16). The incarnation has nullified the ancient distinction between the profane and the holy. Through the human life of God's Son, all that is noble and good in human experience has somehow been recreated and restored by the creative act of the incarnate Word of God.

Christian faith is basically an act of human love and loyalty, whole-hearted self-commitment to Jesus Christ. Faith must establish an interpersonal relationship, which means it must be a candid, selfless, total engagement of ourselves. This is, obviously, not the whole of faith, but only its human side. The other facet of faith, the mystery of Jesus, which we reach out for in our profession of loyalty is not so easily discernible. We grow in awareness of this element only gradually, under the action of the Spirit of God. We see that this was largely lacking in Peter's avowal at Caesarea; his very human reaction upon the mountain of the transfiguration only serves to underscore the supernatural limitations of Peter's profession of faith. Yet both at Caesarea Philippi and upon the mountain Peter offered something significant to Christ. He teaches us a valuable lesson about faith on its human side. "It is fortunate," Peter says, "that we are here! Let us do something. Let us do something *human*. Let us do the best we can to prolong this revelation of your mystery." There is much we can learn here about the necessity of genuine, total engagement for the authentically personal exercise of our own Christian faith.

THE THIRD WEEK

WITH THE OPENING of the third week a turning point is reached *Turning point*
in the practice of contemplation, as it is understood in the Spiritual
Exercises. Until now, the exercitant has been contemplating Jesus
in the activity of his public life, intent upon observing his words
and actions in the Gospel narratives, in order to learn from him a
pattern for Christian living. For through this knowledge of Jesus,
his aims, his mission, his activity, the exercitant may hope to learn
to love him more effectively, and acquire that spirit, those virtues
and attitudes, which a twentieth-century apostolate demands.
Yet this contemplation has not been mere study, even the study of
Scripture, because he has been praying for what he is aware is a
free gift, Christ's grace. He has come to realize that Jesus presents himself to us in the second week of the Spiritual Exercises
as the way to the Father. Jesus is then, admittedly, at this stage
of the retreat, a means to the end which I desire. Jesus however is
not just any means; he is the Way to God. The retreatant has been
putting himself to school to him who is incarnate wisdom, as he
invites men to do in the eleventh chapter of Matthew (vv. 25-30).
The exercitant has been endeavoring to love him as a person who
is good for him; he has been seeking the Christian counterpart of
that love which has been called "enlightened self-interest."

With the third week, however, the very heart of the gospel, the *Love of*
focal point of the good news of salvation in Jesus Christ is reached *Friendship*
with his death and, (in the fourth week) his resurrection. This new
situation demands a significant change of attitude in the approach
to our Lord. One must now endeavor to reorientate radically one's
personal relationship with him. It is not merely that the object of
our contemplation shifts from Jesus' public life to his sufferings
(later it will be the joyful scenes of Christ's risen life). What is
crucial to the success of the Exercises is that the retreatant must
now attempt to rise above his love of enlightened self-interest, the
attitude characteristic of the second week, and begin to love

209

Jesus with the purer love of friendship. He must now beg to advance, with divine grace, from this good (but imperfect, because interested) love of Christ for the sake of his own Christian perfection, to a higher, disinterested love. He must dare now to love Christ for himself, which is genuine friendship. St. Ignatius tells us in the Notes for the Third Week [206] to ask for the grace of sympathy, compassion, the capacity for suffering with Christ, just as later we are to seek the grace of rejoicing with the risen Lord.

This is the beginning of Christian wisdom, because we thereby acquire "real" (as opposed to "notional") knowledge of God's revealed plan for the salvation of man (cf. 1 Cor 2:6-16). To state it in the terminology of St. Ignatius, this is the point in the Spiritual Exercises at which we should begin the *Contemplatio ad amorem;* or, in terms of another famous Ignatian phrase, it is now that we must learn to practice the *Third Degree of Humility.* This *Third Degree,* St. Ignatius says, is "the most perfect humility, since by it I desire and choose by preference poverty with the poor Christ over riches." What gives this attitude its specific differentiation is the "with Christ." I prefer to be rated as useless or foolish for the sake of being on Christ's side, who was first held to be such, than to be accounted wise and prudent in this world. St. Ignatius asserts, in the introduction to the *Contemplation for Obtaining Divine Love,* that such love is characterized by two qualities. Firstly it consists of deeds, not mere words. Just as truth only emerges in a given historical situation, so love is proven authentic, only by action. He tells us, secondly, that love consists of a mutual exchange between two who love each other. He who loves must give himself truly to the person he loves.

Cum Christo   In the writings of St. Paul there are five or six words that have become salient features of his technical, theological vocabulary. These compound verbs, which Paul probably coined himself, are distinguished by the fact that they begin with the Greek preposition *syn* (with). I suffer with Christ; I am nailed to the cross with Christ; I die with Christ; I am buried with Christ. I am raised from death with Christ; I ascend, or rather, I am carried into heaven, and am seated with Christ at the right hand of the Father. This is one of Paul's characteristic ways of underscoring the necessity of my personal participation in the redemption.[1] I must assimilate to myself, I must somehow experience, with God's grace, the prin-

---

1 For the Greek terms, cf. D.M. Stanley, S.J., " 'Become imitators of me': the Pauline Conception of Apostolic Tradition," *Studia Biblica et Orientalia, Volumen II: Novum Testamentum* (Rome, 1959), 294 n. 3.

cipal events by which Christ has saved me, since, by undergoing them Christ has transformed certain basic human experiences into a "new creation." Death, before Christ met death, meant simply separation from the God of the living, and so led to an undesirable state of misery—Sheol. That is why the psalmists so frequently pray to be delivered from death, as it was conceived in the ancient beliefs of Israel. However, once God's Son become man passed through death, he made possible to the believer a totally new experience—Christian death, now become the most important event in the whole Christian existence.

It is of paramount importance to grasp the element of novelty which is introduced into the contemplations of the third and fourth weeks of the Spiritual Exercises. This new orientation is achieved by a quite perceptible shift of accent, directing our attention and our desires towards a totally new existence "with Christ."

JESUS INSTITUTES THE NEW COVENANT IN THE EUCHARIST
Luke 22:7-20

The day of unleavened bread arrived, on which it was necessary to sacrifice the paschal lamb. [8]Accordingly, Jesus sent off Peter and John with these instructions, "Go and make preparations for us to eat the passover supper." [9]So they said to him, "Where do you wish us to make the preparations?" [10]He told them, "As you are entering the city, you will suddenly come upon a man carrying an earthenware water jar. Follow him into the house he enters, [11]and inform the owner of the house, "The master asks you, 'Where is the guest-room where I may eat the paschal lamb with my disciples?' [12]The man will show you an upstairs room, spacious and furnished. Make your preparations there." [13]So they went off and found things just as Jesus had told them; and they prepared the passover supper.

[14]And when the hour had arrived, Jesus took his place at table surrounded by the apostles. [15]Then he told them, "I have been longing eagerly to eat this paschal lamb with you before my Passion. [16]I assure you, I shall not any longer eat it, until it finds its fulfillment in the kingdom of God." [17]Taking a cup, he said, after giving thanks, "Take this and share it with one another. [18]I assure you, I shall not drink the product of the vine from now on, until the kingdom of God becomes a reality."

[19]And taking bread, he broke it, after giving thanks, and gave it to them saying, "This is my Body, to be given on your behalf. Do this in memory of me."

[20]Similarly, the cup also, at the end of supper, saying "This cup is the new covenant sealed with my Blood, to be shed on your behalf."

Chapter 21

LAST SUPPER: CHRIST IN THE
PRIEST'S LIFE

THE LAST SUPPER in the Synoptic tradition signifies Jesus' in- *Second Method* auguration of the new covenant. In the Exercises it functions as the *of Prayer* foundation-contemplation of the third week, inducting us into the new stage of Christian life in which we love Christ for himself. It is on this occasion in the fourth Gospel that our Lord admits the Twelve to a wholly new relationship with himself, "I shall no longer call you slaves, but friends" (Jn 15:15). The slave cannot share the personal thoughts and feelings of the master. He does not enjoy a genuine interpersonal relationship with him.

To advance to this love of friendship with Christ, I must, in prayer and by the experience of his grace, try to share Jesus' sufferings, and so gain a real knowledge of what my redemption cost him.

For our contemplation of the institution of the Eucharist, we might use the Second Method of Prayer [249-257], which is suggested for times of fatigue. You recall that this simple recipe for prayer consists of reflecting meditatively upon the words of a text.

Four words in the Mass of the Roman rite sum up Christ's actions at the Last Supper, when he created the Eucharist as the instrument of his new covenant: *accepit* (he took); *benedixit* (he blessed); *fregit* (he broke); *dedit* (he gave).

These four words, I believe, indicate also Christ's action in the lives of us who are called to share his priesthood. These four words describe the dynamic operation of Christ the priest in my priestly life, as indeed they be applied to the divine action throughout the whole course of sacred history as recorded for us in the Bible.

Accepit—he took. At the Last Supper, Jesus took bread, he *"He Took"* took wine, the most common, ordinary, inexpensive items of diet in the ancient Mediterranean world. Every man, rich or poor, had bread and wine upon his table. They were, so to say, the "meat and potatoes" of the Mediterranean world in Jesus' day—ordinary things, yet essential. This gesture of Jesus recalls God's utterly

213

free choice of the Hebrews, a motley mob of unruly, runaway slaves, fleeing under Moses' leadership from the tyranny of the Pharaoh, a disorderly crowd of rebellious expatriates, whom the prophet would later describe rightly as "not a people" (Hos 2:23). Culturally, if one compares them with the civilizations which surrounded them in the ancient Near East, the Hebrew tribes had little to recommend them. Religiously, if one accepts the evidence of the book of Exodus, with its ominous silence about the Hebrews' cult of God in Egypt, they had still less to recommend them. And yet this was the people that Yahweh chose as his "acquisition" (*segullāh*). Why this choice, this preference? Only God can tell us why, as he has done in Deuteronomy 7:7-8, a passage I have already quoted: "It was not because you were the greatest of all peoples that Yahweh set his heart on you and chose you (for you were the smallest of all peoples), but it was because Yahweh loved you that Yahweh rescued you from a state of slavery, from the power of Pharaoh, king of Egypt!"

Similarly, of all the bread that lay to hand upon that table in the upper room on the occasion of his last supper with the Twelve, Jesus chose one loaf, one particular piece of bread for the lofty privilege of being changed into himself. Of the many cups of wine standing there in the flagons at that momentous Passover meal, Jesus picked out a single cup of wine. The mystery that lies hidden in that divine choice of Christ!

Likewise, in my life he has chosen me as his servant, his collaborator, his companion. He is now choosing each of you as his priest, one of "the stewards of the mysteries of God," as Paul puts it (1 Cor 4:1). I was—God knows, I still may well be—so ordinary, so undistinguished. How many others could I point to as more worthy than I, who am so weak and sinful, at times perhaps even perverse. I have so little to recommend me to myself—let alone to the Lord! The awful depths there are in this mystery of the divine choice of myself! Yet what grounds for hope and optimism, what grounds for faith and confidence in the divine wisdom and the divine love of Jesus Christ. Even under the old covenant, as we see in the instance of Samuel the priest-prophet, God made choice of men for his own hidden purpose. "I will raise up for myself," God says of Samuel, "a faithful priest, who will act according to what is in my mind and in my heart; and I will build for him a sure house; and he will continue before the face of my Anointed forever" (1 S 2:35). Our Lord's selection of myself contains no less a promise: "You have not chosen me," he says, "I have chosen you." Perhaps in moments of disenchantment I may be tempted to think that, if Christ were capable of making a mistake, he certainly made one when he chose me to be a Christian, when he chose me to be a religious, when he chooses me, now, to be a priest. It is in just such moments of disillusionment, as if to answer just such cynicism, to rebut such humanly superficial judgments of myself, that the words of him who is wisdom incarnate remind me that the origins of my vocation lie with Christ, not with myself. These words of Jesus "put me in my place," so to speak. For I have not chosen myself: I have not even chosen Christ; he has chosen me. And in this dialogue of love, the only response the divine initiative asks of me is the acceptance of this privilege with faith, with trusting confidence, hope, above all, with love. If only I can succeed with his divine favor in accepting fully the divine wisdom of Christ's choice of me.

Benedixit—he blessed. Consider the dynamic thrust of Jesus' blessing at the Last Supper, the creative power of a divine benediction that could change mere bread and wine into himself. In the strength of that hallowing of the incarnate Word, "by whom all things were made and without whom nothing was made," the bread and wine which Jesus held in his blessed hands became his body, blood, soul, and divinity. What only a moment before had been a thing, a common, everyday article of diet, became a divine Person, the incarnate Son of God.

Even so, by the creative power of Yahweh, through the covenant he had made with the Hebrews on the mountain of Sinai, a group of independent, liberty-loving, restless, nomadic tribes became a people, God's people. As God would later say through the prophets, "You shall be my people, and I will be your God" (Ez 36:28). It was the divine blessing alone, only the divine favor which formed Israel as God's own son (Hos 11:1), as God's first-born son (Ex 4:22), God's well-beloved son. It was not ties of blood, though these existed, nor tribal organization, nor common political cause; it was God's word alone, only his revealed will, which provided the cohesive force that made Israel one people.

In my own life as a Christian, as a priest, as a religious, it is the infinitely powerful blessings of Christ, continually imparted, that constitute the only effective answer to my doubts and fears and scruples about the wisdom of his divine choice of myself. I should remember this: Christ has not only taken me; he has also blessed me. His *accepit* is accompanied constantly, mercifully, by his *benedixit*. He chose me—yes! But he does not leave me as he found me; because he blesses me as he blessed the bread. He blesses me with the creative gestures of the Christian sacraments. He once blessed me at baptism, taking what was ordinary human clay, stained with the universal sin of all the children of Adam, and transforming it through the breath of his grace into a true son of his own heavenly Father, capable of sharing with him the heritage of the Father's house. The power of Christ's blessing in the sacrament of penance, turning an enemy into a friend! The power of his blessing in the Eucharist, imbuing me with the divine power of loving my neighbor as myself—indeed, loving my neighbor as Jesus has loved me!

Now I consider especially the power of that blessing in the sacrament of the priesthood, making a priest out of an ordinary man, bestowing on him the same power that Jesus himself exercised at the Last Supper, giving to this man's lips the force that can change bread and wine into the Eucharist, giving to his hands the healing dynamism that can bless, to wash away sin, the creative strength to anoint the sick and prepare them for their last journey home to the Father.

"He Broke"   *Fregit*—he broke. After consecrating the bread by his blessing at the Last Supper, Jesus divided it up in order that it might go round the circle of his disciples, that it might be sufficient for all of them; in order, in short, to make it adaptable to their needs. This is "the bread given for the life of the world" (Jn 6:51b). This is the bread which "if a man eat, he shall live forever" (Jn 6:58).

This divine principle of adapting, forming man we see operative throughout the long course of Israel's history. God led them by his all-pervading, inerrant direction through the vicissitudes of their wandering in the desert and into the land of promise. He gave them a king when they demanded to be like the other nations. He later destroyed the monarchy during the Babylonian captivity, after a brief flicker of imperial glory under David and Solomon. He destroyed the monarchy in order to bring his people to a surer hope in that future king, the new David. By the mouth of his prophets God rebuked and disciplined his people. Through these divine spokesmen he formed the conscience of Israel, elevating it slowly but surely to a higher morality, to a deeper social responsibility, to a more transcendent religious spirit.

In my priestly life also Christ aims to make me adaptable, to make me the instrument joined to himself that is expendable, effective for the salvation of men. However, there is one serious obstacle that stands in the way of this divine purpose, threatening to make me unadaptable, unsuitable as an instrument of grace: my own selfishness. Consequently that egotism of mine must be transformed: it has to die and be raised to a new existence, if I am to act, in Paul's phrase, as a "collaborator of Christ and a steward

216

of the mysteries of God" (1 Cor 4:1). Accordingly, to assist me by his gracious favor to attain the purpose of my priestly vocation, Christ treats me as he treated the bread at the Last Supper. He tests me, sends me suffering in various ways to transform me gradually into the image of himself. For his Father's plan, as Paul saw so clearly, (Rom 8:29) is that Christ "should become the eldest among a large family of brothers." Has he not told me that, "unless the grain of wheat die, it simply remains all by itself" (Jn 12:24): it remains isolated, incapable of reproducing more like itself.

And here I must not overlook one salient feature of Christ's act of breaking the bread at the Last Supper because it teaches me the profoundly positive purpose of whatever suffering, in whatever form, our Lord may choose to send me during my priestly life. The point is this: Jesus did not break the bread until after he had blessed it. Only through the previously conferred power of this divine blessing did the breaking of the bread acquire any significance. Suffering is not designed, in God's providence, merely to frustrate my life, to destroy my humanity, to hobble my personality, but to perfect it after the pattern of Christ's own experience, as the author of Hebrews tells us. "Son of God though he was, he learned obedience in the school of suffering; and being thus made perfect, he has become, for all who heed him, the cause of eternal salvation" (Heb 5:8-9).

Dedit—he gave. At the Last Supper, Jesus gave the consecrated bread and wine, transformed into himself, to the Twelve, and through his apostles to us all, for the salvation of the world. "Having loved his own who were in the world," John tells us in his Gospel, "he loved them unto the end—unto perfection" (Jn 13:1). "Your fathers ate manna in the desert," Jesus had told the Galileans, "but they are dead! The bread which comes down from heaven is such that whoever eats it never dies. I myself am this living bread which has come down from heaven. . . . What is this bread, which I am to give? It is my flesh for the life of the world" (Jn 6:49-51).

Jesus' final gesture upon the cross is the gracious symbol of the plenary fulfillment of this promise which he made that day by the lake of Galilee. Every Christian, but more particularly every priest, should contemplate this last and loveliest gesture of the crucified hands of Christ. He flings them wide upon the cross to embrace the whole world; and only then I see that those hands are empty, because he has given me all he has. He has loved me unto the end, unto perfection. He has given me himself in the Blessed Sacrament!

Israel's history, we also know, ended no less dramatically, no less salutarily. It would seem that when all God's other gifts had failed to obtain their desired effect upon the chosen people, God gave them his only Son. The Father, Paul says in Romans 8:32, "did not spare his own Son but surrendered him for us all. How then, with this gift, has he not lavished upon us all," that he has to give?

Like the bread, I too, Christ's priest, am given to men as the sign of their salvation. I too am given for the life of the world. This is the ultimate meaning of my priesthood, of my priestly life, which Christ himself chose and blessed and transformed and molded for his own sacred purpose. In the *Roman Pontifical*, during the rite of priestly ordination, the bishop is directed to enjoin upon the candidate for the priesthood to "become what you do." "*Agnoscite quod agitis,*" he says ("Pay attention to what you are doing"). "*Imitamini quod tractatis*" ("Imitate this holy business, this action you carry out"): "*quatenus mortis dominicae mysterium celebrantes*" ("insofar as you celebrate the mystery of the Lord's death") "*mortificare membra vestra a vitiis et concupiscentiis omnibus procuretis*" ("you must attempt to procure the mortification of your members from vices and evil desires"). The priest must then in his life realize what, in imitation of Christ at the Last Supper, he effects each morning at the altar. The priest is to live by doing what he does at Mass.

What does the priest do in the Mass? In collaboration with Christ, the priest makes the offering of the Church: he offers the Church's sacrifice of herself, all she is and all she hopes and aspires to be. He offers this sacrifice through, and with, and in "Christ Jesus who died, or rather (as Paul says) who was raised, who is moreover at God's right hand, who indeed pleads our cause" (Rom 8:34). It is by changing the symbols of the Church's self-oblation into Christ, Christ the risen Lord who is present in the sacrament of the altar, that the priest learns how to live his own priestly life—*imitamini quod tractatis*. This means he must allow Christ to transform his personality, to take over his very person, not by subjugation, not by enslavement, but through the sweet dynamism of his grace—and this for men's salvation, for the life of the world.

THE COMMANDMENT TO ISRAEL
Deuteronomy 6:4-5
Hear, O Israel, Yahweh is our God, Yahweh alone! You must love Yahweh your God with your whole heart, with your whole soul, and with all your strength.
Leviticus 19:18
You must love your neighbor as yourself: I am Yahweh!
JESUS CONFIRMS THE COMMANDMENT
Mark 12:28-31
Now one of the scribes . . . asked Jesus, "Which is the first commandment of all?"
29Jesus replied, "This is the first: 'Hear, O Israel! The Lord our God is Lord alone! 30Therefore you shall love the Lord your God with all your heart, with all your soul, with all your mind, and with all your strength.' 31This is the second, 'You shall love your neighbor as yourself.' There is no other commandment greater than these."
PAUL'S INTERPRETATION
Galatians 5:14
For the entire Law has been fulfilled through the command, "You must love your neighbor as yourself."
Romans 13:8-9
The man who loves his neighbor has fulfilled the Law. 9For, "You must not commit adultery." "You must not commit murder," "You must not steal," "You must not covet," and any other commandment there be, has been summed up in this, "You must love your neighbor as yourself."
JOHN'S INTERPRETATION
John 13:34
This is my commandment: that you love one another, as I have loved you.
1 John 2:7-10
Beloved, it is no new commandment I write for you, but an ancient commandment which you possessed from the beginning. The ancient commandment is the word which you heard. 8Yet it is a new commandment I write for you—what is verified in him and in you. . . . 10The man who loves his brother remains in the light. . . .
1 John 3:11-23
For this is the news which you heard from the beginning: that we love one another. . . .
23And this is his commandment, that we believe in the name of his Son, Jesus Christ, and love one another according to the commandment he gave us.

THE NEW COMMANDMENT

Jesus' Passion, IN MAKING CONTEMPLATIONS on the Passion of our Lord, we
Paschal Mystery cannot, I think, afford to forget that the Passion narratives in the
Gospels were composed by their authors in the light of their experience of the paschal mystery, and hence these records of
Jesus' suffering and death must always be understood in the light
of his resurrection. For it was only through their paschal
faith, under the impulse of the Pentecostal Spirit, that the apostles
were able to create the kerygma, the primitive preaching, and
make the news of Jesus' death good news. It is no accident that, in
the New Testament, the word "gospel" is applied primarily to the
apostolic preaching. Only in a secondary and a derived sense is
the term predicated of the preaching of Jesus during his public
ministry. The principal reason for this usage is the fact that Jesus
proclaimed that the reign of God was come, during his ministry,
in his own Person. It was left to the apostolic Church to announce
that God's dominion was definitively realized by Jesus' death
and resurrection. Consequently, we must, in the contemplations
on Christ's Passion in the Spiritual Exercises, endeavor to recall
continually that the death and the resurrection are really inseparable, even though St. Ignatius appears to have separated them into
the third and fourth weeks. Actually, as we have already implied,
this Ignatian division is more methodological[1] than real, or theological. St. Ignatius makes a real separation of the second week
from the last two, which have a single aim—the development in
the exercitant of the love of friendship with Christ as Redeemer.

Another point to recall in contemplating Jesus' Passion is how
conscious the evangelists seem to have been of the fact that what
redeemed us was the voluntary character of Jesus' act of obedience
so freely and lovingly given to the Father. Throughout each of
these accounts of the Passion, we find the sacred writers stressing

---

1 It is in fact significant that the opening lines [219] of the text in the
Spiritual Exercises at the beginning of the fourth week are clearly a
repetition of those which terminate the third week [208]. I am indebted
for this illuminating observation to Father William Peters, S.J.

the willingness of Jesus in accepting, in all its concrete reality, the specific kind of death decreed by his Father; his supernatural fore-knowledge of what was to happen to him; and his awareness that, at every moment, he was in complete control of the situation.

Finally, it may be helpful also to note the manifest intention of the evangelists to involve their reader personally in the story as he progresses through it. These authors help him, in other words, to make what St. Ignatius has called the "composition of place," to become involved in the episodes that he contemplates, and thus aid him to make a total commitment of himself to Jesus Christ. An illustration of this concern of the evangelists to engage the reader personally may be found in some of the questions, or the sentiments expressed by the various actors in the drama, which are meant to evoke a reaction in the reader. There is, for instance, Judas' question at the Last Supper, "Is it I, Lord?"; Peter's pro-testation somewhat later, "I will never betray you"; Jesus' question in the garden, "Friend, what have you come to do?"; Pilate's avowal, "I am innocent of the blood of this holy man"; finally, the supremely important occasion for the reader's act of Christian faith after reading the narrative of Jesus' death, provided by the centurion's admiring assertion as he stood by the cross, "Truly this man was the Son of God!"

After these prolegomena, which may help our contemplations of the third week, we may take up the subject of this conference, the meaning of "the new commandment" which Jesus, according to the fourth Gospel, left his disciples on the eve of his departure from this world.

"Hear, O Israel, Yahweh is our God, Yahweh alone. You must love Yahweh your God with your whole heart, with your whole soul, and with all your strength." This quotation from the sixth chapter of Deuteronomy (vv. 4-5) expresses the way in which Is-rael was bid to respond in the dialogue of love, which is the old covenant, the sacred history of God's people. She must respond with her whole heart. In the Bible the heart does not symbolize, as among occidental peoples, the emotional, affective side of man, but rather that part of man which is most truly himself, most truly unique. Thus it includes his intellectual activity, which is the reason for the strange sounding phrase of the psalmist, employed in the Introit of the Mass of the Sacred Heart, "the thoughts of his heart." The Semitic concept of "the heart" also includes the will; and thus it is close to our western notion of the person, all of which, the commandment says, must be given unreservedly to God. The Hebrew term, which is rendered by "soul," in our text actually

The Old Commandment

221

means "life," or "life-principle." Thus, everything within us that makes us alive must be devoted to the service of God; and this with "all our strength."

I am sure there is no one here who labors under the misapprehension that the God of the Old Testament was a God of fear. Israel's God revealed himself constantly to her as a God of love. One has only to read a few pages of the prophet Hosea to be convinced of this truth. And this God asked for the love of Israel in return, as we see from this quotation of Deuteronomy. Yet this response of love, as Israel was well aware, to be genuine had to be translated into action. It had to be validated by reverence for Yahweh, by devoted service to him, by obedience to his commandments. Israel seems to have been convinced that there was something she could and should give Yahweh, which he, as her covenant-partner, wanted and even, in a sense, needed. As St. Ignatius remarks, love consists in a mutual exchange.

But on the other hand, and this was Israel's dilemma, she knew that Yahweh was not like the gods of the Gentiles, which a man might carry around in his pocket. These gods were helpless, of no use even to themselves: "they have mouths, yet they cannot speak; eyes, yet they cannot see; ears, yet they cannot hear!" (Ps 135: 16-17). Yahweh, by contrast, was a living, acting God. The transcendence of God is brought out very strikingly in the passage of Isaiah 40:12-27, where the prophet declares that the God who created the heavens and the earth has no need of any dwelling made by man; he is in no way dependent upon his creatures. He is no nature god, who dies annually, and requires to be resuscitated by a ritual like that carried out in Babylon, for example, on the New Year's feast between the king and the hierodule. God declared in the Old Testament that he did not need Israel's sacrifices and good works. The prophets are continually reminding their people that God is the Holy One—the "totally other." How then could Israel really give Yahweh anything?

In the nineteenth chapter of Leviticus (v. 18), there is another commandment with which you are very familiar: "You must love your neighbor as yourself: I am Yahweh!" By "neighbor," undoubtedly, was meant a fellow Israelite. But what is interesting here, I think, is that this command to love the neighbor is based upon the nature of God. "You must love your neighbor as yourself, for I am Yahweh!" God's transcendence somehow demands that the Israelite love his neighbor. That Israel was aware of this and articulated it to a degree will be seen from a careful examination of the decalogue, the epitome of Israel's reply in the covenant dialogue with her God.

The most astonishing feature of the decalogue is that most of it deals, not with what we might think of as man's relations with the Deity, but with his duties towards his neighbor. Almost all the commandments have to do with social life and social justice. Only the first two commandments are exclusively aimed at what would today be called religious or cultic observances. Even the third commandment, which demands that man keep the Sabbath holy, is understood in the Mosaic legislation as an ordering of human living. It was regarded as a humane measure, to give serfs and hired help one day in the week to rest (Dt 5:14-15). This commandment also was intended to set bounds upon man's desire for acquiring possessions. It limited human avarice by reminding the Israelite that Yahweh was master of time; hence one day in the week must be set aside and offered to God (Ex 20:11).

The rest of the decalogue deals with man's relations with his fellowman; and the same is true of the code of the covenant, as I pointed out before, since it is concerned almost entirely with what we should call "secular" and social questions. Indeed, it was the passion for social justice as well as the humanity of her legislation that distinguished Israel's law code from those of her neighbors.

Thus it was that Israel endeavored to solve her problem of what she might give God, by following out the command of Leviticus 19:18, that the neighbor must be loved as oneself. You will recall that during his public ministry, Jesus merely repeats these two commandments in the little dialogue with the lawyer, and declares that they sum up the Old Testament spirituality as a preparation for the coming of God's reign in history (Mk 12: 28-34).

When we turn to Paul, we discover, surprisingly perhaps, that the apostle has made a further abridgement of our Lord's already simplified version of man's relationship to God, which had reduced religion to two commandments. Paul sums the Christian life up in one commandment. "You brothers," he writes to the Galatians, "have a vocation to liberty. Only do not let it be an occasion to return to the natural; but become slaves to one another through love. For the entire Law has been fulfilled [brought, that is, to its prophetic consummation] through the command: 'You must love your neighbor as yourself'" (Gal 5:13-14). And lest we might think this was a slip of Paul's pen, we find him restating this same doctrine in Romans: "Owe no man anything, except the debt of mutual love. The man who loves his neighbor has *fulfilled* the whole Law. For 'You must not commit adultery,' 'You must not commit murder,' 'You must not steal,' 'You must not covet,'—and

223

any other commandment there be, has been summed up in this: 'You must love your neighbor as yourself.' Love towards one's neighbor works no evil; and hence love is the fulfillment of the Law" (Rom 13:8-10). Such is Paul's interpretation of the aim and the orientation of the Mosaic legislation. It is much as we have already surmised. The whole thrust of the old law was towards promoting a deep love of one's fellow man. In short, what Paul seems to say is that the only way we can do God's will, the only way we can love God effectively, is by loving our neighbor.

New Commandment in John

Our Lord, on the eve of his Passion, is represented in the fourth Gospel as giving his disciples a "new commandment." "This is my commandment: that you love one another, as I have loved you" (Jn 13:34). What is new about this new commandment? We must, first of all, inquire which Greek term for "new" is employed in this injunction. For there are two words in the Greek New Testament which mean "new": *neos* and *kainos. Neos* signifies new, in the sense of "just off the assembly line"—like a new car, that is probably full of "bugs" that have yet to be worked out. This is the term with which the evangelists describe the "new wine,"—it is freshly made (Mk 2:22). Such newness is obviously not a desirable quality; it rather suggests immaturity, a lack of perfection. Consequently, St. Luke, who seems to have been something of a connoisseur, in recording this saying of Jesus about new wine, adds an observation of his own: "No man who is used to drinking old wine will take the new; 'for,' says he, 'the old is better' " (Lk 5:39).

In the fourth Gospel, however, the "new" commandment is qualified by the term *kainos,* which means "new," in the sense of novel, unprecedented. It denotes something that interrupts the ordinary course of events, the continuity of history; hence something which involves a completely fresh start, and so implies a creative act of God. The *new* covenant, the *new* commandment demand the use of *kainos*—it is a creative beginning by Christ. This new commandment Jesus will promulgate through his inauguration of "the new creation" at his death and resurrection. He intends it to replace the two commandments that he mentioned during his public life.

Observe that this new commandment is simply, "that you love one another, as I have loved you" (Jn 13:34). Later, in this same discourse, Jesus will speak of the greatest love a man can display. Amazingly enough, he does not speak of our loving God, but of love for other human beings. "Greater love than this no man has," Jesus declares, "than that he lay down his life for his friends" (Jn 15:13). This new commandment, which he announces at the

224

Last Supper, he considers to constitute an essential part of the new covenant, which he makes with us through the mediation of the Twelve. The Blessed Eucharist is the instrument of covenant-making: it is through it men are to be given the power to love one another. In this new commandment nothing indeed is said explicitly about loving God; yet through it Jesus provides mankind with a solution to this problem of mutual exchange, which is the essence of love. He tells us that there is something we can give God: our love for one another.

When the Word became flesh, the Son of God became dependent upon other men in a very real sense, whereas he had been, in the bosom of the Godhead, supremely independent of all creation. Yet once his work of redemption was accomplished, after his death and resurrection, our Lord returned with his sacred humanity to his rightful place at the Father's right hand; he no longer needed men's help, as he had during his mortal life. He cannot be personally benefited any more by actions of love towards him. It is for this reason that he has given us a new commandment, which his death and resurrection have given us the capability of observing—the divine imperative that we love one another as he loved us. For, if St. Ignatius is correct in asserting that love consists in action rather than in words, and that it consists in a mutual exchange between those who love, then I must give God something if I claim to love him in reality. Yet the only return I can make to God in exchange for what he has given me, Jesus tells us, is to love my fellow man. "Love one another as I have loved you." Jesus' love, of course, being divine, was creative; but Jesus' love was also human, and, as human love, it was efficacious since it has redeemed mankind.

The human love then that he desires from me, which he declared to be the hallmark of the Christian must somehow be efficacious. It has become effective in Christianity because, as a result of the death and resurrection of Jesus, we are somehow identified with him in a way in which we were not before. In dying and rising Christ has somehow assumed to himself all mankind. Someone has stated, not inaccurately, that Jesus rose with his Mystical Body. This is the event which has conferred its novelty, its utter newness upon this new commandment of Jesus; because his death and resurrection have created a totally new possibility for our truly loving God—by loving one another. There was never anything man could do directly, effectively to love God, until Jesus, by dying and rising, provided a new possibility. And for this purpose he had given the new commandment, that we might truly love God his Father and himself in his risen state by showing love,

225

by our lives, for one another. This, quite simply, is the great good news of the gospel—the message of love that is efficacious towards God because it is love for man.

You will recall that in his preamble to the *Constitutions*, St. Ignatius declares that the only thing that keeps the Society together effectively, the sole source of our unity, is the love of God, which, as Paul says, "is poured forth into our hearts by the gift of the Holy Spirit" (Rom 5:5). He is this love which Ignatius believed had created and which will sustain the Society. You know St. Ignatius' own words, which you have heard so often: "It is the interior law of charity and love, which is to preserve, govern, and direct in God's holy service this least Society of Jesus, just as he deigned thereby to bring it into existence."[2] This profound act of confidence in the presence of the Spirit of Christ, which Ignatius made as founder of the Society is meant to be our daily credo also. Despite the spots and the wrinkles, the maladjustment of certain Renaissance trappings that the Society has carried with her somewhat awkwardly into the twentieth century, we must continue to believe that the Spirit of Jesus remains present among us; and that this same Spirit, in his own good time, will quicken us anew for the work of that personal self-reform, which is the very foundation of any reformation of the Society on the institutional level. Moreover, this same Spirit of love will quicken the Society so that its *aggiornamento* may be realized according to the will of Jesus himself. But it is imperative that we remember that this "interior law of love," which St. Ignatius believed to exist in us as a body, demands a response from each one of us: that we love one another.

Pauline Hymn to Love It is striking that when Paul comes in first Corinthians, chapter thirteen, to speak of this "most excellent way," he appears to be talking primarily, though he does not say so explicitly, about our love of one another, rather than about the love of God. "And now I will show you the most excellent way. I may speak the language of men, even of angels; yet, if I am without love, I am merely a loud gong or a clanging cymbal." Paul does not mean a noisy sort of person. In chapter fourteen, where he is talking about musical instruments, he says that gongs and cymbals produce but a single note, so that nobody can tell what tune is being

2 "Although the Supreme Wisdom and Goodness of God our Creator and Savior are what must preserve, direct, and carry forward in his divine service this least Society of Jesus, just as that Wisdom and Goodness designed to begin it; and on our part the interior law of charity and love which the Holy Spirit writes and engraves upon hearts must help more toward this end than any exterior constitution . . ." (The Preamble to the *Constitutions of the Society of Jesus*.)

played: they emit no intelligible sound (1 Cor 14:7-8). "I may possess the gift of prophecy, know all mysteries, have all knowledge, I may have faith enough to move mountains, but if I am without love, I am nothing. I may give away all I possess, even hand over my body to be burned; yet if I have no love, I am utterly useless."

Paul now goes on to describe the many faces of this Christian love we must display towards one another. "Love is patient; love is kind and free from envy. Love never puts on airs, is never conceited or rude, is never selfish, nor easily offended. Love keeps no score of injuries, takes no morbid pleasure in wickedness, but delights in the truth. Love is able to bear anything: there are no bounds to its trust, its hope, its endurance" (vv. 4-7).

Paul ends with a magnificent hymn in honor of the primacy of love. "Love will never come to an end. What prophecy there is will eventually be terminated. Ecstatic prayer likewise will cease to exist. The knowledge men have will vanish. For our knowledge and our prophecy alike are imperfect, and the imperfect will vanish when perfection is realized." [Let me illustrate what I mean.] "When I was a child, I spoke as a child, had the interests of a child, thought as a child. When I grew up, I had no time for childishness. At the moment, we can see only obscure reflections like those in a mirror [you may recall that the ancients used polished bronze as mirrors]; but then we shall see face to face. My knowledge is now imperfect. Then it will be complete, like God's knowledge of myself. In a word, there are three things that will last for eternity: faith, hope, and love. But the greatest of them all is love" (vv. 8-13).

Chapter 23

THE MASS: SCHOOL FOR
THE RELIGIOUS

Mass, School THE GOOD NEWS of Christianity comes simply to this, that as a
of Christianity result of Jesus' death and resurrection we can now love God effectively only by loving one another. St. John asserts this truth in
very strong language by saying that, "If a man claims to love God
and hates his brother, he is a liar" (1 Jn 4:20). Probably the greatest difficulty with Christianity is that it is so utterly human, so
astonishingly simple. The real novelty of the Christian gospel is
the revelation that I must find God in Christ, not "out there," and
not merely "in here," in the sense of inside myself; I find Christ
upon the face and in the heart of humanity.

Someone has said that the Mass is the school of Christianity;
and so the Mass must be the locus of my Christian activity, in
which I learn how to love Christ by loving my fellowman. I must,
with grace, endeavor to see that the only possibility open to me,
since Christ's glorification, of loving him effectively—as indeed
I must—is to love him in that dimension of his personality, so to
speak, which he acquired by his death and resurrection. It is certainly true that through his glorification he has gone forward into
the new life with the Father, beyond the reach of my own love. Yet
by this identical saving event he has acquired that "Body, which
is the Church" (Col 1:18); and so has provided me with a completely new and effective way of responding to this new commandment of loving my neighbor. This very truth he disclosed to his
disciples when, at the moment of his ascension when he seemed
to be leaving them forever, he promised to remain with them
and among them until the termination of history (Mt 28:20). The
mystery of Jesus' ascension signifies a revolution in the whole
idea of religion. It means that the way I find the sacred is in what
was formerly thought of as the profane. It means that the successful quest for God is to be carried out in the world of men, through
human experience. As St. Mark has pointed out, the good news
of the gospel is to be found in Jesus' redefinition of the "common."
That evangelist tells us that "thus he declared all food clean" (Mk

228

7:19), thereby giving men a new insight into the significance of the secular, the profane. There is indeed such a reality as "the world." It is where the reign of Christ is unknown. It is the Church, which acknowledges Christ as Lord, whose lofty privilege it is to proclaim that lordship to the world. For "the world" is that sector of mankind which does not know him. It is the duty of the Church to announce the good news of the gospel "to every creature" (Mk 16:15).

The gospel includes the divine cult. Thus the liturgy has, in a certain true sense, regained its original meaning of "public affairs," the business of life. Its chief aim is to provide the grounds for our gradual growth in the awareness that we are truly "sons of God." *Familiaritas cum Deo in oratione* is the purpose of public worship, which is orientated towards giving us a deeper "sense of family." This means that our Christian fellowship, a truly genuine human fellowship of mutual love, is the experience through which we learn how the Father has really loved us. How does the Mass efficaciously create this union of wills in us, which is the carrying out of Jesus' command to us?

We might recall here that religious are simply Christians whose entire life is ordered totally to the full actualization of the exigencies of the baptismal grace which they have received. In baptism, as Paul teaches (Rom 6:3-5), we die and rise with Christ; that is, we experience sacramentally our involvement in our Lord's act of redeeming us. In consequence of this initiation we must endeavor to experience in our daily living this dying and rising with Christ which is our preparation for uttering that final saving "yes" to the Father—our own act of dying to rise at the *parousia*. The religious then is someone who has adopted a way of life in which all is ordered to the perfect flowering of this baptismal grace. Thus the aim of the religious life coincides with the aim of any Christian life. The religious obligation to attain perfection does not, as end, differ from that of the ordinary Christian: the religious is not bound to attain a different kind of perfection from that imposed as goal upon the ordinary Christian. When Jesus said, "Be perfect as your heavenly Father is perfect" (Mt 5:48), this commandment was addressed to all his followers, not merely to some sort of elite.

The distinction between the religious and other Christians is not a discrimination between those consecrated to God and those not consecrated. The very word "laity" reminds us that they are by definition the people (*laos*) of God: *plebs tua sancta*. In the kingdom of God there is no division into first class and second

class citizens—at least on the basis of the goal to be achieved.
Mediocrity is proposed to no one in the Christian Church as
the purpose of the Christian life.

What then is the distinction between the status of the religious
and that of other Christians? The difference lies in the means taken
to arrive at the common Christian goal of perfection: the exploitation of the baptismal grace. The means taken by religious
men and women, as the Church declares in approving their constitutions, are ordered completely to arrive at that perfection
incumbent upon all Christians. This total orientation of human
life towards the supreme goal laid down by Jesus Christ does
not consist merely in subjecting oneself to a number of rules. This
could simply mean that the religious has more possibilities for
committing faults and imperfections than his brothers and sisters
in the Church—hardly an advantage in the path towards perfection! It is rather that by entering the religious state the Christian
freely takes part in what might be called a "conspiracy of wills,"
in striving to attain the common purpose of the Christian life.
He enters into a special Christian fellowship where all the members are personally involved in the task of assisting one another to
the realization of the fullest possible actuation of the baptismal
grace.

Sense of Family   In the Mass the initial steps taken as a preparation for the public worship of the Father are meant to impress the participants
with the keen sense of forming a community. Such an intention,
of course, is implicit in the very fact of their assembling together
to celebrate the Lord's Supper. But this desire for communion
with one another, this acquisition of a "sense of family" must
become more deeply conscious. The Rule of St. Benedict[1] describes the aim of the monastic life as consisting in *stabilitas in
congregatione*—the inauguration and successful achieving of this
special Christian fellowship which is the essence of the religious
state. The Mass aims at giving us a sense of solidarity, a sense of
belonging. Belonging to whom? To Christ as our brother, to God
as our common Father. We start out towards this goal, however,
by trying to make more real to ourselves the Christian sense of
belonging to one another. We endeavor to become conscious of
our existence as a community here and now, as a specific group
gathered to celebrate the Eucharistic liturgy in a special place on
a particular day.

1 *The Holy Rule of St. Benedict*, ch. 4 lists this among the "instruments of
good works."

How do we acquire at Mass this sense of community? We begin by the public confession of our sins to one another. Sin is divisive —the most anti-social element in human life, as the story of the tower of Babel illustrates so graphically (Gn 11:1-9). Sin effects our isolation from one another and cuts us off from this fellowship. Hence we must try to rid ourselves of sin, if we would attempt to create the sense of family. We should not permit ourselves to forget that our reception of the sacrament of penance is an act of public worship, because thereby we return sacramentally to the Christian fellowship of the Body of Christ.

Confession of Sins

A second and more positive means of realizing this family spirit is by prayer, the prayer of petition, by which all of us unite together, pool our personal needs and aspirations, and address ourselves as a family to the one Father through the one Jesus Christ in the one Holy Spirit. The familial petition that we offer in the Collect is a public expression, through our *Amen*, of our common desire for this sense of belonging to one another here and now.

Prayer of Petition

The solemn proclamation of the word of God in the Epistle and in the Gospel is the third of these formative elements in realizing our fellowship at this stage of the Mass. The unity produced by the proclaimed word of revelation is a feature of sacred history, testified to by the repeated experience of Israel. The runaway slaves that Moses led to the mount of Sinai had had in the beginning little or no sense of community. The only factor that brought them into the desert and kept them there despite hardships and misfortune was fear of reprisals by the taskmasters of Egypt. But when Moses came down from the mountain and proclaimed to the people God's covenanted word, we behold a new phenomenon. Israel was thereby created from this oddly sorted group of Hebrews. At a later age, after the Exile, when the people, returning to a desolated homeland, had lost this sense of their solidarity and unity to a large extent, Ezra the scribe "stood up on a raised wooden platform which they made for the purpose," and read to the people from the book of the law for eight days continuously. The purpose of this act was simply to recreate the fellowship that was Israel (Neh 8:1-18). We see a similar phenomenon in the history of the primitive Church (Acts 2:42). That communion of heart and mind, which Acts considers to be the hallmark of the Jerusalem Church, was caused by their constant devotion to the teaching of the apostles. At this early stage in the life of the Church, there were no New Testament

Proclamation of the Word

Scriptures. In their stead the preaching or instruction of the apostles, the oral transmission of Christian doctrine within the community, transformed these Jewish Christian converts into the Christian family or fellowship.

Gift-giving

The last way in which, at Mass, we express symbolically our desire for union of wills, for fellowship with one another, is through the gifts brought to the altar at the Offertory. Our gifts consist of bread and wine—symbols of life, since in the Mediterranean world, at least in Jesus' day, they constituted the principal items of diet. This bread has been produced by the molding together of countless grains of ground wheat, just as the wine has been produced by the crushing of numberless grapes. Thus while these offerings do indeed symbolize each one of us—our personal ideals, our needs, our aspirations, yet they represent principally our collective desire to belong to one another.

*Christ's
Consecration*

Yet all four of these gestures, expressing our desire for an increased sense of community, are merely the preliminary steps in preparation for the central action of the Mass, which is the Consecration. For it is through the Consecration that the instrument of covenant-making by which Jesus established the new covenant at the Last Supper appears in our midst: the now glorified body, blood, soul, and divinity of Jesus Christ. It was by means of bread and wine become himself that Jesus struck a covenant, through the mediation of the Twelve, with the future Christian people, and so instituted the Mass.

This desire of ours to belong to one another, which is the Christian expression of our quest for God, is necessarily a dialogue between the community and the Father. We cannot carry it out successfully by ourselves, but only through the Son incarnate. We, the congregation assembled for public worship, cannot effect this *divinum commercium* by ourselves, even when united as the *plebs sancta*.

On the other hand, because the Father and the Son have so ordained, God cannot do it by himself. It is for this reason that we cannot remain passive, we cannot approach God empty-handed to ask him to produce this miracle of fellowship among us. By his divine ordination each of us must come, bringing what the Father desires: myself, my life, my needs, above all my longing for communion with those present with me at Mass. Hence the necessity of my gifts. I offer God a token or symbol of this communal desire.

By the priestly act of consecration, the memorial of Christ's

232

death and resurrection, these gifts are transformed into the glorified Lord, who is now become "life-giving Spirit." In the fore-
Mass it was our unity of wills, our common Christian purpose,
which we set out at the beginning of the liturgy to achieve, which
made it clear that these gifts stood for all of us, stood for that
oneness of mind and heart which we desired to increase. Yet this
desired fellowship was of itself a fragile, unstable communion,
since it was only the effect of our weak, creaturely wills. Such a
community as we then constructed could only be as effective and
actual as the wills that desired it within the group present at
Mass. At the Consecration, the gifts which symbolized this will
to oneness are transformed, "transubstantiated" into the risen
Christ himself. And by this very event the fellowship symbolized
by these gifts is transformed also. Our collective will to oneness
is taken over by Christ and recreated by his gift of the Holy Spirit
into a new unity, because this conspiracy of our human wills is one
united with his single will-act, by which he redeemed us, by which
he effected our at-one-ment. We may here recall that the sufferings of Christ's passion and death, as well as the joys of his
resurrection, were but external symbols also. They were the ex-
teriorization of that invisible act of will by which he redeemed
us. Thus the goal of our common quest for Christ, and for the
Father in Christ, is to unite our feeble, inconsistent hearts (*nutantia corda*)[2] with all the other hearts in the Christian community
present at Mass, in the hope that the risen Lord will unite them
with his own eternal act of self-offering to the Father, his redeeming will made present in the Eucharist.

There is, of course, one final stage in the Mass: the sacramental
realization of our communion with God in Christ, which effectively
produces in the community a renewed "sense of family." St.
Paul has reminded us that in pagan religions, as also in Judaism,
the sacrificial meal was the normal accompaniment of sacrificial
cult (1 Cor 10:18-21). Holocausts, where the victims were entirely
destroyed in order to devote them totally to the service of God
and place them entirely outside the profane, were relatively in-
frequent. In the majority of Israelite sacrifices, particularly in the
thanksgiving offering, part of the victim offered to God was
given back to the worshiper, so that he with his family and
friends might hold a sacrificial meal and so become "table com-

---

2 Cf. the prayer over the gifts for the fifth Sunday after Epiphany: We
   offer this sacrifice to you, O Lord, to atone for our sins. Mercifully absolve
   us from our wrongdoing and exert your power over the inconstancy of
   our hearts.

panions" with God. Paul says, speaking of this kind of sacrifice in Israel, "Is not he who partakes of the victim made a partaker of the altar?" (1 Cor 10:18). The altar in Israel stood for God; accordingly, this fellowship in the sacrificial meal signified communion with Yahweh.

By analogy, then, as Paul conceives it, the cup from which we drink and the bread which we break in the Mass is fellowship with the body and blood of the risen Christ (1 Cor 10:16). This sacred meal, inasmuch as it is communion with the risen Christ, produces in us the dynamic presence of the Holy Spirit, the gift of the Father's love for us "poured out in our hearts" (Rom 5:5). It is his operation which recreates our Christian fellowship, making us aware that we are all sons of the heavenly Father (Gal 4:6).

St. Paul tells us also of another important aspect of the Mass. "As often as you eat this bread and drink the cup, you proclaim the death of the Lord" (1 Cor 11:26). The Mass is proclamation, like the gospel; it is divine Word, like the gospel. It is the heralding of Christ's death as revelation of the lordship of Jesus Christ, which indeed was the burden of the gospel. In the Mass then, we depose our Christian testimony to the joyful truth that Christ's redemptive activity is still being deployed in our world. Yet this quest for God in Christ, through the Lord's supper, Paul tells us also, is a continuing quest. We do not achieve the goal suddenly, or all at once; and when we come upon it we do not grasp it in its entirety. Consequently, all our Christian lives, we must continue to "proclaim the death of the Lord until he comes." This Eucharistic epiphany of Christ as Lord, like the coming in his earthly life, is calculated mainly to stir up our desire for his final coming at the close of history. When he thus comes in glory, our Lord will effect the resurrection or the transformation of our body (1 Cor 15:23; Rom 8:23). That is to say, he will bring us all within the full range of God's redemptive plan for us; and this, even on the material side of our personality. Meanwhile, our participation in the Eucharist continually brings us closer to this wonderful climax of the redemption. Holy Communion truly affects us even on the corporeal side of our human nature. Its quality as food is a real and efficacious sign of a gradual process: the spiritualization of our bodily personality. This is difficult, if not impossible to understand; yet we must not think of it as a kind of dissolution or evanescence of the material components of our nature. The action of the Holy Spirit does not destroy the material or bodily side of our humanity, causing it to dissolve and disappear. The Spirit comes more fully into my life as a human being, whose body is a component part of my personality. Indeed, as Paul asserts

234

(2 Cor 3:18), the term of this gradual spiritualization is the reproduction in us of the image of Christ, who is the image of the Father: "and all of us, reflecting the glory of the Lord in our unveiled faces, are being transformed into his image from one degree of glory to another, by the Lord who is the Spirit."

In Holy Communion the risen Christ comes to take over my body, my heart, my will, myself. He comes to transform this very human need which I have of belonging to the other members of the Christian community. He comes to make this desire for fellowship efficacious, sacramentally efficacious, because it is his intention to make use of my personality in my world of the twentieth century in realizing his plan for the redemption of my contemporaries. Thus the "real action" that results from Holy Communion is the ultimate purpose of this most Blessed Sacrament. To this goal the real presence of Christ is subordinate. My transformation into Christ, which is also the goal of my religious life, is to be experienced sacramentally in the Mass. This means that I am given an effective aid to insert myself into that conspiracy of wills which marks me off as a Christian who is also a religious; a man, more conscious than the ordinary Christian, of the necessity of organizing my whole life around the one fundamental Christian goal, the full exploitation of the baptismal grace which is in me. Because I am a social being, because I need the aid of fellowship, the help of other men who have this same awareness and this same aim, Christ comes in the Mass to me as a religious to strengthen this conspiracy of wills, the most significant feature of my religious life.

Thus we return to this notion of fellowship with which we began—*stabilitas in congregatione*, as St. Benedict calls it. This it is which provides the pattern for Christian salvation. I am not intended to go to God in Christ as an isolated individual. I must go in the universal fellowship of the Christian people; and within that universal fellowship I live my life within my own religious family. The chief means by which I am taught to discern this route, along which my quest for God in Christ must be pursued, is my daily participation in the Eucharistic liturgy, carried out in union with my religious brethren.

Chapter 24

THE LITURGY OF HOLY THURSDAY

Character of the THROUGHOUT THE SOLEMN CELEBRATION of the Lord's Supper
Meal in Ancient at which we shall shortly be present, the social aspect of the
Near East Blessed Eucharist is very much to the fore. On this holy day
there is but one Mass in which the whole of our religious family
is meant to participate together, since the Church wishes to remind
us of the meal-character of the Eucharistic liturgy by making this
anniversary of its institution a genuine family feast. Cicero saw
in the Roman *convivium,* or banquet shared by friends, a far
superior symbol of social significance to the *symposion,* or drinking bout of the Greeks. Eating together promotes as well as symbolizes real friendship in a more effective manner than merely
drinking together.

We should remind ourselves however that in the ancient world,
particularly in the Semitic cultures, a meal was not merely a social
event; it possessed in addition a sacred and religious character
which is difficult for modern man to appreciate. Thus, for instance, the gesture of Melchisedek in "offering bread and wine"
(Gn 14:18) to the sheik of Sodom and Abraham and Lot after their
return from battle meant something more, in the cultural context of the time, than the provision of a collation for these tired,
victorious warriors. We cannot properly assess the significance
of this act of oriental hospitality unless we remember that among
these peoples the meal was also a sacred rite. Hence it provided
a most suitable occasion for Melchisedek's blessing of Abraham
(vv. 19-20). Accordingly, the Fathers of the Church exhibit a
sound instinct for the theological meaning of this meal when
they consider it a type of the Blessed Sacrament. The ancients regarded the meal, in which man's social needs as well as the merely
physical demands for nourishment were satisfied, as a genuine
form of divine worship, expressive of man's religious attitudes.
Recently Mrs. Solange Hertz in a delightful book, which expresses vivaciously a housewife's reactions to the Bible, *Come
Down Zacchaeus,* has shrewdly observed how frequently the

236

sacred writers advert to male interest in eating. The most important occasions involving men in the Scriptures are somehow connected with the enjoyment of a meal; and when our Lord on the eve of his own passion and death instituted the new covenant with the Twelve, he did so by providing them with a meal—a transcendently sacred meal, the Blessed Eucharist.

The entrance hymn for today's liturgy takes its inspiration from a passage in Paul's letter to the Galatians: "May I never glory in anything except the Cross of our Lord Jesus Christ, through which the world has been crucified for me once for all, as I also remain crucified together with the world" (Gal 6:14). The theme then of this Introit is the redemptive death of Christ, but the saving function of Jesus' resurrection in addition to the Cross has been more explicitly set forth than in the Pauline passage. "It is our duty to glory in the Cross of our Lord Jesus Christ, for it constitutes our salvation, our life, our resurrection. Through it we have been saved and set at liberty." We are thus reminded of the intimate connection which exists between the Eucharist and the central act of man's redemption, the death and resurrection of our Saviour.

Introit

The Collect, which admittedly is rather lengthy, may not at first seem to mention this aspect of our Christian fellowship, which constitutes the central theme for today's liturgy. However, the mention of Judas' treachery recalls the pathos which this tragic betrayal communicated to the atmosphere of love and union, which is the salient feature of the scene depicted in the thirteenth chapter of the fourth Gospel, when our Lord waits until Judas leaves the room before he institutes the Eucharist and begins his farewell discourse to the faithful disciples. The mention of the Good Thief in the Collect commemorates a bandit who professed a desire for fellowship with Christ, and recalls our Lord's promise to him: "I assure you, today you will be with me in paradise" (Lk 23:43). The desire for fellowship with Jesus Christ is the dominant motif in the conversion of the Good Thief. When we ask that our Lord may grant us a share in the grace of his resurrection, we are praying for the re-creation of his Mystical Body, the whole Christ. This is the grace of the resurrection. It was in order to inaugurate the Mystical Body, the Church, that Christ rose from death. This is the marvelous favor that God has done us through this phase of the central act of our redemption.

Collect

The Epistle is a selection from Paul's letter to Corinth (1 Cor 11: 20-32), where he complains that, instead of developing this feeling

Epistle

237

of fellowship, the celebration of the Lord's Supper was the occasion for certain abuses which produced the very opposite effect, divisions within the community. The touching practice of sharing their earthly goods with one another by the Jewish-Christian community of Jerusalem is called in Acts *koinōnia*, a word which means "fellowship." The first members of the Jerusalem community shared their earthly possessions with one another as a preparation for the celebration of the Eucharist. They hoped that by thus giving one another whatever they had at their disposal, they might be better prepared to receive Christ, and to profit by the grace of his presence when he came to them in the breaking of the Bread. This community of goods was intended as an effective sign of an essential Christian attitude, the longing for fellowship. Later when this experiment in primitive communism broke down, through bad management or for whatever reason, it was never repeated in the same form in the history of the Church. Yet it seems that in certain communities, as for example at Corinth, a common supper, or community meal was instituted precisely to provide a symbol of this "communion," or Christian fellowship. In the Pauline passage which concerns us, Paul is attacking certain abuses because, he says equivalently, these Christians are not participating in the fruit of the redemption brought to us in the Eucharist, which is basically a social attitude.

Gospel   The Gospel (Jn 13:1-15) provides a very striking scriptural exemplification of this fellowship, or "sense of family," which today's feast seeks to communicate to us. As you know, John's account of the Last Supper omits the narrative of the institution of the Eucharist. He chooses rather to stress two points which evidently caught his attention: firstly, Jesus' washing of the disciples' feet, and secondly, that new commandment which we reflected upon this morning, "that you love one another as I have loved you." When you read the thirteenth chapter of John—the part that we will hear in the Holy Thursday liturgy—I am sure you have observed, as I have, the seemingly exaggerated build-up for this very simple action of Jesus. The opening verses of this Gospel passage recapitulate the Johannine theology of the redemption, and the evangelist twice insists strongly that Jesus is completely aware of what is to happen to himself. He asserts that Jesus does what he does, that is he washes the feet of his disciples, with the full knowledge that his hour to leave the world has come. He is leaving the world, and he is going home to the Father. Yet Jesus' departure from this world is not like the death of anyone else, since this is the event by which Jesus will redeem mankind. Hence John

238

reminds us that "he loved his own unto the end," that is, unto perfection. The sacred writer draws our attention to the fact that Jesus is fully conscious at this moment that the whole work of the redemption has been committed into his hands by the Father, and that it is in the light of this awareness that our Lord prepares to wash his disciples' feet. This appears, as I have said, to be an elaborate introduction to what turns out to be a very ordinary service which Jesus performs for his disciples. The author insists that Jesus is aware of the whole divine economy of the redemption: that he has come from God upon this very mission, that he is now to return to the Father.

Why does John stress this *pedilavium*? He intends, I believe, to underscore for his readers one very important aspect of our Lord's redemptive work: Jesus did not die and rise in order to prevent, or even excuse us from sharing personally in this saving experience. If we are to be redeemed, we must, in our turn, undergo death and resurrection, which in Christ are now become an essential Christian experience. On John's view, Jesus washes the disciples' feet as a symbol of their future participation in his death and resurrection. But this Christian sharing in the redemptive act is specified by the very nature of Jesus' symbolic action on this occasion. To wash the feet of the disciples is, for the Master, an act of service, indeed a very special act of service, since it is a demonstration of love. *Exemplum dedi vobis:* it is an example of fraternal love. Accordingly, when Peter demurs, Jesus must explain to him that he cannot be aware of the significance of this action of the Master. Otherwise, he would not refuse to cooperate in this mimed prophecy. And indeed, at this juncture Peter is incapable of understanding the sense of what is being enacted by Jesus, since our Lord's death and his resurrection lie hidden in the future.

Peter's refusal to let Jesus wash his feet permits our Lord to explain that Peter, without intending to do so, would be cutting himself off from all fellowship with his Master in the supreme act by which he will accomplish Peter's redemption. "If I do not wash you, you have no part with me!" (Jn 13:8). But Peter still misunderstands. All he knows is that he loves Jesus dearly, and he wants to be associated perpetually with him. And so he asks to be washed entirely, to be given a bath! "Lord, not merely my feet, but also my hands and head" (Jn 13:9). Jesus' reply to this well-intentioned but incomprehending request by Peter is not easy to grasp. In fact, because of the difficulty of now ascertaining with any certainty what our evangelist originally wrote, it is well nigh impossible to comprehend. The verse caused trouble for centuries, as the Vulgate text testifies: *Qui lotus est, non indiget nisi ut pedes lavet, sed est mundus totus* (Jn 13:10). Some copyist felt it was necessary to insert an explanatory note to the effect that the man who is washed needs simply to wash his feet, and he is completely clean. But this *"nisi ut pedes"* is almost certainly an interpolation, based upon misunderstanding of the original text. What Jesus appears to mean is that the man "who has taken a bath" by the reception of Christian baptism is not to "bathe" again, since of its very nature, as the rite of Christian initiation, baptism can never be repeated. However if the Christian is defiled by sin, "he has only to wash, and he is completely clean once more." By washing we are to understand, in some sense, the exercise of the Church's power, committed to her by Christ, of forgiving sin. Jesus' action, as has been said, is a symbolic one; and its significance is not to be sought in washing. It is rather a symbol of mutual service, a symbol of fraternal love. He appears to be saying equivalently that it is only by effectively loving one another that we are enabled to involve ourselves personally in the great movement of the redemption, itself initiated by the love of the Father and the Son, which is the death and resurrection of Jesus. Thus, while the evangelist does not record Jesus' act of instituting the Eucharist, still by means of this narrative of the washing of the disciples' feet by our Lord, he reminds his reader of the primary purpose of the Christian celebration of the Lord's Supper. It is the sacramental re-presentation of that new covenant of love, which Jesus made with the Twelve at the last meal he shared with them in this world. The Mass is a memorial, a re-presentation, and it is truly sacramental. This means that, by doing what Jesus did at the Last Supper in obedience to his express command to bless and eat the bread and wine, we may obtain the grace of loving one another, as he has loved us. For by celebrating the Lord's Supper we ensure our participation in the grace of having our fraternal love caught up into the great act of filial love by which Jesus has redeemed us. We are thus empowered to inaugurate, through this fellowship of the Eucharist, the process which prepares our definitive final fellowship with his own death and resurrection through which we are to be totally redeemed.

This lesson of service and mutual love of the brotherhood is so central to the rite of Holy Thursday that these words of Jesus, *"Exemplum dedi vobis . . .,"* are repeated at the Communion versicle. The rubrics of the Missal suggest that this theme be prolonged and emphasized by the chanting of one of the most beautiful psalms in the Old Testament, Psalm twenty-three: "The

Lord is my Shepherd," It has been chosen because, in the opinion of the Fathers of the Church, it contains allusions to the two great sacraments of Christian fellowship, baptism and the Eucharist. The "refreshing waters" to which God leads his people were understood to be baptism (Ps 23:2), as also the anointing with oil (v.5). The "banquet for me in the sight of my foes" (v.5) was interpreted as a type of the Eucharist. What is perhaps even more significant for these sacramental themes is the atmosphere of special intimacy with Yahweh which breathes throughout the entire poem. It is this sense of fellowship which dominates the Postcommunion prayer. "Fortified by this lifegiving nourishment we beg you, O Lord, that by the gift of your immortality [the Eucharist] we may one day enjoy the full possession of this mystery, which during our mortal life here below we re-enact through Christ our Lord."

JESUS' PRAYER IN GETHSEMANI
Mark 14:32-42

And they reach a villa which was called Gethsemani, where he says to his disciples, "Sit down here while I pray." 33Then he took Peter, James and John along with him; and he became bewildered and anguished. 34He says to them, "My heart is near breaking with sorrow. Remain here and stay awake." 35He advanced a short distance, and fell prostrate upon the ground, praying that, if it were possible, this Hour might pass him by. 36He kept saying, "*Abba* (dear Father!), you can do everything. Take this cup away from me. Yet it must be as you wish, not as I wish."

37When he returned, he found them asleep; so he said to Peter, "Simon, you are asleep? Could you not stay awake even for an hour? 38Stay awake, and pray that you be not subjected to the trial. Your spirit is fervent, but poor human nature is weak."

39And again he went to pray, employing the same words. 40Once again he found them asleep on his return; their eyes seemed to have heavy weights upon them, and they did not know what to say to him.

41When he returned a third time, he said to them, "Still asleep? Still enjoying your rest? Enough of this! the Hour has come: see, the Son of Man is being handed over into the power of evil men. 42 Get up! Let us be on our way. See, my betrayer is here."

Chapter 25

GETHSEMANI: DRAMATIZATION OF
CHRISTIAN PRAYER

I SUGGEST that for our contemplation we take the experience of *Reconstruction* Jesus in the garden of Gethsemani, which we usually refer to as his *by the Synoptics* "agony." Luke is the one who uses this term, which means simply a struggle. Each of the Synoptics has his own way of recounting this episode (Mt 26:30-46; Lk 22:39-46; Mk 14:32-42).

In the Passion account of the fourth Gospel there is no agony. Through John's scene in the garden, as we shall see when we come to contemplate his version of the Passion, there breathes a quite different spirit. John however has not omitted this struggle of Jesus. We find a description of it in that scene where Jesus meets "the Greeks," probably Hellenistic Jews, who have come on pilgrimage to the temple for one of the great feasts (Jn 12:27-30).

The agony in the garden, as it is narrated by the Synoptics is, from the literary point of view, similar in character to the account of Jesus' temptations in Matthew and Luke. That is to say, we are dealing here with an experience of our Lord, personal to himself, and unobserved by any other human being, as were his temptations. Consequently, we may expect that for the composition of this scene, the evangelists have been forced to reconstruct it from the scanty data which they received from the oral tradition. We know, in fact, that of the Twelve, all of whom except Judas accompanied him to the garden, only three remained within seeing distance of this struggle: the two brothers, John and James, Zebedee's sons, and Peter. We know also from the accounts that all of them fell asleep. Besides, it would seem more natural that when Jesus was praying to his Father, he would have done this not aloud so as to be heard, but simply, as we ourselves pray and as he himself recommended that we pray to the Father, in secret, silently.

From certain indications in the accounts of this prayer of Jesus in Gethsemani, it would appear that the evangelists or the tradition on which they relied, had utilized the prayer which Jesus taught his disciples, the Our Father, in putting together the el-

243

ements of this scene. The struggle itself forms a pendant, and runs in parallel to that other scene at the start of his ministry when Jesus encountered temptation. Now he has reached the climax of his career: then he was starting out. Then he had to reject the offer of Satan, the preternatural demonic help that seemed capable of guaranteeing the success of his preaching. Now the issue is clear: he has rejected Satan from the beginning; they are declared enemies; in consequence, he now stands alone to engage in the trial, the temptation, the eschatological test of strength (*peirasmos* in New Testament Greek).

Throughout the Old Testament and in some of Paul's writings we discover references to this definitive struggle, pictured frequently as occurring at the end of history as a necessary preliminary to the definitive establishment of the reign of God. In this trial Jesus, as the incarnate Son, must stand alone and engage in this combat with evil. He seeks at times during this prayer the human consolation of fellowship with his own. They fail him in this, as you are aware. But what makes this terrible testing so intolerable is his awareness that he is asked to accept this cup of suffering from the one hand, from the one person closest to him, his heavenly Father.

In the New Testament there is a term which means "to hand over" (*paradidonai*). It is used of Judas' act, where it is usually translated "to betray." It is used of the action of the Jewish religious leaders in committing Jesus to the Romans for crucifixion. It is used however in its most profound, theological sense of God the Father, who hands over his Son out of love for the world to effect man's redemption. John alludes to this, you remember, in the third chapter, the sixteenth verse of his Gospel. St. Paul also refers to this in Romans 8:32. In both texts the typology employed is that of the sacrifice of Abraham recounted in the twenty-second chapter of Genesis. "God so loved the world," John says, "as to hand over his well beloved Son." And Paul says in the passage I read earlier, that God loved the world so as not to spare even his only Son. The phraseology is borrowed from the account of Abraham's sacrifice. In order to appreciate the poignancy, the tragedy, and hence the meritorious character of this act of Jesus, and the love involved in this act of his Father, we might profitably recall here that story of Abraham's sacrifice, which we commemorate each morning in the second prayer after the Consecration, to see how the author of Genesis brings out the fatherly love that Abraham displays towards his son Isaac. On the one hand, he is faced with the terrible demand on the part of his God, that he sacrifice his only hope at becoming the father of many nations:

244

for Isaac is the only child, the only son he has. Yet Abraham, out of faith and confidence in God, accepts this terrible demand. On the way up the mountain, however, we are given precious evidence of the tenderness of Abraham for this small son of his. You will notice that while he allows the little boy to carry the wood for the sacrifice, the father himself carries the other two instruments, the fire and the knife, for fear the boy might hurt himself. As they journey up the mountain, the child asks his father where they are to find a victim for the sacrifice: and Abraham makes a prophecy which is not fulfilled in the sequel. "God, my son," Abraham says, "will provide a lamb for the sacrifice" (Gn 22:8). In the event, it is actually a ram that is found caught by its horns in a thicket which they offer as victim to God. For it will only be through the sacrifice of Jesus by his own Father, that that prophecy of Abraham will be fulfilled, that God would provide a lamb for the sacrifice.

Jesus begins his prayer, according to Mark 14:36, with the word "*Abba.*" It is an Aramaic word meaning "father." But what is significant is that this was the term which the children of a Palestinian family used toward their father. No Jew in addressing God ever dared use this word because it was too familiar. They prayed to God as the Father, the-One-in-Heaven; they did not say "*Abba.*" Jesus alone could say "*Abba,*" because he was aware of his own unique filial relationship with the heavenly Father. It is very hard to translate the word into English, so as to suggest that sense of familiarity. It really only could be accurately rendered by some such term that we use affectionately for our own fathers—"dad" or "papa." At any rate, it is significant that Jesus during his earthly life is the only one in the Gospels who ever addresses God with this familiar term.

It is equally important to recall that twice in Paul's letters, after the death and resurrection of Jesus, in speaking of the prayer characteristic of the Christian, the apostle uses this same Aramaic term. The first passage is in Galatians (Gal 4:4-6). "When the fullness of time had come, God sent his Son born of woman, made subject to law, to redeem those subject to law, so that we might receive the adoptive sonship." Then he adds in verse 6: "The proof that you are sons is that God has sent the spirit of his Son into your hearts, crying 'Abba' (dear Father)." And in Romans, Paul repeats this idea. "In reality," he says (Rom 8:14-17), "All those who are led by the Spirit are sons of God. For indeed you have not received a spirit of slavery to make you fall back into fear. You have received the Spirit of adoptive sonship by which we cry

'*Abba*' (dear Father). The Spirit personally unites himself with our own spirit in attesting to the fact that we are God's children. If children, then heirs—heirs of God, and heirs together with Christ, provided that we really suffer with him in order that we may be glorified with him." St. Paul does not appear to be speaking here of any mystical prayer, of that kind of experience given to relatively few Christians. The whole tenor of the passage suggests that he assumes this to be the normal experience of every Christian in prayer, the awareness of his adoptive sonship.

In his agony Jesus asks the Father to take away this cup, and immediately he adds: "Yet it must be as you will, not as I will" (Mt 26:39). He has come to this struggle, to do battle by facing this terrible trial, together with his disciples; and as he takes leave of them, both Matthew and Mark tell us, he is overwhelmed by a sea of the deepest emotions. Matthew says: "Jesus now began to show sorrow and become distressed from shock" (Mt 26:37). Mark's expression is even stronger: "He was bewildered with terror and distressed from shock" (Mk 14:33). Jesus is represented by both writers as exclaiming that he has come near to dying from sorrow (Mt 26:38; Mk 14:34). This indeed marks the beginning of that final eschatological struggle with evil of which Mark, as we saw, made us aware all through his Gospel.

Prayer of the Christian   The prayer of Jesus on this occasion, the evangelists would seem to suggest, was closely patterned after the prayer he had taught his disciples—the Our Father. We have one version of it in Luke 11:1-4; and Matthew has included another form of it in his Sermon on the Mount, where he gives his theology of prayer (Mt 6:9-13). Very probably the variations in the two accounts are to be attributed to the fact that they were created in two different liturgical settings. Luke may well have taken his from the Antiochian liturgy, Matthew perhaps from that of Palestinian Christianity. Indeed we know that from very early, perhaps before the end of the first century, in one liturgical rendition of this prayer, the words, "For thine is the kingdom, and the power, and the glory, forever. Amen" were added (cf. 1 Chr 29:11). These words continue to be recited in the Byzantine liturgy when the priest and people recite the Our Father.

The Christian is bid to pray to the Father in heaven. He is taught to present his petition in a threefold form, that God's dominion may become a reality in earthly history. The words "hallowed be thy name" are the first formulation of it. By this phrase we ask that we be consecrated, "hallowed" to the name, that is, the Person of God. Our consecration to God's service, our personal commitment to him as members of the people of God, should be as perfect as is humanly possible.

Our petition is then formulated another way—this time, in terms of the kingdom. "May your kingdom become an earthly reality"—may it descend from heaven into history. This idea of the coming of God's kingdom from heaven into the world of men is to be seen already in the Old Testament prophets, particularly in the Second Isaiah, when he speaks of the definitive, eschatological good news that is become reality through the action of God (Is 52:7). The prophet puts it quite simply: "Yahweh has become king!" This is the Deutero-Isaian gospel. The reign of Yahweh in history is about to become actuality: it will soon become contemporary reality.

"May your will be carried out." This expression of our prayer is much more positive than some may realize. It does not mean the passive acceptance of a plan already formulated by God. Rather, it is a promise of our personal, active collaboration with the heavenly Father in making the divine plan a meaningful, dynamic reality in our own lives and in our contemporary situation.

The words "on earth as in heaven," as Origen once suggested, are probably to be taken as applying equally to all three formulae. Heaven is conceived in the Old Testament as the place where the reign of God is perfectly realized. Consequently, our prayer for the descent of God's reign into history expresses the desire that the earthly realization of the divine will may emulate the heavenly reality.

After this triple formulation of the single main petition, we now petition for the means to help us in achieving the principal goal of the Christian life. "Give us this day our daily bread." Undoubtedly this was originally meant as a request for the temporal needs of the Christian. Yet, from the fact that this prayer (as we see from the *Didachē*) was used in the Eucharistic liturgy from very earliest times—probably indeed from the apostolic age —this verse has also been understood by the Church as a petition for the Eucharistic Bread, as its customary insertion into the most solemn part of the Mass would appear to indicate. From time immemorial it has formed part of the preparation for Holy Communion.

We next ask the heavenly Father for forgiveness. Matthew follows Jewish idiom, and expresses sin in terms of debt: "Forgive us our debts as we also forgive our debtors." Luke expresses it differently. "Forgive us our sins, just as we forgive whatever any man owes us." In English we use the term "trespasses," an archaic English expression that has come down to us from the pre-Reformation period. It means very much the same as sin. By this petition we obviously do not mean to compare our ability to forgive offenses against ourselves with God's forgiveness of our sins. The Father's forgiveness of sin in us is a creative act immeasurably beyond our creaturely powers. We simply ask to be allowed, according to our potentialities, to imitate the Father by forgiving our debtors, pardoning those who have wronged us.

The next petition, the final one in Luke's version, "Lead us not into temptation," has nothing to do with what we normally think of as temptation. Temptation in that sense is included in the last petition of Matthew's *Pater Noster*—"Deliver us from the evil one." What we now ask is that we may be spared exposure to the awful eschatological testing which Jesus is now enduring in Gethsemani. Luke perhaps makes it clearer by saying, "Do not subject us to trial"—that terrible testing which, the Bible teaches, is to be the prologue to the definitive establishment of God's reign (Ez 28:2ff.; Ez 38—39; Is 14:13-14; Dn 7:23ff.; 8:9ff.; 11:-36ff.). In the Synoptic description of the scene in the garden, Jesus warns the disciples to pray that they should not be exposed to that frightful trial (Mt 26:41; Mk 14:38; Lk 22:40). This is what he now faces himself: the ultimate struggle to the death with the powers of evil. This it is which causes his "agony." Knowing the death-dealing nature of the ordeal and our own weakness, our Lord taught us to pray his Father to spare us its horrors.

The final petition according to Matthew, not included by Luke, reads, "Deliver us from evil," or, "Deliver us from the Evil One." It is impossible to say which translation is the more exact; but in any event it comes to the same thing. We beg to be delivered from the forces of evil, from Satan.

The Our Father was the prayer, our evangelists seem to suggest, which Jesus himself prayed during this supreme crisis in his earthly life in Gethsemani. What made the struggle so painful was his awareness that he had been asked to accept this dreadful experience from the hand of his Father. He had, in consequence, to accept it out of love in a spirit of filial obedience. As a man, he found it exquisitely painful to stand bereft of human companionship and solace as he engaged in this final trial. We recall that the two greatest theologians of the New Testament, Paul and John, have caught the poignancy of the drama of our redemption, when they compare God the Father to Abraham and Jesus to Isaac in their enactment of the tragic sacrifice on the mountain. It was his trust in God, when faced with such a terrible demand upon his father's love, that made Abraham "the father of all believers," and gave him the privilege of becoming type of God the Father

248

in the most significant act that history has known, the work of our redemption.

The disciples, alas, are incapable of assisting Jesus in this struggle. Partly because of their own human weakness, but more because of the Father's will, it is upon Jesus alone that the burden of this trial must fall. That our Lord will infallibly win the victory does not, at this stage, make the ordeal any easier to bear. What does make it more tolerable is his consciousness of his unique relationship as Son to the Father; the fact that when he prays, he has the filial right to say "*Abba*." By this filial prayer, as by the victory achieved through his death and resurrection, Jesus Christ has won for us Christians the right to say "*Abba*" also, to address God in the familiar, trusting fashion, in which Jesus himself as the only-begotten Son could do. I say that he has won this right for us through his death and resurrection; for one consequence of this redemptive act was his sending the Holy Spirit into the heart of every Christian, enabling us to say "*Abba*" through the inner dynamic power of the Spirit of the risen Christ. Our Lord has sent the Spirit of God into our hearts to testify to the fact that, as Christians, we are in reality sons of his Father by adoption. This divine adoption is a reality, because it entails the personal presence of the Holy Spirit. Yet this gift of the Father was only possible as a consequence of Jesus' struggle in the garden, the eschatological ordeal by which he initiated the battle with evil which would culminate in victory on the cross and in his resurrection.

Chapter 26

THE PASSION ACCORDING TO ST. JOHN

MODERN NEW TESTAMENT SCHOLARS are agreed that the earliest attempts to compose written accounts of the good news contained in the apostolic preaching in the primitive Church produced pre-Gospel accounts of Christ's Passion and resurrection. Moreover, these literary compositions were created for the express purpose of being proclaimed in the Eucharistic liturgy. In short, the immediate literary progenitors of our canonical Gospels were liturgical recitals of the central act of man's redemption, which was also the focal point of the primitive kerygma. This recital began with Jesus' action at the Last Supper by which he instituted the Holy Eucharist, continued with the narrative of his sufferings and death, and came to a triumphant, joyous climax in the announcement of his resurrection. It was in consequence basically a story of the victory of God's paternal love, rejected by mankind, whereby he "was in Christ reconciling the world to himself" (2 Cor 5:19). When these narratives were proclaimed in the "breaking of the Bread," they were believed to possess a reality far beyond that of a mere historical recall of significant past events. Such a liturgical *anamnēsis* was, in some mysterious way, a real occurrence. It was their awareness through Christian faith of the event-character of this proclamation which accounts for the joyous, exultant nature of the Eucharistic celebrations in the primitive community of Jerusalem, alluded to in Acts. "Daily they kept up their faithful attendance in a body at the temple and broke the Bread in the privacy of their own homes. They shared the food with one another with utterly unaffected joyfulness" (Acts 2:46).

This traditionally festive quality attaching to every celebration of the Eucharist should not be lost sight of, if we are to have a proper appreciation of the meaning of the Mass; and this important feature must always be allowed to display itself, even in the Lenten liturgy and requiem Masses. It was with this point in mind that Vatican II, in the Constitution on the Liturgy, called for a reform of the burial service. "The rite for the burial of the dead should express more clearly the paschal character of Christian death. . ." (No. 81). However, that is not the point with which we are concerned here. It is rather the joyful, victorious note attaching to the primitive Christian recitals of the Passion and resurrection at the Holy Eucharist, which has significance for our approach to the Ignatian contemplations of these sacred events. For we can never afford to forget that from the very beginning of Christianity the Church has always contemplated Christ's sacred Passion in the light of his resurrection. In her eyes, therefore, the Passion and resurrection constitute but two phases, two aspects, of the unique saving event in Christian sacred history.

This indivisible character of Jesus' death and resurrection is not easily grasped by our western, modern mentality. Yet the New Testament authors constantly reveal a deep awareness of it. The heart of the kerygma for Paul is expressed in a lapidary formula containing the quintessence of the apostolic tradition: "that Christ died for our sins according to the Scriptures, and that he was buried, and that he has been raised the third day according to the Scriptures" (1 Cor 15:3-4). In any reformulation of it, Paul reverently safeguards this unicity. Thus he declares to the Roman community that the real object of Christian faith in Jesus Christ is the fact that "he was handed over for our sins, and raised for our justification" (Rom 4:25). Moreover, Paul is very much aware that the Eucharistic liturgy itself is, in a most realistic sense, a kerygmatic presentation of this central saving event. "As often as you eat the Bread and drink from the cup, you proclaim the death of the Lord, until he comes" (1 Cor 11:26). It is of the very nature of the Eucharistic celebration that it is a proclaiming, like the preaching, of the death of the risen Christ, "the Lord." To announce, by breaking the Bread, the redemptive character of Jesus' death is, in fact, to profess the basic tenet of the Christian credo: "Jesus is Lord!"

The indivisible unity of the death and resurrection of the Church's Lord, which made the kerygma good news, or gospel, is reflected beyond all question in the Gospel accounts. Even in Mark, where the story is one of almost unrelieved tragedy, Jesus' resurrection is seen to constitute an essential part of the narrative. Jesus' very act of dying is portrayed as a triumph over sin and death itself. Matthew, by employing the language of apocalyptic, presents the same truth in most dramatic fashion (Mt 27:51-53). Yet it is undoubtedly in the fourth Gospel that we see the most perfect expression of the apostolic belief in the unified character of the Christ-event. And it is for this reason that we now suggest John's Passion, in its entirety, as the best example of an *historia* (in the Ignatian sense) for the present contemplation. St. Ignatius prescribes, in the exercises of the third week, that even the exercitant who desires to shorten the time he devotes to the contemplations of Christ's sufferings, should spend a whole day contemplating the whole of it [209]. This prescription by the author of the *Spiritual Exercises* would seem, in part at least, to be dictated by his awareness of the need to impress the exercitant with the truth that this whole series of humiliations and sufferings formed but a single saving event. And if St. Ignatius rarely appears to consider the resurrection as an integral part of this unity in the *Exercises*, its inclusion here is unquestionably demanded by developments in the contemporary theology of the redemption, which has so successfully returned to the primitive Christian viewpoint by refusing to separate Christ's resurrection from the consideration of his redemptive death.

While we have selected the fourth Gospel as the basis for our contemplation of the entire Passion because of the deeply theological nature of its narrative, it should not be forgotten that its author has the right to claim our attention because his narrative is based upon a personal, apostolic experience of the Passion, which is independent of the Synoptic tradition. This important feature of the Johannine Gospel has recently been demonstrated most convincingly by Dr. C. H. Dodd in his book, *Historical Tradition in the Fourth Gospel*.[1] Thus John's account puts us in close touch with the various scenes of Jesus' suffering and death. We should not fail to appreciate the fact that this author, in addition to a deeply theological interpretation of this moving story, appears frequently to be nearer the events he records than do the Synoptic evangelists. As Father Roderick MacKenzie, rector of the Pontifical Biblical Institute in Rome has observed, "The Johannine narratives are 'first-hand,' in a way that the Synoptic accounts are not; the former have not passed through the process of standardization and oral repetitions which tended to strip the Synoptic material of inessential details."[2] Awareness of the "immediacy" of this Passion account will undoubtedly aid us in bringing home to ourselves the reality of the events accomplished "under Pontius Pilate." For to ensure our successful prayerful contemplation of the Passion there is nothing so imperative and instructive as a continual rereading of the text. This return to the sources is as essential to the task we have in hand as it is to sound biblical scholarship.

1 C.H. Dodd, *Historical Tradition in the Fourth Gospel* (Cambridge, 1963).
2 R.A.F. MacKenzie, *Introduction to the New Testament*, 2d edition (Collegeville, Minn., 1965), 30.

By way of introducing ourselves to such a fruitful consideration of St. John's Passion story, it may not be out of place here to
recall some of the predominant theological themes which presided
over its composition. The principal theme is that of the definitive
revelation of the kingship of Jesus Christ. Through his Passion
and his resurrection, John tells us equivalently, our Lord has entered upon his reign. There are three variations on this theme
which play a significant role in John's narrative of the Passion. It is
the initial step in Jesus' return to the Father. It is also the beginning of his exaltation, his "being lifted up." And it is the inauguration of his "glory." It may be helpful to enlarge briefly upon these
motifs.

It has long been observed by commentators on the fourth
Gospel that the phrase, "the kingdom (or reign, or dominion) of
God," so characteristic of the Synoptic Gospels occurs but twice
in this book—and that in a single episode: Jesus' conversation
with Nicodemus (Jn 3:3, 5). In noting this strange phenomenon,
the exegetes point out quite rightly, that, if the formula is so rarely
employed, the reality is presented in Johannine terminology as
"eternal life." Yet, after taking cognizance of the accuracy of these
observations, the reader of St. John's Gospel should advert to the
importance the evangelist attaches to the conception of Christ as
king. Jesus is given the title "King of Israel" by Nathanael in the
series of testimonies (Jn 1:49) which the author has collected in
the first chapter of his Gospel, in order to remind the Christian
reader of the various facets of Jesus' mission and person. The reaction of the crowd, fed miraculously with bread by Jesus in the
wilderness, is presented (by John alone) as a desire to make him
king (Jn 6:15). Jesus is acclaimed as "king of Israel" by the crowds
on the occasion of his messianic entry into Jerusalem (Jn 12:13).

It is however in his narrative of the Passion that our evangelist
stresses the idea of Jesus' kingship. One thinks immediately of
the inscription nailed to the head of the cross, a trilingual, and
consequently universal, proclamation to the world of Jesus' royalty
(Jn 19:19-20). The evangelist records Pilate's refusal to accede
to the request of the Jewish religious leaders that the announcement be altered to suggest that Jesus' claim to kingship was
unfounded (Jn 19:21-22).

The theme of kingship is brought out even more dramatically
by John's presentation of Jesus' trial before Pilate, which the author has with great care set in the place of honor at the very
center of his whole account. He passes over the hearing before
the highpriest and the Sanhedrin in order to focus the reader's
attention upon the dialogue between Jesus and the Roman pro-

curator. It is here, as we shall have occasion to observe presently, that John defines with the utmost precision the meaning of our Lord's royal prerogatives.

Return to the Father Theme

As we have remarked, there are three variations on this basic theme in the fourth Gospel which contribute to our understanding of its Christological import. The first of these is the conception of Jesus' redemptive work as a return to the Father. John begins the final section of his Gospel by observing that the hour had come for Jesus' "passing from this world to the Father" (Jn 13:1). Our evangelist dwells with emphasis upon our Lord's consciousness of the fact. He tells us that our Lord was "aware that the Father had put sovereign power into his hand, and that he had come forth from God and was going home to the Father" (Jn 13:3). This statement, of course, is simply a recapitulation of the prologue to the fourth Gospel (Jn 1:1-18), wherein the coming of the Word is described as a cyclic movement. It begins in the heart of the Trinity, and continues through the coming into this world of the Word of God in creation and in the *tōrāh*. It comes to a climax with the incarnation, and eventually—after the incarnate Word bestows upon those who have found faith in him the divine "power to become God's children" (Jn 1:12-13)—it becomes a return to the bosom of the "God no man has ever seen" (Jn 1:18).

Exaltation Theme

A new variation on this theme is developed through the idea that the first stage in Jesus' journey home to God is accomplished by his "lifting up" at the crucifixion. "As Moses lifted up the serpent in the desert, so the Son of Man must be lifted up, in order that each one who believes in him may possess eternal life" (Jn 3:14-15). The bronze serpent was characterized by the author of the book of Wisdom as "the sign of salvation" (Wis 16:6). As such for John it was a type of the definitive salvation brought to man by the crucified Lord. This elevation of Jesus indeed contains the revelation of the mystery which, during his earthly life, surrounded his person. "When you have lifted up the Son of Man, then you will know that *I am!*" (Jn 8:28). Since the time of Moses, "I am," as the evangelist is fully aware, was a divine name. For Yahweh had declared in response to Moses' question, "Who shall I say sent me?" (Ex 3:14), "I am that which I am. Go to the people of Israel and say 'I am' sent you." For our evangelist, it is the sweet attraction exerted by the crucified Christ that has given the apostolic preaching of the death and resurrection its character as good news. "And I, when I am lifted up from the earth, will draw all men to myself" (Jn 12:32). After he has told the story of Jesus' crucifixion, John will cite a prophecy found in Zechariah which reminds the reader of this universal attractiveness of Christ upon the cross: "They shall look at him whom they have pierced; and they shall mourn for him, the way one mourns for an only son; and they shall weep for him, the way one weeps for the firstborn" (Za 12:10).

The third variation on the theme of Christ's kingship in John's **Glory Theme** Passion narrative is the theme of Jesus' "glory." It is one of the most characteristic insights of our evangelist to have perceived that the glorification of Jesus begins, not with Easter Sunday, but with the Passion. This conception dominates the discourse in which Jesus bids farewell to his faithful disciples. "Now is the Son of Man glorified, and God is glorified in him. If God is glorified in him, God will glorify him in himself, and he will immediately glorify him" (Jn 13:31-32). Jesus' self-offering to his Father begins on the same note. "Father, the hour has come. Glorify your Son in order that the Son may glorify you!" (Jn 17:1). This "glory" of Jesus lies actually in his supreme act of self-revelation, his death and resurrection. Since it is through the operation of "the other Paraclete," the Holy Spirit, that the disciples are brought to possess "the whole truth" of Jesus' divinity, the Spirit's proper role is to glorify Jesus. "He will glorify me, because he will take what is mine and announce it to you" (Jn 16:14). In the Old Testament the *kābōd* or "glory" is a technical term denoting any palpable, tangible manifestation of God's protective presence. The theophany at the burning bush (Ex 3:2) may serve as an illustration of this divine "glory." The inaugural vision of Isaiah is another example. This latter John construes as referring to the "glory" of Jesus Christ: "Isaiah said this, because he had seen his glory and had spoken of him" (Jn 12:41). In the eyes of the apostolic Church, Isaiah had spoken of Christ most meaningfully in the celebrated fifty-third chapter of his book, where he describes the vicarious death of the Servant of Yahweh "for the many" and God's exaltation of his faithful Servant. For this reason the whole story of Jesus' Passion, as it comes from the pen of St. John, is glory-filled. It is presented as the freely and deliberately chosen means which the incarnate Word, upon command of his Father (Jn 10:18), adopted to redeem mankind. It signifies moreover the chief means through which the divinity of Christ is revealed to the believer. On John's view, Jesus' death is supremely significant as a perfect act of self-revelation.

When we pick up the text of St. John's Passion, we should be **The Garden** impressed by the careful way in which he has respected the historical character of the events he records, without failing to appreciate the highly original manner in which he has succeeded, by a most judicious use of the Old Testament, in providing his reader with an insight into their meaning for Christian faith. As Jesus leaves the room in which he has celebrated the Last Supper with his disciples, he appears to walk backward through Israel's sacred history. "He went out," John informs us, "to a place beyond the torrent Kidron" (Jn 18:1)—a remark that recalls the path David took when fleeing from his rebellious son Absalom (2 S 15:23). David has already appeared as a type of Christ in John's account of the Last Supper, where Jesus' announcement of Judas' treachery was made by means of a citation from Ps 41:9, "The man who eats my bread has lifted up his heel against me" (Jn 13:18). The traditional rabbinical interpretation of this verse saw it as an allusion to Ahithophel's conspiracy with Absalom against King David. John accordingly views Judas as the new Ahithophel who treacherously betrays the new David.

Jesus, John tells us, "went out to a place, where there was a garden." The evangelist however, does not, like the other sacred writers, record the name Gethsemani—"the olive-press." Such an apt designation this is for the scene of Jesus' terrible struggle, so graphically depicted by the Synoptics. John omits all reference to this "agony," since he has anticipated it in the episode where "the Greeks" seek to interview Jesus (Jn 12:20-30). In the incident we are considering John appears to suggest that the garden in which Jesus is to score his first triumph over his enemies is the terrestrial paradise in which the Creator had placed Adam after molding him from the soil of the earth (Gn 2:15). Jesus, it would seem, is the new Adam, who prepares for the confrontation with "the ancient serpent" (Ap 12:9), Satan. For John has taken the trouble to inform us earlier in his narrative that, as Judas took the morsel of bread at the Last Supper, "Satan entered him" (Jn 13:27).

Now Judas, amply supported by a detachment of soldiers and the temple police, makes his way to the garden where Jesus stands ready for them, since "he knew perfectly all that lay ahead of him" (Jn 18:4). He awaits, as the Light of the world, the cowardly advent of the darkness. Since the moment of confrontation has come, Jesus "went towards them and asked, 'Whom are you seeking?' 'Jesus the Nazarene,' they replied. Jesus says to them, '*I am*'!" When Jesus utters the divine name, his would-be captors trip over one another and fall to the ground. It is only after the question is repeated and answered a second time that our Lord submits to the indignity of his arrest. Yet even then he issues orders to the soldiery as to his own servants. "If you are seeking me, let these men go unmolested" (Jn 18:8). He permits himself to be taken by force solely because such is the Father's will, part of the divine plan for his glorification and the redemption of mankind. "This is why the Father loves me: because I surrender my life to receive it back again. No man takes it from me: I myself surrender it of my own accord. I possess the authority to surrender it: I possess the authority to receive it back again. Such is the command I have received from my Father" (Jn 10:17-18).

Even Jesus' own disciples, as Peter now illustrates, are powerless when they attempt to interfere with God's eternal plan for the world's salvation. Peter's misguided action in cutting off the ear of Malchus, a retainer of the highpriest (Jn 18:10-11), provokes a remark from Jesus which is an echo of the Synoptic "agony" in the garden. "Sheathe your sword. Am I not to drink this cup which my Father has given me?"

"They took him first to Annas," John tells us (Jn 18:13), a deposed highpriest without any authority to interrogate Jesus, whose curiosity Jesus refuses to satisfy, and who with gross injustice permits his servants to maltreat the prisoner. Our evangelist also alludes to the official hearing before the supreme tribunal of Judaism, which appears to have been convened at daybreak (Jn 18:24-28). Thereby, John sheds light upon the anomalous tradition, recorded by Matthew and Mark, concerning two "trials" before the Sanhedrin (cf. Mk 14:53-65; 15:1). Neither of these writers provide any plausible reason for the second meeting, nor do they explain how, in contravention of Jewish law, a trial involving a capital charge could be held during the night. Moreover, they make no attempt to account for the indignities and abuse showered upon the captive Jesus. The fourth evangelist appears to provide a solution to these questions by making it clear that the first hearing before Annas was unofficial. By observing that this evil old man still retained the title of highpriest, John seems to suggest the source of the confusion in the oral tradition followed by Mark and Matthew. The memory of two assemblies, each presided over by "the highpriest" (actually Annas in the first instance, Caiaphas in the second), had created the impression that the Sanhedrin had been present on both occasions. John's treatment of these episodes serves to remind us of the solid historical tradition upon which his account of the Passion is based. At the same time, his omission of any description of the formal trial before the Sanhedrin is the result of John's theological viewpoint. The sentence pronounced upon Jesus by this Jewish juridical body is of no moment; for judgment has already been passed—upon the very men who presume to judge Jesus. Already in the twelfth chapter of this Gospel, Jesus has declared: "Now is the judgment of this world. Now the ruler of this world is to be expelled!" (Jn 12:31). Indeed, as John is well aware, the task of dispelling the ambiguity of history falls to the Spirit of Truth, the Paraclete who vindicates, for the Christian, the justice of Jesus' claims. "And when he comes, he will convict the world on three counts: sin, justice, and judgment. . ." (Jn 16:8-10).

Jesus and Pilate   It is the solemn session held by Pilate which commands the attention of our evangelist, thereby profoundly influencing his presentation of the entire Passion. It is Pilate, not "the Jews," who is regarded as the instrument of divine providence for the salvation of mankind. The dialogue between Jesus and the Roman procurator falls into two sections, punctuated by the scourging and the crowning with thorns. This painful incident, providing as it does a startling example of Johannine irony, serves to underscore the dominant theme of the kingship of Jesus.

The first half of the hearing begins with Pilate's inquiry into the charge brought against the prisoner. Since it is inconceivable that the Jewish religious authorities would not have briefed the procurator on the accusations against Jesus and their intent to have him executed, it was probably Pilate's desire to humiliate "the Jews," by making them admit publicly that their real grievance was based upon religious grounds. To their confident, insolent reply, "If he were not a criminal, we should not have handed him over to you," Pilate rejoins, "Take him yourselves and crucify him!" (Jn 18:29-31). He thus forces Jesus' accusers to the humiliating admission that they no longer possess the *ius gladii*, the effective authority to mete out capital punishment.

Pilate now turns to interrogate Jesus. "You are then king of the Jews," he says, employing the political title which obviously figured in the Jewish indictment. The only adequate and accurate expression of Jesus' kingship is the title accorded Yahweh in the Old Testament, "King of Israel." Because of the ambiguity arising from the form of Pilate's question, Jesus calls for further elucidation. Was the phrase employed by the Roman procurator simply the result of his ignorance of what must, to a pagan, seem a very subtle distinction, or has he accepted the Jews' insinuation that Jesus is guilty of sedition? Pilate, now nettled, demands to know what crime, whether real or specious, Jesus has committed.

"My kingdom is not of this world," Jesus answers; and he attempts to give his judge some notion of the distinction between

258

being "King of the Jews" and being "King of Israel." He presents Pilate with an argument which any pragmatic Roman bureaucrat is capable of appreciating. "If my kingdom were of this world, my servants would be fighting to prevent my being handed over to the Jews. In point of fact, however, my kingdom has no such origin" (Jn 18:36).

"Then you are a king!" asks Pilate; and Jesus endeavors to clarify this all-important concept of his royalty. "I am indeed, as you say, a king. For this was I born and for this I came into the world: to give testimony to Truth!" (Jn 18:37). Jesus' whole mission is to establish the reign of God in history. By his very presence upon earth and particularly through the events of his public ministry, God's dominion has at last become present in history. Since he is the kingdom of God incarnate, he is born to be king. Yet, given the fact that Jesus has inaugurated God's reign here below by proclaiming the gospel, his kingly function can also be described as "testimony to Truth," that is, to the divine reality now present in history in himself and his mission. Pilate's puzzled query, "What is Truth?", is actually the principal question posed by John throughout his Gospel. We must be able to answer this question for ourselves if we intend to be Christians. Truth in the fourth Gospel is a reality in the existential order. Truth is something one does (Jn 3:21), something one lives. It is indeed the self-revelation of God in Christ, and as such it is the source of Christian existence.

This section of Jesus' hearing closes with a suggestion by Pilate that, as he finds no grounds on which to condemn the prisoner, he will release him.

The second half of the trial follows Jesus' crowning with thorns and Pilate's foolish attempt to satisfy the blood-lust of the crowd by displaying the pitiful figure of the accused, "still wearing (as John emphasizes) the crown of thorns and the purple cloak" (Jn 19:5). By threatening to stop the hearing, on the grounds that Jesus was not guilty of any capital offense, the procurator forces the religious leaders to confess their real motive for demanding Jesus' execution. "We have a law, and according to that law he must die, because he has made himself Son of God!" (Jn 19:7).

Pilate's recorded reaction to this statement is one of even greater fear than he has felt up to this point. He appears to realize however vaguely, that he is involved in something quite beyond his ken. So he asks Jesus, "Where do you come from?" This question, like that of the Jews at Capharnaum after the miracle of loaves (Jn 6:25), cannot be answered satisfactorily without a comprehension which is aided by Christian faith. Consequently, Jesus does not reply. The sequel shows that Jesus' silence is justified, indeed, is an act of mercy. Pilate does not realize that the power he possesses over the prisoner has come to him in reality from God, who "so loved the world as to give his only begotten Son" (Jn 3:18). "You would have no power over me at all, were it not given you from above. In consequence, he who handed me over to you is guilty of greater sin" (Jn 19:11). Who is it that is meant here? While it is difficult to be certain, it would appear to be a series of persons (the religious leaders, Judas), all tools of Satan, upon whom the responsibility chiefly falls.

The procurator makes one more attempt to release Jesus; but "the Jews" play their trump card by insinuating that they will indict Pilate before the imperial tribunal if he dares let Jesus go free (Jn 19:12). The Roman official weakly goes through the formality of condemning Jesus to crucifixion. However he cannot resist one last derisive taunt. "There is your king!" (Jn 19:14) at which the highpriests, stung by the humiliating insult, finally abjure their faith in the God of Israel as their own acknowledged king. "We have no king but the emperor!" (Jn 19:15).

Scene on Calvary

The evangelist hurries over the journey to Calvary and the actual crucifixion. But he takes time to point out that, by carrying his own cross upon his back, Jesus fulfills Old Testament typology set forth in the story of the sacrifice of Isaac (Gn 22:1-14). The kingship of Jesus is proclaimed to the world by the governor's inscription. John, by historicising a passage from the psalm, which had foretold our Lord's suffering and death (Ps 22:18), describes how the soldiers divided up Jesus' clothing. A seamless robe was part of the regalia of the Jewish highpriest (Sir 50:11). Jesus, John tells us equivalently, is not only king; he is also priest at this supreme moment of his earthly career.

At this moment also, "the mother of Jesus" reappears for the first time since the Cana episode. She is asked to make the greatest sacrifice of her life: to exchange her son for "the disciple whom Jesus loved," who represents the body of the Christian faithful. It is as if her divine maternity were not enough, in the Father's plan: Mary must become the mother of the Church (Jn 19:25-27).

The end now comes quickly; and Jesus shows in the last moments of his mortal life that he is entirely in command of the situation. "It is consummated!" he cries: my work for the world's salvation is now completed. This is the hour of his glorification, in John's eyes, and consequently Jesus is now empowered to bestow the Spirit upon the Church, which is being born of his Passion. Earlier, the evangelist had declared that "the Spirit was not yet, because Jesus was not yet glorified" (Jn 7:39). Now Jesus has been glorified: now therefore is the moment, in the fourth Gospel, of "Pentecost." "And bowing his head, he handed over the Spirit" (Jn 19:30). Jesus' dying breath, breathed forth upon the head of his mother and the beloved disciple is the supreme sign, for John, of the glorified Christ's gift of the Spirit.

Jesus dies also as the new paschal lamb, as that "lamb for the sacrifice" predicted by Abraham (Gn 22:8), as the Suffering Servant of Yahweh executed "like a lamb led to the slaughter" (Is 53:7). Pilate had passed the death sentence at the very hour when the priests in the temple area were beginning the slaughter of the lambs used for Passover (Jn 19:14). Jesus now fulfills the prophetic element in the rubrics for the sacrifice of the paschal lamb (Ex 12:46). John may also have in mind the psalmist's description of the persecution of the just man (Ps 34:20).

As befits his royal character, Jesus' burial is presented as a truly kingly interment—indicated by the enormous quantity of spices used (Jn 19:39). More important still is John's observation that the manner of this burial was in accord with Jewish (not Egyptian) funeral practice. For the Egyptian method of mummification demanded the mutilation of the corpse. The body of Jesus, already glorified and soon to rise, must remain intact. Its integrity could in no way be marred or sullied. *The Tomb*

"Now there was a garden in the locality, where Jesus had been crucified," the evangelist tells us; "and in the garden, a new tomb in which no one had been laid to rest. It was there, accordingly, out of respect for the Jewish day of preparation, that they laid Jesus, since the tomb was nearby" (Jn 19:41-42). After his labor of redemption, the new Adam rests in a garden. However it is not the same as the garden (Gethsemani), which symbolized for John the earthly paradise. It is a new garden with a new tomb, a symbol of the celestial paradise, which, according to Luke, Jesus had promised to share with the good thief "This day you will be with me in paradise!" (Lk 23:43).

The kingship of Jesus, with its subordinate themes of "lifting up," of "glory," of the going home to the Father, and of the "new Adam," has presided over the structuring and interpretation of John's Passion narrative. The evangelist has transformed the grim and tragic elements in this story by focusing upon them the glorious light of the resurrection. The Passion is above all, for John, an act of Jesus' self-revelation as the Son, and by that very fact a revelation of the Father, the "God no man has ever seen." For, as Jesus once reminded Philip, to see the Son in Jesus Christ by Christian faith is to behold the Father (Jn 14:9). Jesus dies to reveal the Father's love for the world, and he does so by giving us the greatest proof that any man can give his friends (Jn 15:13). Indeed, the ultimate in this revelation of the divine love of Father and Son for us is the gift of the Holy Spirit, symbolized by the last breath which Jesus drew. To all this, we can only cry out, with the centurion beneath the cross, "In very truth, this was God's Son!" (Mk 15:39).

YAHWEH'S LOVE FOR ISRAEL
Deuteronomy 7:7-8

It was not because you were the greatest of all peoples that Yahweh set his heart on you and chose you (for you were the smallest of all peoples), 8but it was because Yahweh loved you. . . .

Isaiah 49:14-15

And Sion said, "Yahweh has forsaken me, the Lord has forgotten me!"

15"Can a woman forget the infant at her breast, so as not to cherish the son of her womb? Even if there might be found one who would forget, I shall never forget you!"

THE FATHER'S LOVE FOR US IN CHRIST
Romans 8:32

How is it possible that he, who did not spare his own Son, but handed him over on behalf of us all, has not with him given us everything?

John 3:16

For God so loved the world that he gave his only-begotten Son, that every man with faith in him might not perish but have eternal life.

1 John 4:9-10

God's love was manifested among us by this fact, that he sent his only-begotten Son into the world that we might live through him. 10This is the meaning of that love: not that we loved God, but he himself loved us first, and sent his Son in atonement for our sins.

DEVOTION TO THE SACRED HEART
OF JESUS

Problems
and Objections

THE ERA PRECEDING the Council of Trent was a creatively fruitful age in Catholic theological thinking. To take some examples from scriptural studies—it was the period when Spain, thanks to the illustrious leadership of Cardinal Ximénez de Cisneros, produced what was actually the first modern critical edition of the New Testament in Greek, as well as the celebrated polyglot Bible of Alcalá. Indeed, the fathers of the Council of Trent demonstrated their awareness of the Church's need for accurate editions of the Scriptures, both in the original languages and in the venerable versions of antiquity. They wisely commissioned scholars to produce critical editions of the Hebrew Bible, the Septuagint, and the Latin Vulgate. Because of various circumstances, only one of these projects could be completed—the critical edition of the Septuagint. Yet this notable achievement was a very creditable piece of work, and it is still regarded as valuable by modern scholars.

Shortly after this theological renaissance in the sixteenth century, however, a decline set in, a decadence in theological and philosophical thought within (and perhaps also to some degree) outside the Church, which would continue for almost two centuries. The scholastic system, produced by the great minds of the Middle Ages, suffered an eclipse. At the same time anti-clericalism and a profoundly anti-religious spirit gained momentum throughout Europe. There was born an age of intense, ruthless individualism, which was ultimately to issue in movements like the French Revolution. Seventeenth and eighteenth century France also witnessed an extravagant romanticism, when royalty, instead of concerning itself with the social and economic plight of thousands of its subjects, would disport itself by playing at being shepherds and shepherdesses. Yet this was the age when divine Providence saw fit to confront the world, through St. Margaret Mary, with the devotion and the doctrine of the Sacred Heart.

For some time now in our century many people have been
264

questioning the relevance and meaningfulness of this devotion. And, indeed, it must be confessed that, in what may be called its classical expression at least, it seems to have little or no appeal to modern Catholics. Yet because the Society of Jesus has had and ought to continue to have a great interest in and concern for this very devotion, we may reflect upon some of the ways in which the devotion to the Sacred Heart may be revitalized and given a more contemporary appeal.

to whom?

Why is it that the devotion to the Sacred Heart, as it has been handed down to us, appears to be outmoded and unattractive? The basic reason, I suggest, is that its seventeenth, or even nineteenth century formulation neglected one very fundamental feature of the gospel, namely, that the death and resurrection of Christ must be proclaimed as simply two facets of the central redemptive event. Moreover, any popular devotion to be solid, and so capable of surviving, must rest four square upon a realistic view of the Christian mystery. Now it is clear to any Christian that the Christ who now exists, whom the Church acknowledges as her Lord, is the risen and exalted Christ, the Master of history and Lord of the universe. Finally, if the proclamation of the gospel is to achieve its purpose today or in any age, the historical events involved in man's redemption must be presented in all their saving significance,—which means that in speaking of Jesus' sufferings during his earthly life, we must, like the evangelists, present them in the light of his subsequent glorification. There were many Jews and some Romans who, upon Calvary, witnessed the crucifixion of the Son of God. They experienced everything that could be apprehended by the human senses. But they missed the one thing necessary if these occurrences are to be presented as good news: the *propter nos et propter nostram salutem.*

To whom?

Another cause for decline in this devotion may be discovered in the fact that the intensely individualistic piety, which was a hallmark of the age in which the revelations were made to St. Margaret Mary, has lost its allure in times like ours, characterized by a growing consciousness of social relationships, of social values, of the need of social reforms. We are all nowadays very much aware of the social dimension of man, not only in psychology and anthropology, but especially in religion. Ours is an age which highly values interpersonal relationships. Accordingly the Church in the twentieth century has preached the doctrines set forth in the social encyclicals. She has proclaimed the universal kingship of Christ; she has come to view herself as the Mystical Body of Christ, as the people of God; she has, with considerable anguish on the part of many of her children, reformed the liturgy to emphasize the social character of the Christian cultus. She has moreover finally felt the imperative need, under the inspiration of John XXIII, for dialogue with other Christian churches, indeed with non-Christians, and even, with "the world!" All of these tendencies and ideals, characteristic of modern man and modern Christians, must somehow be allowed to play a role in the refashioning of devotion to the Sacred Heart.

To say these things is to admit that the Sacred Heart devotion must create new forms of prayer and of practise if it is to speak to the men of today. Let us take, by way of example, the practice of reparation to the Sacred Heart. To a degree at least, its classical expression was the outcome of a piety that strikes us today as sentimental. It was based upon certain theological principles whose value at best is highly dubious. Immediately there comes to mind the conception (so often depicted in nineteenth century devotional art) of Jesus as "the lonely prisoner of the tabernacle." The Christ of the Eucharist is the risen and exalted Christ, whose office, as St. Ignatius rightly observes in the first contemplation of the fourth Week of the *Exercises* [224], is to comfort and console us—not to be consoled by our poor attentions.

Indeed there is a certain well-founded scepticism displayed by theologians of our day about the value of my efforts to console Jesus, retroactively so to speak, during the period of his mortal life—granting that he could foresee my well-intentioned actions through some kind of knowledge that might provide consolation. Again, some theologians question whether my endeavors today to compassionate the mortal, suffering heart of the earthly Jesus are not somewhat presumptuous. Can I be sure that my distracted attempts to offer consolation were not, in their poverty, a cause of greater suffering to him?

Haurietis Aquas   Certainly it seems clear that, if devotion to the Sacred Heart of Jesus is to be given new life in our day, this can only be accomplished by a radical return to the sources: to divine revelation recorded in the Bible and to authentic Christian tradition. This was the way indicated by Pius XII in his encyclical *Haurietis aquas*,[1] a document written expressly to show how this devotion can be reformulated in terms which will be meaningful for mod-

---

1 "Indeed, if the evidence on which devotion to the wounded Heart of Jesus rests is rightly weighed, it is clear to all that we are dealing here, not with an ordinary form of piety which anyone may at his discretion slight in favor of other devotions, or esteem lightly, but with a duty of religion most conducive to Christian perfection." Pius XII, encyclical "Haurietis aquas" in *Acta Apostolicae Sedis,* XLVIII (May, 1956), 346; tr. in *Catholic Mind,* LIV (August, 1956), 464.

ern Christians. That such updating is necessary may be inferred from the pope's unequivocal statement that devotion to the Sacred Heart is not one among many pious practises laudably cultivated by Catholics, but it is something which touches the very essence of Christianity. This assertion deserves our reverent consideration, not only because it has emanated from the highest authority in the Church, but also because we as Jesuits are committed by our Institute to the preservation and spread of devotion to the Sacred Heart in our day and in our world.

For our present purpose of reminding ourselves of the real nature of this devotion, we may follow the methodology indicated by the late Holy Father in *Haurietis aquas,* and attempt to present a brief and rapid review of what the Bible reveals to us concerning the love which God our Father has displayed towards us his children in both Old and New Testaments.

It was through the establishment of his covenant with Israel that Yahweh revealed his love for this people. It was in terms of this same covenant that eventually God would disclose his universal love for all men. In the ancient Near East, the sociological phenomenon known as a *berīth* or covenant assumed various forms and was ratified by numerous rituals. It could be made between equals, or between a powerful king and his vassals. It consisted essentially in a solemn giving of promises by both parties involved, and its effective observance and perpetuity were safeguarded by oaths and imprecations (in the event of its violation). By expressing her unique relationship with almighty God in the form of a covenant, Israel demonstrated her unshakeable belief in God's free and preferential choice of her as his *segullāh* or acquisition. God declared his love for her above all the nations of the earth by entering into a pact whereby he became Israel's kinsman-God—a relationship which, short of the future incarnation of God's Son, was as personal and intimate and "familiar" as any relationship could possibly be.

It is not surprising that Israel's spirituality, as it developed and was expressed by her prophets, Hosea, Jeremiah, Ezekiel, and others, drew its inspiration and vitality from the primordial fact of the covenant, which on his own initiative and out of love for her Yahweh had made with this people. This divine love of preference is a love that was not always accepted by Israel. Indeed it often appears in the prophetic writings as a rejected love, a violated love, a love betrayed by the numberless and continuing infidelities of God's people. At best it is a love only imperfectly and sporadically reciprocated. It is then a love which suffers frustration throughout Israelite history.

Yet even a rapid review of the pertinent Old Testament texts will impress us with the faithfulness and tenderness of this divine love of Yahweh for Israel. "He [God] came upon them in the steppe-country, in the howling waste of the desert. He surrounded them, brought them up, guarded them like the pupil of his eye. As an eagle incites its nestlings, hovering over its little ones, so Yahweh spreads his wings to catch them, bears them up on his pinions" (Dt 32:10-11). This dramatic and moving description of the loving watchfulness of the divine protective presence over Israel during her wandering in the desert is reminiscent of a passage in Hosea, in which that prophet recurs to this earliest experience by Israel of her God's love in order to proclaim the future renovation of the covenant. "Because Israel was a child and I loved him, I called my son away from Egypt. . . . It was I who taught Ephraim to walk; I took him in my arms. Yet he was unaware of the care I took of him! . . . I will cure their infidelity: I will love them with all my heart; for my wrath has turned away from them. I will be like the dew for Israel; he shall grow like the lily . . . his beauty shall resemble that of the olive tree. . ." (Hos 11:1—14:6).

Perhaps the most tender expression of God's love for Israel is to be found in a passage of Deutero-Isaiah. "And Sion said, 'Yahweh has forsaken me, the Lord has forgotten me!'—Can a woman forget the infant at her breast, so as not to cherish the son of her womb? Even if there might be found one who would forget, I shall never forget you!" (Is 49:14-15). The author of the Canticle of Canticles employs the image of married love to portray most feelingly God's deep affection for his people. "Like a lily among the thorns, so is my loved one among women" (Ct 2:2). "My lover belongs to me and I to him, who pastures his flock among the lilies" (Ct 2:16). "Set me like a seal upon your heart, like a seal upon your arm; for inexorable as death is love, as relentless as the netherworld. The flames of passion are a blazing fire. . ." (Ct 8:6).

When, through the prophet Jeremiah, Yahweh foretells the striking of a new covenant, the prediction is set in the context of God's undying love for his people. "I have loved you with an everlasting love, and therefore will I draw you to me, taking pity on you" (Jer 31:3). "'Behold! the day shall come,' says the Lord, 'when I will make a new covenant with the house of Israel and with the house of Judah. . . . This will be the covenant that I will make with the house of Israel after those days,' says the Lord. 'I will set my law within them, and I will write it upon their hearts; and I will be their God, and they shall be my people . . .

for I will forget their iniquity, and remember their sin no more!' "
(Jer 31:31-34).

The superiority of the New Testament revelation of divine love
over anything found in the sacred literature of Israel may be
gauged by the fact that it is made through the unique Son of
God, Jesus Christ. Jesus' most striking and attractive exposition of
God's love for mankind is presented in Matthew's Sermon on the
Mount. It is noteworthy that almost every time God is mentioned
in this sermon by Jesus, he is called "my Father," "your Father,"
"the heavenly Father." Jesus' proposed renovation of the *tōrāh*
(Mt 5:21-47) is inspired by his desire to reveal mankind's new
filial relationship to his Father. Jesus' message is summed up in
the final injunction, "Be perfect as your heavenly Father is perfect"
(Mt 5:48). It is by acting as the loving Father of mankind that God
reveals his perfection to us. Consequently the perfection demanded of every Christian is to be conceived in terms of the
Christian's new status as an adoptive son of God.

Jesus beautifully portrays God's fatherly concern for all his
children by reminding us of his provident care of "the birds in
the sky" (Mt 6:26), and his prodigality in arraying "the lilies of
the field" (Mt 6:28-30). Jesus teaches us to persevere in the prayer
of petition, the purpose of which is not to tell the Father something he is not already aware of (Mt 6:8), but rather to impress
ourselves with the goodness, wisdom, and bounty of the heavenly
Father (Mt 7:7-11). Jesus insists that the Father's love excludes
no one, not even those who are hostile to him (Mt 5:45).

The theophany at Jesus' baptism, preserved in the Synoptic
tradition, reveals the boundless love of the Father for his Son as
man (Mk 1:10-11). This same message is communicated to the
three privileged disciples who witness Jesus' transfiguration (Mk
9:7). The moving prayer of Jesus to the Father recorded by Matthew and Luke (Mt 11:25ff.; Lk 10:21ff.) gives us a profound
glimpse into the mysterious, divine love which unites them. Indeed, in the fourth Gospel, Jesus assures us that his Father loves us
men with the same love with which he loves his incarnate Son
(Jn 17:26).

St. Paul discloses the creative dynamism of the Father's love for
mankind, which through Baptism communicates the Spirit of divine adoptive sonship. "When the fulness of time was come, God
sent his Son, born of a woman, made subject to law, in order that
he might redeem those under law, in order that we might receive
adoptive sonship. The proof that you are sons is the fact that God
has sent the Spirit of his Son into our hearts crying, '*Abba!*' (dear
Father)" (Gal 4:4-6). Indeed this gift of the Spirit means that the

very love of God is poured out into our hearts (Rom 5:5). Paul's contemplation of the truth that God loves us as our Father forces him to cry out: "How is it possible that he, who did not spare his own Son, but handed him over on behalf of us all, has not with him given us everything?" (Rom 8:32).

The other great New Testament theologian of the love of God is St. John, for whom God is simply "Love" (1 Jn 4:8). In the fourth Gospel, the work of the redemption is a work of divine love. "God so loved the world as to give his only begotten Son" (Jn 3:16). The evangelist thinks of Abraham's sacrifice, when the patriarch, to show his loving obedience to his God, was ready to sacrifice his only begotten son, Isaac (Gn 22:1ff.). God the Father's love of the human race has brought him actually to sacrifice the incarnate Son, Jesus Christ. Our Lord in his turn has loved us enough to lay down his life for us (Jn 15:13). Indeed this very love is the source of our divinely-bestowed power to love one another as he has loved us (Jn 13:34).

In fact, in the New Testament the principal "motive" (if one may speak of God as motivated) for the work of man's redemption on the part of the Father or the Son is love. Certainly there is no hint to be found on any page of the New Testament of that appalling notion, found unfortunately in the sermons of preachers of the seventeenth century, that God acted out of vindictive justice, demanding the death of his Son, or that the Father was punishing Christ upon the cross instead of punishing sinful man. To represent the redemption thus is to betray the teaching of our inspired writers, who state that the Father is the originator of Christ's saving work out of love of his Son and out of love for men, and that Christ accepted his mission of redemption out of love of the Father and for mankind. It is this divine love of the Father incarnate in the divine-human love of Jesus Christ, which is the object of devotion to the Sacred Heart. To make our response of love to this loving heart of Jesus is simply the practise of Christianity, nothing more, nothing less.

But how, one may well ask, does one make a proper response of love to God the Father, or even to the incarnate Son now exalted in glory at the Father's right hand? If, as St. Ignatius notes in the *Contemplation for Obtaining Love*, love consists in mutual exchange or sharing, what can we possibly give God, what can we really share with his glorified Son?

Practise of Reparation   This question leads us to our final consideration: the practise of reparation to the Sacred Heart of Jesus. Once it is seen, as we have shown, that this devotion is actually directed to the risen and exalted Lord Jesus, who retaining in glory his sacred humanity continues to love man with a human as well as divine love, what can we give him who is universal Lord? There can be no doubt that Christ glorified is truly beyond the reach of any "reparation" we could make to him personally.

Yet by the very fact that he rose from death with his human nature, he has created that body which is the Church. St. Paul, contemplating this truth, saw a totally new possibility: "Now I take joy in the sufferings on your behalf," he writes to the Colossians, "and I complete what is lacking in the tribulations of Christ in my flesh on behalf of his body, which is the Church" (Col 1:24). There is a sense in which the risen Christ, in that new dimension of himself acquired at his resurrection, has need of my love, my reparation. The truth is that I make reparation to him by my practise of fraternal love towards the suffering members of his body. The message of the New Testament is that Christ now risen is more involved in history than he was during his mortal life; and part of that involvement is the suffering he endures through the tribulations of mankind upon earth—all members, at least potentially, of himself. Today when men are so deeply aware of the poverty and anguish of their fellowmen, so anxious to alleviate effectively the evils that afflict mankind, what better means can be proposed, what more efficacious motivation can be presented than devotion to the Sacred Heart of Jesus correctly understood and rightly practiced?

THE FOURTH WEEK

IN CERTAIN RESPECTS the contemplations of the fourth week *Paschal Mystery* have a common aim with those of the third week. Here it is still the spiritual *amor amicitiae* which is sought: Christ is to be loved for what he himself now is. Of course, significant changes in technique are to be made, as St. Ignatius indicates in the Notes [226-229]. More important, there is a totally new approach to be taken in these contemplations, as will be indicated in the following chapter. Above all, the risen Lord's new office as "consoler" is to be profoundly appreciated [224].

It is crucially necessary that the Ignatian division of Jesus' death and resurrection into separate "weeks" should not be permitted to distract the exercitant from the essential unity of these two events. They are simply two facets of the central paschal mystery: the *transitus Domini*. For the truth is that our Lord's death, resurrection, ascension, exaltation, and his sending of the Holy Spirit, while separated in our time-space world, constitute a unique saving event, the principal object of the Christian faith.

It should be remembered that until relatively recently the resurrection of Christ did not receive the attention in theology or in popular devotion which it demands. Catholic reaction in the sixteenth century to the denial of the universally efficacious character of Jesus' death in making satisfaction for mankind ended by concentrating attention almost exclusively upon this aspect of the redemption. In answer to another error, the Church underscored the nature of the Mass as "a memorial of Christ's Passion," and as a sacrifice; and the causality of the resurrection in the sacramental symbolism of the Eucharist, as also its nature as a meal, tended to be forgotten. This led in turn to the (to us) less than meaningful attitudes and practices enshrined, in the seventeenth and following centuries, in the classical forms of the devotion to the Sacred Heart.

The balance has now been restored in our age with the promulgation by Paul VI of the Constitution on the Sacred Liturgy, which underscores the paschal character of the Christian life and emphasizes repeatedly the dynamic influence of Christ's resurrection upon the existence of the people of God. The Mass is declared a memorial of our Lord's death and resurrection (No. 47); the other sacraments provide a stream of divine grace, flowing from the paschal mystery (No. 61). The faithful are bid consider the paschal character of Christian death (No. 81). In her celebration of Sunday, the Church preserves the memory of "the resurrection of the Lord, together with his blessed Passion" (No. 108). The continuity between Good Friday and Easter Sunday is to be portrayed by "the paschal fast" (No. 110). Devotion to the mother of God derives its main inspiration from the fact that in Mary the paschal mystery has been completely actualized; she is in consequence "a faultless image" of the Church, symbolizing all that "she herself desires and hopes wholly to be" (No. 103).

Relevance of Resurrection Theology

The doctrine of the resurrection of the body, an integral part of Christian faith in Jesus' own resurrection, as Paul demonstrated for the Corinthians (1 Cor 15), appeals to the men of our times, so vitally interested in the material side of human personality. To speak of "saving our souls" to a world agonizing about the riddle of man's relationship to matter is to risk consigning the gospel of Christian hope to oblivion. Any spirituality that would, even by implication, view man as an angelic spirit endowed only with the spiritual dimensions of intelligence and will, is obsolete. Modern psychology has made us only too conscious that by far the greater part of human life is led on other levels than those of thought and will. It is the total view of man, which is the biblical view, that can arouse the interest and elicit the response of Christian faith from modern man. It is the message of Easter, that man is to be redeemed even in the material aspects of his personality, which contemporary man finds appealing. And this is the basic thrust of the fourth week of the Spiritual Exercises.

We may take one feature of the mystery of Christ's ascension into heaven to exemplify the modern relevance of the paschal mystery. The apostolic kerygma declared that the Son of God, who, to redeem mankind, had assumed our human nature and became like us in all save sin, chose, upon his return to the Father, to retain his humanity for all eternity. The exalted Lord exhibits in glory the spectacle of redeemed man. This tenet of the apostolic *credo* assures us today of the continuing contemporaneity of the Lord Jesus and of his total, enduring humanness. It reveals that our primary Christian vocation is to become fully human, and warns that any spirituality which would tend to dehumanize, is by that fact suspect of being bogus. It announces the very good news that Christ, as Lord of History, is to be found, not in retreat from this world, but in the daily round of our most banal human experiences. He, the risen Lord Jesus, confronts me personally in my own existential situation. "Go down into the city!" the angels had warned the disciples who witnessed Jesus' ascension—that is where you will find the Spirit. "Why stand you looking up to heaven?"

Chapter 28

THE CONTEMPLATIONS OF THE FOURTH WEEK

Forms of Resurrection Narratives

THE EXERCISES OF THE FOURTH WEEK are contemplations of the appearances of Christ after his resurrection. The Gospel narratives of these experiences fall into two main categories: the appearances of Jesus to those, who if they were not to be the official witnesses to the resurrection, were very close to our Lord in affection, united to him perhaps by some sort of family tie; and his appearances to "the Eleven" who were destined to constitute the apostolic college in the primitive Christian Church. Under the first heading come the various accounts of appearances to women, whether as a group (Mt 28:9-10; [Mk 16:9-11]; Lk 24:1-11) or singly, as to Mary Magdalene (Jn 20:11-18), and also the meeting with the two disciples on the road to Emmaus (Lk 24:13-35). The second type of narrative, the appearances to those who were to be the source of the apostolic testimony, include the accounts of Jesus' revelation of himself on the day of his resurrection (Lk 24:36-49; Jn 20:19-23 [Mk 16:14-18]) or shortly thereafter (Jn 20:24-29), in Jerusalem, or in Galilee, upon "the mountain" (Mt 28:16-20), or by the lake of Tiberias (Jn 21:1-14).

Instead of proposing here one or other of these episodes, I should prefer that each person chooses one for himself. The following discussion of the very real problems connected with any of these contemplations is simply a series of animadversions, intended to aid the exercitant in his approach to these difficult, but supremely important contemplations.

The Paschal Faith

The apostolic experience of the presence of the risen Christ was of a very different character from the experience of Jesus' public ministry. The evangelists all make it clear that during the period when the disciples followed Jesus in Galilee and Judea, listening to his instructions, observing his method of preaching, witnessing his miracles, they grasped very little of the real meaning of what they saw and heard, since the mystery surrounding his Person was impenetrable for them. Until the risen Christico

278

imparted to them the Spirit of Truth, these faithful followers of Jesus were without Christian faith. The principal significance of these confrontations with the risen Christ for the apostolic group (and consequently for the present-day Christian who contemplates these happenings) lay in the birth and gradual maturation of genuine Christian faith. Accordingly, unless the exercitant is deeply conscious of the peculiar character of these episodes, which he is to contemplate during the fourth week, and can appreciate how different they are from the events of our Lord's earthly life, he is exposed to the risk of failing to comprehend the paschal mystery, with the result that he is unable to perceive the paschal character of the Christian life, which he is called to lead.

Now no one who has thoughtfully contemplated the Gospel scenes depicting the return of the risen Christ to his own after the first Easter morning can have missed a certain indefinable aura of unfamiliarity, even—let us admit it—of unreality surrounding the figure of our Lord. As we read the evangelists' accounts of these meetings, we inevitably discover to our great discomfiture that everything appears much the same, except the risen Christ himself. In the upper room in Jerusalem on the first Easter Sunday evening (Jn 20:19-25), one senses the uncertainty, indeed the terror, of the disciples. The remains of the fish they had cooked is real enough to taste (Lk 24:42). But he who is discovered standing without warning in their midst seems almost a total stranger, and though we are ashamed to confess it, he strikes us as ghostly, even weird. In fact, the uneasiness and incredulity which the disciples display on this and other similar occasions communicates itself to us as we ponder these episodes; and we too are in need of Jesus' reassuring word, "Peace! it is I; stop being afraid." The reader undergoes the same unwanted, embarrassing reaction to the scene by the lake of Tiberias. The frustration of the disciples who have spent the night in fruitlessly fishing, their fatigue and hunger, are very genuine. The smell of the fish frying upon the coals at the lakeside is most real. Yet the Jesus who stands on the shore remains in a very true sense a person of mystery. Like the disciples we know somehow that "it is the Lord!"; but like the disciples we dare not ask, for we are dimly aware that, if it is he, he is not the Jesus of Nazareth whom we have beheld in our contemplations of the second or the third weeks. Mary Magdalene's inability to recognize, in the stranger who accosts her in the garden on Easter morning, her beloved Master, is, we feel, a most understandable mistake (Jn 20:11-18). We should have committed the same error ourselves.

Moreover, there is another feature of these narratives which the careful reader will not fail to have noticed. Jesus comes suddenly and without any explanation into the group of disciples or the women. One moment he is apparently absent, and the next moment he is among them without warning. Even more striking perhaps is the sudden, unexplained way in which he departs. The evangelists never elucidate: they know no more about it than we do. Only in one instance is there any reference in the Gospels to Christ's departure on these occasions. This is in the Lucan account of the incident at Emmaus, where the two disciples suddenly recognize the Lord in the breaking of bread, the evangelist simply says, "He vanished into thin air!" (Lk 24:31). It is uncanny somehow, the reader feels, despite himself.

The Notion
of Presence

The difficulties which confront us in these contemplations might be expressed another way. Frequently, in making the Spiritual Exercises, one finds that while the points given for the first three weeks are helpful, yet there is often a sense of bewilderment or disillusionment felt in attempting to make a success of the fourth week exercises. Something, it seems, is not right. There is a difficulty which can be successfully solved only if we can discern the purpose behind these continued post-resurrection appearances. One might have thought it would be sufficient for Christ to have manifested himself alive, after his death, but a single time. It is necessary to see the pedagogical purpose at work in these repeated appearances to the disciples. There is a lesson of paramount importance for our grasp of the Christian mystery which the risen Lord wished to teach all Christians: a deeper insight into the concept of presence. Hence it is of considerable moment that we become conscious of the air of unfamiliarity, even unreality, which haunts these scenes. It is no less necessary that we realize that in these same encounters the disciples are really certain, despite their misgivings, that it is really he who is among them—the "historical Jesus," the master whom they had known and followed so loyally during his mortal life.

We should not miss the purposefulness of this divine schooling of his disciples by Jesus, their induction into the mystery of Christian faith. The risen Lord is attempting to make them (and through them, ourselves) experience the reality of his presence in history, even though he remains unseen. The various writers of the New Testament provide evidence that this was no easy lesson to master. We see in Acts and from the writings of Paul that the Christians of the apostolic age were preoccupied with the thought and the desire for the final "return" of their Lord in glory. The author of Acts is probably quoting a very ancient source, which antedates even his own work, when he represents Peter as announcing the exalted Christ as the one "whom heaven must hold until the era of the restoration of all things" (Acts 3:21). Yet, Matthew assures us that, if the primitive Church yearned for the parousia of the Master, she was very much aware that he was present in her midst, especially during her liturgical reunions (Mt 18:19-20); for she kept fresh the memory of his unfailing promise of his abiding presence "until the end of the age" (Mt 28:20). One of the most significant effects of the coming of the Pentecostal Spirit upon the community was the consciousness of the first disciples that they now formed a new collectivity, "the Israel of God" (Gal 6:16). Still, if they were cognizant through their newfound faith of the risen Christ's dynamic presence through the operation of his Spirit and while they knew that he was present also in the "breaking of the Bread," the celebration of the Lord's Supper, as Paul testifies, makes them look forward the more ardently to his return in glory (1 Cor 11:26). The Eucharistic acclamation, "Maranatha" (1 Cor 16:22), reveals how effective a reminder was the sacred liturgy that Jesus would one day return to them—perhaps to find them partaking of this ritual meal, as he had so often come to them after his resurrection in connection with a repast. This attitude towards the Blessed Sacrament from the earliest years of the Church's life reveals the very real tension that has always been felt by Christians between their belief in the real sacramental presence of the risen Christ, or his presence in the Church through the operation of his Holy Spirit, and the unshakeable hope that he is one day to return to them—a hope which implies that somehow he is absent.

Certain special features of Christ's post-resurrection appearances indicate unequivocally that we cannot approach the contemplation of these occurrences as we did those of Jesus' earthly life. Nor should we look to obtain the same fruit from them as in the earlier weeks of the retreat. We see, for example, that the disciples never again return to the same delightfully human intimacy with the Lord which they had in "the days of his flesh." It is St. Mark particularly who gives us such a profound insight into the reality of Jesus' human nature by his candid portrayal of the whole gamut of emotions which he could display, his ever varying reactions to the different groups he met, his constantly changing attitudes toward his own disciples. Now, however, everything is new: the risen Christ without displaying any emotions inspires a deep peace and trust and belief in the hearts of his dearest friends.

Unique Character of the Paschal Experience

It should not be forgotten, moreover, that after his resurrection our Lord appeared only to his own disciples. He makes no attempt to overawe his opponents, to convince his enemies that he is again alive. How helpful to Christian apologetics it might have been, had Christ confronted Pilate or Caiaphas in his glorified state! The Gospels however attest that Christ had no such intent. He appeared not to convince the unbelieving that he was alive, for the new life he possessed was not a return to his former mode of existence. He had now gone forward into a completely different life with God. He returned to his devoted followers to create in them, whose love and loyalty to himself opened them to such an unprecedented favor, the grace of Christian belief. In these scenes, then, which we are now contemplating, we should constantly recall that we are assisting at the genesis of the apostolic faith.

It is most significant that the risen Jesus did not manifest himself in the first place to the Eleven who were to be the official witnesses to him within the Christian community (Acts 4:33) and before the world (Acts 1:8). The Gospel record makes it clear that he first revealed himself to the faithful women who had been united to him by the strongest bond of affection. One cannot but admire the sure and authentically Christian instinct which led St. Ignatius to propose as the first contemplation of the fourth week, our Lord's appearance to his blessed Mother. Who could have been nearer to him than she, both in natural affection and in the gifts of divine grace?

These contemplations of the risen Christ can teach me much about the spiritual life within me and its ultimate orientation. In the first place, I begin to see the truest meaning of the term "spiritual"—one found constantly upon the pages of the Bible: that which is completely dominated by the Spirit of the risen Christ. Thus I come to an ever deeper realization that it is my total self, even on its material side, that is to be redeemed by Christ and consecrated totally and irrevocably to him. I learn, moreover, that the fundamental message of the *praeconium paschale* is this: that the Son of God has chosen to remain human for all eternity. The paschal mystery means that all the authentically human facets of man's existence, lived at the various levels of imagination, pulsating emotions, intelligence, and will are, as the consequence of Christ's resurrection, destined to go forward into eternal life. Thus I begin to appreciate the paschal character of the Christian life. I discern the basic sense of my vocation as a Christian: to be thoroughly human, to be most truly myself. If the Son of God has chosen to remain man forever, then how can I, who strive to follow him who is "the Way," reach him by any spirituality that would dehumanize me?

My contemplation of the risen Christ would be incomplete if it did not result in a deeper appreciation of the dynamic power which has been unleashed in history through him. This theme is central to the last, and only prophetic book of the New Testament, the Apocalypse. The seer of Patmos, its author, develops certain implications of the statement of the exalted Christ, "I was dead: and behold, I am alive for evermore!" (Ap 1:18).

In the first place, he presents the risen Christ as the undisputed master of history. He never tires of repeating, by means of various images and symbols, the idea that Jesus Christ, having gone forward into eternal life, is not less, but infinitely more involved in the events which occur in our world than ever he was when he walked the hills of Galilee. The universal power he now exercises "in heaven and upon earth" (Mt 28:18) is to be seen, by the eyes of Christian faith, in everything which happens to the Church in the world and to each member of the Church. The reign of Christ has been inaugurated by his exaltation; and if while time endures our Lord must continue to vindicate his royal claims, if "he must reign until he puts all his enemies beneath his feet" (1 Cor 15:25), he remains even now in control of history. By his resurrection the kingdom of God has become a terrestrial reality.

A little reflection upon this truth that Christ, now elevated to heavenly glory and apparently absent from our world, is in reality actively involved in our history, reveals to me a conception of heaven which stands in marked contrast with the usual, popular notion of it as a "place of rest." The author of the Apocalypse, and indeed the other inspired writers of the New Testament, habitually present heaven as our participation in this reign and mastery of the risen Christ over the course of the world's history.

Heaven then, as these writers view it, is not a kind of perennial "old folks' home." It is not simply a place of retirement and celestial repose for the senior citizens of the kingdom of God. It is true that the author of Hebrews represents the blessed life after death as a participation in the "sabbath" (the rest or repose) of the Creator, into which the Christian hopes to enter with his leader, Jesus Christ. Yet the context of this development within the whole treatise, which we call the epistle to the Hebrews, indicates that the divine Sabbath-rest must not be misapprehended as inaction or passivity. The Word of God himself, who shares this repose of God, is declared to "sustain the universe with the dynamism of his mighty word" (Heb 1:3). Moreover, now that his work of redemption is completed by his arrival in the heavenly sanctuary, the exalted Christ never ceases to make intercession for mankind by his offering of the celestial sacrifice through which we are redeemed (Heb 9:11-28).

The Christian prophet who wrote the Apocalypse reminds the persecuted churches to whom he writes that their glorified Lord, now risen as priest and king (Ap 1:13), holds the direction of the Church's life in his all-powerful hands. Nothing can happen to her except by his express will, whether it be prosperity or persecution. And what is perhaps even more striking, the blessed martyrs, already "at rest from their labors" (Ap 14:13), have been granted a share in this royal and priestly power of "the Lamb that has been slain": "he has made us a royal house, priests for his God and Father!" (Ap 1:6). This means that their heaven consists in their active participation in the glorified Christ's direction of history.

This truth is dramatically presented by the author in a scene in which he portrays the efficacy of the prayers of these saints under the symbolism of incense placed upon the burning coals of the heavenly altar before the throne of God (Ap 8:3-5). The prayer of these blessed martyrs demanded that divine retribution be visited upon "the inhabitants of the earth" (God's enemies), who had put them to death (Ap 6:10). When the angel has offered the prayers of God's people mixed with incense and they are accepted by God, the angel hurls the burning coals down upon the earth, and the result is a series of catastrophes heralded by seven trumpets (Ap 8:5ff.). Thus does the author of this book show how the martyrs, who are with God, still take an active part in the history of this world. Towards the close of the Apocalypse, by means of the celebrated "reign of a thousand years," we are told explicitly that the blessed in heaven "reign together with Christ," that is, they participate in the glorified Christ's rule of the universe during the lifetime of the Church on earth (Ap 20:4-6).

This conception of the joys of heaven as a deeper involvement in history is also suggested by Jesus' parable of the Talents (Mt 25:14-30). It will be remembered that the reward bestowed by the master upon his return is not a vacation, nor is it honorable retirement with a pension for their services. Because they have been faithful in a small way, they are to be put in charge of greater affairs. Their reward is a larger share in the master's interests. The Lucan version of this same parable (Lk 19:11-27) underscores this point even more effectively. The faithful stewards, who have succeeded in doubling the investment entrusted to them by the king, are put in charge of the administration of five or ten cities.

Thus Jesus makes it clear that he will recompense the faithful Christian by permitting him, after death, to assist him actively in promoting the kingdom of God in this world.

There is a further consequence of Jesus' resurrection and exalta- tion, which we see in the attitude which the apostolic Church displays towards Jesus' earthly history. Nowhere in the Gospels is there any sign of nostalgia for "the good old days" of our Lord's public ministry, when the disciples had enjoyed such human familiarity with him. The primitive Church never looked back to this period as an ideal, a golden age that had been lost. From Pentecost the Church is characterized rather by a looking forward to the final reunion with the parousiac Christ at the close of history. While it is true that the apostolic Church preserved in the Gospels the record of the principal events of Jesus' earthly career, still these were of interest to her only when interpreted in the light of her paschal Christian faith. Or, alternatively, these historical incidents were employed by the evangelists principally to assist their readers to grasp more fully the central announcement of the good news: the signification of Jesus' passion and resurrection. The Gospels are correctly described as a passion-resurrection story with an introduction.

I believe that it is no accident that the first literary contributions to what was to become the New Testament were letters, not the Gospels. The fact that Christian sacred literature begins with Paul, rather than the Synoptics or John, is a clear indication that the fundamental interest of the first Christians was in the contemporary Christ, the Christ, whom they knew to be risen, who was present in his Church through the activity of his Spirit, who would one day come to judge the living and the dead. This deeply Christian attitude to our Lord as the dominant figure in contemporary history is one which I need to cultivate in my own spirituality, if it is to be relevant and meaningful today.

My prayer should be oriented to the contemporary plan of salvation, to present-day sacred history. As Nadal put it, my prayer as a Jesuit should "favor execution,"[1] my principal aim in prayer must be to seek my own point of insertion into salvation history in this age of the Church.

Thus the contemplations of the fourth week warn me of the perpetual necessity of maintaining a contemporary outlook, of keeping up to date; for I am surely called to imitate the perennial *aggiornamento* which I see incarnate in the risen Christ. There

1 Cf. page 152 and note 4.

can be no return to the past, no turning back of the clock, no romantic wish that I could have heard Jesus preaching during his public life, or witnessed his miracles. The risen Lord himself reminds me of this truth through his last word to Thomas in the fourth Gospel, when he pronounces a final beatitude upon those of us who are privileged to have been born in the age of the Holy Spirit. "Blessed are they, who have come to the faith without seeing!" (Jn 20:29). Far from regretting what we may have missed of the special experiences of the Twelve during Jesus' mortal life, we are actually to be deemed "blessed," because we live in the age of the outpoured Spirit.

In conclusion I might recall that I have the consolation of knowing that the risen Christ is the one, who not merely directs the course of the history of this world, but also my own personal life. He is interested in me, in my achieving real success as a human being, because he has chosen to remain human himself for eternity. Because he is concerned about my "humanity," he carried back into the mystery of the Godhead a human nature like my own. His humanity is indeed now perfected by the operation of the Holy Spirit; yet it remains nonetheless truly human. During his post-resurrection appearances, he showed the disciples the reality of his risen body by eating, by insisting that Thomas touch him. And we can be fairly sure that Christ did this not principally to prove that as the "Christ of faith" he was still to be indentified as the "Jesus of history." His purpose was a far more salutary one: to show the disciples that, incomprehensible though it may be for us at the present time, man may hope, indeed must hope, to enjoy God even on the corporeal and material side of his total personality.

The contemplation of the episodes in the risen life of Christ, as I said in the beginning, cannot be conducted in the same manner as those concerned with the mortal life of Jesus. The knowledge that is now sought is markedly different from that involved in the imitation of Christ. It is a deeper, more "contemplative" knowledge that leads the Christian into the love of friendship with the risen Lord. I must now learn to look for "the new sky and the new earth" present in creation as a consequence of Jesus' death and resurrection. For the dynamic power inherent in the glorified humanity of the risen Christ is not confined to the little land of Palestine, to a brief lifespan in the first century of our era. The Lordship of Christ is universal, cosmic. It spreads out like the rays of the sun to enlighten the whole of creation. Moreover he has now become an entirely new way to the Father. The fact that he has gone ahead of us does not at all indicate any intention to exclude us from sharing in his redemptive experiences of dying and rising. We too through death and resurrection must one day go home to the "God no man has ever seen." How this is to be we do not really know, for we have as yet no experience of it. We have met no one who has passed along this road to the Father—except the Lord Jesus and his blessed Mother. Through the prayer of faith we can be touched at very rare, and very precious moments, in such a way as to learn however feebly, "the power of his resurrection" (Phil 3:10).

CHRIST AS THE LAST ADAM
1 Corinthians 15:21-22

For since through a man [came] death; so also through a man [will come] resurrection of the dead. 22For just as in Adam all die; so also in Christ all will be brought to life.

1 Corinthians 15:45-49

Thus Scripture also states, "the first man, Adam, became a living being." The last Adam became a life-giving Spirit. . . . 47The first man was from the soil of the earth: the second man from heaven. 48Those made from the earth are of the same nature as the earthly man: those who are heavenly possess the same nature as the heavenly man. 49And just as surely as we have borne the image of the earthly man, so too shall we bear the image of the heavenly man.

Romans 5:12-21

That is why, just as by a single man Sin entered the world, and through Sin, Death; and so Death has passed to all men, by the fact that all have sinned. . . . 14Death was king from Adam to Moses, even over those who did not sin by a transgression like that of Adam—the type of he who was to come. . . . 19For just as, through the disobedience of one man, the rest were constituted sinners, so also, through the obedience of one man, the rest will be constituted just. . . . 21Thus, just as Sin was king in Death, so Grace was to reign by justice for life eternal through Jesus Christ our Lord.

Colossians 3:9b-11

You have put off your old man with his habits, 10and you have put on that New Man, constantly being renewed in view of perfect knowledge in the image of his Creator, 11in whom there is no "Greek and Jew," "circumcised and uncircumcised," "barbarian, Scythian," "slave, freeman," but Christ, all in all.

Ephesians 4:22-24

You [must] put aside your old way of living, the old man, who is constantly being corrupted by deceptive desires. 23Become new by the Spirit [who dwells] in your mind; 24and put on the New Man, created by God in justice and holiness and truth.

Chapter 29

THE LAST ADAM

THE CHRISTIAN MESSAGE of salvation acquired its character as *Articulation of* "good news" from the experience of the risen Christ, which the *Christian Faith* "original eye-witnesses" (Lk 1:2) were privileged to enjoy. This experience to which the first disciples responded by the commitment of Christian faith resulted in the acquisition of a totally new knowledge of Jesus Christ, the significance of his earthly life, and above all, of his death. To interpret and articulate their newfound belief, the apostolic college under the guidance of Peter had recourse to "the Scriptures," the sacred literature of Israel, finding there certain images and themes, through which God's gracious, saving acts performed for the chosen people had been expressed.

Accordingly, in the summaries of the primitive preaching recorded in the Acts of the Apostles, we find various historical figures from Israel's past and certain key events in her experience of God's activity on her behalf employed by the earlier Christian evangelists in order to set forth the significance of Jesus' redemptive work. He is depicted as the answer to the divine promise made of old to Abraham (Acts 3:25-26). His exaltation "at God's right hand" is proclaimed as the accomplishment of the dynastic oracle, given by Nathan the prophet in God's name to David (Acts 2:30 31; 13:23), that a son of his royal line should inherit his throne forever. In his speech before the Sanhedrin, Stephen the protomartyr interprets Old Testament history in the light of the death and resurrection of Christ, and thereby discovers a series of famous Israelites who may serve as types of the crucified and risen Lord Jesus. In addition to Abraham (Acts 7:2-8), there is Joseph (Acts 7:9-16), Moses (Acts 7:17-40), and especially the prophets (Acts 7:52).

One of the themes most prominent in the Christology of the apostolic age was that of the suffering and glorified Servant of God, of whom the Second Isaiah had sung so poignantly and mysteriously. The kerygma of the Jerusalem community had first applied this motif to Jesus as the Servant "glorified" (Is 52:13) by

289

the God of the patriarchs (Acts 3:13) through his resurrection and ascension (Acts 3:26). Jesus was regarded as the Servant against whom Herod and Pilate, with the collaboration of Jews and Romans, had conspired and contrived to execute (Acts 4:27-28). The earliest inspired authors of the Gospels, in their turn, expressed Jesus' predictions of his sufferings and death in terms of the Isaian Suffering Servant (cf. Mk 8:31; 9:31; 10:33-34).

Paul's Originality in His Use of Genesis   When we turn to the writings of Paul, whose initial experience of the risen Christ differed notably from that of the Twelve, who had been favored with a particularly close association with Jesus during his public ministry, we soon discover that his approach to the Christian mystery is unique. Paul's conversion by the Damascus road had brought him face to face with the exalted Lord, who stood revealed to him as Son of God (Gal 1:16). It was only in response to his query of amazement, "Who are you, Lord?" that Paul learned to identify this celestial, divine person with the humble, despised rabbi Jesus of Nazareth (Acts 9:5). From his reminiscences of this extraordinary event, we see Paul attempting to describe its wholly unprecedented character by comparing it with God's creation of light (Gn 1:3): "because the God who said, 'Light shine out of darkness' [is he] who caused light to shine in our innermost self, to impart the illuminating knowledge of the divine glory in the face of Christ" (2 Cor 4:6).

Indeed, Paul appears to have been the first Christian theologian to make use of the early chapters of Genesis to body forth his very personal insight into the mystery of Christ. The teaching of our Lord himself, reported in the Gospels, provides little precedent for the use of these images and motifs. Jesus' unequivocal prohibition of divorce (Mk 10:6-7; Mt 19:4-5) constitutes his single recorded reference to the opening chapters of Genesis. Only rarely too do the prophetic writings of the Old Testament allude to the creation in presenting Israel's hopes of the eschatological salvation. The final conversion of God's people was thought of as demanding a creative act of God (Jer 31:22). The Second Isaiah depicted the hoped-for return from the Babylonian exile as a new creation (Is 43:17-18). The Third Isaiah at a later date poetically described God's definitive saving action as the creation of a new sky and a new earth (Is 65:17; 66:22-23). It is only in late Judaism that the figure of Adam is used as a vehicle of theological teaching by certain of the sapiential writers (Sir 17:1ff.; 49:16; Wis 2:23-24; 9:2-3; 10:1).

We obtain a hint from the résumés of Paul's preaching to pagans in Acts, which may partly explain his highly original preference for these themes of creation. When Paul preached to Jewish audiences, he was accustomed to introduce his version of the gospel with a review of Israel's history (Acts 13:16-25). In addressing Gentiles, however, he had to begin with the doctrine of the one true God. Thus at Lystra, Paul asserts that the God of Israel is the sole source of all creation, the one "who made sky and earth and sea and everything in them." He alone regulates, by his loving providence over mankind, the natural cycle of the seasons, as he also directs human history in accordance with his own designs (Acts 14:15-17). At Athens, Paul repeats the truth that Yahweh is "the God who made the earth and everything in it" (Acts 17:24), "the one who gives to all life and breath and everything" (v. 25), who "made from a single common origin the whole race of mankind. . . ." (v. 26). The latter part of this citation probably contains an allusion to Adam, who as common parent gave to the human race its basic unity.

The first appearance of what has come to be regarded as Paul's characteristic presentation of Christ's redemptive work appears in first Corinthians, a letter from the middle years of his literary activity. Of the several pastoral problems to which Paul addresses himself here, the most important undoubtedly was the hesitation, on the part of certain members of the Corinthian community, in accepting the crucial doctrine of the eschatological resurrection of the just. This doubt the Corinthians appeared to have combined, inconsistently enough, with an orthodox faith in the resurrection of Christ himself; and Paul was quick to point out that a denial of the resurrection of those "who have died in Christ" was tantamount to a denial of one of the central events announced by the traditional Christian gospel (1 Cor 15:3-4). What these wavering Corinthian converts did not grasp, it appears, was the social character of our Lord's death and resurrection. Jesus did not die as an isolated individual: he involved mankind in his death; or rather, he created the possibility of our involvement in his death. As Paul would later write to Corinth, "One died for all: therefore all have died" (2 Cor 5:14).

The Risen Christ

To counter the doubts in the Corinthian Christians concerning their personal involvement in Christ's resurrection, Paul first declares that "Christ has been raised from death as the first fruits of those who have fallen asleep" (1 Cor 15:20). His reference is to the ancient ceremonial dedication of the first fruits prescribed in the Mosaic law (Lv 23:10-14). This act constituted a solemn obligation for Israel, since it was an acknowledgement of God's exclusive ownership of the land and its produce. At the same time, this

291

oblation of the first fruits was in effect the consecration of the whole harvest to Yahweh. Paul was aware that this significant ritual had been carried out in the temple on the very day when Jesus rose from death. The risen Lord is rightly called "first fruits of those who have fallen asleep," not merely because he has initiated the universal resurrection of the just, but also because his own glorified humanity will one day effectively realize in us this final object of Christian faith and hope.

At this stage of his argument Paul introduces Adam for the first time in his letters. "For since through a man [came] death, so also through a man [will come] resurrection of the dead. For just as in Adam all die, so also in Christ all will be brought to life" (1 Cor 15:21-22).

To appreciate the scope of the antithesis which Paul here sets up between Adam, the sinful parent of the human race, and Jesus Christ, "who was handed over for our sins and raised for our justification" (Rom 4:25), we must recall the comprehensive or "global" character of the biblical concept of death. When, as here, Paul speaks of death in the context of sin, the term does not connote merely physical death. It includes also what we seek to express by the phrases "spiritual death" (grave sin), and "eschatological death" (eternal punishment). The total reality of death for the Old Testament writers comprised in fact complete and final separation from the living God of Israel. Such indeed was the destructive effect of Adam's sin upon the entire human family, as Paul will declare in a later letter (Rom 5:12ff.). The purpose of Christ's resurrection then was to undo the baleful influence of Adam upon mankind. The life which he wills to bestow upon all, who are to be united with him by their own glorious resurrection, is life in its fullest sense. It is eternal life, indeed, and its communication will affect the Christian even on the material side of his person. To assert in its fullness the Christian belief in the efficacy of Jesus' redemptive resurrection, Paul says equivalently, it is not sufficient merely to accept the Greek philosophical argument for the soul's immortality.

Paul returns to the contrast between Adam and Christ somewhat later in this same chapter, in order to expand upon this truth. "Thus Scripture also states, 'the first man, Adam, became a living being.' The last Adam became a life-giving Spirit" (1 Cor 15:45). Paul cites the second creation-account given in Genesis (Gn 2:7), in order to recall the origins of Adam from the earth, and to remind the Corinthians that Adam's origins have left their mark upon all his children. "The first man was from the soil of the earth . . . those made from the earth are of the same nature as the

earthly man . . . we have borne the image of the earthly man . . . ."
(vv. 47-49). Paul is leading up to his final point: "I tell you this,
brothers: flesh and blood cannot inherit the kingdom of God"
(v. 50). The human nature which we have all received from Adam
is powerless to attain the fullness of that divine life which communion with God demands. Human nature must somehow be
empowered to transcend its earthly limitations no less than its
sinfulness.

It is precisely as risen that Christ possesses this power to enable
man to qualify for "the kingdom of God." He has, through his own
resurrection, achieved the definitive status to which all men are
destined. Hence, he is "the last Adam," the eschatological man,
in whom the total effect of his own redemptive work is forever
incarnated. Paul denominates the glorified Lord as "life-giving
Spirit," in contrast with Adam, who at his creation from the earth
"became a living being." In so describing Christ, Paul does not
intend to imply that this transformation of his humanity has made
it immaterial. By calling Christ "life-giving Spirit," Paul asserts
that the Lord is, in his risen state, the source of the Spirit, whose
operations in us are henceforth identified with his own (2 Cor
3:17-18). There is a very real sense in which "the Lord is the
Spirit." In the Nicene Creed, the Church means to underscore this
same truth when she applies the two characteristically Pauline
epithets for the risen Christ, "the Lord and the life-giver," to the
Holy Spirit.

Christ's function as "life-giving Spirit" is defined by Paul in the
passage we have been considering with the help of another idea,
which he took from the first account of creation in Genesis: man's
fashioning in "the image and likeness" of God. "Just as surely as
we have borne the image of the earthly man, so too we shall bear
the image of the heavenly man" (1 Cor 15:49). The risen Christ,
who has assumed the office of the creative Spirit of God (Gn 1:2),
will work the transformation of the Christian in his own image
by effecting the resurrection of the just, through which the ultimate state of man's glory is to be realized even in man's bodily
parts.

Paul continues to fill out the details of this picture of Christ
as the "last Adam" in the celebrated section of Romans, where he
treats the problem of the origins of human sinfulness (Rom
5:12ff.). He institutes the contrast between the first parents of mankind and the risen Lord by calling Adam "the type of him who
was to come" (Rom 5:14). Adam's personal act of disobedience
led, in some mysterious way, which Paul himself does not make
altogether clear, to the sinfulness found in his descendants (vv.

12-15). This evil inflicted upon humanity by the transgression of Adam was to be remedied by the saving obedience of Jesus Christ (v. 19). This life-giving obedience was actualized on Paul's view (although he does not expressly say so here) by Jesus' acceptance in all their concrete circumstances of the two greatest events in his earthly career, his death and resurrection, through which he has been constituted "the last Adam."

Structure of Pauline Soteriology We may at this point present a synthesis of the principal features of Paul's personal thought concerning man's redemption. He fixes his attention almost exclusively upon the two-faceted event which forms the heart of the gospel: Christ's death and resurrection. Paul does not include the incarnation, as John was to do in the fourth Gospel, as a positive part of the redemptive event. For Paul, the coming of God's Son into the world is considered simply as his entry, so far as that was possible for one who was sinless, into the sinful family of the first Adam. It was a necessary presupposition to his labor of redemption. He had to associate himself intimately with sinful mankind, if he were to give the Father what rebellious man was incapable of rendering to him: one act of filial, obediential love. Hence for Paul, the Son of God came "in the likeness of sinful flesh" (Rom 8:3); he was "born of a woman, made subject to law" (Gal 4:4).

By accepting his death in all its concrete reality from the hand of his Father, Jesus Christ destroyed forever the sinful solidarity which had bound humanity to the first Adam. For he freely "became obedient even to death, yes, death upon the cross" (Phil 2:8), as the one effective, redeeming representative of the whole race. By his resurrection, Christ created a new, supernatural solidarity of grace, thereby creating the possibility of an entirely new relationship for man towards God as his Father, through his union with the unique Son of God. "And he died for all, in order that the living might no longer live for themselves, but for him who died and was raised for them" (2 Cor 5:15).

Yet in order that man personally might attain this salvation, he must pass through the ultimate redemptive experience, Christian death, the "new creation" that became a reality in Jesus' own death. The possibility of attaining this crucially necessary experience, Paul teaches, is initially opened to the individual human being through baptism, the sacramental participation in Jesus' redeeming death (Rom 6:3-4). Yet another experience, participation in Jesus' resurrection, which his baptism also makes possible, is also needed for the completion of man's salvation: and it is to occur at the parousia (1 Cor 15:23ff.).

Thus the emphasis in Paul's thought is not upon the vicarious nature of Jesus' redemptive work, although that element is not absent, but rather upon the efficacy of Christ's death and resurrection in involving man in a totally new human experience. For this he is prepared here below by the Christian sacraments, principally by Baptism and the Eucharist. Ultimately however he is saved by being totally conformed through death in Christ and resurrection to Christ, who exhibits in himself the definitive form of redeemed human nature as "the last Adam."

Closely connected with the theme of "the last Adam" is another motif which has a significant role in the soteriological thought of Paul. It too comes from the creation stories of Genesis, where man is described as being created in "the image and likeness" of God, inasmuch as he is destined to "have dominion . . . over . . . all living things" (Gn 1:26-28). God, supreme Lord of creation, graciously bestows upon man a share in his universal dominion of his creatures; and hence man can be said to be made in the divine image. That Paul is indebted to this passage of Genesis for his theological theme of the image is clear from its first appearance in his writings (1 Cor 11:7-8), where the context contains several allusions to God's creation of man. Here the Christian is denominated "the image and glory of God," a conception which will continue to be exploited by Paul in subsequent letters.

The risen Christ, the "last Adam," is proclaimed in Paul's gospel as "the image of God" (2 Cor 4:4), for Paul views the Christian existence in this world as a continuous process of transformation into this aspect of Christ. "All of us, while with unveiled face we reflect, as in a mirror, the glory of the Lord, are being transformed into the same image with ever-increasing glory, as by the Lord [who is] Spirit" (2 Cor 3:18). Later, in writing to Rome, Paul sets forth God's plan for man's salvation in terms of this same theme. "Those whom he [God] had known from the beginning, he also predestined to be shaped in the image of his Son, that he might be the first-born of a large family of brothers" (Rom 8:29). Man is saved by being molded "in the image of His Son," who as risen is himself "the image of the invisible God" (Col 1:13). It is only through being raised from death to glory in his total personality, with and through Christ, that man arrives at the goal for which he was created: true sonship with the Father. Thus by means of this image theme Paul is enabled to present the redemption, not as an impersonal or magical process, but as a progressive growing into a very real interpersonal relationship, that of son to father, with God in Christ.

The Last Adam

Themes
in Colossians
and Ephesians

In Paul's later letters, from his Roman captivity, Christ appears as "the new man," a phrase synonymous with that of "the last Adam"; and here again the image motif recurs in combination with this conception. Through his baptismal experience and by the baptismal grace, the Christian "has put off the old man with his conduct, and has put on the new Man, who is continually being renewed in the image of his Creator in order to know him fully" (Col 3:9-10). It is, as we have just seen, only by knowing God as his Father that this fullness of knowledge is arrived at. Thus Paul exhorts the Ephesians to strive for "the knowledge of the Son of God," which for him is "mature manhood, that full measure of development found in Christ" (Eph 4:13). Christian spirituality is simply the unfolding of an ever-increasing consciousness of our relationship as sons and daughters to the Father. And the pattern which must be followed is that of the risen Christ as "the last Adam," as Paul adds a few lines further in this same letter. "You must put aside your old way of living, the old man, who is constantly being corrupted by deceptive desires . . . and put on the new Man, created by God in justice and holiness and truth" (Eph 4:22-24).

It is an unwritten axiom of the biblical view of sacred history that "the end must correspond to the beginning." We see this viewpoint functioning in the attempts by so many New Testament writers to return to the origins of Israel's history. However they do not go back beyond Abraham or Moses. It is the religious genius of Paul which exhibits an unprecedented originality of thought by returning to the very beginnings of the cosmos to seek inspiration in the creation stories of the opening chapters of Genesis. His presentation of Christ as "the last Adam" epitomizes his view of Christian eschatology. For Paul, our human nature has attained its definitive perfection in the exalted Christ; and it is through the power unleashed in history by God's raising of Jesus that our own future redemption is to be accomplished at the *parousia*. Yet the process is not a mechanical one: it involves the Christian in a most personal experience, his individual participation in the "new creation," which is Christian death. This death in Christ becomes in Pauline spirituality the most crucial event of our earthly existence. It is by saying "Amen" to the Father as our Father that our final access to God is opened up for us. This union will be completed ultimately only with one further act of filial obedience, our bodily resurrection, by which we are made eternally conformable to "the last Adam," Christ our brother, "the image of the invisible God." "The Son of God, Christ Jesus, whom we have announced among you, you did not find wavering between 'Yes' and 'No' . . . for to all God's promises he supplies the 'Yes' which confirms them. That is why we voice the 'Amen' through him, when we give glory to God" (2 Cor 1:19-20).

THE BODY OF THE GLORIFIED CHRIST
1 Corinthians 12:12-27

Just as the body is one, even though it has many organs—all the organs of the body, many as they are, constitute one body—so also is Christ. [13]For all of us were baptized into one body, be we Jew or Greek, slave or freeman; and all of us drank the one Spirit.

[14]For in reality, the body does not consist of one organ, but of many. [15]Suppose the foot were to say, "Because I am not a hand, I am not part of the body." Would it for that reason cease to be part of the body? [16]Suppose the ear were to say, "Because I am not the eye, I am not part of the body." It would not for all that be any less part of the body.

[17]If the body were all eye, where would the hearing be? If it were all hearing, where would be the sense of smell? [18]As a matter of fact, however, God has set the various organs, each with its own individual function, in the body, as he willed.

[19]But if the whole consisted of a single organ, where would the body be? [20]As it is there is a plurality of organs, but one body. [21]And so the eye cannot say to the hand, "I have no need of you." Nor again, the head cannot say to the feet, "I have no need of you." [22]Indeed, the seemingly weaker organs are actually all the more necessary; [23]those parts of the body we deem less honorable, we surround with greater honor; our uncomely parts we grace with greater comeliness than our comely parts, [24]which have no need of that. God has, in fact, assembled the body, bestowing particular dignity upon the humbler parts, [25]so that there be no disunity in the body, but all its organs may feel the same concern for one another. [26]Consequently, if one organ suffers, all the organs suffer: if one is in good form, they all rejoice together.

[27]Now you are Christ's body, each constituting one of its organs.

Chapter 30

THE CHURCH, BODY OF THE
RISEN CHRIST

THE MEMBERS of the primitive community of Jerusalem regarded   *Baptism and*
baptism as the rite of initiation into the new Israel. It was through   *Faith in Paul*
the administration of this sacrament that those who joined the
apostolic group from the day of Pentecost were given a share in
the Pentecostal graces of the Holy Spirit (Acts 2:38). St. Paul
views baptism constantly as the incorporation of the Christian into
Christ. How close this union appeared to him may be gauged
from the description given to the Galatians, if we recall that the
ancients always regarded clothing as in some real way identified
with the wearer. "All of you, because you were baptized into
Christ, have been clothed with Christ. There is no 'Jew and
Greek,' 'slave and freeman,' 'male and female;' for all of you constitute a single Man in Christ Jesus" (Gal 3:27-28). How realisti-
cally Paul viewed this union between the baptized and the risen
Christ—a union which involved the Christian in his total personality, as it also included the glorified body of the risen Lord—
may be seen from a remark he made in writing to Corinth after
citing the verse in Genesis, which presents marriage as a union
of "two in one flesh" (Gn 2:24). "The man who cleaves to the
Lord is one spirit [with him]" (1 Cor 6:17). Later, in Ephesians,
Paul expresses the effects of the baptismal grace as a breaking with
the sinful family of the first man and an initiation into the solidarity created by the risen Christ as the last Adam. "You must put
aside your old way of living, the old man, who is constantly being
corrupted by deceptive desires, become new by the Spirit who
dwells in your mind; and put on the new Man, created by God
in justice and holiness and truth" (Eph 4:22-24).

Paul's use of the metaphor of clothing and even that drawn
from the physical union of man and wife indicates how vividly
real to him was the closeness of the bond that united the Christian
at his baptism to the risen Christ. These figures of speech however
should not be permitted to obscure the intensely personal character of this union. This will be seen to be the more necessary

when, as is our intention here, we come to study the characteristically Pauline conception of the Church as the Body of the risen Lord.

Here it may be helpful to remind ourselves of the peculiarly Pauline view of Christian faith. For Paul, faith is the total self-giving of the baptized to the supreme Lord of the cosmos, the glorified Son of God. It is a passionate and personal surrender of all that a man holds dear, particularly his innermost self, a total dedication to him "who died and rose in order to be Lord of dead and living" (Rom 14:9). We have perhaps the classic description of it in the opening lines of Romans, where it is called "the obedience of faith" (Rom 1:5). The genesis of this warmly human attachment, so full of loving trust and confidence in the person of Jesus Christ, may be traced back to Paul's first meeting with the Lord Jesus on the Damascus road.

The New Testament data regarding Paul's conversion-experience (that in Acts and in Paul's own letters) make it clear that the apostle's introduction to Christ was unique in the annals of the early Church. The sudden confrontation with one whom, until that very moment, Paul had thought of as "a curse" (Gal 3:13) was a violent, blinding experience. He himself was to refer to it years later as a "capturing" by the Son of God (Phil 3:12). It would be no exaggeration to say that our Lord "took by storm," at their very first encounter, this one-time persecutor of his nascent Church. How deeply and intimately this crisis affected Paul may be judged from his own characterization of it to the Galatians as God the Father's revelation of "his Son *in* me" (Gal 1:16).

As a result of this tremendous experience, which shattered forever Paul's former dreams of making a name for himself as a zealot and transformed his whole notion of religion, faith for the Apostle of the Gentiles was not predominantly intellectual, but a wholehearted commitment of self to the person of Jesus Christ. It differs notably from the conception of faith found in Johannine literature, which is much more contemplative in character.

Paul still had much to learn about Christ after this initial meeting with him on the Damascus road: the elements of Christian belief contained in the apostolic kerygma, as well as the various traditions concerning Jesus' life and teaching, which would later be enshrined in the Gospel records. No doubt he acquired this from the catechesis transmitted to him by Ananias. Yet it remains incontrovertibly true that, even before Paul had been received into the Christian community through the administration of baptism by Ananias in Damascus, he had capitulated wholly to the compelling attraction of the glorified Son of God; and the fundamental shape of the Christian mystery in Pauline spirituality was thereafter determined unalterably. It was constructed, as he tells the Colossians, upon the supernatural reality of "Christ within you" (Col 1:27).

The distinctive character thus stamped upon Pauline Christology should not be overlooked. On the view of this great mystical theologian of the apostolic age, Jesus' resurrection was not to be thought of principally as a personal reward for his obedience to his Father. This was indeed the way in which it was habitually presented by the Jerusalem kerygma. "The God of Abraham and Isaac and Jacob, the God of our fathers, has glorified his Servant Jesus . . ." (Acts 3:13). "Therefore did God in turn immeasurably exalt him, and graciously bestow on him the Name, out-weighing every other name . . ." (Phil 2:9). By contrast, Paul will assert of Christ that "he was raised for our justification" (Rom 4:25). In the work *De Fide Resurrectionis,* attributed to St. Ambrose, we find this same line of thought further developed, "For if he [Christ] did not rise for us, then he did not rise, since he had no personal reason for rising. . . . For himself, the resurrection was not necessary, since the bonds of death did not hold him captive; because, though as man he was dead, still in the city of death he was free!" This same passage contains the very poetic but deeply theological passage: "*Resurrexit in eo mundus, resurrexit in eo caelum, resurrexit in eo terra. Erit enim caelum novum, et terra nova.*"[1]

Paul's most characteristic presentation of the risen redeemer is expressed through the title, "the last Adam" (1 Cor 15:45), which we have already considered. Christ rose as the inaugurator of a new human family, a new race. His loving obedience to the Father erected a totally "new creation" upon the ruins of the old solidarity, binding mankind to the protoparent, marring it with Adam's sin.

The Church as Christ's Body

Paralleling the development of this theology of the redemption in Paul's letters, may be seen a concept of the Church which is closely related to it. The Church is simply the Body of the glorified Christ. We can trace the origins of the idea back to Paul's conversion-experience, when the divine being surrounded with the light of glory, who met Paul on the Damascus road, identified himself as "Jesus, whom you are persecuting" (Acts 9:5; 22:8; 26:15). In some mysterious way the Son of God, who remains human for all eternity, was actively present through his disciples in the world. He was still a personage contemporary with Paul

1 J. P. Migne, *Patrologiae Cursus Completus. Series Prima, Tomus* XVI, column 1344, n. 102.

himself, having acquired at his exaltation a new dimension, so to speak, the members of the Church, to which Paul at his baptism by Ananias was admitted. As a consequence of his later missionary career and his continued reflection upon the meaning of the Christian mystery, Paul came to realize, as we stated earlier, that the individual Christian was inducted by baptism into a union with the humanity of the risen Christ, which was so all-embracing as to be almost one of identity. Being one with our Lord, each Christian is united to all other Christians "in Christ Jesus." This is the mystery of the Church as the Body of the risen Christ.

The first complete expression of this insight occurs in the twelfth chapter of Paul's first letter to Corinth. If the insight was unprecedented in Christian thought, the literary expression of it was inspired by a fable, which was already ancient when Aesop added it to his celebrated collection. Livy had recorded it in his history of Rome. At a much later date Shakespeare was to insert it in his play *Coriolanus* (Act I, scene 1). It may help us to appreciate Paul's conception of the Church, if we recall the fable.

At a crisis in the Roman Republic when the *plebs*, or common people, had seceded, and civil war threatened to cause great damage to the body politic, the aristocracy, or *equites*, in their concern for the common weal, dispatched Menenius Agrippa, on account of the authority he enjoyed with the common people, to parley with them. Menenius Agrippa finally brought the people round to see how suicidal was the course upon which they were embarked. He achieved this by telling them the following fable.

At one time, the various active members of the body became seriously annoyed with one organ, which to all appearances sat idly in their midst like a queen, waited upon by all the rest. This lazy organ (the belly), they decided, must be taught a lesson. So the hands, the feet, the head, teeth, and throat conspired to starve this do-nothing organ into subjection. Each of them in turn refused to pass food along to the belly. The first day or two, everything went well. Indeed, there was no question but that the belly was feeling noticeably miserable. By the third day, however, the other organs discovered to their alarm that they themselves were exhausted and ill. Thus this drastic experiment taught them the salutary lesson that, because this one organ had a very different function from the others, this did not mean that it was useless, or that they could get along without its collaboration. They eventually realized that in fact it performed an essential function for the good of the whole body.

If we turn to the Pauline passage, which depicts the Church as the Body of Christ, we can recognize allusions to this ancient fable. "Just as the body is one, even though it has many organs—all the organs of the body, many as they are, constitute one body—so also is Christ. For all of us were baptized into one body, be we Jew or Greek, slave or freeman; and all of us drank the one Spirit. For in reality the body does not consist of one organ, but of many. Suppose the foot were to say, 'Because I am not a hand, I am not part of the body.' Would it for that reason cease to be part of the body? Suppose the ear were to say, 'Because I am not the eye, I am not part of the body.' It would not for all that be any less part of the body. If the body were all eye, where would the hearing be? If it were all hearing, where would be the sense of smell? As a matter of fact, however, God has set the various organs, each with its own individual function, in the body, as he willed" (1 Cor 12:12-18).

In this first phase of Paul's development, by which he has attempted to delineate the kind of unity with which the Church is endowed by God, we discover what at first may seem to be a somewhat startling truth. We Christians, members of the risen Christ, form one body precisely in virtue of what makes each of us totally different from one another: our own uniqueness as a person, our distinctive character as an individual human being. It is this very uniqueness which renders our union in Christ a necessity, since we stand in need of one another as persons. At the same time, it is this individual distinctiveness which is each one's greatest contribution to the good of the whole Body of Christ. It is this very quality which makes it possible for each to bring something to the community or fellowship, which no other person can contribute.

In the paragraph which follows in the Pauline passage we are studying, the apostle develops another aspect of the Church, which has been given a certain prominence in Vatican II. It is known nowadays as the principle of subsidiarity, which asserts the need for permitting the collaboration of all in the common enterprise, in accordance with the position and capacities of each individual. "But if the whole consisted of a single organ, where would the body be? As it is there is a plurality of organs, but one body. And so the eye cannot say to the hand, 'I have no need of you.' Nor again, the head cannot say to the feet, 'I have no need of you.' Indeed, the seemingly weaker organs are actually all the more necessary; those parts of the body we deem less honorable, we surround with greater honor; our uncomely parts we grace with greater comeliness than our comely parts, which have no need of that. God has, in fact, assembled the body, bestowing particular dignity upon the humbler parts, so that there be no disunity in the

303

body, but all its organs may feel the same concern for one another. Consequently, if one organ suffers, all the organs suffer: if one is in good form, they all rejoice together. Now you are Christ's body, each constituting one of its organs" (1 Cor 12:19-27).

In this second half of his development, St. Paul dwells upon the complementary roles which the various members of the Church are called upon to play for the good of the entire body. True unity in Christ demands that each be given scope to make that particular contribution which he alone can make. Only thus can Christians provide what is lacking to the completeness of the whole Christ (Col 1:24). Authentic Christian unity takes its rise from the individual exploitation of the baptismal grace by each Christian. Thus this union is created out of the infinite variety exhibited by the various members of the Church. It is, as a consequence, far removed from any sort of deterministic uniformity.

It is instructive to observe that Paul evidently considered the Greek term "unity" (*henotēs*) too bloodless and impersonal, too coldly abstract. We find it employed only twice in all his correspondence (Eph 4:3,13). The designation which the apostle prefers is *koinōnia*, or fellowship. The Christian vocation is in his eyes a gracious summons by God the Father "into fellowship with his Son" (1 Cor 1:9); and the Church itself is simply "the fellowship of the Holy Spirit" (2 Cor 13:14; cf. Phil 2:1). The Spirit, the bond of unity within the Church, as the love of the Father for the Son, imparts the intensely personal character to Christian fellowship in Christ. We need perhaps to remind ourselves in our day that the unity of the Church is a God-given reality, which does not depend upon the efficiency of her organization, nor upon the coercive force of her laws, and certainly not upon any enforced standardization by which each person is turned out of the same mold. The Christian fellowship depends primarily upon the indwelling Holy Spirit who unites each Christian with the risen Christ and with the rest of the faithful. In brief, the unity of the Church depends upon that fraternal love imparted by the Holy Spirit.

Achieving Christian Unity   We must endeavor to reflect profoundly upon this truth and illustrate it by the lives we lead, if we are to work effectively to promote Christian unity. Only in this way can we hope to correct the terrifying caricature of herself which the Church has at times, unfortunately, presented to other men. Because of the distorted image which some Catholics have harbored of the Church to which they give their allegiance, she can appear as a tyrannical machine, crushingly ruthless in her striving for self-preservation, jealous to increase the centralization of her power, oppressive and absolutist in the inexorability of her legalistic regime.

Paul's conception of the Church, as we have seen, springs from a deep conviction of the unique character of each person who enters the Christian fellowship. Once again however we must remind ourselves that this value-judgment is not based merely upon the natural dignity surrounding the human person. It arises really from the salutary divine necessity under which the Son of God put himself by the very fact of his becoming man. This was nothing short of a freely chosen act of self-limitation on the part of the divine Son. He did not become *homo in genere, homo universalis,* but an individual member of a particular race, who lived within the narrow limits of a relatively short life-span at a definite period of the world's history, whose activities were confined within a very tiny sector of the earth's expanse. By deliberate choice, the Son of God excluded himself from large areas of space and time, and limited severely his own personal field of achievement. Instead of accomplishing the redemption entirely by his own infinitely efficacious operation throughout the course of history, he chose out of divine condescension to invite human collaboration.

This precious lesson, as we have already had occasion to observe, was one which Paul learned in the very hour of his conversion to Christianity, when the risen Lord had revealed to him that, though exalted in glory, he was still actively present in the world through the existential reality of his Church. By the very circumstances of his admission into the Christian community, Paul was taught the salutary truth that, by the will of Christ, men are to be saved by other men. Despite the unprecedented nature of his experience by the Damascus road, it was not the risen Lord, but a member of the Christian brotherhood in the city of Damascus, Ananias, who baptized the convert Paul and made him a Christian.

In my own world of the twentieth century Jesus Christ has need of my cooperation, if his redemptive activity is to go forward. There are certain things which I as a distinctive personality can add to the Church's work today—a contribution which Christ cannot make by himself, since he has chosen to rely upon me. Thus the Church depends, for her life, upon an elaborate set of interpersonal relationships binding all Christians together in Christ. Paul has said it in much simpler, more effective fashion: "You are Christ's Body, each constituting an organ of it!"

We should, in closing, recall briefly the later development of the Pauline theme we have been considering. The apostle came to realize, it would seem, that one important detail was missing in the picture of the union of all Christians in Christ, which he had pre-

Church as Christ's Spouse

305

sented to the Corinthians and later to the Roman communities (Rom 12:4-8) with the help of an ancient Mediterranean fable. By adapting it as a kind of parable, Paul had insisted upon the intimacy of the union (one of quasi-identification) of all with Christ. In Colossians and Ephesians he expressly adverts to the distinction between Christ as head and Christians as his body (Col 1:18), the completion of Christ (Eph 1:23).

This distinction permits Paul to speak of the relationship of love, which binds the risen Lord to the Church. For love demands a certain otherness and personal confrontation between lover and beloved. It is only after an extended discussion of this aspect of the Christian mystery in the fourth chapter of Ephesians, that Paul will finally dwell upon the love relationship existing between Christ and his spouse the Church. "He had himself graced some with [the vocation of] apostles, others with that of prophets, others again with that of evangelists, still others with that of pastors and teachers, in order to perfect God's people for a work of service, the building up of the body of Christ, until we all reach that oneness of faith, the profound knowledge of the Son of God, as the fully mature Man, the full measure of the completion of Christ, that . . . we may grow in all things into him who is the head, Christ. For from him, the whole body, closely joined and fitted together . . . according to the measure [of cooperation] of each single organ continues its development towards the building up of itself through love" (Eph 4:11-16).

This dynamic love, by which Christ redeemed man and created his Church, is the dominant motif of the closing section of Ephesians. "Therefore become imitators of God as beloved children; and live a life of love, as Christ also has loved you and handed himself over for us, an offering and sacrifice to God in the odor of sweetness . . . Christ is the head of the Church: he is himself the saviour of his body . . . Christ loved the Church and handed himself over for her sake, in order that he might make her holy by cleansing her in the bath of water with the word. . . . For no one ever hates his own flesh, but he provides for it and cares for it, just as Christ [acted towards] the Church, since we are organs of his body" (Eph 5:1-30).

THE ATONEMENT, WORK OF THE FATHER
AND THE SON
Romans 8:1-4

Consequently, there is no condemnation for those in union with Christ Jesus. [2]For the law of the Spirit of life in Christ Jesus has freed you from the law of Sin and of Death. [3]God, by sending his own Son in the likeness of sinful humanity and on account of Sin, condemned Sin in that humanity—a task impossible for the Law, seeing it was reduced to utter helplessness by sinful human nature—[4]in order that the justice of the Law might be fulfilled in us, whose conduct is governed, not by sinful human nature, but by the Spirit.

"THE LAW OF THE SPIRIT OF LIFE IN CHRIST JESUS"

Paul on the Function of Mosaic Law

PAUL CHARACTERIZED his own version of the apostolic kerygma as "a scandal to Jews and folly to pagans" (1 Cor 1:23), and even today his admirers are forced to agree with his critics that his ability to disconcert his readers was not the least noteworthy of his talents. In fact, although his thought may at other times be obscure or tortuous, Paul is unmistakably clear when he is most disconcerting. Thus in defining the purpose of the Mosaic law for the Galatians, he will simply say "it was brought in with a view to transgressions" (Gal 3:19), a comment which scandalized generations of copyists and commentators, as the history of its transmission and interpretation demonstrates.

It is just such a disturbing remark of the apostle which we wish to consider here, because of its significance for a genuine Christian (and Ignatian) spirituality. In his correspondence with the Corinthian community Paul once stated in a somewhat offhand manner, "The letter kills: it is the Spirit that gives life" (2 Cor 3:6). One might be inclined to think that this startling, lapidary statement was a slip of the pen. Yet, as Père Stanislas Lyonnet has shown,[1] this epigram is an accurate summation of Paul's attitude towards law—not merely the Mosaic law, but law as such.

As if to put an end to all discussion concerning the true meaning of this statement of St. Paul, St. Thomas Aquinas, citing the authority of St. Augustine, comments upon the aphorism with his customary serenity in a way that is not calculated to reassure the legalistic mentality. "By the term 'letter' must be understood any line of Scripture which remains exterior to men, even the moral precepts of the Gospel" (*Summa Theologica* 1a-2ae, q. 106, a.2).

Disturbing as this viewpoint may appear to some, it particularly deserves our prayerful consideration as we contemplate the mysteries of the fourth week. For it was validated ultimately by the

1 Stanislas Lyonnet, S.J., "Liberté du chrétien et loi de l'Esprit selon saint Paul," *Christus* N⁰. 1 (1954) 6-27; cf. also "La Morale de saint Paul," *Catéchistes* (1953) 149-159.

joyous event of Christ's exaltation. It might be more precise to say that it owes its creation to the risen Christ's gift of the Holy Spirit. It is in this context, at any rate, that it was perceived and formulated by Paul. "The law of the Spirit of life in Christ Jesus has freed you from the law of sin and of death" (Rom 8:2). Accordingly, it is not out of place at this point of the retreat to review a problem which remains a perennial one for the Christian and, even more especially, for the religious: the relation of externals to the interior Christian life.

Jesus himself occasionally refers to this problem in the Gospels, where he condemns the bankruptcy of the religious spirit of contemporary Judaism. Not a few of the Pharisees in first century Palestine, it appears, attached more importance to certain human customs and regulations than they did to the will of God (Mk 7:6-13; Mt 23:1-36). Paul encountered this same tendency in certain judaizing Christians, who attempted to indoctrinate the Galatians with the false view that the observance of the Mosaic code was a necessary means for the Christian's salvation. In his letter to his young converts in Galatia, Paul denounced this error as tantamount to a denial of the universal efficacy of Christ's redemptive death. He did not hesitate to assert the orthodox view in a most forthright manner, since he was deeply angered by the disturbance caused among his neophytes. "Remember, I, Paul, am telling you: if you have yourselves circumcised, Christ can help you in no way whatsoever. . . . You people, who propose to be justified by law are finished with Christ! You have fallen from grace" (Gal 5:2-4). Later, Paul would write to the Romans: "What has become of your grounds for self-confidence? It is ruled out. By what kind of law? The law of works? By no means! By the law of faith. For we are convinced that a man is justified by faith, apart from works of law" (Rom 3:27-28). Reminding us, as they undoubtedly do of the old faith and/or good works controversy debated so fiercely at the time of the Reformation, these words may seem to be as disconcerting as his remark to the Galatians.

Yet the problem to which Paul addresses himself is one that has constantly reappeared throughout the course of the history of the Church. That it is still with us may be seen from such recent phenomena as the Traditionalist Movement. It is further exemplified by those who never miss Mass on Sunday, simply because there is a law which enjoins such an observance. Yet such people appear to be devoid of what one thinks of as the genuinely Christian spirit: they lack charity towards others, or fail to include the virtue of justice in their business ethics. There are others who multiply devotions without ever seeming to exhibit the very fundamental virtue of devotion. In the history of Christian spirituality, a decline in the spirit of genuine prayer has usually been accompanied by an exaggerated multiplication of vocal prayers.

This difficulty also manifests itself among religious. It is not inconceivable that there are some religious who never break a rule, yet are never really charitable, for it is quite possible to be uncharitable in the way one keeps the rules. There are those who may carry out what the superior commands with great scrupulosity, without ever being truly obedient. It is quite feasible to avoid any technical violation of the vows of poverty, for instance, without acquiring the true spirit of poverty, which has been well described as "being happy with nothing" (where the emphasis is upon the word "happy"). These random examples indicate that the problem which concerns us is that of the correct attitude towards the structures affecting the Christian and the religious life, whether it be commandments or canon law, or the religious rule or prescriptions for the observance of the vows.

New vs.
Old Testament We may begin our discussion of this vexing problem by seeking to determine just what distinguishes most fundamentally the religion of the New Testament from that of the Old. The first answer that comes to mind is that Christianity proposes a more perfect code of morality, a set of norms more exacting than those which obliged the Israelites. To contrast the two religions in this way, however, is to assume that they are essentially two law codes, a view which does not do justice to the description of Christianity provided by the New Testament. In her liturgy for the feast of Pentecost, the Church regards it as the annual commemoration of the creation of the "new law," but a "law" written upon the hearts of the faithful by the Holy Spirit, "the finger of the Father's right hand" (*Veni Creator Spiritus*). The reality underlying this metaphor, "the new law," it would seem, is not legislation, but the indwelling presence of the Spirit within the Church and within the individual Christian—the prodigal gift of divine love "poured out in our hearts" (Rom 5:5).

This impression is confirmed by the answer given to our question by the *Summa Theologica* (1a-2ae,q.107,a.1ad2). "Although the Old Law imposed precepts of charity, yet through it was not given the Holy Spirit, by whom 'charity is poured out in our hearts,' as is stated in Romans 5:5." Elsewhere, St. Thomas states his view with even greater precision. "It is the Holy Spirit himself who is the New Testament by effecting love in us, the fulfillment of the Law" (*In 2 Cor cap.3, lect.2*). "It is proper to God to act by operating upon the interior of the soul, and thus it was that the New Testament was given, because it consists in the outpouring of the Holy Spirit" (*In Heb cap.8, lect.2*).

We are now in a position to grasp the basic difference between the Old and the New Testaments. They are to be distinguished as an external law or ethical code, on the one hand, and a totally new dynamic force, interior to man, on the other. Indeed, where the immediate relationship of the Israelite was to a thing, however holy (the God-given covenant stating Israel's obligations to Yahweh), the Christian is, by the grace of God, placed in a totally unprecedented interpersonal relation to the Holy Spirit. It is the presence of the Spirit, within the Christian, which provides the power for his supernatural activity as well as the guidance to act in accordance with the divine will.

We might remind ourselves here of another question, quite similar to the one which we have been discussing. What is the difference between the religious state and that followed by the Christian laity? We must beware of couching our reply primarily in terms of the obligations imposed upon religious by the vows and the rules. For to call the religious state a higher way of life simply because it is a better regulated life might merely mean that religious have more occasions for falling into imperfections, and even into sin than their Christian brothers and sisters in the world.

And here we may turn with confidence for a specific answer to a man who surely possessed the heart and mind of St. Paul, Ignatius Loyola. In his preamble to the *Constitutions of the Society of Jesus,* St. Ignatius makes a profound and very moving act of faith in the Holy Spirit's presence within the Society, by asserting his conviction that the Spirit of Christ is the main cohesive force which binds the members together in fellowship and aids them to realize the Christian ideal held out to them for God's greater glory. "It is the interior law of charity and love, which the Holy Spirit is wont to write and imprint upon our hearts, rather than any exterior constitutions," he says, which must govern and maintain in existence the religious order he has founded.[2] In the course of reading the *Constitutions* of the Society, however, with its numerous, detailed directives for the admission of novices, the formation of the young religious, the system of checks and balances upon the power of the General, one might receive the impression that St. Ignatius had forgotten all about his initial act of faith in the guidance of the Holy Spirit. Yet the repeated ref-

2 Cf. page 226, note 2.

erences throughout the *Constitutions* to the Spirit as "the unique unction of divine Wisdom," or "the sovereign providence and direction of the Holy Spirit," permit no room for such misunderstanding as to the identity of the real guide and promoter of the Society of Jesus.

This primacy of the Holy Spirit in Ignatian spirituality is of course most evident to anyone who has properly grasped the real originality of the *Spiritual Exercises*. Merely to read this little book, which has been admired for its economy of expression, the logic and psychology of its graduated arrangement in four "weeks," even the novelty of certain meditations or contemplations, is to experience a certain disillusionment. To appreciate their special worth, the Spiritual Exercises must be made under the direction of a competent guide. The principal reason for this is the danger of missing one of St. Ignatius' most striking contributions to Christian asceticism: the discernment of "spirits." The two sets of rules, which he appends to his book, contain directions for discerning "spirits" during the first and second weeks of the Exercises, and are actually, in the mind of the author, one of the book's most significant and essential sections. In fact, it may be truly said that a good deal of the justified criticism directed against Ignatian spirituality in our day stems from the neglect of this discernment of spirits on the part of those who give the Spiritual Exercises. No degree of adherence to "the letter" of the author throughout the rest of the book can compensate for a neglect of "the spirit" of the Exercises, found only through careful and competent application of these rules by both director and exercitant.

Primacy of the Spirit in Pauline Spirituality   We have had occasion earlier in the retreat to point out how characteristic of Pauline spirituality is this idea of discernment. Paul is very much aware that there cannot be any ready-made program for the Christian life, which regulates the conduct of the Christian down to its least details. He regards the Christian as a "spiritual" man, one who is attuned to the movements of the Holy Spirit within him. "Live by the Spirit," he tells the Galatians, "and you will not carry out the desires of the flesh. For the flesh by its desires is in opposition to the Spirit, while the Spirit by its desires fights the flesh. . . . But if you are led by the Spirit, you are not under law. . . . Now the harvest of the Spirit is love, joy, peace, patience, kindliness, goodness, faith, gentleness, self-control; and against these things there is no law!" (Gal 5:16-23).

This passage presents the ideal Christian life, in which a man is totally "inner-directed," by the power and the inspiration of the Spirit. For those who attain such a high ideal, there is no need to be "outer-directed," by the coercion of any laws or regulations. Indeed, this interior dynamism may be called "the law of the Spirit" (Rom 8:2), because for such a perfect Christian the Spirit has replaced any kind of law, not only showing him how he is to act in any given situation, but also bestowing upon him the power to carry out God's will in any specific instance. Such perfect freedom to live without distraction or hindrance from "the desires of the flesh" and without external pressure from law St. Paul has described, in the paragraph immediately preceding that we have just cited, as the carrying out of the single command, given by Jesus himself, "You must love your neighbor as yourself" (Gal 5:13-14).

Paul had already given to the Corinthians a magnificent description of the Christian life as simply a series of variations upon the theme of love. "Love is patient, love is kindly, love feels no envy, love is not boastful, does not put on airs, is never rude, nor selfish, nor touchy. It keeps no score of wrongs, does not rejoice over wickedness, but delights in truth. It can face anything: its faith, its hope, its endurance know no bounds" (1 Cor 13:4-7).

The apostle can describe this same ideal Christian existence as a progressive realization of that divine sonship to which all men are called by the Father. "Those who are led by the Spirit of God are God's sons. The Spirit whom you have received is not a spirit of slavery reducing you once more to fear, but the Spirit of our adoptive sonship, in whom we cry, '*Abba*' (dear Father)" (Rom 8:14-15). We may say that the whole ascetical ideal of St. Paul, as also for St. Ignatius, is orientated towards attention to the workings of the Holy Spirit, who directs and aids the adoptive sons of God to an ever deeper awareness of their relationship to the heavenly Father. The immediate, concrete means to this filial obedience and love is, of course, the love of all men as our brothers. It is essentially through our experience, in all our actions, of this solidarity with one another, that we can, by the grace of Christ, experience the supreme truth that God is our Father. When the Christian arrives at a perfect awareness of these relationships, he has no need of any law to indicate how he must act or to coerce him into so acting.

Yet Paul, like Ignatius Loyola, took a realistic approach to human existence. If Ignatius, after asserting his belief in the guidance of his Society by the Spirit of God, could admit that even "reason itself teaches us in the Lord" that regulations and constitutions are a necessity, given the ordinary human condition, so Paul also realized that law has a necessary role to play in the life of the majority of Christians. For both these great mystics were fully conscious that, while the ideal Christian has no need of law, the greater number do require its aid for the simple reason that they are not yet perfect, not yet able to interpret correctly the voice of the indwelling Spirit. "We know," Paul wrote to Timothy, "that the law is an excellent thing, if a man treats it as law, recognizing that law is intended not for the saint, but the sinner and rebellious, the impious and the sinful, the irreligious and the worldly. . ." (1 Tm 1:8-9).

We begin to see the solution for the problem we have been discussing of the relation of structures, whether in the Church or in a religious community, to the spiritual life of the individual. If we were saints, if we had attained the maturity of the Christian ideal, there would be no need of structures like law or rule to support and sustain our interior life. Law intervenes to repress some existing disorder, or to guarantee by its sanctions that disorder may not arise again. It is, as Paul once declared, like the *paidagōgos*, the slave in Greek city-state society, who took the son of the house to school, where he was taught by the master. The apostle had the Mosaic law in mind, when he made this remark to the Galatians, but the same holds true for any kind of law or regulation. "Thus the Law was our 'pedagogue' leading us to Christ, in order that we might be justified by faith. With the advent of the faith, we are no longer under a 'pedagogue' " (Gal 3:24-25). There is no need, I am sure, to remind ourselves that Paul speaks here of the Christian ideal. In those moments when we are through our sinfulness rendered incapable of hearing the voice of the Spirit within us, the external impetus of laws and rules can be an efficacious help towards that exercise of brotherly love which is the essence of Christianity. Yet St. Paul and St. Ignatius are there to remind us that Christian morality advocates obedience to law merely as a substitute for the infinitely higher direction of the Holy Spirit; and thus of necessity it takes on the character of a concrete manifestation of love towards other persons—towards all men as our brothers, towards God as our Father.

ISRAEL'S CREDO IN YAHWEH
Deuteronomy 26:5-9

My father was a wandering Aramean, who went down into Egypt. It was with a small household that he went there to seek refuge. But there he became a great nation, mighty and numerous. ⁶The Egyptians maltreated us, tyrannized over us, and oppressed us with hard labor. ⁷We cried out to Yahweh, the God of our fathers; and Yahweh heard our cry, he saw our wretched state, our labor and our oppression. ⁸So Yahweh brought us out of Egypt with mighty hand and outstretched arm, by awesome power, with signs and miracles. ⁹He led us here and he gave us this country, a land flowing with milk and honey.

PAUL'S VISION OF THE REDEMPTION OF THE CREATED UNIVERSE
Romans 8:18-29

I believe that the sufferings of the present time are not worthy to be compared with the glory that will certainly be unveiled before our eyes. ¹⁹For the [material] creation, with eager expectancy, awaits the revelation of the sons of God. ²⁰The creation was subjected to a state of frustration, not by its own fault, but by him who condemned it [to its present state]. ²¹Yet always there was hope, because the very creation itself will be set free from its enslavement to corruption, and [enter] upon the freedom of the glory of the children of God. ²²For we know indeed that the whole of creation groans with the pangs of childbirth until the present moment.

²³Indeed, that is not all! We ourselves, possessing the first fruits of the Spirit, also groan in our turn within ourselves, expecting the [divine] adoption, that is, the redemption of our bodily personality. ²⁴It is by hope that we have been saved. . . .

²⁶In like manner also, the Spirit comes to the aid of our impotence. For we do not know how to petition as we ought; yet the Spirit himself intercedes for us with yearnings beyond expression.

²⁷[God] the searcher of hearts understands the intent of the Spirit, how he intercedes before God on behalf of the saints.

²⁸Indeed we know that God makes everything collaborate for the good of those that love him, that is, those called in accordance with his design. ²⁹Those whom God had known from the beginning, he also predestined to be shaped in the image of his Son, that he [the Son] might be the first-born of a large family of brothers.

CONTEMPLATION FOR OBTAINING LOVE

A New Approach AT THE END of the little book of the *Spiritual Exercises,* St. Ignatius has added an exercise which he called *Contemplation for Obtaining Love,* which is at once the crown of the retreat and a bridge to enable the exercitant to return to his ordinary round of duties. It is actually a method of prayer which can be easily employed; and it is simply a specific example of St. Ignatius' favorite technique for "finding God in all things," which must be considered one of his most precious contributions to Christian spirituality.

As outlined by St. Ignatius this exercise is an application to the Christian life of the great theological synthesis created by medieval scholasticism. I am asked to recall the benefits in the order of creation and of grace which God has conferred upon me; to consider how God himself exists in everything around me, and so gives himself to me in these creatures; to reflect upon the fact that God sustains these gifts in existence, and so may be said to "labor" for their conservation; and finally, through the grateful contemplation of these marks of the divine favor, to return in humility and gratitude to the giver of such good gifts, "that I may in all things love and serve his divine Majesty."

Since the almost technical terminology employed by St. Ignatius in his exposition of this magnificent contemplation may be less congenial to the modern mind, by reason of its scholastic frame of reference, I suggest for your consideration another approach drawn from the contribution of modern scholarship to our understanding of the Bible. Accordingly, we shall reflect in the first place upon the manner in which through the historical process almighty God has revealed himself to man. Then we shall consider how man is called to act as a mediator in the redemption of the material creation, and thus find a way through his work to collaborate in the divine plan of making the kingdom of God a reality in this world, thereby effecting his own return to God himself, with the grace of Christ.

316

It was Israel's preeminent privilege, through the religious genius of her prophets and priests, to obtain an insight into the action of God in her own history, and so give to the world in the Old Testament the inspired record of divine revelation. The beginning of Israel's history as a people dates from her unique experience of God at Sinai. For it was here through the mediation of Moses that the recalcitrant Hebrews, who had run away from their Egyptian taskmasters, were confronted with the God of history, who chose them as his *segullāh*, his cherished possession. No people achieves nationhood without a sense of its destiny, a sense of the direction of its history. They must arrive at an appreciation of the purposefulness of the events in which they are involved. This implies an awareness that this series of occurrences affecting their national history began somewhere and is tending in a certain direction. Israel obtained this sense of history through her experience of Yahweh's action on her behalf in the exodus from Egypt. The term "exodus" here includes the Hebrews' successful escape from the power of the pharaoh, their crossing of the Red Sea, their meeting with God at Sinai, and their entry into the promised land of Canaan.

Actually the settling of the people in Palestine, recorded in the books of Joshua and Judges in the simplest, most schematic form, went on during a period of some two hundred years, when by infiltration and intermittent forays, the Israelites managed to stake out a claim to the land which Yahweh had promised to give them, and finally set up some sort of tribal confederacy in Palestine. This amphictyony was held together initially only by a common belief in the one God, Yahweh. In time of national emergency charismatic leaders arose throughout this early period to organize defense and lead the people in war: the judges. About the time when Israel was making this attempt to settle in Canaan, another group of newcomers from the islands across the Ionian Sea, the Philistines, were laying claim to the land north and west of Palestine. Accordingly, to insure their somewhat precarious hold upon their own hard-won territory, the people of Israel demanded a king. They felt that they needed strong, permanent leadership for a more effective and efficient direction of their campaigns against these marauders to the north and west. The sporadic leadership given by the Judges was an obstacle to the people's security, for Israel's military successes depended upon the presence of such God-given commanders.

At last, with Saul as king there was a more assured hope that the Israelite position in the promised land might be consolidated. Saul, however, after a few years' reign, was supplanted by David under whom the kingship acquired a new aura of prestige in the eyes of all Israel. For that politically astute monarch had the genius to unite in his own new capital, Jerusalem, the seat of royal power and the center of Israelite cult. The throne with the presence of the ark became the focus of national pride. In the psalms, the holy city was soon to become a symbol of eternal life with God himself. In Solomon's reign, the Davidic kingdom attained imperial dimensions. Yet after a relatively brief period of brilliance, a schism at the death of Solomon split the nation into the northern and the southern kingdoms. The northern kingdom, Israel, was to survive as a sovereign state scarcely two centuries, when the Assyrians overthrew its government and carried off its citizens into exile. Judah, the kingdom in the south, survived for another century and a half, but in 587 B.C. her king also was forced to capitulate to the Neo-Babylonian, Sargon II, and the tragic period of the Babylonian captivity commenced.

Yet it was precisely in this half-century of exile and humiliation, with the collapse of the monarchy, the ruin of the temple, and the disruption of the sacrificial cult of God, that Israel began to reflect upon the vicissitudes of her history. Prophet and priestly scribe had the faith to perceive the divine hand at work, not only in the halcyon days of national aggrandisement, but even in the hour of disaster and defeat with its subsequent insecurity. "God," said the prophets, "has visited his people!" in order to make them return in trust and humility to himself. Thus it was in exile, under the inspiration of a priesthood dispossessed of its primary cultic functions, that the Old Testament, as we know it, began to take shape, with the collection and editing of the laws and traditions, legends and sagas, and chronicles of Israel.

When the Jews returned, as the prophets had promised, from this captivity, they came back to a land destitute and barren, to a capital city, whose walls had been leveled, whose temple had been desecrated. Yet with deep faith and boundless confidence, under the leadership of the priesthood (for the princely house was permanently deprived of its power by the Persians), the Jews set about rebuilding their national fortunes. Never again however would the Davidic monarchy recover the throne: its destruction was one of the lasting effects of the Babylonian captivity. It was at this period that Israel, her hopes of an earthly king frustrated, learned from her prophets of a royal figure, hidden as yet in the far-distant future, who one day would come as Yahweh's emissary and vice-gerent to establish God's kingdom definitively.

The significance of Israel's story as sacred history, that is, as the record of God's self-revelation, should not escape us. It was in many respects comparable, though undoubtedly less spectacular from the viewpoint of world history, to the national history of almost any other people. Yet, it was Israel's reaction of faith to the events of her national history which gave to its written record a unique character: it was a national history written not to glorify the nation, but the nation's God. Whatever is known about the God of the Old Testament was revealed through the historical process by which Israel became a nation, together with those ups and downs of her national fortunes encountered during the regnal period, the Babylonian exile, and its sequel, the reconstruction.

Israel's lesson to us is simply this: that in order to disclose to men his existence, his designs upon the world, and his providential care of his people, God does not need to interfere with the processes of history. He shows man his face from within that history itself, if only man has the insight of faith to read the sacred significance that is hidden within the chain of events.

In the New Testament record of Christian sacred history, it is the event known as Pentecost which best corresponds to Sinai. *God's Overtures of Love to the Apostolic Church* This may seem at first sight surprising, since of course the whole earthly life of Jesus Christ— his incarnation, birth, the experiences shared by the Twelve of his public ministry, his death and resurrection—had preceded this coming of the Spirit upon the infant Church. Yet the creation of historical writing depends upon the perception of the pattern within the interaction of personalities and occurrences which otherwise remain ambiguous and unmeaningful. Before Pentecost the disciples had indeed heard Jesus and seen his miracles. They had followed him with love and loyalty; and even after his death and resurrection they had remained together, animated by their hope in a mysterious promise which he had given them of their future baptism with a holy Spirit. Yet through all this they did not know who he actually was —the Son of God incarnate.

Pentecost brought them this realization, and with it their consciousness of their new identity as a people, the new Israel, possessing a universalist mission to all men. Pentecost marked also the inauguration of the apostolic practice of the Christian sacraments. In short, it was Pentecost that gave the Church her Christian sense of history, enabling her to see the "good news" which was contained in the earthly life of Jesus of Nazareth, attested by "the original eyewitnesses." Once again, we observe that the Christian revelation, like that made to Israel, came through an insight of faith into the significance of the historical process.

319

Yet there was much of what we now call the Christian revelation which still remained hidden or obscure in the first days of the Christian community of Jerusalem. The series of historical events, which we designate as the apostolic age had yet to unfold, revealing new facets of the Christian mystery. These were to be recorded under divine inspiration in the letters of Paul, the Acts of the Apostles, and other writings, in which the Church would recognize the finger of God revealing himself to her. A number of incidents preserved in this sacred literature enable us to see how the risen Christ, enthroned at God's right hand, continued to be active in history, revealing to his Church the whole complex of religious truths which together form the object of the Christian faith.

Sometimes it was a trivial incident that enabled the apostolic group to see the direction which these divinely directed events were taking. An insignificant disagreement between Hebrews and Hellenists over the distribution of the common fund in Jerusalem —no more than a family quarrel—would lead to the special vocation of Stephen, giving him the opportunity to voice the conviction that the Church could not remain merely a Jewish-Christian community, but must, by the will of Christ, stand forth in the world as a "sign raised amongst the Gentiles." The sequel to Stephen's death, according to the inspired author of Acts, was the conversion of Paul, the apostle of Greek-speaking Asia Minor and part of Europe. The wealth of experience which Paul garnered from his spectacular career as a missionary taught him (and through him, the Church) many truths about Christianity. Not the least of these was the ability to discern what was essential to the Christian life from the cultural, racial, and historical milieux in which the Church was born. Thus it was that the dialectic of history once again served as a medium for the communication of God's will to mankind.

The Gospels are the record of the way in which the early Church, under the guidance of the Holy Spirit, contemplated the meaning of Jesus' earthly life. She saw, for example, in Jesus' choice of the Twelve, the manifestation of his intention to bring her into existence under the direction of the apostolic college. She interpreted Jesus' merciful feeding of the crowds in the wilderness as a parable-in-act of the blessed Eucharist. She perceived in many of his sayings, preserved in the memory of the apostolic witnesses, a depth of significance which even they had not suspected when they heard Jesus utter them. And through the writings of certain privileged members of the apostolic generation, the Church was able to hand down through the centuries the inspired record of this historical process, which, with the Old Testament, constitutes our Christian revelation.

I too in my own day am meant to participate in this salvation history through my reaction of faith to the series of happenings which affect me in prosperity or adversity, for better or worse. To a certain degree I also am able to see the hand of God working to form me, to lead me along the way known clearly only to himself. My reflections upon the mysterious ways by which Yahweh worked through history to reveal himself to Israel, by which the risen Christ, under the new covenant, actively directs the destiny of the Christian people, should help me find my personal point of insertion into the contemporary divine plan for the salvation of the world. And this brings me to the second consideration in my contemplation for obtaining love: man's role in the redemption of the material creation.

In this age of specialization the Jesuit priest, who is also a scientist, literateur, or artist, has a particularly difficult vocational problem which his ancestors in the Society of Jesus did not have, or did not, at any rate, feel so acutely. He is a religious and a priest, and at the same time a botanist, philologist, psychologist as well. He is faced with the puzzling enigma of a double vocation. How can he pursue the quest for God successfully by means of this twofold calling? Is not the priesthood in danger of becoming merely a matter of personal, private devotion for a man most of whose time, interest, and energy is devoted to work in the study or the laboratory? He appears to be attempting the impossible: to reconcile a layman's occupation with that of a cleric and a religious.

Yet, if one considers the difficulty carefully, it resolves itself into a question whose solution is imperative in every Christian life, although it may appear easier to solve in some instances than in others. The fundamental problem is a profoundly theological one: the significance of man's work in this world for the kingdom of God. St. Paul provides a helpful clue to this problem in a passage in which he describes the cosmic effects of Christ's redemptive work. While Paul's answer does not strip away entirely the mystery surrounding the redemption of the material creation, he does assert beyond any doubt that the irrational creatures, with whose existence man's life in this world is so intimately involved, constitute, in addition to man himself, an object of the redemption wrought by Jesus Christ. And the prayerful consideration of this truth will provide no little help in answering the problem of the double vocation which we have been discussing.

The Redemption of the Material Universe

"I believe," Paul asserts, "that the sufferings of the present time are not worthy to be compared with the glory that will certainly be unveiled before our eyes. For the [material] creation, with eager expectancy, awaits the revelation of the sons of God. The creation was subjected to a state of frustration, not by its own fault, but by him who condemned it [to its present state]. Yet always there was hope, because the very creation itself will be set free from its enslavement to corruption, and [enter] upon the freedom of the glory of the children of God. For we know indeed that the whole of creation groans with the pangs of childbirth until the present moment. . ." (Rom 8:18-22).

Despite the rather poetic form of this passage, it seems clear that Paul intends to assert that the entire created universe is orientated towards a destiny closely bound up with the redemption of man himself. For man in his total person possesses a very real solidarity with the material creation. This fact was perhaps more evident to a writer like Paul, endowed as he was with the Semitic (and biblical) view of salvation. For the Bible nowhere considers that man will be admitted to eternal happiness as a kind of disembodied spirit. Man is to be saved in the totality of his being, on its material as well as on its spiritual side. If then man's body is destined, through the glorious resurrection, to participate in that divine adoption, which is the ultimate goal of the redemption (Rom 8:23), the material world itself is also ordained to share "the freedom of the glory of the sons of God." Moreover, because of his relationship to the material as well as to the spiritual world, man's divinely conferred vocation is to act as mediator of its redemption for irrational creation. This point of view confers a new set of values upon human work, upon the significance of culture, as the divinely ordained way back to the God who created both man and the material universe.

Theology of Work

If we turn to the opening chapters of Genesis, we discover that the author exhibits a fairly well defined theology of work. In the first place, there is a certain penal or penitential aspect to man's work. "Through you the earth shall be cursed; you shall gain your livelihood from it in suffering as long as you live. . . . You shall earn your living by the sweat of your brow. . . ." (Gn 3:17-19). We are told that in consequence of man's sin, the work by which he must wrestle a livelihood from the soil will always present a toilsome side, thus enabling man to make reparation for the original sin.

Yet such was not, according to our author-editor, the primordial character of human work. If we examine the second chapter of

Genesis, we discover another value attaching to man's work. For already in Eden, the garden of God, Adam was given by his Maker the vocation of working with his hands. "Yahweh God took the Man, and put him in the garden of Eden to till it and take care of it" (Gn 2:15). Thus even before the fall of man, the human condition included work as one of its essential components. Indeed, in this "garden of delights" man's work would seem to possess a kind of recreational quality. For man's situation in God's own garden—a place man had no right to be, except by the favor of the Creator—would indicate that this appointed task was intended to be a joy for man.

Still these two aspects of the work of man's hands, which we have called the penal and the recreational, are not its only, or perhaps even its most basic characteristics. The priestly author of the first chapter of Genesis provides the most theologically satisfactory answer to our question, through his explanation of how man was created in "the image and likeness of God himself" (Gn 1:26-28). "So God created mankind in his own image. . . . Then God blessed them, and God said to them, 'Be fruitful, multiply, fill the earth, and subdue it! Exercise dominion over the fish in the sea, the birds in the sky, the domestic animals, and all the living things, which creep upon the earth.' "

We are accustomed to seek an explanation of this statement that man was created in God's image in man's endowment with the spiritual faculties of will and intelligence. While such a view is undoubtedly correct, it is not that of the inspired writer just cited. In his eyes, God, supreme, unique Lord of the universe, may be said to have made man in his own image, because he imparted to the human race a share in his divine direction of the material world. The author represents this vocation of man to exercise dominion upon earth over all things as a command issued by God, in order to underscore its value and to show how essential work is for man himself. This "image of God," after which man was created, the author notes somewhat later in his book (Gn 5:1-3), was not effaced by the fall; for Adam, created in the divine likeness, is said to have begotten Seth "in his own likeness." Thus this obligation to collaborate with God in the governance of the world remains an inalienable human right, a responsibility which man may never abdicate. The writers of the New Testament, like Paul, will simply specify this obligation further, by showing that man is by his mastery of the material world to cooperate in the realization of the kingdom of God throughout the course of history.

Thus it would appear that the achievements of man's mind and man's hands in science, art, literature belong, in the plan of God, to man's mediatorial role in the redemption of the material universe. This divine mission, of course, can only be successfully undertaken in love, for it is an axiom of Christian spirituality that "flesh and blood cannot inherit the kingdom of God" (1 Cor 15:50). Moreover, it seems clear from Paul's repeated affirmations that there is to be some final transformation of the material world as it exists at present (1 Cor 15:51-52; 2 Cor 5:17; cf. 1 Thes 4:17). Other New Testament writers repeat the same idea in speaking of "the new sky and the new earth" (Ap 21:1; 2 Pt 3:13).

The typically Stoic dogma of the destruction of the world by a universal conflagration (*ekpyrōsis*), in my opinion, is not to be found in the New Testament. The passage in 2 Peter 3:10-12, which might appear to teach this doctrine, is simply a description, in the language of apocalyptic, of the universality and effectiveness of the divine judgment, symbolized throughout the Bible by fire. Indeed, that this eschatological divine judgment will effect the transformation mentioned by Paul (and not the destruction of the material universe) is indicated by the author of this very passage, when he adds, "It is the new sky and the new earth, where justice will dwell, that we await according to his promise" (2 Pt 3:13).

Enough has been said, I believe, to indicate the place, in such a divine scheme of things, for a priest-scientist, a priest-artist, who by his devoted, unremitting fidelity to his committed task, promotes the coming of the kingdom of God with his contribution to human culture. Moreover, does not such a religious or such a priest, through his function as mediator in the redemption of the material creation, most surely encounter Christ, the Master of history, in that work? The problem of the priest-specialist is, in the last analysis, not really one of a double vocation, of two callings, which at best might run parallel and so not collide with each other. It is rather one particularly effective way of teaching men the true significance of their common calling to exercise dominion as a collaborator with the supreme Lord over the material creation. For by such work man authenticates the divine image in which he was created, and ultimately succeeds, as St. Ignatius would have him do, in "finding God in all things."

Reference matter

SUPPLEMENTARY NOTES

GLOSSARY OF TERMS

INDICES

SUPPLEMENTARY NOTES

Note A

TABLE OF REFERENCES TO THE TEXT
OF THE SPIRITUAL EXERCISES

It is suggested that this series of references to the *Spiritual Exercises* may prove useful to anyone following an eight-day retreat with the help of the considerations given in this book. It may also indicate to what extent fidelity to the spirit, if not always to the letter, of the Ignatian structure has been a constant concern of the author. Indeed, he attempted to employ the principle of adaptation [18], which St. Ignatius appears to have esteemed highly, out of consideration for the particular group of exercitants for which this retreat was originally composed and for the liturgical season (Passiontide) during which it was first given.

THE FIRST WEEK
FIRST DAY

1) ELECTION OF ISRAEL: Read the Annotations [1–20] with special attention to those which stress the personal involvement of the retreatant through faith in God's Word [2, 3, 5, 10, 20].

2) INITIAL ATTITUDES TO PRAYER: It is helpful to recall the opening remarks of St. Ignatius [1], as well as his description of man's relationship to his creator [23].

3) PRAYER OF THE CREATURE: The various points in the Examination of Conscience [24–42] may be profitably reviewed.

4) FAITH FACES THE HUMAN PREDICAMENT: The principle of Christian wisdom which underlies the "indifference" advocated [24] by St. Ignatius may be pondered; also the rules for discernment of spirits for the first week [313–327].

SECOND DAY

5) LOVE WHAT YOU FIND! St. Ignatius considered the principle of

"the more," enunciated in the closing lines of the Foundation [23], to be of crucial importance to the exercitant.

6) SIN IN THE BIBLE: It is significant that St. Ignatius intended, through the first exercise of the first week [45–54] to ensure the exercitant's involvement in the dialectic of salvation history.

7) REPENTED SIN: The cross of Christ remains the divine judgment upon the history of mankind [53]. St. Ignatius intends the retreatant to impress this truth upon himself through reflection upon his own personal history of sin [59–61; 71]. The celebrated Ignatian virtue of spiritual discretion may be seen to operate in the remarks on corporal penance [82–89], in the notes on scruples [345–361], and in the general examination of conscience and confession [43–44].

THE SECOND WEEK

The purpose of this phase of the *Spiritual Exercises* is described by St. Ignatius [127, 130, 131, 133]. It is further clarified in the rules for discernment of spirits for the second week [328–336].

8) PALM SUNDAY [287]: The consideration on the *Kingdom of Christ* is actually a kind of foundation for this week [91–98]. Note may be taken of the readings now proposed for the retreatant [100].

THIRD DAY

9) CONTEMPLATIONS OF SECOND WEEK: St. Ignatius is not insensitive to the fact that one must contemplate the earthly life of Jesus *sub specie Crucis* [cf. particularly 116], for he is well aware that it is the Christ-event *par excellence* which imparts its saving significance to Jesus' entire life. It is helpful to recall here the nature of the Ignatian *contemplatio* [47; 114–116].

10) INCARNATION [101–109]: The attempt to induct the exercitant into specifically Christian salvation history should be carefully noted [102, 103, 106, 107, 108].

11) INFANCY NARRATIVES [101–134; 262–272]: Here more than anywhere in the *Spiritual Exercises* perhaps one senses the profound difference between medieval and modern piety. Accordingly, more adaptation is needed, if these exercises are to be made meaningful to the modern mentality.

12) NATIVITY [110–117; 264–265]: This contemplation is actually intended as a prolongation of that on the incarnation.

FOURTH DAY

13) BAPTISM OF JESUS [158; 273]: The meditation on *Three Classes of Men* [149–156] should be considered in connection with this contemplation, so that its particular function in the retreat may be appreciated.

14) TEMPTATIONS OF JESUS [161, 274]: The meditation on *Two Standards* [136–147] corresponds closely to the aim of this contemplation.

15) IGNATIAN PRAYER: The salient features of Ignatian spirituality may be gauged by solidly grasping the import of the *Kingdom of Christ* (cf. especially the first prelude [91]), *Two Standards* (cf. particularly [146]), and above all, the Contemplation for *Obtaining Love* [234–237].

16 SERMON ON THE MOUNT [161, 278]: This is the source of Jesus' teaching, which has inspired the Ignatian doctrine on *Three Degrees of Humility* [164–167], the *vera Christi Domini nostri doctrina* of the *Two Standards* [145].

FIFTH DAY

17) THE TWELVE [275, 281]: This contemplation brings out the special significance of Jesus' strategy in *Two Standards* [145].

18) FEEDING OF MULTITUDE [283]: With this contemplation the exercitant begins to look forward to the third week. The event is described by all the evangelists as a parable-in-action of the institution of the Eucharist.

19) OUR LADY: It is instructive to observe her place of privilege in the *Spiritual Exercises,* which indicates St. Ignatius' fidelity to the traditions of the primitive Church [63, 147, 102–108, 208, 218–225, 248, 273].

20) TRANSFIGURATION [284]: This contemplation with its very mysterious character provides an appropriate introduction to the third week, where the climax of the apostolic kerygma, the death of Jesus, is to be contemplated. It may be helpful to reflect now upon what St. Ignatius says about retreat resolutions [189].

THE THIRD WEEK

The striking change in the technique of contemplation is to be carefully noted [195–197, 289]. The *Rules for Eating* [210–217] may be usefully adapted to other problems.

SIXTH DAY

21) THE LAST SUPPER [190–199, 289]: The second method of prayer is described by St. Ignatius [249–257].

22) THE NEW COMMANDMENT: It will be profitable to reflect upon the very shrewd observations on the authentic character of real love made later on by St. Ignatius [230–231].

23) THE MASS: It will be recalled that the frequent hearing of Mass

is strongly encouraged [355]. Useful considerations at this point in a retreat will be found in the rules for *Distributing Alms* [337–344].

24) LITURGY OF HOLY THURSDAY: In an age like the Renaissance, St. Ignatius' attitudes towards the liturgy might well be considered extra-ordinary: cf. his rules for *Thinking with the Church* [352–370].

SEVENTH DAY

25) GETHSEMANI [200–203, 290]: Once again it is the achievement of a truly personal involvement in sacred history [203] which is a main preoccupation in the *Spiritual Exercises.*

26) PASSION OF ST. JOHN [291–298]: Ignatian insistence upon devoting at least one exercise to the contemplation of the entire Passion of our Lord should be recalled [209].

27) THE SACRED HEART: This devotion, which according to Pius XII expresses the essential devotion proper to the Christian life (*Haurietis aquas*), is reflected throughout the *Spiritual Exercises*, even if it be nowhere expressly named. It is germinally present in "the more" [23], in the colloquy with Christ on the cross [53], or with "God our Lord" [61], or in connection with hell [71], where God "so loving and merciful" is addressed, this devotion to the Sacred Heart is echoed in the self-oblation which climaxes the consideration on the Kingdom [97–98], as it is also in the third prelude to the Incarnation, with its request for more intimate knowledge of the Godman and deeper love of him [104]. In *Two Standards* the exercitant seeks the grace to imitate Christ in actual poverty and in enduring insults and injustice [147], an attitude characteristic of the *Third Degree of Humility* [167]. The third week is devoted especially to the continued contemplation of the rejected love of Jesus [195–197], while the fourth week recalls the office of the risen Christ, as the consoler [224]. The *Sume ac Suscipe* at the conclusion of the entire *Exercises* articulates the highest form of devotion to the Sacred Heart [234].

THE FOURTH WEEK

The goal of this, often most difficult stage in the *Spiritual Exercises*, may be gathered from the notes [226–229].

28) CONTEMPLATIONS OF THE FOURTH WEEK: The attitudes to be cultivated by the exercitant at this point are described tersely but comprehensively [223–224].

EIGHTH DAY

29) THE LAST ADAM: While retaining in many respects the piety characteristic of his age, St. Ignatius frequently displays a kind of connatural appreciation of the great insights of Pauline soteriology [223–224].

30) THE CHURCH, BODY OF THE RISEN CHRIST: Father Jerome Nadal, credited by St. Ignatius with a profound grasp of the *Spiritual Exercises,* does not hesitate to assert in one of his conferences that the kingdom of Christ is actually a meditation on the mystical body.[1]

31) LAW OF THE SPIRIT: Nowhere perhaps does the thought of St. Ignatius accord with that of St. Paul so strikingly as in his rules for the *Discernment of Spirits* [313–336].

32) CONTEMPLATION FOR OBTAINING LOVE [230–237]: In many respects, this exercise for "finding God in all things" is most characteristic of Ignatian spirituality. The optimistic, incarnational theology of a Père Pierre Teilhard de Chardin undoubtedly derives its inspiration from this source.

Note B

SELECT BIBLIOGRAPHY OF RECENT SCRIPTURAL STUDIES

The purpose of this brief bibliography is to supply books on the Bible, which may assist the retreat master in orientating himself in the direction of modern scriptural studies. The list may also provide helpful suggestions for private reading during time of retreat.

GENERAL BACKGROUND

L. F. Hartman, *Encyclopedic Dictionary of the Bible* (New York: 1963); John L. McKenzie, *Dictionary of the Bible* (Milwaukee: 1965); J. Dheilly, *Dictionnaire Biblique* (Paris: 1963).

NATURE OF REVELATION

Luis Alonso Schökel, *The Inspired Word* (New York: 1965); Hans Urs von Balthasar, *Word and Redemption* (New York: 1965); W. Bulst, *Revelation* (New York: 1965).

LITERARY FORMS

Luis Alonso Schökel, *Understanding Biblical Research* (New York: 1963); Jean Levie, *The Bible: Word of God in Words of Men* (New York: 1961).

OLD TESTAMENT

R. A. F. MacKenzie, *Faith and History in the Old Testament* (Minneapolis: 1963); John L. McKenzie, *The Two-Edged Sword* (Milwaukee: 1956);

1 For the text of Nadal's conference, cf. Maurice Giuliani, "Texte Ancien," *Christus* No. 1 (January, 1954) 91-100.

Frederick L. Moriarty, *Introducing the Old Testament* (Milwaukee: 1960); P. Drijvers, *The Psalms, Their Structure and Meaning* (New York: 1965); H. Renckens, *Israel's Concept of the Beginning* (New York: 1964); Bruce Vawter, *Path Through Genesis* (New York: 1956); *Conscience of Israel* (New York: 1961).

THE GOSPELS

X. Léon Dufour, *Les Evangiles et l'Histoire de Jésus* (Paris: 1963); Maisie Ward, *They Saw His Glory* (New York: 1956); A. Bea, *The Study of the Synoptic Gospels: New Approaches and Outlooks,* edited and translated, J. A. Fitzmyer (New York: 1965). R. E. Brown, *The Gospel According to John I-XII* (Garden City: 1966).

NEW TESTAMENT SPIRITUALITY

J. Guillet, *Jesus Christ, Yesterday and Today: Introduction to Biblical Spirituality* (Chicago: 1965); W. Grossouw, *The Spirituality of the New Testament* (Westminster, Md.: 1960); A. Richardson, *An Introduction to the Theology of the New Testament* (New York: 1958); R. Schnackenburg, *The Church in the New Testament* (New York: 1965); *The Moral Teaching of the New Testament* (New York: 1965).

PAULINE THEOLOGY

L. Cerfaux, *La Théologie de l'Eglise suivant S. Paul²* (Paris: 1965); *Le Christ dans la théologie de S. Paul* (Paris: 1951); *Le Chrétien dans la théologie paulinienne* (Paris: 1961); W. Grossouw, *In Christ: a Sketch of the Theology of St. Paul* (London: 1960); F. X. Durrwell, *The Resurrection* (New York: 1961); *In the Redeeming Christ* (New York: 1963); D. M. Stanley, *Christ's Resurrection in Pauline Soteriology* (Rome: 1961).

JOHANNINE THEOLOGY

W. Grossouw, *Revelation and Redemption: a Sketch of the Theology of St. John* (Westminster, Md.: 1955); C. H. Dodd, *The Interpretation of the Fourth Gospel* (Cambridge: 1958); F. M. Braun, *Jean le Théologien et son Evangile dans l'Eglise ancienne* (Paris: 1959); R. E. Brown, *New Testament Essays* (Milwaukee: 1965).

BIBLICAL THEMES

J. Guillet, *Themes of the Bible* (Notre Dame: 1958); X. Léon Dufour, *Vocabulaire Biblique* (Paris: 1962); J. B. Bauer, *Bibeltheologisches Wörterbuch* (Graz: 1959); T. Maertens, *Bible Themes—a Source Book* (Bruges: 1964) 2 vols.

Much useful material may also be found in the following periodicals: *The Bible Today* (Collegeville); *Worship* (Collegeville); *The Way* (London); *Bible et Vie Chrétienne* (Gembloux); *Lumière et Vie* (St. Alban-Leysse).

COLLECTIONS OF ESSAYS

Barnabas Ahern, *New Horizons* (Notre Dame: 1963); John L. McKenzie, *Myths and Realities* (Milwaukee: 1963); R. W. Gleason, editor, *A Theology Reader* (New York: 1966); Sr. M. Rosalie Ryan, editor, *Contemporary New Testament Studies* (Collegeville: 1963).

Note C

SELECT BIBLIOGRAPHY ON THE
SPIRITUAL EXERCISES

We give here only a few references to critical editions of the text, to the helpful classical commentaries, and to some recent books which deal with one or other aspect of the *Spiritual Exercises*.

CRITICAL EDITIONS OF THE TEXT

Exercitia Spiritualia in *Monumenta Historica Societatis Jesu: Monumenta Ignatiana*, ser. 2 (Madrid: 1919); Alfred Feder, S.J., *Des heiligen Ignatius von Loyola Geistlichen Uebungen nach dem spanischen Urtext Uebertragen*[2] (Regensburg: 1922); José Calveras, S.J., *Ejercicios Espirituales, Directio, y Documentos de San Ignacio de Loyola* with a *Glosa y Vocabulario de los Ejercicios*[2] (Barcelona: 1958).

ENGLISH TRANSLATIONS OF THE TEXT

Elder Mullan, *The Spiritual Exercises of St. Ignatius* (New York: 1914); The Benedictines of Stanbrook, *The Spiritual Exercises of St. Ignatius Literally Translated* (London: 1928); Joseph Rickaby, S.J., *The Spiritual Exercises of St. Ignatius Loyola*[2] (London: 1936); Thomas Corbishley, S.J., *The Spiritual Exercises, a New Translation* (London: 1963); Louis J. Puhl, S.J., *The Spiritual Exercises of St. Ignatius: a New Translation* (Westminister, Md.: 1963).

USEFUL COMMENTARIES

A. Ambruzzi, S.J., *A Companion to the Spiritual Exercises of St. Ignatius*[3] (Bangalore: 1938); Jaime Nonell, S.J., *Analyse des Exercices Spirituels de S. Ignace de Loyola*, E. Thibaut, translator (Bruges: 1924); Erich Przywara, S.J., *Maiestas Divina: Ignatianische Frömmigkeit* (Augsburg: 1925); *The Divine Majesty*, T. Corbishley, translator (Cork: 1951); Ignacio Iparraguirre, S.J., *A Key to the Study of the Spiritual Exercises*, J. Chianese, S.J., translator (Calcutta: 1955); Gaston Fessard, *La dialectique des Exercices Spirituels de S. Ignace de Loyola* (Paris, 1956); Hans urs von Balthasar, *Die Exerzitien* (Einsiedeln: 1959).

333

RETREATS BASED ON THE SPIRITUAL EXERCISES

F. X. McMenamy, S.J., *Eight-Day Retreat,* William J. Grace, S.J., editor (Milwaukee: 1956); W. II. Longridge, *Retreats for Priests according to the Method and Plan of the Spiritual Exercises of St. Ignatius* (London: 1962); Karl Rahner, S.J., *Spiritual Exercises,* Kenneth Baker, S.J., translator (New York: 1965).

IGNATIAN SPIRITUALITY

Louis Peeters, S.J., *Vers l'Union divine par les Exercises de S. Ignace*[2] (Louvain: 1931); Hugo Rahner, S.J., *The Spirituality of St. Ignatius Loyola,* F. J. Smith, S.J., translator (Westminster, Md.: 1953); Hans Urs von Balthasar, *Prayer,* A. V. Littledale, translator (New York: 1961); *Contemporary Thought and the Spiritual Exercises of St. Ignatius Loyola,* Robert F. Harvanek, S.J., editor (Chicago: 1963); Karl Rahner, *The Dynamic Element in the Church, Quaestiones Disputatae 12,* W. J. O'Hara, translator (New York: 1964); Joseph de Guibert, S.J., *The Jesuits: their Spiritual Doctrine and Practice: a Historical Study,* W. J. Young, S. J., translator, George E. Ganss, S.J., editor (Chicago: 1964); cf. Chapter 3, "St. Ignatius' Spiritual Writings," 109—151.

GLOSSARY OF TERMS

'abba (Aramaic), "father," familiar form of address in first-century Palestinian Aramaic-speaking families; avoided, out of reverence, in addressing God.

'ādām (Hebrew), "man," "mankind," conceived as a concrete group.

'adāmāh (Hebrew), "soil, earth," considered in popular etymology as derivation of *'ādām* (Gn 2:7).

'Adōnāi (Hebrew), "my Lord," a grammatically inexplicable form, employed commonly in Psalms and Isaiah as a divine name for Yahweh, in order to distinguish it from the common Hebrew form *'adōnī* ("my lord"), the form of address for human superiors.

agere contra (Latin), "react against," a phrase from the *Spiritual Exercises* [97].

aggiornamento (Italian), "updating," term employed by John XXIII, which epitomizes his hopes for Vatican II.

'almah (Hebrew), "maiden, young woman of marriageable age" (Is 7:14).

amor carnalis Christi (Latin), "carnal love of Christ," an expression of St. Bernard (cf. Sermon 20 on the Canticle of Canticles), who sees the incarnation as an attempt by Christ to "draw all the affections of carnal men, who are only capable of loving carnally, to a redeeming love of his own flesh, and so lead them by degrees to spiritual love."

amor spiritualis Christi (Latin), "spiritual love of Christ," from St. Bernard (cf. his treatise, "On the Love of God"), who views it as a fourth degree of a process of transformation, which begins with "carnal" love (involuntary love of self without merit or blame), through a love of God for my own good, and a realization that God is worth seeking for himself, to a love of God for himself.

amphictyony (from the Greek word for "neighbor"), a confederacy of city-states, convened at a religious sanctuary, e.g., Delphi. The term is applied by some scholars to the loose union of the twelve tribes of Israel, united by their common faith in Yahweh. In early times they gathered at Shechem or Shilo, later at the temple in Jerusalem.

335

anamnēsis (Greek), "remembrance, recall, memorial," used in N.T. in connection with the Jewish Day of Atonement (Heb 10:3) and with the Eucharist (1 Cor 11:24; Lk 22:19). Justin employs it to designate the Eucharist as a "recall" of the saving work of Christ.

'anawīm (Hebrew), "afflicted, poor," designated in O.T. the large class of the people reduced to indigence under the monarchy by the oppression of the wealthy. In post-exilic psalms the term acquires a religious sense, becoming synonymous with pious; in the beatitudes (Mt) it signifies those conscious of their need of God.

apocalyptic (from the Greek word for "revelation"), a term applied to a type of literary expression dealing with the final phase of world history. It endeavors with the aid of symbolism, often obscure and sometimes fantastic, to depict God's final intervention.

berīth (Hebrew), "pact, covenant," a solemn ritual agreement by which individuals or clans became like blood brothers promising to support, protect, or avenge their partners. It included awesome imprecations on any violation of the agreement. Israel conceived her special relationship to Yahweh as a covenant; Jesus instituted the Eucharist as an instrument of the new covenant.

bisrī (Aramaic), "my flesh," the term undoubtedly employed by Jesus at the institution of the Eucharist.

commercium divinum (Latin), "divine exchange," a phrase descriptive of God's dealings with fallen man in Christ.

compunctio cordis (Latin), "piercing of the heart," a picturesque description of total response to the gospel (Acts 2:37 Vulgate).

confessio (Latin), "praise," especially addressed to God for his wonderful works on behalf of Israel. Psalm 135 is a superb example of such a "confession."

contemplatio (Latin), "contemplation," a term used in the *Spiritual Exercises* [1, 2, 4] for the form of mental prayer whose object is the events of sacred history, especially the life of Jesus.

convivium (Latin), "banquet, social feast."

dābār (Hebrew), "word, thing, event." For the Hebrews the spoken word possessed an independent, dynamic reality and also a dianoetic value since the name of a thing or person imparted to them their full reality. Nothing can exist without a name; to name something is to possess mastery over it.

devotio (Latin), "a consecrating, allegiance." In the terminology of St. Ignatius, it denotes the total gift of a man to Christ.

diathēkē (Greek), "last will, testament," in the Septuagint a translation of Hebrew *berīth*, "covenant." It was so employed because it indicated that the covenant was not a contract, the result of an agreement between two equal parties.

dicta et facta Jesu (Latin), "words and deeds of Jesus."

didachē (Greek), "Teaching (of the Apostles"), the title of a book written, probably by an apostle, between 50 and 70 A.D. in

Palestine or Syria, quite possibly at Antioch (J.-P. Audet, O.P.). Its original title was most likely *Didachai tōn apostolōn* ("Instructions of the Apostles"), and its general doctrinal coloring is Matthean. It contains treatises on Christian spirituality, baptism, prayer (including the text of the *Pater Noster* with the doxology), the Eucharist, etc.

diptych (from the Greek word for "folded double"), ancient writing tablet; altar piece, hinged, with two pictures; a literary device, setting in parallel two persons (e.g. John the Baptist and Jesus in Lucan Infancy narratives), or scenes (e.g. Passover meal and institution of Eucharist in Lk 22:14-20). It is characteristic of Luke.

dokimazein (Greek), "test, discern," an important activity of the Christian life in Paul's ethical teaching, carried out with the aid of the indwelling Holy Spirit. St. Ignatius' codification of this essential Christian operation in the *Spiritual Exercises* (Rules for the Discernment of Spirits [313-336]) is probably his most original contribution to Christian spirituality.

doxa (Greek), "glory, radiance," a technical term in the Septuagint, where it translates the Hebrew *"kābōd,"* i.e. any tangible manifestation of the divine protective presence; in John it signifies Jesus' self-revelation through his miracles and especially his death and resurrection, his "glory" *par excellence.*

'Ebed Yahweh (Hebrew), "Servant of God," a title given to Israel in Deutero-Isaiah (Is 42:1ff., 49:1ff., 50:4ff., 52:13-53:12). The precise identity of the "Servant" is much disputed. The title is applied to Jesus in the N.T., and also, by Paul, to himself.

ekpyrōsis (Greek), "conflagration," a term used by the Stoic philosopher Zeno to denote the final "conversion into fire" of the present world.

'elōhīm (Hebrew), "gods, God," a plural form used with singular sense to denote the one God of Israel; also with plural meaning to designate the gods of the Gentiles. Israelite use of this originally pantheistic term to signify God shows that "the linguistic resources of Hebrew were not sufficient to express the singular Israelite conception of the divine being" (John L. McKenzie).

Elohist (from the Hebrew term for "God"), a name given in modern scholarship to an unknown writer of the northern kingdom of Israel (or better perhaps to a tradition), the so-called "E" source of the Pentateuch. The patriarchal history in this source denominates God as *'Elōhīm,* placing the revelation of the divine name Yahweh in the time of Moses. Composed at the end of the eighth century B.C. or even later, it is more recent than "J" (see Yahwist). It begins with the story of Abraham. Stylistically it is less vivid than "J," and the characters are more stylized. The conception of God is less anthropomorphic than "J," and there is more effort to "edify." It is influenced by the spirit of the prophets: the patriarchs' relationship with God is presented

337

as covenantal. More interest is displayed in northern heroes like Jacob, Joseph, Joshua. After the fall of Samaria (721 B.C.), priestly scribes in Jerusalem combined "E" with "J."

'Elyōn (Hebrew), "most high" (God), the name for the deity worshiped by Melchizedek (Gn 15:18), identified (v. 22) with Yahweh, the God of Abraham.

'emeth (Hebrew), "truth, reliability, faithfulness," one of the two principal characteristics (see *ḥesed*) of the God who had made the covenant with Israel.

'enōsh (Hebrew), "man," a poetic term which designates human nature in all its creaturely weakness and inconsistency.

episkiazein (Greek), "overshadow," used in the Septuagint of the cloud, symbolizing the divine presence (Ex 40:35), as also at Jesus' transfiguration in the Synoptics (cf. Mt 17:5 par.). It is employed to designate the divine presence in Mary (Lk 1:35).

eschatology (from the Greek terms for "word" and "last things"), a word susceptible of several meanings, depending upon the view taken of the "End-time," i.e. whether it be the final phase of history, or the termination of history. In the N.T., the "End-time" is sometimes presented as beginning with Jesus' death and resurrection (Acts 2:16; Mt 27:50-52); elsewhere (1 Cor 15:24; Ap 19:1ff.), as taking place at the close of history.

eschaton (Greek), "last thing," a term used (especially by C. H. Dodd) to designate God's definitive act of redemption and self-revelation in Jesus Christ and hence already operative in history.

et elevatis oculis in coelum (Latin), "and raising his eyes to heaven," a phrase introduced into the historical recital of Jesus' institution of the Eucharist in the Mass of the Roman rite. It may have been taken from an early Latin rendering of Mt 14:19 or Mk 6:41, or from the introduction to Jesus' priestly prayer (Jn 17:1), where the Vulgate reads *"sublevatis oculis in coelum."*

eucharistein (Greek), "be thankful, give thanks," employed in N.T. chiefly in religious sense. Its later Christian meaning, "to celebrate the Eucharist," may be reflected in Mt 26:27 par., Jn 6:23.

eulogein (Greek), "praise, bless," also used to describe Jesus' actions at the Last Supper (Mt 26:26).

exodos (Greek), "going out, away," of Israel's exodus (Heb 11:22); also of Jesus' death and resurrection (Lk 9:31).

familiaritas cum Deo (Latin), "sense of (belonging to) God's family," a phrase found in the *Constitutions of the Society of Jesus* (723, 813).

fidelitas (Latin), "faithfulness, fidelity," a term which renders the Hebrew word *'emeth* in the new Latin psalter of Pius XII.

Form Criticism, English rendering of German *"Formgeschichte,"* which designates a technique of Gospel criticism aimed at tracing the history of the development of the literary forms, by which the sayings and narratives of Jesus in the Gospels were reformulated in the primitive Church. This evolution is attributed to the various "life-situations" (*Sitz im Leben*) of the early Church, in which the dominant interest was apologetic, liturgical, ethical, doctrinal, or historical.

gō'ēl (Hebrew), "kinsman, redeemer," used of Israel's covenanted God in O.T. (cf. Ex 6:6; Is 43:1).

gōūm (Hebrew), "Gentiles, pagans," as opposed to the Jews, a post-exilic distinction made for religious and political reasons.

gratia Christi (Latin), "grace of Christ," a theological phrase used to indicate that all God's grace throughout sacred history comes through Christ.

henotēs (Greek), "unity," a rare word in N.T., but particularly frequent in Ignatius of Antioch.

ḥesed (Hebrew), "loving kindness, condescension," a word which, with *'emeth* characterized Israel's God. Like the Latin *pietas*, it suggests God's fatherly concern for his people.

historia (Latin), "narrative, points," a word employed in the *Spiritual Exercises* [102] for the brief résumé of the mystery to be contemplated, given by the director.

imitatio Christi (Latin), "imitation, following, of Christ," a prominent theme in the *Spiritual Exercises* of the second week. It is not to be conceived merely extrinsically, or psychologically, or moralistically. Basically, it is the full exploitation of the baptismal grace given to each Christian.

ischyros (Greek), "strong man," employed in gospels of Satan in parables where Jesus appears as the "stronger man" (cf. Mk 3:27 and Mk 1:7).

kābōd (Hebrew), "glory," originally "weight, heaviness," a technical term, originating in the Pentateuch, for some external manifestation of the divine protective presence, e.g. the pillar of cloud, fire in the exodus from Egypt.

kainos (Greek), "new," in the sense of "extraordinary" i.e. (N.T.) without the imperfection implied by *"neos"*; hence the result of a divine intervention, something remarkable, unprecedented.

kairos (Greek), "favorable time." In the Bible it denotes the "time of salvation," not postulated by preceding events but wholly in the power and decision of God. Yet this eschatological *kairos* does coalesce with the whole salvation history which by God's design leads up to it. Since God's judgment and salvation are revealed at every moment of salvation history, the present moment recapitulates the past and can be denoted as a *kairos*.

kerygma (from the Greek word meaning "proclamation, heralding"), a term used for the apostolic preaching, gospel: the message of hope to a despairing world that God in the death and resurrection of Jesus Christ has definitively wrought universal salvation.

koinōnia (Greek), "fellowship, communion, community," in N.T. it signifies communal sharing of possessions (Acts 2:42); participation in the body, blood of Christ (1 Cor 10:16), in the sufferings of Christ (Phil 3:10), in the Holy Spirit (2 Cor 13:13), in the Church as "fellowship of his Son" (1 Cor 1:9); also a relief fund for Jerusalem poor (Rom 15:26), this text being source of the phrase, "the communion of saints."

kosmos (Greek), "world," as man's habitation, adorned with the results of human labor; the earth in contrast with heaven; the pagan world (Rom 11:12); mankind (Mt 18:7); world at enmity with God, ruined by sin (Jn 12:31; 1 Cor 11:32); also object of God's loving redemption (Jn 3:16; 2 Cor 5:19).

laos (Greek), the (chosen) "people," nation of Israel as consecrated to God's service (Lk 2:32); also of the Christian people (Heb 4:9; 1 Pt 2:10).

lectio divina (Latin), "sacred (spiritual) reading," a phrase used in the Rule of St. Benedict (cc. 48, 49) for the important monastic exercise of meditative reading of Scripture.

magisterium (from the Latin word for "magistery"), the teaching office and teaching body in the Church.

magnalia Dei (Latin), "the mighty deeds of God," in the Vulgate translation of Acts 2:11.

maranatha (Aramaic), "Come, our Lord!" or, "Our Lord is coming!," probably a Eucharistic acclamation (the only surviving fragment) from the first-century Palestinian liturgy (1 Cor 16:22).

Massāh (Hebrew), a station in Israel's march through the desert where they "tempted" God (Ex 17:1ff.), which is the meaning of the Hebrew term.

meditatio (Latin), "meditation," a term used in the *Spiritual Exercises* [45, 55, 136, 149] to denote prayerful reflection upon truths of the faith, in contrast with the *contemplatio*.

metanoia (Greek), "change of mind" in religious sense, "conversion, repentance," employed in N.T. to denote the authentic reaction of faith to the preaching of the kerygma; hence the essential purpose of the apostolic preaching.

misericordia (Latin), "mercy, loving kindness," the Vulgate translation of Hebrew *hesed*.

mystery (from the Greek term for "secret") in the N.T. does not denote a secret rite (as in Greek mystery religions), but the mystery of God's saving plan (Mk 4:11; Col 1:26ff.) revealed in the gospel, i.e. God's invisible operation in history (Ap 10:7). The paschal (or Christian) mystery was worked out first in Jesus' humanity by his death and resurrection, and must effect in each Christian a similar transformation, which is inaugurated in the Church by the sacraments.

neos (Greek), "new," in the sense of imperfect, immature (Mk 2:22), the "new man" who still must develop spiritually (Col 3:10).

nephesh (Hebrew), "vital principle, self," the whole psychic reality of man, often mistranslated "soul." It is not opposed to "flesh," as a basic principle of the human composite. It can also mean "person," for which Hebrew has no special word.

nutantia corda (Latin), "faltering hearts," a phrase found in the Secret of the Mass, which is the fifth left over from those after Epiphany.

paidagōgos (Greek), "custodian, guide," the slave whose task was to take the boy to school and supervise his conduct.

paradidonai (Greek), "hand over, betray," used in N.T. of those who cooperated in Jesus' death sinfully; then of God (Rom 8:32), of Christ himself (Gal 2:20).

parousia (Greek), "presence, coming," also used to denote the visit of state of a reigning monarch in the "common" Greek of N.T. times. Paul originally applied it to Christ's second coming. It does not, strictly speaking, mean "return."

parthenos (Greek), "virgin," used (N.T.) of Mary (Mt 1:23; Lk 1:27), of the Church (2 Cor 11:2).

pedilavium (Latin), "the maundy, washing of the feet," in the liturgical celebration of Holy Thursday. There was a tendency among some early ecclesiastical writers to consider it a sacrament.

peirasmos (Greek), "trial, test, temptation (to sin)," used to designate the terrible, eschatological testing of God's people.

pietas (Latin), "dutiful love," towards parents, gods, fatherland; also of parental loving relationship to children; hence it is used to translate the Hebrew *ḥesed* with reference to God.

plebs tua sancta (Latin), "your holy people," a phrase from the first prayer after the Consecration in the Mass of the Roman rite, where it designates the faithful, the laity.

praeconium paschale (Latin), "paschal proclamation," a phrase found in the blessing of the deacon, as he prepares to sing the *Exsultet* during the Easter vigil. *Praeconium* is found in Tertullian with the sense of "preaching."

propter nos et propter nostram salutem (Latin), "for our sakes and for our salvation," from the Nicene Creed.

Redaktionsgeschichte (German), "history of Gospel-redaction," a recently created form of Synoptic criticism, which arose as a reaction to *Formgeschichte*, in which the focus of interest is centered upon the individual evangelist's editorial work. A study of the history of this redactional activity reveals the personal view (theology, or spirituality) taken by each writer of the earthly career of Jesus. This movement was actually anticipated by Pius XII in *Divino afflante Spiritu*, when he called upon scholars "to show what is the theological doctrine . . . of each book . . ." (#29), and "to discern the distinctive genius of the sacred writer. . . ," since "the chief law of interpretation is that which enables us to discover and determine what the writer meant to say. . . ." (#38).

reformatio vitae (Latin), "reform of life," a phrase which describes one of the aims mentioned in the *Spiritual Exercises* [189, 343], when the exercitant is already fixed in a state of life.

sarx (Greek), "flesh," a term which frequently signifies "human nature," or "a human being."

341

segullāh (Hebrew), "acquisition, valued property," a title given to Israel only in O.T., as the result of Yahweh's election of her (Ex 19:5; Dt 7:6; Mal 3:17). It is employed also of the Church in N.T. (1 Thes 5:9; Eph 1:14; 2 Pt 2:9).

Septuagint (from the Latin word for seventy), the name given the most widely used Greek translation of the O.T., made by Alexandrian Jews between 250 and 130 B.C. The name comes from a legend that seventy-two men from Jerusalem translated "the Scriptures" at the request of Ptolemy Philadelphos in seventy-two days on the island of Pharos near Alexandria. Actually it is not the work of one man, nor was it created as a single project; hence its quality is uneven. It is important because it is the first interpretation of the O.T. strongly influenced by Greek ideas, because it often witnesses to other (older) witnesses of the original Hebrew text, and above all, because it became the Bible of the Christian Church. Other ancient Greek versions of the O.T. were made by Aquila, Symmachus, Theodotion.

Sheol (Hebrew), "underworld, abode of the dead," a word represented in Greek by *Hadēs*. It is a place of darkness and dust, of complete joylessness, where the living God is not present. Until in late Judaism when belief in the resurrection of the body arose, Israel possessed no other concept of the after-life.

simul in actione contemplativus (Latin), "contemplative even while engaged in action," Nadal's phrase to describe St. Ignatius' particular gift of prayer, defined by the saint himself as "finding God in all things."

Sitz im Leben (German), "life-situation, context in the life (of the apostolic Church)," a technical term in Form Criticism, used to designate the particular circumstances or focus of interest which led to the reformulation or adaptation of some saying or incident preserved in the oral traditions concerning the earthly life of Jesus.

stabilitas in congregatione (Latin), a phrase found at the end of c. 4 of the Rule of St. Benedict, which is difficult to translate. It appears to mean something like "continuing commitment to community."

Stoicism (from the Greek word *stoa*, "portico"), the noblest of the pagan philosophies current in the Greco-Roman world in the first century of the Christian era, and for that reason the most serious obstacle (together with Judaizing) to the spread of the gospel in the apostolic age. Their god was *logos* (reason), a kind of world soul animating the cosmos. The goal of man's moral life was to become attuned to this *logos* by natural efforts at dominating his passions and emotions. The wise man thus attained *apatheia* (which might be translated as "indifference," but is totally different from the Ignatian concept in the *Spiritual Exercises*). All men are brothers insofar as they participate in the same *logos*. The term of the evolution of the cosmos was a universal conflagration (*ekpyrōsis*).

sub specie Crucis (Latin), "in the light of the Cross," i.e. as the ultimate divine judgment upon history.

Summa Contra Gentiles (Latin), a manual of Christian apologetics written by St. Thomas Aquinas for use in Spain by those attempting to convert Jews and Moors, the full title of which is *Summa de Veritate Catholicae Fidei contra Gentiles* ("A Compendium of the Truth of the Catholic Faith against Unbelievers"). It was composed at Rome in 1261-64 at the request of St. Raymond of Peñafort.

Summa Theologica (Latin), "A Compendium of Theology," the title of St. Thomas Aquinas' greatest work, uncompleted at his death. It was written at Rome and Naples, 1265-72, designed to be a complete treatise on Catholic theology (and philosophy). The classic expression of the medieval Christian world view.

symposion (Greek), "drinking party."

synthēkē (Greek), "compact, agreement, treaty."

testimonium apostolicum (Latin), "apostolic testimony, witness of the apostles," which was given to outsiders in the kerygma to convert them to Christianity, and also to those within the Church (*didachē*) to deepen their insight of faith into the Christian mystery.

theophany (from the Greek terms for "God" and "appearance"), "a manifestation of the divine presence," often through some tangible sign, e.g. the burning bush seen by Moses, the inaugural vision of Isaiah, Jesus' experience after his baptism in the Jordan.

tōrāh (Hebrew), "divine response (in general)," customarily relayed by priests; hence "priestly instruction." The word is practically synonymous with revelation in O.T.

transitus Domini (Latin), "passover of the Lord," the Vulgate rendering of a phrase in Ex 12:11.

Veni Creator Spiritus (Latin), "Come, Creator Spirit," first line of an ancient hymn from the eighth or ninth centuries, the most widely sung hymn after the *Te Deum*. It is still the sequence of the Masses of the octave of Pentecost.

vera Christi Domini nostri doctrina (Latin), "the true teaching of Christ our Lord," a phrase from the *versio litteralis* of the *Spiritual Exercises* [164; cf. also 145].

veritas (Latin), "truth, sincerity, reliability."

veritas salutaris (Latin), "saving truth," a phrase rejected after considerable discussion in the final formulation of the Constitution *Dei Verbum*, c.4, #11. It was finally replaced by a most significant clause, which describes the peculiar character of the truth found *in the sacred books* (thus dispelling the ambiguity of what the writer *meant*) as that "truth which God has willed to enshrine in holy writ for the sake of our salvation."

Vulgate (from the Latin word *vulgata* [*versio*], "common translation"), the name given St. Jerome's universally accepted Latin version of the Bible, which replaced other, earlier Latin translations made in the early western Church. St. Jerome revised the old Latin version of the Gospels in 383-84 A.D. (the rest of the Vulgate N.T., already existing in 406, is not St. Jerome's work), and between 390 and 405, he translated the entire Hebrew canon from that language in Palestine. Except for Judith and Tobit, he did not translate or revise the old Latin version of the deuterocanonical books. In 1546 the Council of Trent declared the Vulgate to be the "authentic" text of the Bible for the Latin Church, i.e. a safe source of Catholic doctrine, being free from error in faith and morals.

wie es eigentlich gewesen war (German), a phrase of von Ranke articulating his claim for historiography as the description of an event "as it really happened."

Yahwist (from the Hebrew divine name, Yahweh), the creator of an ancient written narrative (called "J" from its use of Yahweh as divine name) embodying the traditions of the southern kingdom of Judah, which became an important source of the Pentateuch. Composed probably under David or Solomon as an expression of the newly-born national consciousness of Israel, its style is lively, rapid, earthy. Its presentation of the Deity is anthropomorphic, while containing a lofty notion of God. The narrative begins with the primordial fall of man and stresses rather pessimistically the continuous subsequent degradation of humanity. God intervenes to save man through the promise given to Abraham. The author is gifted with a deep insight into human psychology; he is mainly interested in Judahite heroes.

Yēsu'a (Hebrew), "Jesus = Yahweh is salvation."

SCRIPTURAL INDEX

GENESIS (Gn)

1:1-2, 42, 293
1:2, 133
1:3, 290
1:3-4, 69, 96
1:26-28, 295, 323
1:28, 15, 144
2:7, 292
2:15, 256, 323
2:19, 134
2:24, 299
3:1, 63
3:1-19, 57, 61
3:15, 65, 191
3:16, 145
3:17-19, 144, 322
5:1-3, 323
5:3, 48
7:2, 180
7:14, 180
9:6, 48
11:1-9, 231
11:3, 116
12:10-20, 179
14:18, 236
14:19, 29
14:19-20, 236
10:11-12, 189
18:20-33, 37
20:1-18, 179
22:1, 244, 270
22:1-14, 260
22:8, 245, 261
26:6-11, 179
35:10, 20
35:21, 123
41:55, 193

EXODUS (Ex)

3:1, 98
3:2, 121, 255
3:14, 254

4:22, 143, 215
4:23, 118
7:17-21, 141
12:46, 261
14—15, 56
19:1, 69
19:12-13, 108
20:1—23:33, 31, 104
20:11, 223
20:19, 108, 124
23:20, 131
32, 68
32:1-8, 143
32—34, 72
33:11, 108
33:18, 69
33:20, 108
34:28, 141
40:34, 114, 188
40:34-35, 101

LEVITICUS (Lv)

19:18, 219, 222, 223
23:10-14, 291

NUMBERS (Nm)

11:4-34, 143
20:1-13, 143

DEUTERONOMY (Dt)

5:1-3, 10
5:14-15, 223
6:4-5, 219, 221
6:13, 141
6:16, 140
7:6-8, 103
7:7-8, 22, 214, 263
8:3, 140
26:5-9, 315
32:10-11, 268

345

GENERAL INDEX

353